SOCIAL SCIENCE IN THE

CRUCIBLE

SOCIAL SCIENCE IN THE CRUCIBLE

The American Debate Over

Objectivity and Purpose,

1918–1941

MARK C. SMITH

Duke University Press   Durham and London   1994

To Georgia and to Cameron, Evan, and Marika
who joined the parade along the way

© 1994 Duke University Press   All rights reserved   Printed in the United
States of America on acid-free paper ∞   Designed by Cherie H. Westmoreland
Typeset in Trump Medieval by Keystone Typesetting, Inc.   Library of Congress
Cataloging-in-Publication Data appear on the last printed page of this book.

Contents

How profoundly ignorant B. must be of the very soul of observation! About thirty years ago there was much talk that geologists only ought to observe and not theorize; and I well remember someone saying that at this rate a man might as well go into a gravel-pit and count the pebbles and describe the colors. How odd it is that anyone should not see that all observation must be for or against some view if it is to be of any service!

CHARLES DARWIN to Henry Fawcett, September 18, 1861

The question whether the data of the social sciences are identical with or analogous to, the data of the physical sciences or the other question whether the method of the physical sciences is readily applicable to the data of the social sciences . . . are dogging the steps and haunting the dreams of American students and . . . a disruptive conflict over them is approaching. When the conflict breaks in full force, it may split American intellectual life as wide open as the introduction of humanistic learning into Western Europe at the time of the Renaissance.

CHARLES A. BEARD, "The Social Sciences in the United States"

INTRODUCTION

Probably no area of study has ever had a more Whiggish history than American social science. Whig historians such as Thomas Carlyle and pre-Kuhnian historians of science systematically analyzed historical incidents as they appeared in the light of a perfect present. They criticized or praised events and individuals according to whether they seemed to aid or hinder progress toward a present that had achieved a sound stasis of solved conflict. Certainly the history of American social science shares this presentism. Most histories of the different disciplines judge past works of social science and their authors in terms of whether they represented positive or negative steps toward a social science that reproduced models of the natural and physical sciences. These historians have valued works according to how well they eliminated moral statements and feelings and replaced them with quantitative data. For example, a historian of economic thought quickly dismissed Adam Smith's precursors as "prescientific" and welcomed the "rigorous, mathematical" statements that had replaced the squabbles of past schools. As early as 1894, a University of Chicago graduate student in sociology polled the leading practitioners in the field and found that although few could agree even on the subject matter of their discipline, thirty out of forty accepted it as a true science. By 1919, the sociologist Luther L. Bernard could proudly proclaim, "We, as scientific workers in sociology, are so definitely launched upon the trend toward objectivism and definiteness of measurement in scientific method that it is needless to argue in its defense." As the social theorist Richard Bernstein ironically concluded, "One could write the history of social science during the past hundred years in terms of declarations that it has just become, or is just about to become, a scientific enterprise."[1]

Yet many historians of social science have gone beyond the Whiggish approach of Carlyle or historians of science such as George Sarton and I. M. Cohen. Carlyle, Sarton, and the early Cohen, at least, compared past events according to an existent period or scientific theory. Conversely, none of the social sciences has ever achieved a commonly agreed-upon theory. Economists continue to debate the functioning of the economic system and the key problems of the discipline and the best methods of solving them. Social scientists from all the disciplines choose their research topics based on a combination of scholarly significance, available research funds, and personal experiences and interests. No majority from any of the disciplines has ever actually accepted an antinormative, quantitative theory of technique or any other paradigm. Indeed, many thinkers have attributed the ongoing vitality of the American social sciences precisely to this constant challenge of existing assumptions and conceptions. The absence of a consensual paradigm has not, however, prevented most historians of social science from proclaiming its existence.

The reasons for the adoption of such a paradigm vary. Early practitioners of the discipline such as Bernard, his wife, Jessie, and the sociologist Floyd Nelson House apparently accepted the scientistic perspective so completely that they could not conceive of everyone not accepting it in the near future. More recent historians have recognized the consensual paradigm as a myth but continue to write as if it existed. George Stocking, Jr., the preeminent historian of American anthropological thought, defended "presentism" in the history of the social sciences as the best means of teaching current practitioners about their history and about previously acquired data and conclusions, and he referred specifically to paradigmatic shifts. The social theorist Paul Lazarsfeld went beyond this to praise the myth of the accepted paradigm as the best way to lead to the actual adoption of one. Once the profession assumed that the paradigm exists, practitioners could act upon it and do the type of small-scale, empirical research that such consensus encourages. This, in turn, would further strengthen the validity and common acceptance of the theory. One of the most extreme, and certainly most ironic, examples of the Whiggish view of social science is Edward Silva and Sheila Slaughter's *Serving Power*, in which the two authors examine the creation of academic social experts who provided quantitative studies to corporate and government leaders in the early part of the twentieth century. Silva and Slaughter openly opposed this and berated social scientists for abandoning the early reformism of their disciplines in order to serve the status quo. Yet nowhere did they seem to recognize that many social scientists could and did continue to act as critical social activists. That is, Silva and Slaughter accepted social scientists' universal adherence to a theory which they themselves hate and which has never been held by most social scientists.[2]

This book criticizes the Whig interpretation of the social sciences during the interwar years from 1918 to 1941. The 1920s and 1930s are key decades for the history of the social sciences in the United States. According to the commonly accepted interpretation, during this period a true quantitative, antinormative science of society emerged, later reaching its culmination immediately after World War II. Certainly many pressures existed that encouraged the development of such a perspective. No graduate student of the day could be unaware of the multitude of academic freedom cases during the progressive and World War I years in which professors, including prominent tenured ones from all the disciplines, were fired or "disciplined" through the threat of dismissal for their stands on controversial political and social issues. At the same time that their outspoken stands threatened the livelihood of those willing to speak, the demand for technical data by governments and private businesses rewarded value-neutral experts with high-paying and high-status occupations. In addition, in the 1920s several major foundations began to fund social science research generously. The directors of these foundations favored small-scale, empirical research, which they believed could have an immediate impact on society and which had previously been too expensive for most social scientists because of the high price of technical equipment and trained researchers. Thus the objective, scientific study of society became attractive for professional as well as for theoretical reasons. While historians had characterized the period from 1870 to 1920 as an ongoing debate between social advocacy and scientific objectivity, they saw the 1920s and 1930s as representing the triumph of the objective service intellectual.

Despite the undeniable allure of the scientistic position, many social thinkers rejected it and attempted to develop an alternative theory. Certainly neo-Thomists such as Robert Hutchins and Mortimer Adler and Catholic legal theorists from such law schools as Notre Dame, Georgetown, and Fordham rejected the entire concept of the scientific study of society and called for social thinkers to recognize the existence of a priori natural laws. The dominant service intellectuals were relatively unconcerned with such opposition, at least until the late 1930s. They found a far greater threat among their fellow social scientists who accepted the validity of the ideas of social science and the scientific method but rejected the developing amoral science of technique, with its lack of attention to normative concerns and elevation of empirical methods to a position of prominence. Those in the opposing group, whom I call the purposivists, insisted on the need for preconceived goals and ends for social science and for social scientists' personal participation in their selection. This conflict raged throughout the social sciences and appeared in journals, lectures, books, private letters, and even the presidential addresses of the professional societies.[3]

The debate can best be understood through David Hollinger's concept of the discourse of intellectuals. Hollinger argued that intellectuals share a community of discourse with established boundaries and assumptions. For true interaction to occur, the participants must share certain beliefs, values, language, and, especially, questions. Discourse in this sense is a social as well as an intellectual activity. These shared factors made the debate all the more important and contributed to the bitterness it generated. While both sides could quite easily dismiss the manifestos of a Hutchins or Adler as completely misguided and even incomprehensible, they could not so easily ignore each other's conclusions. Each group argued with some validity that it reflected the true faith of American social science. Each identified the same individuals as seminal thinkers in its tradition. Indeed, each group desired essentially the same ultimate ends for its professions. Yet the two disagreed on such essential issues as research topics of importance, appropriate research methods and their correct utilization, and the proper subject matter of the individual disciplines and even of social science itself.[4]

The central question dividing the two groups seemed to be a simple one: What is the proper role of the social scientist in relation to his or her knowledge of society? In other words, how should social scientists use their knowledge, and indeed, should they have any say at all in its utilization? Should the correct role of the social scientist be that of a technical expert who provides information and advice to whomever requests it? Or should the social scientist go beyond understanding and analyzing society and use scientifically derived information consciously and personally to help create a better society more suited to humankind's basic needs and desires? How can one reconcile either the delivery of information exclusively to political and economic elites or the determination of social and political goals by a self-determined elite of social scientists within a democracy? Indeed, is it reasonable for social scientists to play any pedagogical role in complex societies? Despite the assertions of service intellectuals, the question went well beyond the matter of alleged bias or objectivity. The issue was, as the historian Robert Bannister said of a group of sociologists of the period, "what [social scientists] thought social science was in the first place." Moreover, its participants believed fervently that the result of the debate would determine not only the direction of social science for the present but for the future as well.[5]

Indeed, social science during the 1920s and 1930s represents not a triumph of the objectivist social science approach but rather the crystall-ization of opposing perspectives. The social and economic pressures of the time served as torches burning the social sciences into a core residue within the crucible of academic and professional institutions. This resi-due, moreover, was a fine ash of two chemically pure and separate ele-ments, the very normative cores of the opposing positions on the proper use of social science. American social scientists were forced during the 1920s and 1930s, more than at any other time in history, to face the central dilemmas and needs of their profession.

The debate within 1920s and 1930s social sciences reflects a central and continuing facet of American social and cultural thought. Tradition-ally, thinkers in the United States have had to deal with the purposive aspect of inquiry. The question has always been, What is the goal of thought? For what purpose is one conducting the inquiry? Lewis Coser noted that intellectuals throughout world history have chosen from sev-eral strategies in their utilization of social knowledge. Some have used the knowledge to attain power through political office or leadership of a mass movement. Others have advised men of power or provided them with ideological justifications for their preconceived decisions. A final group, the most common Western tradition, have used their information to become critics and intellectual gadflys. Service intellectuals could justify their selection of the second option because they believed that the mere accumulation of data led necessarily to social reform and bet-terment through a more complete understanding of society. The pur-posivists, who followed the third tradition and maintained their role as critical outsiders, reproached the service intellectuals for their naive op-timism by pointing to the mixed experiences of social reformers during the progressive and war years. The abandonment of reform during the 1920s and the intellectual bankruptcy of the nation's leaders, as evi-denced by the economic and social collapse during the Great Depression coupled with the rise of totalitarianism and its use of technical social scientists and their knowledge, further strengthened the beliefs of the purposive group and caused some service intellectuals to reconsider their views.[6]

The perception of the social scientist as an intellectual, an individual who attempts to deal with the core values and questions of a culture, is an important one. The Whiggish nature of social science history has

derived largely from the tendency of writers to construct purely inter-
nalist studies of the social science disciplines. They view each discipline and its practitioners as existing in a social vacuum, reacting only
to books and articles by other specialists and occasionally to the ideas
of other academics. Clearly, however, individual social scientists read
newspapers, react to ongoing social and political problems, and are influenced by personal crises and experiences, like all human beings. The
central question of the proper use of social knowledge was held in common and discussed by every social scientist as well as by journalists,
philosophers, clergy, and ordinary men and women who would never
consider themselves intellectuals. Social scientists in the 1920s and
1930s were not only intellectuals in a narrow, professional sense but
intellectuals grappling in incisive and sophisticated ways with some of
the most timely social dilemmas of the day.[7]

One cannot separate service intellectuals from purposivists by age or
institutional affiliation. Many of the latter came from the new generation of social scientists who had come of age during the 1920s, but others,
including several of the leaders, were of the same generation who had
developed the objective perspective of the service intellectuals. A few of
the purposive group retained their independence by giving up their university connections, but others occupied positions in such bastions of
scientistic thought as Columbia and the University of Chicago. The debate over the proper role of the social scientist involved the conflict of
two of America's most widely cherished values: the utility of the scientific method and the normative goals of social thought. Indeed, these two
concepts represented the two core components of American social science. Consequently, one can find mutually contradictory statements on
the issue from almost every major thinker of the period. As Charles Beard
expressed it in 1934, "Everywhere the learned world is split into 'schools'
and rare indeed is the savant who does not appear to be at war with
himself in his own bosom."[8]

I have chosen to analyze this central debate largely through the work
and lives of five representative thinkers for several reasons. First, as
Beard's quote attests, by taking quotations out of context one could
pigeonhole almost any thinker into either side of the debate. Nevertheless, when one studies the work of an individual thinker in its entirety
and in the context of his or her behavior, a clear position almost always
emerges. Second, since this discourse took place equally on social and
intellectual planes, it is necessary to reconstruct the institutional environment of universities, research institutes, philanthropic founda-

tions, and government agencies and commissions to fully understand the dimensions and implications of the conflict. Although I am not asserting that any of the social scientists assumed ideas or research methodologies purely on professional or economic considerations, clearly such factors affected them. Finally, my hope is that by integrating the biographical elements of personality, social class, career and career goals, and political loyalties with a careful analysis of written works I will broaden the study of the history of social science beyond disciplinary analysis and goals and reach a more sophisticated perspective of how social scientists interact with their culture.

The issue of representativeness in general is, of course, problematic. Since the debate over social scientists and their role occurred in all the disciplines, my primary goal was to choose figures who together would cover as much of the spectrum of social science as possible. Included here are chapters on economics, sociology, political science, history, and political psychology, as well as substantial sections on neo-Freudian social psychology, legal education and realism, public administration, civic education, and the culture and personality school of anthropology. My second aim was to choose individuals who were intellectual leaders in their profession, whose work represented a significant contribution to knowledge, and who took an active role in social and political affairs. Finally, I chose five individuals for whom the question of the purpose of social research was a central theme in much of their writing and activity: historian and political scientist Charles Beard, economist Wesley Mitchell, political scientist Charles Merriam, sociologist Robert Lynd, and political scientist and neo-Freudian Harold Lasswell. In both the scope and clarity of their thought, these five provide telling insights into the crucible of 1920s and 1930s social science.[9]

Since the debate over the proper role of the social scientist turned directly on the possibility and desirability of objectivity, I have been compelled to examine my own methodology. In his introduction to *That Noble Dream* Peter Novick wrote eloquently about the dilemmas and ironies involved in writing "objectively" about the lack of objectivity of other historians. As a historian, I have been trained to examine events and ideas in terms of their changing cultural setting and assumptions. Yet my former career as a clinical social worker makes me appreciate the attraction of verifiable proofs that allow absolute solutions to specific problems. Certainly the external pressures of postwar economic and social conversion and the Great Depression, along with the need for research funds and the pressure from foundations and governmental bodies for specific types of information, made the service intellectuals' desire to achieve a standard of knowledge unassailable to outside criticism greater than at any previous period in the history of American social science. Yet their methodology oversimplified both the scientific method and the complexity of society and often ignored the practical and political consequences of their research choices. Although the purposivists were often philosophically limited and perhaps even naive, their vision of a probabilistic universe and the openness of history and culture more closely mirrors contemporary and my own thinking about society and the role of thought.

This is not to say that my viewpoint is not finally a personal one. Beard argued that one doing social research needs to be as objective as humanly possible while recognizing the inevitability of personal biases and freely admitting them to one's audience. I think this is basically sound advice. I freely admit my anger at the complacent (and I believe lesser) heirs of Mitchell and Merriam who unreservedly accepted the status quo and scornfully rejected the value and even the possibility of significant social change. As a child of the 1960s and 1970s, I have shared the frustration of being denied already forged weapons in the battle for a more desirable society, and I accept Robert Lynd's definition of social science as "an organized part of the culture which exists to help men in continually understanding and rebuilding his culture . . . [and] an instrument for furthering men's purposes." I feel the purposivists, for all their limitations, represented a positive movement toward a more constructive view of social change and action. I recognize that many readers will have different opinions and goals from my own and trust that my perspective will not deny the utility of this work for them.[10]

I've often wondered when I was most arrogant in writing such a book— in its first manifestation in the late 1970s, when secondary sources were limited largely to disciplinary histories, or in its present form in the late 1980s and early 1990s, when relevant works seem to appear on a monthly basis. Early in my research, I was most influenced by Edward Purcell's remarkably astute *Crisis of Democratic Theory* and Barry Karl's *Charles E. Merriam and the Study of Politics*. In this latter stage I have especially appreciated two excellent institutional histories, Guy Alchon's study of the National Bureau of Economic Research and Donald Critchlow's examination of the Brookings Institute, for helping to confirm my earlier perspectives on organized social science.[11]

Like everyone else in the field now and for the foreseeable future, I have grappled mightily with two magnificent recent books, Peter Novick's study of the American historical profession, *That Noble Dream*, and Dorothy Ross's *Origins of American Social Science*. I see this work as complementary and supplementary to those two, while still differing from both in approach and conclusions. Like Novick and unlike Ross, I have placed objectivity and the role of the social scientist as the central defining issues. Such a perspective concentrates on the ongoing conflict within the profession(s) and thus implicitly critiques the unilinear model of progress envisioned by the disciplinary historians. Ross's reliance on the shared concept of American exceptionalism results, for all her criticism of Hartzian liberal consensus and disciplinary histories, in an alternative vision of ideological concurrence. Like Ross and unlike Novick, I explicitly treat history as social science and view all the social sciences as reflecting a common discourse of beliefs, assumptions, and questions. By concentrating on the question of the proper role of social scientists, I have been able, unlike Ross, to extend this integration into the fields of anthropology and social psychology. Finally, the key difference is my intensive analysis of a much more limited period and number of individuals. It is my hope that such an approach coupled with extensive analyses like those of Novick and Ross will result in a more thorough and insightful history of American social science.

Although many books seem to engage in interminable odysseys before sailing into the harbor of publication, this manuscript has had an especially long and colorful one, wandering through years of teaching in Germany and Japan and even a career shift to clinical social work before docking at its original harbor at the University of Texas at Austin. A large number of people from various professions and locations along the way have contributed important insights and suggestions. I especially thank June and Sid Axinn, Sally Clarke, George Glaser, Dave Haney, Herb Hovenkamp, Bruce Hunt, Mike Lauderdale, Luci Paul, Richard Pells, the late Tom Philpott, Steve Pyne, Elspeth Rostow, Woody Smith, and Alex Vuccinich. This work also reflects the unconscious contributions of innumerable students from many nations who had their greatest impact when discussing issues seemingly far removed from the subject of this work. Bob Abzug and Brian Levack were instrumental in providing me with the opportunity to return to academic life and encouraging me to expand and finish this work. Larry Malley and Rachel Toor, my editors at Duke, have consistently believed in this work and given support when I needed it most. Bob Crunden and Bill Goetzmann, my earliest mentors, have long served as patient sources of information on an incredible range of subjects far removed from their specialties. My greatest direct debt is to Jeff Meikle, who as fellow graduate student, present colleague, and long-suffering friend has read this manuscript more times than either of us would like to remember. Most of all, however, this book belongs to my wife, Georgia Xydes, whose patience, good humor, and strength have navigated us through the writing of this book and far greater and more important crises and joys.

I

AMERICAN SOCIAL SCIENCE: MORALISM AND

THE SCIENTIFIC METHOD

American social science has always suffered from an ambivalence found in its very name. As science it represents the amoral, empirical, antitheoretical approach of the technical method that Daniel Boorstin among others has championed as the characteristic nature of American thought and action. Scientific method deals with how to do things and do them most efficiently; it is unconcerned with the issue of what to do. Yet social science is also social thought and thus contains, especially in America, a traditional consistent concern for social welfare and the directing of society toward preconceived moral ends. Since the time of the Mayflower Compact and John Winthrop's "A Modell of Christian Charitie," American thinking on society has possessed this normative concern for the welfare of individuals within society. As heir to both traditions, American social scientists have attempted to integrate the two. Yet from the time social science was founded in the late nineteenth century, the elements of social advocacy and scientific neutrality have conflicted with each other.[1]

Puritans' thinking about society was by definition concern for moral issues. Their goal in establishing a new "commonwealth" was to protect the one true church in its Babylonian exile, and they consciously attempted to create a moral and virtuous society in which the church could flourish. John Winthrop reminded his fellow settlers that "wee ought to account our selves knitt together by this bond of love, and live in the exercise of it. . . . Wee must beare one anothers burthens, wee must not looke onely on our owne things, but allsoe on the things of our brethren." After all, the goal was to be a model "citie on a hill" which other nations could emulate and copy.[2]

Although Puritan thinking differed from that of the Enlightenment in almost every imaginable way, they did share this emphasis on the absolute need for a moral society. Enlightenment thinkers maintained that mankind, especially uneducated natural man, possessed a moral sense which caused him to choose and do the ethical thing. One of the chief reasons the American revolutionaries wanted to separate themselves from the mother country was their belief that England had become corrupt and that a conspiracy was under way to make colonial society over in that corrupt image. Since it was possible to mold individuals through social control, the only protection for the virtuous American people was a separation from corrupt Europe and the creation of social and political institutions that would protect and even help create virtue.

Nineteenth-century American social thought retained this conscious moralism and engaged in cyclical periods of social and religious revivalism when citizens perceived materialism and industrialism threatening their visions of a moral society. Many of the followers of the Jacksonian movement were attracted by the movement's attempts to regain the moral simplicity and virtues of the Founding Fathers. Moral and social reformers of the 1830s and 1840s advanced the theory of perfectionism, which would produce sinless individuals through the creation of a perfect society. Its most prominent spokesman, Charles Finney, exhorted his listeners to "be ye perfect even as your Father in Heaven is perfect." Utopian thinkers were less optimistic about the possibility of reforming current American society, but they believed that perfect individuals could be created through the establishment of new communities totally separated from ongoing society. The British industrialist and philosopher Robert Owen found great support in the United States for his attempt to create a "new moral world" in his community of New Harmony.

Owen's communitarian plans are useful for understanding the interaction between this moral strain and the technological perspective. Owen believed his new moral order would succeed because of its rational and scientific basis. He maintained that he had developed his plans through twelve years of scientific testing in his mill community of New Lanarck, Scotland, and he believed he could simply apply these proven methods of social control to the American environment. Owen, like other Enlightenment figures, believed strongly in the power of the environment. Indeed, he matched the later behavioral psychologist B. F. Skinner in the extremity of his views: "Any general character, from the best to the worst, from the most ignorant to the most enlightened, may be given to any community, even to the world at large, by the application of proper means; which means are to a great extent at the command and under the control of those who have influence in the world of men." A truly moral society could be achieved only through the discovery of the scientific laws governing society and their subsequent use by political leaders. Although many of Owen's contemporaries may have opposed the extremity of his environmentalism or the validity of his "laws," few would have disagreed with his search for these laws and the need for a moral society. Enlightenment figures pointed to science and the scientific method as the major liberating forces for the times, and few doubted that society was any less amenable to understanding and control than the physical universe. Even earlier critics of rationalism such as the Puritan ministers Increase and Cotton Mather honored science as positive support in their goal of the good society. Morality and science were inextricably linked.[3]

The immediate precursors to professionalized social science in the antebellum United States were threefold: university courses in moral philosophy, pre–Civil War southern followers of Auguste Comte, and inventors and users of statistics for social research purposes. Each retained the connection between moralism and science found in earlier American social thought.

Foremost among these precursors were the first purely social thinkers in American institutions, the teachers of moral philosophy in the colleges during the early nineteenth century. Every college, whether or not it was church supported, had a senior course in moral philosophy, often taught by the president, which interpreted social life in the context of the reigning moral philosophy of Scottish commonsense realism. This final course demonstrated the alleged interconnections of metaphysics, ethics, logic, natural law, rhetoric, politics, and political economy through man's innate moral sense. Moreover, since commonsense realism relied completely on the senses, all of these fields were necessarily composed of facts. This alliance of theology and Baconian science led to the creation of natural laws that were, in the words of historian of philosophy Daniel Wilson, "both descriptive and prescriptive." Francis Wayland, president of Brown University, declared in 1837 that "the principles of political economy are so completely analogous to those of Moral philosophy that almost every question in the one may be argued on grounds belonging to the other."[4]

The first Americans to use "social science" to describe their work were a group of pre–Civil War apologists for southern society and slavery. George Frederick Holmes, George Fitzhugh, and especially Henry Hughes found in the positivism of Auguste Comte a justification of southern culture through a science based on facts and scientific verification. Hughes and Fitzhugh compared the stable social structure of the South with the chaotic and haphazard North and argued that the former was exactly the type of normative ethical society advocated by Comte. Each individual in southern society had a necessary role in its operation, drawing all into a functioning, interdependent moral community. Hughes in particular then set out to prove the reality of this perspective through facts.[5]

Clearly, social facts, including facts arranged in a quantitative manner, existed in pre–Civil War America, even in the unbookish South. Moreover, despite the common belief that all early American social thought was theoretical and nonempirical, significant statistical work also existed. James Madison championed a thorough national census from the time of the Constitutional Convention, and each decennial census included more data and was methodologically more sophisticated. As early as 1811, the *Niles Weekly Register* devoted itself to accumulating and publishing economic and social statistics. It soon had numerous competitors, including several, such as the highly respected *DeBow's Review*, that concentrated on the South. The medical and life insurance professions collected and published vital statistics on births, deaths, and the like. Finally, a great demand existed for what the Belgian mathematician Adolphe Quetelet termed "moral statistics"; figures on such social problems as poverty, crime, and insanity. A group of well-to-do New England reformers were the primary movers behind the 1839 establishment of the American Statistical Association, whose constitution stated succinctly that "every rational reform must be founded on thorough knowledge." Reform could not be achieved without scientifically derived information, and the purpose of these data was clearly to bring about such reforms.[6]

The social survey movement of the late nineteenth and early twentieth centuries grew out of this empirically derived social research and followed the examples set by British surveys, especially those of Charles Booth. The well-to-do Booth, disbelieving available statistics on the number of the London poor, pioneered in developing methods of enumerating them and describing their lives in quantitative terms. Finally, he identified the social factors that had caused their poverty. The American social survey movement concentrated on this latter aspect. Surveys gathered empirical information on social problems to discover the reasons behind abnormal social disorder. The social survey was, more than everything else, "a social diagnosis" concerned with locating and noting the extent of the problems and then, hopefully, bringing about solutions. Beginning with the Pittsburgh survey of 1908, this mixture of empiricism and moralism became omnipresent in American life. In the twenty years between 1908 and 1927, practitioners of the method completed at least 2,775 surveys of American communities.[7]

As even this short survey shows, American social thought reacted quickly in both moral and scientific terms to the threat of social disorganization. The Civil War followed this pattern. Responding to the suffering of northern soldiers and the breakdown of the authority of traditional social institutions, a few members of the traditional northeastern social elite founded the United States Sanitary Commission to handle the coordination of medical and personal relief for the Union Army. Although a concern for the soldiers' problems certainly influenced the commission's actions, a deeper motivation lay in their belief in the need for discipline and strengthening of traditional moral beliefs and institutions in this time of crisis. In 1865, several leaders of this organization, including the reformer Samuel Gridley Howe, met under the auspices of the Massachusetts Board of State Charities to establish a society modeled on the melioristic British Social Science Association to study and correct the social abuses of the day. This became the American Social Science Association (ASSA), the first official American social science society and "the mother" of all modern social science organizations.[8]

In the years after the Civil War the ASSA became part of an attempt by the established northeastern gentry to retain their position of social authority over increasingly visible and powerful parvenu industrialists and robber barons. Seventy-three percent of the officers and primary members of the ASSA had been born in New England, and nearly that percentage actually lived there. Thirty-five percent of the leaders were professionals, and another 32.5 percent were prominent businessmen. This did not, however, detract from the social reformism of the organization. In contrast with the emerging national leaders, the ASSA represented local elites who saw increasing economic inequality as a serious threat to social stability and a moral society. Members of the society universally condemned Herbert Spencer's social Darwinism and laissez-faire. The constitution of the association proclaimed its activist purpose "to aid the development of social science and to guide the public mind to the best practical means of promoting the Amendment of Laws, the Advancement of Education, . . . the Reformation of Criminals and the Progress of Public Morality." Members favored the scientific study of society and collection of data because they felt that scientifically derived *true* facts would necessarily lead to social reform. Science and humanitarian sentiment were synonymous. Should a conflict arise between the two, however, United States Commissioner of Education and prominent ASSA member John Eaton made clear what the stance of the organization would be in a declaration to the 1886 annual meeting: "Let the warning cry fill the air of scientific associations, from meeting to meeting, that science is our means, not our end."[9]

The career of the ASSA's perennial executive secretary and national spokesman, Franklin Sanborn, demonstrates the normative goals of the association. A Harvard graduate, Sanborn had founded a school in Concord before the war with the aid of Ralph Waldo Emerson and Bronson Alcott and played prominent roles in several reform and abolitionist organizations, including the secret group that provided funding for John Brown's raid on Harper's Ferry. After the war he turned to social science as the best hope for social reformation. Sanborn clearly combined ethical goals and the scientific gathering of facts in his vision of social science: "To learn patiently what is—to promote diligently what should be—that is the double duty of all the social sciences." Sanborn became an expert on social problems and charities and one of the first professors of social science in America. At Cornell, Sanborn gave an activist course on social problems and their solutions and led frequent field trips to prisons, insane asylums, and urban slums. Sanborn declared that "social science . . . by its very nature rushes to an application. . . . We are pupils in such a school as that of Mr. Squiers, where the first class in hydraulics daily took a turn at the pump."[10]

The ASSA is called the mother of social science organizations because it was the source of many groups that formed around specialized subjects, such as the study of governments, and then broke away. Members of these splinter organizations had come to reject many of the ASSA's core beliefs. First of all, they rejected the possibility of an all-encompassing unity of knowledge. The only way to achieve true knowledge, they believed, was to concentrate on a limited area and study it intensively. The ASSA, on the other hand, like the moral philosophers of the early colleges, held that all knowledge was one and could be understood only as a unified whole. Second, and related to the first, the splinter groups had come to believe that the ASSA would never gain the social prestige and authority they desired. They had reluctantly concluded that the organization could claim no special expertise or reason why the public should automatically accept or even consider its views. Even worse, radicals such as Daniel DeLeon, Henry George, and Stephen Pearl Andrews called themselves social scientists and based their various forms of socialism on many of the same American traditions of evangelicalism, civic duty, community, and brotherhood as the academic social scientists. Social scientists feared that such shared identification with the radicals would bring the entire movement into disrepute. In 1878 the ASSA sought to merge with the newly formed Johns Hopkins University in an attempt to share in its prestige, but Johns Hopkins President Daniel Coit Gilman rejected the plan, even though he was a past president of the ASSA, because of the organization's reformist reputation.[11]

Social scientists' desire to achieve community respect and acceptance reflected the nineteenth-century breakdown in local authority. Communities no longer accepted the opinions of local elites without question, and national bodies of expertise were still developing. Scientists, lawyers, and doctors were turning to a culture of professionalization as part of a strategy to win societal acceptance of their authority in limited areas of expertise. Certainly the culture of professionalization possessed attractive qualities for the emerging social sciences. The most commonly accepted list of attributes of professional work is the presence of research-based systematic theory, community acceptance of professional authority, community sanction through certification or other institutional means, the existence of a regulative code of ethics, the development of a professional culture through requirements for professional training and membership in professional organizations, and the creation of a tight community through shared social and educational experiences. Social scientists sought the goal of community acceptance of their authority most, but they also recognized the advantages gained by separating themselves from the political radicals and "benevolent amateurs" of the ASSA. The absolutely objective use of the scientific method could simultaneously serve as a code of ethics and create a research-based theory with far greater claims on validity and public trust.[12]

Codes of ethics were especially attractive in the late nineteenth century, when the crisis of authority gave rise to numerous quackeries and pseudosciences. The social sciences could prove their objectivity by insisting that anyone properly trained in the scientific method could validate their results by repeating the research. Being objective served a double purpose for social scientists: it distinguished them from suspect political reformers, and it gave them knowledge and methods unavailable to but accepted by laypersons. The establishment of professional organizations based on specialization and scientific research aided in the development of a professional culture, but the key element was the alliance between the expanding universities and the social sciences. The university provided training, shared social experiences, and even unofficial certification and sanction. Once the universities accepted social scientists, the middle-class public quickly followed suit. In turn, the social scientists aided the reputation of the universities through their practical and highly visible social service. By the 1890s, the social scientists' drive toward respectability and popular acceptance had succeeded beyond anyone's expectations.[13]

This first generation of professionalized social scientists had three central beliefs. First, they believed in the objective use of the scientific method as the only way to understand, analyze, and, later, control society. Scientists had made rapid strides in describing and explaining physical and organic life and had become effective opponents of superstition and ignorance. The application of science to social issues seemed not just self-explanatory but absolutely essential. Johns Hopkins President Ira Remsen declared shortly after the turn of the century that "the intellectual progress of a nation depends upon the adoption of scientific methods in dealing with intellectual problems. . . . We need it [the scientific method] in every department of activity." Second, they continued to insist on the normative nature of social science and its goal of turning "ethics into action." Many of the first generation of professional social scientists were either former clergy themselves or sons of clergy. Religion by itself had not provided solutions to the ethical problems of society, and so they had turned to social science. Compared with the social reformers of the ASSA, professional social scientists were probably even more personally committed to social change and governmental action. Third, they saw science as synonymous with reform and could not conceive of conflicts between the two. Science was truth, and the truth was by definition moral. Therefore, the scientific method would prove the truth of social scientists' normative opinions. As a widely used college textbook confidently declared, "The purpose of sociology . . . is to formulate a scientific program of social betterment."[14]

The very founding of several of the professional organizations reflected normative goals. Richard Ely, one of the principal founders of the American Economic Association, devised a constitution for the organization that took an activist, pro-state position and prevented laissez-faire economists such as William Graham Sumner and J. Lawrence Laughlin from joining. Among the founders of the organization were such activist radical thinkers as Ely, Edward Ross, Simon Patten, Edward James, Herbert Carter Adams, John Commons, and the social gospeler Washington Gladden. Twenty-five years later, Ely fondly recalled that among the founders of the association "was a striving for righteousness and here and there . . . one who felt a certain kinship with the old Hebrew prophets." While the founders of the American Political Science Association rejected overt political action and scorned the abstract theory of their predecessors, almost all of them worked closely with municipal reform organizations in devising plans for "efficient" and active local and state governments. An episode from the bitter Pennsylvania coal strike of 1901 is an excellent example of the identification of the social sciences with activist liberal goals. In an attempt to settle the strike, President Theodore Roosevelt had set up an arbitration committee, but action was blocked by labor's demand for representation and the employers' consequent threat of a boycott of the negotiations. Roosevelt settled the issue by appointing E. E. Clark, president of the Railroad Conductors Union, to represent labor's interests as "an eminent sociologist." Revealingly, no one, including the social scientists, protested this designation.[15]

Ely and his fellow activists attempted to distinguish themselves as the sole inheritors of the ethical tradition, but neoclassical economists strongly opposed this pronouncement, arguing that the laws of the marketplace reflected not just equilibrium but moral laws of harmony as well. Indeed, economist John Bates Clark, the most important of the American marginalists, abandoned his earlier proregulatory stance in favor of neoclassicism because he felt the latter more accurately reflected his goals of ethical moralism. Few if any of the first generation of social scientists would relinquish either of the twin guideposts of science and moralism.[16]

The universities became the setting for the determination of proper professional standards. Albion Small, chairman of Chicago's Department of Sociology and one of those most committed to the vision of a moralistic, unified vision of society, saw universities and research institutes staffed by wise, disinterested social scientists as perfect tribunals for deciding ethical goals for society. He was confident that such institutions would maintain his conviction that "science is sterile unless it contributes at least to knowledge of what is worth doing." In this he was badly mistaken. By the time of this prediction in 1906, Small was already an anomaly in his outspoken moralism. Beginning in the 1890s, the culture of professionalism and the use of the scientific method had become of paramount importance, especially for the younger generation, and the ethical goals for which their predecessors had instituted the strategy of professionalization receded into the background. The means of professionalization had become, despite Eaton's warnings, the ends.[17]

The reasons behind this vary from individual case to case. Many social scientists, particularly economists, were becoming aware of the impressive results physiologists, biologists, and psychologists were having in their behavioral research and sought to adapt the behavioral interpretation of the scientific method to their own research problems. Also, much of the younger generation, from more sophisticated urban environments, found their predecessors' claims of objectivity ludicrous. Adopting an early version of cultural relativism, objectivist social scientists rejected not only the Christian moralism of their teachers but all value systems as indefensible and insisted on divorcing the scientific means of obtaining information from any predetermined ends.

Although these certainly represented valid intellectual responses to the problem of value neutrality and social ends, they were not sufficient in themselves. Innumerable commentators have remarked on the continued commitment of most American social scientists to liberal activist ends despite their refusal to consider such ends in their research. The reasons behind their rejection of open normative commitment were as much institutional as ideological and reflected the demands the culture of professionalism made on social scientists at the turn of the century. Most prominent among these demands was the requirement by universities and their conservative presidents and trustees that their employees avoid controversial subjects and opinions. Another important influence stemmed from social scientists' continuing desire to serve society despite those restrictions. State and local governments and corporations offered prestigious advisory and technical positions but hired only those who provided empirical, technical data and did not challenge the institution's ideological beliefs. Finally, the sheer cost of obtaining the type of empirical data needed to create a valid science of society forced social scientists, like the practitioners of physical and natural sciences before them, to turn to philanthropic foundations. These foundations and their administrators insisted on their own standards of objectivity and claimed to base their funding of research institutes solely on grounds of practicality and scientific nature. Such determination was, of course, dependent on personal values and experiences, and it necessarily reflected the conservative views of the foundation board members.

The practical nature of the American university, especially as it developed in the late nineteenth century, differed considerably from that found in Europe, where semiautonomous institutions protected from outside interests and dedicated to pure scholarship had evolved. American colleges and universities, on the other hand, were traditionally service institutions. Colonial American society had established Harvard,

Yale, and their successors to provide a native learned clergy for the churches of the new land. In the second half of the nineteenth century, enterprising college presidents such as Charles Eliot of Harvard and Andrew White of Cornell diversified the college curriculum to meet the changing needs of their times. State universities, founded by the Morrill Land Grant Act of 1862, opened agricultural and engineering schools. In contrast with the relatively independent nature of European universities, control of American institutions lay in the hands of hardheaded trustees from the business and political communities who consistently judged scholarship according to their own ideas of practicality and service to society. The social sciences had expanded more rapidly in the United States than in Europe precisely because their advocates had convinced these individuals of the utility of their disciplines. Nevertheless, trustees' conservative political and economic views significantly colored their interpretations of both practicality and science.

University teachers in the United States had always lived under constraints. Certainly individuals who dealt with social and political issues in the late nineteenth and early twentieth centuries had to deal with this problem even more than their predecessors. Eliot himself warned social scientists implicitly in his 1905 Phi Beta Kappa address that since "philosophical subjects" were not established sciences and contained many open, debatable conclusions, professors should never suggest any solutions. By 1915 the first report of the American Association of University Professors Commission on Academic Freedom and Tenure noted that the chief area of academic freedom cases had shifted from religion and science issues to the political and social sciences. Among the social scientists dismissed by conservative presidents and boards of trustees were such prominent figures as Edward Ross, Edward Bemis, John Commons, Simon Patten, Scott Nearing, James McKeen Cattell, and Henry Carter Adams. Even a few conservative thinkers such as Arthur Lathem Perry and William Graham Sumner were seriously threatened. The danger of losing their jobs directly affected the teaching and scholarship of many social scientists. Even Richard Ely, an aggressive champion of ethical goals sheltered at the University of Wisconsin, probably the most liberal university in the nation, abandoned labor and other "popular" issues and took up the "scientific" study of land economics and research for private utilities. Adams, dismissed from Cornell for his support of the Knights of Labor and the Haymarket defendants, later advised his fellow economists to avoid controversial topics and become technical experts for legislators or regulatory commissions.[18]

Adams's retreat to technical expertise was a strategy followed by many social scientists. When used in the service of progressive reforms and commissions, as in Wisconsin under Robert LaFollette, that approach seemed to provide the perfect answer to social scientists' dilemma. They could protect their jobs by concentrating on solidly empirical research and also satisfy their political desires by giving their results to social activists whose goals mirrored their own. They could be ethical, practical, and uncontroversial all at once. This position was especially popular during the Progressive Era, with its equation of technical expertise and efficiency with reform.

The demand for technical service from social scientists reached its height during World War I when the federal government desperately needed to centralize and make the economy more efficient. Although economists and psychologists were especially important for this effort, large numbers of political scientists, geographers, historians, and sociologists were employed as well. The information necessary to plan a war economy simply did not exist. Would-be planners lacked comprehensive figures on inventories, construction, employment, bank credit, retail prices, trade, and almost everything else. Bernard Baruch, chairman of the War Industries Board, bluntly stated that "the greatest deterrent to effective action was the lack of facts." The American Economic Association, while refusing to establish official committees to deal with war problems, urged its members to show the practicality of their expertise, and thousands of its members followed this advice in government service. The American Psychological Association established twelve official committees to deal with the war crisis, and experts in testing set up comprehensive psychological and aptitude-testing programs for the armed forces. Political scientists and historians produced propaganda for the Committee on Public Information and its foreign branches and abandoned any pretense of scientific objectivity. One historian of the subject concluded that American academics were among the earliest and strongest supporters of the war and that their desire to improve their uncertain social status heightened their enthusiasm. During the 1930s the war years were remembered fondly as a utopian time for the social sciences.[19]

Nonacademic employment did not end for all social scientists after the war. Although the government dismissed all but a few of its experts, private businesses, impressed by the results of war work, hired many of them. Companies were particularly interested in intelligence and aptitude testing and "industrial engineering," and they hired psychologists and sociologists who had pioneered in the area during the war. For business, one of the most popular wartime government agencies was the Central Bureau of Planning and Statistics directed by Edwin Gay, dean of Harvard Business School. The bureau's task was to collect and collate statistical information from all government agencies, including the armed services. The Price Division, supervised by Wesley Mitchell, Gay's friend from Columbia University, prepared a massive study of the wholesale prices of more than fifteen hundred commodities for the years 1917–18. Such research permitted both government policymakers and private businessmen to plan production and inventories. When the war ended, leading businessmen joined administrators and social scientists in petitioning for the incorporation of the bureau and its studies into the Department of Commerce. When President Woodrow Wilson refused the request on the grounds that government should not interfere in business, a group of prominent businessmen established the privately funded National Bureau of Economic Research (NBER) under the supervision of Mitchell and Gay to continue the research.[20]

The NBER conducted exactly the type of quantitative research desired by both businessmen and the major foundations. The war emergency had proved the practicality of this type of work, and financial support by business demonstrated its lack of controversiality. The Laura Spelman Rockefeller Memorial Fund was by far the largest contributor to the bureau, providing $1.8 million between the years 1922 and 1943, or roughly half the bureau's budget during those years. Only after the war did such foundations consider social science safe and practical enough to sponsor. In 1914, when several employees recommended that the Rockefeller Foundation fund an earlier version of the NBER, Frederick Gates, John D. Rockefeller, Sr.'s, chief philanthropic adviser, shrilly opposed the plan, claiming that medical research would cure all social problems and that all fundamental economic principles were already known. By 1919, however, former Secretary of State Elihu Root, archconservative chairman of the board of the Carnegie Institute, traced Germany's power during the war to government and private sponsorship of social research and insisted that America must follow Germany's lead or perish in international competition. Indeed, it would be the Carnegie Foundation that would provide the first philanthropic funding for the NBER.[21]

The most important source of funding for the social sciences was the Rockefeller Foundation, especially the Laura Spelman Rockefeller Memorial Fund. Prior to the war, only the Russell Sage Foundation had funded the social sciences to any degree, and it limited its support to social work and charities. In 1914 and 1915 the Rockefellers had hired economist and former Canadian labor minister MacKenzie King, ostensibly to conduct a major research project on the conditions of American labor but in reality to write apologetics for the Rockefeller role during the Colorado Coal War of 1913–14. This approach failed dismally, and both King and the Rockefellers were censured by the congressional Commission on Industrial Relations. Convinced by his personal adviser, Raymond Fosdick, that funding the social sciences represented an excellent way to aid society and improve his public image at the same time, John D. Rockefeller, Jr., noted his desire for the family foundations to enter the field but to distance themselves from the conduct and results of the research funded.[22]

The individual chosen by the Rockefellers and their advisers to find a middle ground for the social sciences was twenty-seven-year-old Beardsley Ruml, a psychometrician with a doctorate from the University of Chicago and the codirector of the government Division of Trade Tests during the war. Ruml had gained foundation experience as chief assistant to his former supervising professor, James Angell, at the National Research Council and the Carnegie Corporation. Ruml's reputation throughout his career was as an "idea man," an individual who came up with innovative solutions to difficult problems. Soon after he was appointed director of the General Education Fund of the Rockefeller Foundation in 1922, he sent out an important memorandum, "Memorial Policy in the Social Sciences," which suggested guidelines for the funding of social science research. The memo advocated strongly that the Spelman Fund consider only empirical research; theoretical and philosophical social scientists were unworthy of financial support because of their lack of practicality. In the past, government, industry, and business had all benefited from empirical research, thus proving its "commercial value." By emphasizing empirical research, the memo continued, the Spelman Fund could increase the marketability of all the social sciences. One important reason why empirical research was so marketable was its avoidance of controversy. The Rockefeller Foundation was especially concerned with this. When the executive committee of the Spelman Fund established the official funding policy in 1924, they concentrated on such issues. They refused to fund organizations concerned with legislation, to become involved in any social or economic reform, to try to influence findings or ever deal directly with researchers, or to fund nonempirical studies. The fund retained this approach throughout its history and in its final report identified its commitment to value neutrality as its greatest legacy. During the seven years that he directed the fund, Ruml disbursed more than $58 million for research in the social sciences.[23]

Commentators have traditionally praised the neutrality of the foundations, but this overlooks the traditional activist role of American social scientists. By insisting on objectivity and refusing to support reform activities, the foundations did impose a de facto political position. Ambitious social scientists consciously directed their research to appeal to the foundations. During the 1920s, every political research institute and group in the country replaced the word *politics* in their titles with *administration* in an attempt to bypass the foundations' fears of social activism and oversized government. Thinkers as different as the scientistic L. L. Bernard and the English socialist Harold Laski complained about the creation of empirical research institutes in seemingly every university in the country and the near-universality of social scientists' pandering to foundation policy.[24]

The institutional pressures intensified the movement toward extreme empiricism and avoidance of moral positions begun by behaviorism and cultural relativism. The social scientist became the service intellectual, an instrument for descriptive reporting and determining the most efficient procedures. The service intellectual never took a position on what should be done but regarded all social and political issues as simple problems of administration. Thurman Arnold, legal realist and Franklin Roosevelt political appointee, argued this position most persuasively. In a democracy the electors vote for leaders to make the difficult, normative judgments for society as a whole. Social scientists should advise these leaders when requested to do so, but their basic function is to serve as "cheerful practical technicians dealing with the facts before them." Arnold's beliefs were echoed by Charles Merriam, chairman of the political science department of the University of Chicago, cofounder of the Social Science Research Council, perennial appointee to federal commissions under Presidents Hoover and Franklin Roosevelt, and by far the most successful supplicant of foundation support. For Merriam, the perfect social scientists were the city managers with their motto "on tap, not on top." Throughout his work, Merriam emphasized "a sharp distinction . . . between scientific fact finding on the one hand and the determination and execution of policies on the other."[25]

The convictions and actions of the service intellectuals were very popular among social scientists throughout the 1920s and 1930s. During the first years of the Great Depression, Congress, looking for a convenient scapegoat, adopted the heavily protectionist Smoot-Hawley Tariff.

The tariff was the highest in American history and, according to most economists, represented exactly the wrong approach to the economic depression. Some leading economists launched a petition drive to urge President Hoover to veto the bill, but most of their colleagues, and especially the leaders of the American Economic Association, refused to support the petition for fear of being considered political and prejudiced. A few years later, Franklin Roosevelt had no better luck in seeking advice from Yale economist James Harvey Rogers, the foremost authority on gold and silver. Rogers allegedly told Roosevelt that *as an economist* he could not give advice on any particular gold policy but could only predict the consequences of Roosevelt's eventual choice. The sociologist George Lundberg saw the role of the service intellectual as the ultimate safeguard for the social science profession. Noting the employment of physical scientists under all types of political regimes, Lundberg argued that social scientists should strive for a similar position: "If social scientists possessed an equally demonstrably relevant body of knowledge and technique . . . , then knowledge would be equally above the reach of political upheaval. The services of real social scientists would be as indispensable to Fascists, as to Communists and Democrats." The ideals of Sanborn, Ely, and Small seemed far distant and irrelevant.[26]

The concrete, physical manifestation of this marriage of empiricism, the universities, government, and the foundations was the construction of the Social Science Research Building at the University of Chicago. Paid for by the Rockefeller Foundation, "Eleven Twenty-six" represented Merriam's and Ruml's vision of the ideal physical setting for the social sciences. First of all, only professors who taught primarily graduate students were allowed to have offices there. Second, floor space was very flexible to allow for the development of cooperative, interdisciplinary research. Third, only two or three lecture rooms existed. Most of the other rooms were filled with galvonometers, calculators, and the like to measure and enumerate data. There was no space at all for books. Even the outside of the building reflected an amoral, empirical perspective. The individual in charge of the "Symbolism" section of the building's committee was the respected sociologist William Fielding Ogburn, whom Chicago had hired away from Columbia to provide a strong statistical approach to social science, and he fulfilled his role in his planning as well as his teaching function. Under the bow window on the 59th Street side of the building, he ordered workmen to chisel, ironically in Gothic script, the inscription, "When you cannot measure . . . your knowledge is . . . meagre . . . and . . . unsatisfactory."[27]

On December 16 and 17, 1929, a love feast of university administrators, national and international social scientists, and foundation officers dedicated Eleven Twenty-six. After a perfunctory dedication by Chicago's neo-Thomist president, Robert Hutchins, the chief speaker rose. Wesley Mitchell represented not only the success of the service intellectuals but, as a member of the University of Chicago's first class in 1892, the success of the host institution as well. Mitchell had won the respect of the academic community not only through his technical work with the government and the NBER but through his early work in institutional economic theory and his 1913 classic pioneering study *Business Cycles*. By 1929, Mitchell subscribed to the position of the service intellectuals. He began his speech by praising the stimulation of his early Chicago years with John Dewey, Thorstein Veblen, and J. Lawrence Laughlin but quickly went on to bemoan his lack of training in statistics. Statistics had proved to be the most important development in contemporary social science, and Mitchell happily noted the new building's technical equipment for such study. To him, the building represented a new age in American social science devoted to the accumulation of data "bit by bit after the succession of the elder sciences" and the replacement of "the man of hunches" with the man of "facts."[28]

The succeeding addresses echoed Mitchell's views. The geologist John Merriam, president of the Carnegie Institute and Charles's brother, advocated adopting the empirical techniques of the physical and natural scientists. He bluntly declared that issues such as the tariff, conservation, and Prohibition would "melt away" once social scientists gathered sufficient data. In the following address, Ruml calmly assured John Merriam and other doubters that social scientists were already true scientists and were approaching success at solving such problems.[29]

The self-congratulations of the service intellectuals were not only self-serving but also premature. Despite their claims and those of later supporters, a significant number of individuals *within* social science continued to deny the validity of their methodological position. Controversy reared its head even at the dedication of Eleven Twenty-six. Charles Merriam, who was away from Chicago during Ogburn's efforts on behalf of symbolism, opposed the absolute deification of measurement and mumbled about taking Ogburn for a ride, Chicago style. University of Chicago economists, who were actually abandoning empiricism at this time to develop the famous theoretical Chicago school of economics, were ruder. Frank Knight declared, "And if you cannot measure it, measure it anyhow." Jacob Viner added, "And if you can measure . . . your knowledge will still be meagre and unsatisfactory."[30]

The underlying conflict also emerged in the celebration's next-to-last address, "Man and the Humanities." Not only was its position among the addresses significant, so was the choice of its presenter, anatomist C. Judson Herrick. Despite his own scientific background, Herrick challenged the assumptions of the conferees and insisted that all the new techniques and instruments were irrelevant without social values. Rather than imitating the physical sciences in ignoring human values and goals, social scientists should serve as a bridge between the sciences and the humanities and develop ways of determining values scientifically. Without these values, all knowledge—scientific or not—was worthless.[31]

Herrick's insistence on the centrality of values was by no means the only one. Nor was his support for simultaneous reliance on the scientific method. The chief opposition to the objectivist position came not from outsiders like Herrick but from within the social sciences, from individuals who shared many of the service intellectuals' assumptions and core beliefs. Although a few were freelance intellectuals, most held positions in prominent institutions and were well known within the profession and often better known than the objectivists outside it. Like the service intellectuals and unlike the neo-Thomists, they believed that the scientific method had to be used to study society. It was not only the best strategy for obtaining socially accepted conclusions; it was the only valid methodological approach for obtaining verifiable knowledge. These critics also shared the traditional concern of social science for practicality.

The key difference between the service intellectuals and their critics was that the latter believed that social scientists could and should take a normative position on social issues. The members of the purposive group shared a strong commitment to the teleological character of social science. To them, the entire purpose of social science involved the achievement of certain moral ends; without this normative aspect, social science was little more than mindless empiricism. Social science, they believed, was a purposive science tied to *specific* moral goals, and individuals who neglected this aspect abandoned their cultural and ethical responsibilities. This did not, however, mean that they rejected the scientific method. According to their understanding of John Dewey's instrumentalism, the scientific method did not preclude predesigned moral ends but actually required them. One could be scientific without renouncing moral judgments. Social scientists must be objective and use the scientific method scrupulously, but they could use the information obtained in pursuit of normative goals. In fact, scientifically determined knowledge aided immeasurably in the selection of specific value goals. After all, social scientists had studied the subject more intensively than anyone else. Who was better qualified to recognize the positive goals to be achieved than the true experts?

In their commitment to specific normative goals, the purposivists clearly demonstrated their disdain for the service intellectuals. Although both sides claimed to be concerned with practicality, each found the specific actions of the opposing group controversial and often provoking. The works that brought out the most anger among the purposive thinkers were Thurman Arnold's *Symbols of Government* and, especially, his bestseller *The Folklore of Capitalism*. In his writings as a legal realist, his famous courses in procedure and trial practice at Yale Law School, his administrative work for the New Deal, his post–World War II practice as the senior partner of the prominent Washington firm Arnold, Fortas, and Porter, and especially in his popular social science work of the 1930s, Arnold laid bare the idolization of technique and the dislike and distrust of normative theory that lay at the base of objectivist social science. Several contemporary reviewers and such prominent later historians as Richard Hofstadter and Howard Zinn called his books the best examples of the technical, New Deal approach to social science and, in Hofstadter's words, "the theoretical equivalent of FDR's opportunistic virtuosity in practical politics."[32]

This elevation of technique to an end in itself came, appropriately, from a legal thinker and legal realist. Legal formalism—the study of law as completely logical, theoretical, and uninfluenced by economics, politics, or personal psychology—continued to dominate the study of law despite the challenges of Oliver Wendell Holmes, Louis Brandeis, and Benjamin Cardozo. Following the ideas of these thinkers, legal realists rejected the analytic approach and demanded that law be studied as it really existed, in all its complexity. Karl Llewellyn, probably the most important theorist of the movement, freely acknowledged the lack of ideological agreement among its members and identified their one common characteristic as an emphasis on method, the "technology of how to perceive law." By emphasizing what law was, many realists engaged in what Llewellyn called "the temporary divorce of 'Is' and 'Ought.'" Arnold's Yale colleagues Walter Nelles and Walter Wheeler Cook finalized the divorce and denied all ethical absolutes for law. As Holmes stated, the single concern of the lawyer was knowing the law and winning the case for one's client.[33]

Arnold, one of the great practitioners of his day, reveled in the practice of law. Beginning as an obscure lawyer in Laramie, Wyoming, he quickly rose to become the dean of the West Virginia Law School and a professor at Yale on the basis of his championing of the importance of teaching legal technique. His Yale lectures on procedure, with their brilliance, circuitousness, and outrageousness (and his basset hound's faithful attendance), became popular institutions. In his second- and third-year courses on trial courts Arnold emphasized details and actions of specific cases, carefully relishing the maneuverings of the opposing sides. He agreed fully with Llewellyn's contention that a lawyer should not be a philosopher or even a social scientist but "a craftsman . . . a specialized technician . . . [with] a specialist's knowledge of abnormal situations and legal techniques." As his good friend William Douglas summarized it, "Practice was his dish."[34]

Identifying contemporary social science with that taught at Princeton twenty-five years earlier and with legal formalism, Arnold savaged social scientists as "preachers," "medicine men," and "a bunch of dodos" living in "a dream world." They were "obsessed with a moral attitude" that hindered practical responses and meaningful progress. To Arnold, normative theory was purely the "philosophical justification" of special interest groups. Ideologies and principles were "found" and "manufactured" in order to maintain morale and offer rationalizations for the group's accession to power. Arnold saw ideas as "symptoms and not remedies," and he categorically dismissed and even insulted individuals who based their arguments on moral or theoretical grounds, saying they were either fools or knaves. Social scientists were by definition such individuals. Even though he was a dedicated New Dealer, Arnold accused the brain trust of attempting to establish a social system based on principles rather than facts. His sole evidence for this unique assertion was that many brain trusters were academic social scientists and therefore must think that way.[35]

Arnold maintained that social scientists could best transcend their alleged inadequacies by following the lead of the legal realists: "A practical or humanitarian attitude develops techniques, and not logical arguments. A rational moral attitude develops philosophies and priests and not technicians." He viewed social and political activity as a Manichean struggle between the "heroic men of skill" and the unregenerate "men of principle" and called for America to follow the Henry Fords and ignore the philosophers. If they did this, technical social scientists might someday approach the high standards of colonial Africa, where one Englishman could "rule ten thousand blacks" by acting practically and unideologically. As for values, Arnold cavalierly dismissed them. "The actual result of dialect definitions of social values is only to create a group of words like fascism, communism, regimentation, bureaucracy, etc., which impede the practical methods of distributing goods." If one could not eliminate abstractions, then one should follow the counsel of Machiavelli and use them to further the goals of one's organization. Arnold followed his own advice in his personal career. After proving in his works the purely symbolic nature of America's antitrust laws and lampooning the hapless "crusaders" honestly attempting to enforce them, he turned around a year later to become the extremely activist head of the Justice Department's Antitrust Division under his chosen leader and organization, Franklin Roosevelt and the New Deal.[36]

The most thorough critique of Arnold's beliefs came from instrumentalist philosopher Sidney Hook. Born in the New York City ghetto of Williamsburg, Hook went to City College and then to graduate school at Columbia, where he studied philosophy with John Dewey. Hook was one of Dewey's closest intellectual disciples and popularizers, and by the late 1930s he was the one individual Dewey allowed to suggest improvements for all his manuscripts before publication. Hook's connections to pragmatism were essential because Arnold, like the other service intellectuals, considered himself a true pragmatist and cloaked himself in its philosophy. In a 1938 *University of Chicago Law Review* analysis of *Folklore,* Hook disagreed. Although he praised the book for its realistic portrayal of the functioning of the political system, Hook claimed that the real issue was whether politicians and social scientists could do away with normative judgments. He adamantly denied Arnold's contention that value judgments were meaningless because it was impossible to test their validity scientifically. Without preconceived values, a social thinker lacked bases for his choices. Arnold argued that decisions should be left to a chosen leader, but that sidestepped the question of how one chose the leader. Without normative goals, one would be reduced to "a kind of Bonapartism" without valid grounds for choosing a Roosevelt over a Hitler or a Stalin. Although Hook clearly recognized Arnold's continued commitment to ethical goals through his New Deal service, he perspicaciously demanded that Arnold explain how he could justify his actions without abstract moral principles. Hook argued that the position of the service intellectual must be either spiritually or intellectually bankrupt.[37]

Hook's critique of Arnold reflects both the strengths and the weaknesses of the purposive approach to social science. Certainly it points out the glaring weaknesses and deficiencies of the service intellectuals' abandonment of ethical goals. Clearly social research needed values. Yet

Hook, like the other purposivists, completely sidestepped the question of where to obtain these values. Like the objectivists, purposive thinkers rejected all a priori values and insisted on experientially based knowledge. But unlike the objectivists, they also insisted on transcending "what is" to reach "what could or should be." The means and location of these normative values remained unclear. The search for values was widespread during the 1930s. Groups as diverse as labor leaders, filmmakers, folksingers, and muralists bitterly criticized the absence of normative concerns in American social and economic thought and tried to develop alternative value systems. Unlike the others, who could present suggestions and symbolic examples of such values, social scientists, by the very nature of their work, had to come up with well-developed, logical answers to such problems.[38]

Purposive thinkers began to look for alternative values in the work of the cultural anthropologists of the 1920s and 1930s. In the past, anthropology's main role for the social sciences had been, in the words of E. B. Tylor, "to expose the remains of crude old culture which have persisted into harmful superstition, and to mark these out for destruction." Beginning in the early 1900s, American anthropologists under the direction of Franz Boas began to investigate thousands of different cultures in depth and to emphasize the totality and common features of all cultures. Developments in anthropology provided purposive thinkers with three possible avenues for the determination of ethical but scientifically based values.[39]

First, and most important, purposive thinkers welcomed anthropological research for the intellectual liberation provided by the recognition of the myriad cultural possibilities. Ruth Benedict wrote in her classic *Patterns of Culture* that "the diversity of the possible combinations is endless, and adequate social orders can be built indiscriminately upon a great variety of these foundations." For a social thinker dissatisfied with the present order, that recognition opened up endless vistas of possible social changes. In a similar fashion, the purposive school turned to works of history as reflections of different patterns of thought and institutions that demonstrated the temporality of the present system and the wide range of choices. "This speaking of the things that are absent" provided the purposive school with possibilities that had not existed for them before.[40]

Anthropology's second contribution was the holistic perspective on society and social problems. The Boasian school's devotion to describing culture in all its manifestations resulted in many clear examples of cultures existing as cohesive wholes. One could not understand one aspect of society apart from the rest. Anthropology had demonstrated "the inescapable interrelatedness of things." Social scientists began to apply anthropological insights to examine the interconnections between the various aspects of modern society to forge a functional perspective.[41]

The recognition of the cohesiveness of culture led to a necessary emphasis on interdisciplinary study. Service intellectuals also called publicly for this type of study. One of the primary reasons for the establishment of both the Social Science Research Council (SSRC) and Chicago's Social Research Building was to encourage such research. Yet few service intellectuals actually did such "impractical" work. The wide scope demanded by interdisciplinary research made the collection of sufficient data to meet the demands of the service intellectuals almost impossible. They chose instead to concentrate on more closely defined and limited projects. Moreover, the lack of clear disciplinary boundaries seemed to threaten their revered professionalism. In 1938, Edwin Nourse, chairman of the SSRC's powerful Problems and Policy Committee, stated that interdisciplinary research had failed to live up to expectations and called for the end of funding. He summed up his low opinion of interdisciplinary work with reference to the council's "highly facetious—at times even ribald—use of the expression 'cross fertilization of disciplines.'" A year later, the council's president, Robert Crane, publicly stated that the council would work through the various disciplines. The purposive school, on the other hand, supported the interdisciplinary movement completely. James Harvey Robinson called it the most positive development in history and the other social sciences during the past thirty years. Beard was the only individual of the day to serve as president of two professional organizations, and throughout his career he continued to work in both political science and history.[42]

A third source of values also came, although somewhat indirectly, from anthropology. When Boas and his disciples first began to study various cultures, they perceived individual members of cultures as being completely molded by social institutions and customs. As ethnologists began to record cultures in detail, it became evident that every society contains a wide range of personalities. This began the culture and personality school, represented by such thinkers as Benedict and Margaret Mead, which investigated the impact of the individual on culture and vice versa. The anthropologist Edward Sapir argued against the concept of a "super-organic, impersonal" culture and asserted that "the true locus of a culture is the individual or a specifically enumerated list of individuals." Adapted by such purposive thinkers as Robert Lynd, the concept of the culturally independent individual provided a means for determining ethical values and evaluating social institutions and cultures. Lynd argued that the most valuable cultural institutions are those that permit the greatest possible emotional and intellectual growth in individuals. Social scientists should judge and further develop these institutions according to their ability to satisfy the basic "human cravings" of all normal individuals. "The responsibility is to keep everlastingly challenging the present with the question: But what is it that we human beings want and what things have to be done in what ways and in what sequence, in order to change the present so as to achieve it?"[43]

The key source for the purposive thinkers' quest for scientifically determined values was the philosophy of pragmatism, specifically Dewey's instrumentalism. The purposivists maintained that Dewey's philosophy, especially as it developed in the 1920s and 1930s, demonstrated how to use the scientific method to determine verifiable, normative values. That is, the scientific method could not only show the *best* way of doing something but also *what* to do in the first place. Their reliance on instrumentalism, with its heavy dependence on the scientific method, was ironic for two reasons. First, it meant that the scientific method was in some ways more important for the purposive group than for the "scientistic" service intellectuals. Second, the service intellectuals also saw pragmatism and especially instrumentalism as the key to their approach to the study of society.

The attraction of pragmatism for social scientists of both schools and its place in their central conflict is clear. From its very beginnings pragmatism concerned itself with the concept of action, specifically with the relationship between action and knowledge and belief: What is it that we know? What do we believe and why do we believe it? And how does this knowledge and belief affect our actions? Pragmatism sees man consciously using his mind to solve problems. William James consistently insisted that "the idea is essentially active" and has "a cutting edge," that knowledge makes a difference in individuals' actions and their situations, and all thinking has a conscious purpose toward which it is directed. As the historian of philosophy John E. Smith lucidly explained, "Behind the thought of major thinkers in the American tradition for the past half-century has been a thoroughly teleological view of things. Thought has a purpose; it is guided by purposes, and its genuine actuality or power in the world is made manifest as a shaper of the future in accordance with plans or ends in view. . . . Purpose is a concept without which pragmatism is unintelligible." Certainly it was a perspective that conformed with the practical orientation of American social science.[44]

Pragmatism began in the late nineteenth century as part of the period's search for verifiable knowledge. Faced with the impact of the evolutionary perspective on a fixed, unchanging worldview, many intellectuals found it difficult to believe anything. If everything was in the process of change, then truth as an unchanging ideal was an impossible goal. Pragmatists accepted evolution but also insisted on the need for belief and action. Charles Sanders Peirce rejected the rationalist belief that thinking is a disinterested pursuit of truth. Rather, for Peirce, thought was a way of "fixating" belief, of achieving thought at rest. James's philosophy and psychology were directed even more toward permitting the individual to act. As a young man, James experienced a series of mental breakdowns and found himself unable to make decisions. His consequent thought sought to liberate the individual through a "will to believe." Once one *knew* something, one could and must act. Knowledge was not a passive affair of testing the reality of the knowing self against the reality of direct experience; it was part of a conscious action directed toward achieving certain ends. In the functionalist psychology of James and Dewey, one literally could not separate thought and behavior; both were parts of a continuous function of the entire organism. As Dewey insisted in his college psychology textbook, "There is no dualism or separation—thought cannot exist independent of acting."[45]

Dewey certainly saw himself as part of this tradition of freeing individuals to think and act: "In a sense my own life of thought has been a struggle to get liberation—freedom from a tradition inherited and still embodied at least in the formulae of civilization." For Dewey, Darwinism, by emphasizing change, had rescued American thought from its reliance on predetermined answers and conclusions. The role of thought was to answer questions and permit action; "mind, whatever else it may be, is at least an organ for service for the control of environment in relation to the ends of the life process."[46]

Dewey's ideas were even more relevant to the needs of social scientists than those of other pragmatists. While the other pragmatic philosophers concentrated on "fixating belief" for individuals, Dewey saw pragmatism as a way of solving social problems. Philosophy must "become a method of locating and interpreting the more serious of the conflicts that occur in life and a method of projecting ways for dealing with them." Indeed, Robert Westbrook recently argued that while most philosophers of Dewey's generation saw epistemological questions and their relationship to the scientific method as the key to their discipline, Dewey saw ethics and its relationship to science as representing the core of philosophy.[47]

Much evidence exists for Dewey's pervasive influence on the social sciences. The noted sociologist W. I. Thomas, who taught with Dewey at Chicago, dismissed a negative comparison of the relative impacts of Dewey and fellow Chicago pragmatist George Herbert Mead. Thomas held that Mead had one central fixed idea, which he kept repeating "as if it were a great profundity"; but Dewey was an intellectual giant, "America's medicine man." If this analogy was not true for all Americans, it surely was for social thinkers and especially for social scientists. Such leading historians of twentieth-century American social and reform thought as Arthur Schlesinger, Jr., and Eric Goldman categorically identified Dewey as *the* central figure in the development of twentieth-century social thought, and a historian of social science claimed with equal conviction that Dewey and his disciple Mead "did as much to shape American social science as any two men."[48]

In the 1920s Dewey consciously turned his primary attention to social thought and specifically to providing a scientific basis for the study of society. In his 1920 *Reconstruction in Philosophy*, Dewey set about to demonstrate that philosophy, despite its claims of universal truth, always reflects the traditions and social conflicts of its age. Rather than bemoan this fact, Dewey applauded it and called for the development of a philosophy that would openly concentrate on contemporary social and moral clashes. During this period he told his Teachers College colleague R. Bruce Raup that he had shifted the focus of his educational and philosophical writings from solving problems in general to solving problems in current society. Dewey had decided to apply his general philosophical conclusions to specific social issues and conflict. He accelerated his already active writing for popular journals, and between the years 1915 and 1935 he wrote 160 articles for the *New Republic* alone.[49]

Moreover, Dewey saw the social sciences as the key agents in this development of a new and better society. He best expressed these beliefs at a 1928 symposium at the University of Virginia on the social sciences. Dewey began his address by noting that while few people regarded philosophy as a social science, he thought it was wise to do so. His "favorite idea" was that modern philosophy should do for the social sciences what seventeenth- and eighteenth-century philosophy had done for the physical sciences. After all, the social sciences as the study of "*the* distinctly human phenomenon" was "of the greatest impact to man."

Philosophy could not provide scientific conclusions, but it could help achieve an "encompassing intellectual perspective" that would enable social scientists to go beyond the description of social activities to their evaluation.[50]

Since the issues of evaluation and connection between knowledge and action were exactly the central issues of social science between the world wars, and since Dewey proposed to solve them in a scientific way, social thinkers naturally welcomed his contributions. Yet Dewey was a "medicine man" for social science in more than one way. Social scientists recognized that he was attempting to cure the evident illnesses of their profession but, like primitive tribesmen, were unclear about how he was doing this. Dewey was never easy to understand, even for other philosophers, and debates always seemed to exist over what Dewey had *really* said about any major philosophical issue. Oliver Wendell Holmes, who admired Dewey's work greatly, asserted that Dewey wrote as "God would have spoken had he been inarticulate but keenly desirous to tell you how it was."[51]

The service intellectuals seized upon an apparent lack of clarity in Dewey's writings on the proper role of the scientific method in the study of society to bolster their position. The purposive thinkers, with Dewey's concurrence, insisted that he believed that social science was a humanistic discipline in which means and ends were inextricably linked. The scientific method involved the actual determination of goals as well as techniques and facts, and these normative ends did not follow automatically from facts and methods. The social scientist must take personal responsibility for goals as well as for the best way of obtaining them. The service intellectuals, on the other hand, argued that Dewey saw two central roles for the scientific method. First, it provided valid knowledge and determined the best methods for the achievement of set goals. Second, sufficient and valid information used in the most appropriate ways showed the proper things to be done. Social scientists could become Arnold's "cheerful technicians," because scientifically determined data and techniques ensured good ends. The central issue between the two groups involved the proper interpretation of Dewey's thinking about the scientific method and its proper application to the study of society. Their differing interpretations of instrumentalism reflected the key difference between the two groups.

Surely the centrality of the scientific method for pragmatism, and especially instrumentalism, was one of its chief attractions for both groups of social scientists. Even if the theories of evolution and relativity had demonstrated the indeterminacy of knowledge, the scientific method restored the validity of inquiry. Philosophers of pragmatism, social scientists, and, indeed, most early twentieth-century intellectuals came to emphasize the importance of methodology. Social scientists and philosophers had independently come to emphasize science for intellectual, cultural, and professional reasons.[52]

Even before the advent of pragmatism, American philosophy had traditionally relied on the scientific method in its attempt to combine theology, metaphysics, and morals. Scottish commonsense philosophy saw itself as incorporating religious views and a scientific worldview, and some commonsense philosophers even referred to their field as "moral science." One of the last of these, James McCosh of Princeton, serenely noted his continued attachment to science despite the apparent heresy of Darwinism: "I believe that whatever supposed discrepancies may come up for a time between science and revealed truth will soon disappear, that each will confirm the other, and both will tend to promote the glory of God." The appeal of the scientific method within the discipline of philosophy was so strong that by the late nineteenth century even the idealist metaphysician Josiah Royce claimed to have used it to prove his theories.[53]

Despite his relative lack of scientific training compared with the first generation of pragmatists, Dewey admired science equally. The scientific method represented to him the highest development of human intelligence, and its function was to test hypotheses for the solution of problems and the control of the individual's environment. Dewey's attachment to science was a central focus throughout his career. Even in his early years he shared the common sentiments of his time and turned to science to prove his beliefs. According to his daughter, Dewey claimed that the most lasting influences of his college years were articles by Darwin, Huxley, and Leslie Stephen in the contemporary English philosophical journals. At Johns Hopkins, one of the chief attractions of T. H. Green's version of neoidealism to Dewey and his mentor, George Sylvester Morris, was its contention that science and idealism corresponded and were even dependent on one another. The scientific method could provide at least some definitive answers to the continuous arguments of philosophy. As he was studying psychology under G. Stanley Hall at Hopkins, Dewey recognized how German advances in physiology were transforming psychology, and in his 1887 textbook, *Psychology*, he tried to integrate physiology and a Hegelian conception of mind and consciousness. Even when science conflicted with Dewey's philosophical beliefs, he retained his conviction of its primacy as a guide for human affairs.[54]

The service intellectuals' attempted appropriation of Dewey as scientific icon stemmed from his tendency to connect technique and moralism through the activity of the scientific method. In a revealingly entitled 1903 article, "Logical Conditions of a Scientific Treatment of Morality," Dewey insisted on the primacy of a "moral interest" to guide the scientific method and the noncomparability of "matters of conduct" and the social sciences. But he then quickly proclaimed an identity of logical procedure. That is, the methods of arriving at moral and technical conclusions are the same. In his later *Theory of Valuation*, Dewey stated that normative judgments are governed by exactly the same "matter-of-fact judgments" as anything else and are different only in subject. The service intellectuals chose to interpret this, despite Dewey's consistent protests, to mean that the use of the scientific method per se would provide not only the proper techniques but also correct and evaluate ends. Proper technique ensured moral conclusions.[55]

The service intellectuals were not alone in this interpretation. Some of Dewey's earliest disciples came to similar conclusions and criticized him harshly for them. The pragmatic philosopher C. I. Lewis denied that it was possible to completely determine ethical knowledge through empirical facts alone. Facts were needed, certainly, but they were never sufficient by themselves. Cultural critic Lewis Mumford explained the dissenters' position eloquently: "Without superimposed values, the values that arise out of vision, instrumentalism becomes the mere apotheosis of actualities: it is all dressed up with no place to go."[56]

The purposive school's continued attachment to instrumentalism stemmed from a different perspective. Both the service intellectuals and Dewey's pragmatic detractors overlooked the strong heritage of moralism evident in pragmatism in general and instrumentalism in particular. Morton White, in *Science and Sentiment in America*, noted the constant tension in American philosophy between Lockean empiricism and the possibility of nontestable spiritual emotions, feelings, and beliefs, and he concluded that in American philosophy the latter always seemed to be dominant. No matter how strong the attachment to nature and science, the ultimate purpose became the positive uses of knowledge and the values of things for human purposes.[57]

This, indeed, was close to a definition of pragmatism. As Louis Hartz noted, "American pragmatism has always been deceptive because, glacierlike, it has rested on miles of submerged conviction." Despite his reliance on the scientific method and his vocal disdain for metaphysics, Peirce desperately sought to replace the "greed philosophy" of classical economics with "the natural judgments of the sensible heart," man's humanity to man. James openly insisted on the primacy of personal and intellectual liberation over any scientific "truths." "Science can tell us what exists; but to compare the worths, both of what exists and what does not exist, we must consult not science, but what Pascal calls our heart."[58]

Dewey carried his insistence on normative goals even further than his fellow pragmatists. As the biographer of Dewey's early life remarked, one can never quite imagine Dewey's thinking without moralism, the often unconscious belief that philosophy determines what should be done. Dewey's moralism evolved directly out of his evangelical upbringing, especially his mother's social concerns. Many of his early essays reveal this combination of religious ideas, ethics, and political activity in their titles: "The Ethics of Democracy," "Moral Theory and Practice," "The Relation of Philosophy to Theology," and "Christianity and Democracy," for example. Dewey adopted neo-Hegelian philosophy in the early 1880s largely in order to construct a unified system that could develop and defend a system of what could and should be. Revealingly, Dewey came to Hegelianism through the work of the British ethicist T. H. Green, who sought to use the Hegelian organic metaphor and emphasis on the group to moderate the individualistic emphases of liberalism while retaining liberalism's concern for individual freedom. Even as Dewey turned to the scientific method to refine and eventually replace his Hegelian perspective, he insisted that it could not replace or create spiritual goals. "The mere fact that the physical universe as such is making toward a certain goal does not decide that man should aim at the same goal."[59]

The need for normative values to direct human activity and help comprehend reality was central throughout Dewey's life. His predominant concern with the application of instrumentalism to education and the development of a scientific logic during the first two decades of the twentieth century may have caused this central concern to be less obvious in his works. Yet in the 1920s the self-admitted error of his support for World War I and American culture's pervasive materialism brought the issue of value clarification to the forefront of his concerns. In his 1929 *Quest for Certainty*, Dewey bluntly declared that philosophy's "central problem is the relation that exists between the beliefs about the nature of things due to natural science and beliefs about values—using that word to designate whatever is taken to have rightful authority in the direction of conduct."[60]

Throughout the 1920s and 1930s Dewey constantly pursued "practical and human" ends to direct the "truncated, blind, and distorted" scientific method. Philosophy needed the scientific method to determine facts, but science by itself was not enough. It could provide liberation from the past but no direction for the future. "The beginning of wisdom is, I repeat, the realization that science is an instrument which is indifferent to the external uses to which it is put." Direction would have to come from philosophy, which was not a mere collection of facts but "a conviction about moral values, a sense for the better kind of life to be led . . . [and for] a desired future which our desires, when translated into articulate conviction, may help bring into existence." Of the twin attributes of science and morality, Dewey clearly stressed the primacy of the latter.[61]

Nor did Dewey hesitate to make clear the implications of his thinking for social science. Throughout the 1920s and 1930s he blasted the same service intellectuals who looked on him as their champion. He stated bluntly that all the myriad problems of contemporary social scientists derived from their unquestioning emulation of a mistaken view of the social sciences. "Observing, collecting, recording and filing tomes of social phenomena" without established normative goals led to a mere massing of facts, which in turn led to an acceptance of "what is" for "what should be" and a conscious disregard for "larger social issues." Dewey considered this to be an abandonment of the teleological nature of social science. "Anything that obscures the fundamentally moral nature of the social problem is harmful, no matter whether it proceeds from the side of physical or psychological theory. Any doctrine that eliminates or even obscures the function of choice of values . . . weakens personal responsibility for judgment and action." Dewey argued that "instead of awaiting an event to know what means to take, we should take measures to bring the event to pass." The proper role of social scientists was to decide the best goals for society and then to use their skills to help bring them about.[62]

Dewey found these goals in his attachment to democracy, a shared way of life dedicated to personal liberty and positive choices which would lead to the development of "composed, effective, and creative" individuals. Such individuals would be free to develop only in a culture based on equality and freedom expressed through popular participation, and Dewey made quite clear that the "money economy" of present-day America did not meet those criteria. Dewey had no use for any scholarship, scientific or not, that did not directly seek democratic ideals and goals. For Dewey, knowledge had to be purposive.[63]

The conflict over the role of social scientists and social knowledge erupted not just in practitioners' respective attempts to qualify as Dewey's disciples but in all aspects of the discourse of the social sciences. One can best recognize the centrality of the debate by analyzing the presidential addresses of the American Economic Association (AEA), the American Historical Association (AHA), the American Political Science Association (APSA), and the American Sociological Society (ASS) for the years 1919–39. Of the seventy-six addresses I was able to locate, thirty-four of them, or 45 percent, deal directly with the question of knowledge and value judgments. The percentages are similar in each of the professions and in both decades. Fifty percent of the APSA addresses concern the social role of social scientists, while the AEA addresses had the lowest percentage with 40 percent. Presidents of the AHA dealt with the topic 45 percent of the time, and the sociologists 44 percent. Forty-four percent of all the addresses during the 1920s concerned this topic, and discussion of this issue increased very slightly to 46 percent of presidential speeches during the 1930s.

Although a majority of the presidents who addressed social knowledge and value judgments in their speeches subscribed to the objectivist position, a significant number did not. Twenty-one of the thirty-four relevant addresses, or 61 percent, accept the role of the service intellectual, while twelve, or 35 percent, clearly belong to the purposive school. The inimitable L. L. Bernard delivered an unclassifiable address, alternately blasting and praising both positions in the same speech. The AHA, in which purposive thinkers had challenged an entrenched objectivist position even before the 1920s, had the most purposive presidential addresses, with four. Revealingly, sociology, which had most recently sought to separate itself from its normative origins and was fearful of public identification with social welfare and social work, had the least, with two. If the service intellectuals had felt as secure as their talks at Eleven Twenty-six indicated, they clearly would have had no reason to constantly assert the methodological superiority of their position and denigrate the claims of the purposive group. Some of them obviously did not feel such a threat. Robert Park used his 1924 ASS presidential address to champion cities as a place for research and insist on the importance of spatial factors in all social research. University of California historian Herbert Bolton repeated his well-known thesis on the significance of borderlands for world history in 1932, and Columbia economist Henry Rogers Seagar compared the benefits of company and trade unions in his 1922 address. This concentration on particular research interests is not surprising. What is surprising is that it occurred so seldom—only one-fifth of the time—while almost half the addresses deal with the single issue of the proper ends of social research.

Nowhere was the debate more heated than within the historical profession. Historians had adopted a policy of strict empiricism several decades earlier than the other social sciences and had sought to fulfill Leopold von Ranke's goal of *"Geschichte wie gewesen"* (History as it was) through the meticulous collection and printing of historical documents without analysis. Similarly, their purposive thrust began earlier as well. A convenient starting date for the beginning of this goal-oriented, self-described New History is 1907, when Charles Beard and James Harvey Robinson published *The Development of Modern Europe.* The authors openly stated in the preface that they had "consistently subordinated the past to the present . . . to enable the reader to catch up with his own times." Within the historical profession, colonial historian Charles Andrews best articulated the empirical, nonactivist approach in his 1924 presidential address, "These Forty Years." Andrews used the opportunity of the fortieth anniversary of the AHA to relate the progress of the discipline and clearly attributed it to the replacement of "vigorous partisanship" with objective, scientific history. "The object of historical study is to understand, not to condemn, . . . preach or revile."[64]

None of the succeeding presidents of the association openly challenged Andrews's views until Robinson became president in 1929. Robinson's address, revealingly entitled "The Newer Ways of Historians," states blandly that the very possibility of scientific history is as irrelevant "as whether glorified spirits are in the empyrean rather than the aqueous heaven." Historians, Robinson said, should discard such useless debates and concentrate on the best opportunity ever offered for connecting the lessons of the past with the creation of present and future policy. Two years later, Carl Becker continued and expanded Robinson's theme in his classic "Everyman His Own Historian." Becker noted the dependence of personal knowledge and opinions on past experience and pointed out that such limitations affect all historians. Facts cannot speak for themselves; they speak only through limited, experientially biased interpreters. One must confront this truth honestly and both admit and accept one's biases. Completely objective, empirical history cannot exist, but historians can and should have normative ideals and goals. After another two-year interval, Beard continued this train of thought in "Written History as an Act of Faith." With characteristic aggression, he called on his fellow historians to "cast off [their] servitude to the assumptions of natural science" and recognize the constant personal choices involved in their work. Since one could not prevent personal biases from affecting one's choice of material and conclusions, one should consciously adopt a "frame of reference composed of things deemed necessary and things deemed desirable."[65]

Many historians reacted with outrage, and furious debates raged within the professional journals, but it was not until 1936 that an AHA president took up Beard's challenge in his presidential address. When the official response did come, however, it attacked the normative position totally and angrily. Charles McIlwain, a professor of English legal history at Harvard, had raged against the "bias" of the New History and called for its "repression" since 1926. In his 1936 presidential address he called Becker and Beard "defeatists" led by "sophistry," "pessimism," and distrust of reason to present history as mere fiction and speculative philosophy. History had no necessary connection with public policy. The proper task of the historian was "with history, not with its application"; historians were really "bystanders" to current affairs, not "physicians."[66]

As president of the American Political Science Association in 1926, Beard also figured prominently in its debate over the issue. Charles Merriam, the 1925 APSA president, had begun his official address with a proud review of the various developments in political research since the founding of the association in 1904. Still, Merriam remained dissatisfied. "After all our advances, it sometimes appears that we are not fully appreciated by our colleagues, either in the world of practical politics or in the higher and brighter world of theoretical science." He thought the way to win wider public acceptance of political science was to follow the conclusions of his friend Wesley Mitchell's AEA presidential address: that "more and more it appears that the last word in human behavior is to be scientific." The APSA had made a good beginning toward this goal but needed to develop more sophisticated quantitative methods to continue its progress.[67]

The association honored Beard, Merriam's chief competitor for influence within the association, the following year. Beard and Merriam had a very competitive relationship. The two exchanged fairly frequent "Dear Charlie" letters full of pleasantries and invitations (never accepted) to visit, but they genuinely disliked each other. Merriam dismissed a potential researcher sent by Beard as "essentially a propagandist," and Beard frequently wrote unfavorable, even snide, reviews of Merriam's books. Beard envied Merriam's access to research funds, and Merriam coveted Beard's far greater popularity with the public.[68]

Beard devoted his 1926 presidential address to an almost point-by-point refutation of Merriam's. The same research that Merriam had praised, Beard condemned as "myopic," "sterile," and lacking the creative imagination needed to solve the significant issues of the day. The over-specialization plaguing the field had come about because of the demands universities and foundations made on researchers. Beard opposed the purely scientific approach in political science because it denied a place for the "man of hunches" who searched for answers to the central problems of the culture. He concluded stirringly, "Let us put aside resolutely that great fright, tenderly and without malice, daring to be wrong in some-thing important rather than right in some meticulous banality."[69]

The debate within the other two professions, economics and sociol-ogy, was more muted, at least on the surface. In his 1921 AEA presi-dential address, Jacob Hollander retrospectively examined the role of economists in the war effort. He pointed out the large number of econo-mists employed by government agencies, regulatory boards, and private agencies during the war, and also emphasized their lack of power. They had done mostly clerical, subordinate work, and "not a single figure was . . . permitted to exercise formative, determining influence on the economic conduct of the war." Three years later, Mitchell implicitly noted Hollander's criticism and claimed that the answer was more and better quantitative research. Edwin Gay, the cofounder with Mitchell of the NBER, and E. L. Bogart of the University of Illinois would later repeat Mitchell's empirical agenda in their respective addresses. Yet, in 1936, the New School's Alvin Johnson would launch a blunt, blistering attack on the policy of concentrating on precise measurement while the na-tion's economic and social structure collapsed. Johnson claimed that since economists refused to make predictions on less than perfect data, politics simply went on without the addition of their knowledge and potential leadership.[70]

The service intellectuals did reign relatively unchallenged within the American Sociological Society. Lester Frank Ward's successor and abso-lute disciple, James Dealey, began the 1920s with a plea for sociology to engage in "eudemics, the science of general welfare" and Frank Han-kins's "Social Science and Social Action" closed out the two decades in 1939. Between them only L. L. Bernard with his bitter attack on founda-tions and research institutes that refused to fund him blemished the ASS's perfect record. In 1925 John Lewis Gillin, a former student of Franklin Giddings, sneered at the earlier "propagandists," "sentimentalists," and other "enemies of sociology," and only half humorously appealed for a "sociological inquisition or holy office by which these fellows can be eliminated." In 1928, William Ogburn, another Giddings student, surpassed even this. In "The Folkways of a Scientific Sociology," Ogburn maintained that the role of sociology was *not* to make the world a better place, nor was it to spread information or help in making policy. "Science is interested in one thing only, to wit, discovering new knowledge." In the future all sociological literature would be "wholly colorless" and devoid of any "interpretation, popularization, and emotionalism." Ogburn's goal was to make sociological articles resemble social science abstracts, complete with supporting data and no pretense at literary style. Journals of physics and sociology would become outwardly identical.[71]

Yet this apparent dominance of the objectivist position is misleading. There was extreme bitterness within the profession over the existence of a Chicago- and Columbia-trained clique that unilaterally chose national officers, articles for the officially sponsored *American Journal of Sociology*, and convention sites. Especially bitter were members from the Midwest and the Pacific states, who tended to retain normative goals and engage in more activist-oriented research. During the years 1931–34, some of the older normative-oriented individuals, such as Missouri's Charles Ellwood and Oberlin College's Newell Sims, teamed up with a group of malcontents headed by Bernard and William Meroney of Baylor University to establish a new official journal, dissolve the objectivist Special Commission on the Scope of Research, and, at least temporarily, wrest control of the organization away from the service intellectuals.[72]

Short presidential addresses can hardly do justice to the intricacies of either position, of course. In the final analysis, individuals made their respective methodological choices based on a combination of intellectual, psychological, institutional, and research reasons. One of the best examples of this is the career of Wesley Mitchell, whose combination of methodological sophistication and commitment to a more egalitarian society ironically led him to develop a very convincing defense of objectivist social science and the role of the service intellectual.

2

WESLEY MITCHELL AND THE QUANTITATIVE

APPROACH

Wesley Mitchell, chief speaker at the dedication of Eleven Twenty-six, was not only a prominent service intellectual, he was also probably the most outstanding American economist of his generation. His *Business Cycles* of 1913 suggested large new areas of profitable research to hundreds of young economists, and one knowledgeable admirer called it the most important work published between Alfred Marshall's *Principles of Economics* (1890) and John Maynard Keynes's *General Theory of Employment, Interest, and Money* (1936). Mitchell cofounded and served as the director of research for the National Bureau of Economic Research and served on numerous governmental commissions, and many organizations showered him with honors. He served as president of the American Association for the Advancement of Science—only the second social scientist ever to be so honored—the American Economics Association, the American Statistical Association, the Social Science Research Council, the Econometric Society, and the Academy of Political Science. In 1947 he became the first recipient of the Francis A. Walker Medal, an award given once every five years to the individual who has made the greatest contribution to the study of economics. According to Alvin Johnson, economist and president of the New School for Social Research, economists unanimously considered Mitchell "the Dean" of the profession. Even Rexford Tugwell, who criticized Mitchell for abandoning normative theory in pursuit of the almighty fact, readily admitted that "he is the best we have." When he died in 1948, colleagues mourned him as the greatest American economic scholar of the twentieth century.[1]

Mitchell's eminence within the profession was not due solely to his very real accomplishments as a researcher. At Columbia and the National Bureau of Economic Research he became the mentor of such diverse and influential thinkers as Arthur Burns, Simon Kuznets, Frederick Mills, Joseph Schumpeter, and Milton Friedman. Moreover, Mitchell served on the board of numerous important government commissions on economic and social issues from 1910 to 1945. The basis of Mitchell's teaching and administrative success was his remarkably calm and even temper. In a profession filled with considerable egos, Mitchell stood out as the one figure who could always get a committee to cooperate and reach a workable compromise. As both secretary of commerce and president, Herbert Hoover inevitably turned to Mitchell when forming advisory commissions and referred to him fondly as "the great umpire." A friend teased Mitchell that his middle initial, C., must stand for "Compromise."[2]

Mitchell's cooperative abilities came from his very self-confident personality. His childhood was by all accounts happy, and his father noted his son's "moderate" nature even in childhood. His wife, Lucy Sprague Mitchell, an important progressive educator, spoke of her husband's "unified personality," and his family doctor called him "the most normal man I ever knew." Mitchell himself often protested his alleged normality but when challenged by his wife to name one unusual trait could only come up with his dislike of tripe. Not surprisingly, he had many friends. When Robert Lynd in the purposive manifesto *Knowledge for What?* chose Mitchell's work as representative of the weaknesses of contemporary social science, he sent several anguished notes to Mitchell expressing his continued attachment to Mitchell as a friend and a colleague. Characteristically, Mitchell replied soothingly.[3]

Much of Lynd's anguish, and that of many other purposive thinkers, stemmed from the fact that Mitchell's commitment to reform often seemed to match or even surpass their own. Certainly his family credentials were good. His father was an abolitionist doctor who volunteered to serve with Negro regiments during the Civil War. His mother's family ran a Chicago station on the Underground Railroad and were close associates of the Lovejoy brothers. Moreover, due to his father's war injuries, the family grew up in tight economic circumstances, and Mitchell never forgot the feeling of being poor. He never adopted the air of noblesse oblige common to so many liberal intellectuals. When Mitchell became involved in settlement work, he didn't lecture to workers on their responsibility to broaden their intellectual horizons; instead, he patiently and joyfully taught carpentry to their children. He encouraged his talented (and very rich) wife to pursue her own career and, according to her biographer, truly deserved to be called a feminist. He worked hard for such reforms as the abolition of child labor, control of natural resources, and government regulation of corporations; criticized the uneven distribution of income; and shared Veblen's belief in and hatred of business's sabotage of production. In 1932, while serving as chairman of President Hoover's Committee on Recent Social Trends, Mitchell quietly but emphatically supported and voted for Norman Thomas.[4]

In addition to Mitchell's personal attraction to reform, many purposive thinkers saw him as the one individual who could merge the insights of his teachers, Dewey and Veblen, to replace classical economics with a new ethically based economics. At the beginning of his career Mitchell produced several seminal articles which challenged the psychological preconceptions of classical economics. Columbia hired him to replace the eminent neoclassicist John Bates Clark, and throughout his career there he gave a famous course on the history of economic theory. Historian of economic thought Robert Heilbroner called Mitchell's lectures the best work ever done in the field. Mitchell was one of the first professional economists to support John Hobson and his theory of welfare economics, and he fought to get Hobson's views and those of socialist economists into print. He also attacked Herbert Davenport's price theory because it abandoned the problem of value which he saw as tantamount to destroying the reason for the existence of economics.[5]

Nevertheless, Mitchell's 1929 dedication address at Eleven Twenty-six was a fair summary of his views. Beginning in the late 1800s with his research on business cycles and becoming more pronounced with his government service during World War I, Mitchell downgraded his concern for normative goals and values to concentrate on an empirical, quantitative economics. His convictions were especially strengthened during the war, when the absence of factual data made determining wartime America's needs almost impossible. The experience convinced him that economists could best serve and reform society by first obtaining enough information on economic activities to understand the system as it actually exists.

The best way to attain this goal, he thought, was by emulating the objectivity of the scientific method and using techniques that allowed other investigators to verify one's results. The method that seemed most applicable, especially in a money economy such as the United States, was quantification. Throughout the 1920s, and especially with the onset of the Great Depression, Mitchell's attempts to quantify became ever stronger, and he began to insist more strenuously that empirical data collected and tabulated according to the scientific method was *the* key to solving the depression.

Despite Mitchell's later criticism of his education at the University of Chicago, his work there provided him with both his early theoretical insights and the later empiricism so admired by his fellow service intellectuals. Foremost among the Chicago influences was the iconoclastic economist Thorstein Veblen. Mitchell chanced to take an introductory course with Veblen during his sophomore year and quickly formed an admiration for him both as a thinker and as an individual. Initially, Veblen attracted Mitchell by his destruction of the economic preconceptions and complacencies of the age. While many students shied away from this "vivisection without an anesthetic" of their personal beliefs, Mitchell eagerly plunged into the study of philosophy, psychology, and ethnology, searching for evidence of the limitations of classical economics. He would later use the critical insights derived from these disciplines to refute the hedonistic basis of orthodox economics. At its most elementary level, Veblen's thought liberated Mitchell from the confines of accepted economic dogma and provided him with a fresh perspective on the study of economics.[6]

Veblen also provided Mitchell with the basic theoretical constructs for his study of "the money economy" and its business cycles. Foremost among these was the distinction between industrial and pecuniary employments. Veblen maintained that business enterprise, dedicated to realizing pecuniary profits from invested capital, dominated the economic life of contemporary Western societies. The making of goods became subordinate to the making of profit. Financiers engaged in "business sabotage" against the "instinct of workmanship" of craftsmen. Money rather than goods became the medium of exchange and value. Mitchell accepted this hypothesis and set out to examine the money economy in depth. Although Veblen had remarked on the need to make detailed, empirical studies of the money economy's institutions, he never did so himself. Veblen the radical remained primarily concerned with disproving the conventional wisdoms of the status quo. It fell to Mitchell the reformer to use such Veblenian concepts as business enterprise, the money economy, and industrial and pecuniary employments to study the fluctuations of the money economy as the key to modern economic life. Despite the growing differences in their approaches to economics, Mitchell always considered Veblen the most original social thinker of the twentieth century and consistently noted his own reliance on Veblen's hypotheses and insights.[7]

The one individual who rivaled Veblen in influence was another teacher with whom Mitchell began taking courses in his sophomore year, John Dewey. Before he encountered Dewey, the skeptical Mitchell had regarded philosophy as dogmatic and boring, but after Dewey's introductory course he began to feel that the Chicago pragmatism of Dewey and George Herbert Mead might actually provide answers to some fundamental questions. Mitchell took philosophy courses throughout his undergraduate and graduate career and won Dewey's respect as a student. Indeed, Dewey helped Mitchell go to graduate school by supplementing Mitchell's meager economics fellowship with a graduate philosophy scholarship. Mitchell thereupon went against the wishes of his adviser, department chairman J. Lawrence Laughlin, and chose philosophy rather than political science or history as his minor field.[8]

From Dewey, Mitchell derived several ideas crucial to his later work; chief among them was Dewey's theory of the process of thought. Mitchell claimed that all of Dewey's courses revolved about this problem, and he early became fascinated with its implications for economics. If, as Dewey argued, habit controls human behavior, then it should be possible to demonstrate that consumers do not make rational choices and economic behavior does not conform to the preconceptions of hedonism. Moreover, if the physical and intellectual environment created these habits of thought and action, then the preconceptions of economic theorists were merely products of specific historical and material circumstances. Mitchell came to insist that scholars studying economic behavior should examine its social background since, "in John Dewey's phrase, 'all psychology is social psychology.'" Like Veblen, Dewey helped to liberate Mitchell from the dogma of accepted theories. In a 1934 letter to Dewey, Mitchell humbly wrote, "There is no one to whom I feel under heavier obligation than yourself."[9]

The third important figure for Mitchell at this time, J. Lawrence Laughlin, differed greatly from both Veblen and Dewey. Laughlin was a dogmatically laissez-faire economist who felt that even John Stuart Mill had strayed from the correct orthodox path. Laughlin believed completely in the classical tradition and attempted to convince his students of its validity. More than most laissez-faire economists, he involved himself in practical concerns, especially those dealing with money and banking. He encouraged empirical research, although Mitchell tartly noted that he simply discarded any facts that did not fit his theory. Laughlin also led the academic opposition to free silver. He composed hard-money pamphlets in the crusade to combat the heresies of "Coin" Harvey and his "school," and he even served for two years as full-time director of the National Citizens League for the Promotion of a Sound Banking System.[10]

Laughlin too provided Mitchell with useful ideas. In his battle against soft money, Laughlin had come to deny the quantity theory of money and had turned to price analysis as a way to prove his hypothesis. Laughlin interested Mitchell in monetary matters and theory and suggested the greenback phenomenon of the American 1860s and 1870s as a case study of the affect of paper money on an economic system. Mitchell's analysis of the greenbacks, combined with Veblen's recognition of why prices are important, led him to his theory of the significance of the money economy and subsequently to his work on business cycles.

Mitchell's study of psychology with Dewey, ethnology and economic institutions with Veblen, and price analysis with Laughlin led him to one conclusion: the key element in understanding the current economic system was the use of money and the pecuniary thinking it creates. "From the use of money is derived not only the whole set of pecuniary concepts which the theorists and his subjects employ, but also the whole countinghouse attitude toward economic activities." Mitchell maintained that one must investigate the institutions of the money economy, especially the processes of making money and making goods, in order to truly understand the functioning of the economic system. He argued that money and the price system served as its motivating force and provided a quantifiable manifestation of individual values and wants. Thus, he thought that Alfred Marshall was correct when he stated that "money is the center around which economic science clusters," although he was right for the wrong reasons.[11]

Once Mitchell had developed this overall view of the economic system, he engaged in few theoretical hypotheses. He occasionally wrote an essay noting the mistaken philosophical or psychological preconceptions of an earlier thinker, but for the most part he saw economic theory as relatively useless. It did aid in the identification of significant areas for study and in the recognition of other investigators' approaches to similar problems. But like Veblen in such essays as "The Preconceptions of Economic Science" and "The Limitations of Marginal Utility," and Dewey in *Reconstruction in Philosophy*, Mitchell regarded theory as a product of and rationalization for its particular historical circumstances. In 1925 Mitchell explained to a Harvard seminar that one can study economic theory in one of two ways. Either one can examine the particular economic doctrines and attempt to determine their validity, or one can try to discover why people came to believe these specific economic ideas. Mitchell chose the latter. He never faulted Adam Smith, David Ricardo, or any of the others for examining the central economic issues of their day and using whatever materials and techniques they had available. On the other hand, he never seriously considered their theories to be accurate reflections of economic reality. What was true for classical theorists was equally true for Veblen and Dewey. All theory, not just classical thought, was a product of its environment and hence susceptible to the historicist technique.[12]

Mitchell's childhood conditioned him to reject the validity of all theories. In an autobiographical letter he noted that he had early in life become intrigued with the strict Baptist theology of his great-aunt and began to explore its logical implications. He soon recognized its weaknesses and tormented her by picking apart the inconsistencies in her beliefs. Studying philosophy under Dewey further aided him in his ability to note the inconsistencies and rationalizations within all theories. "My grandaunt's theology; Plato and Quesnay; Kant, Ricardo, and Karl Marx; Carnes and Jevons, even Marshall were much of a piece." Economic theory, it turned out, had as little to do with reality as did poetry or any other product of the imagination.[13]

Although Mitchell was quite willing to turn the same historicist critique on himself, he never seemed to notice how his own rejection of the utility of abstract theory was itself conditioned by his environment. In this case, the conditioning factor was apparently Mitchell's commitment to reform. Like his fellow service intellectual Thurman Arnold, Mitchell seemed to equate abstract theory with conservative classical theory. His lectures on the history of economic thought were sprinkled with references to cases of economic theorists justifying their personal views and economic interests through deduced "scientific laws." For example, in the 1870s the English economist Francis Edgeworth advocated increased taxation of the poor on the grounds that Bentham's felicific calculus "proved" that aristocrats had greater pleasure needs and enjoyment than peasants, and therefore the greatest possible good would ensue from *their* use of the wealth. Mitchell concluded not only that such a position was almost criminally irresponsible, but also that no theorists really believed their positions anyway. When he began to study the quantity theory of money controversy, he discovered that the adherents of the quantity theory did not really believe that the amount of money in circulation was the sole influence on prices. Nor did their opponents seriously believe that the quantity of money did *not* affect prices. Yet his adviser, Laughlin, advocated policies on such purely theoretical grounds. Laughlin had even initially tried to direct Mitchell's research on greenbacks to serve his own propagandistic purposes. Revealingly, one of the few times Mitchell ever expressed anger in public was in a 1945 talk entitled "Fifty Years as an

Economist," in which he declared that any economist who offered recommendations on purely speculative grounds was guilty of "intellectual dishonesty . . . [and] professional malfeasance."[14]

Mitchell seemed to believe that the scientific approach alone could overcome rationalizations and acts of self-interest. The central needs of economics, for him, came to be the accumulation of sufficient facts to create an empirically testable theory. Theory, to be useful, must "take hold of phenomena by their handles." The immediate task was to gather data on such diverse phenomena as wage rates, employment and unemployment, interest rebates, profits, expenditures of personal income, and savings, and then to try to determine the interconnections among them.[15]

Yet here again Mitchell did not follow through on his own self-proclaimed historicism. As Dewey and Charles Beard pointed out for social science objectivity in general and Lynd for Mitchell's work specifically, empirical work also contained elements of rationalization and self-interest. As Dewey (if not Veblen) consistently pointed out, all thought is conditioned environmentally, and there is no escape from this central truth. Therefore, the task of the modern thinker is to emulate the Platos and the Adam Smiths of the past and identify the central issues of the day and attempt to solve them in the most ethical and efficient way possible. Accumulating data and using the scientific method can help thinkers draw better conclusions, but, for better or worse, the personal element will always be present.

Rexford Tugwell, Mitchell's Columbia colleague and friendly critic, chose Mitchell as the representative practitioner of an economic methodology he termed "analytical economics." Analytical economists seek to understand the economic system by engaging in minutely detailed statistical investigations of group behavior and attempting to discover correlations. Tugwell argued that in their search for uniformities of economic behavior, analytical economists piled up mountains of data and often lost sight of which facts they wanted and why they wanted them.[16]

Most of Mitchell's admirers would accept Tugwell's description, if not his criticism, of analytical economics as a fair analysis of Mitchell's goal. By collecting literally thousands of factual studies, Mitchell hoped to construct a verifiable theory of business cycles, and eventually of the money economy. Through his activity in the National Bureau of Economic Research and the Social Science Research Council, Mitchell actively encouraged a generation of young economists to follow his path. With sufficient economic data, one could understand the economic system, make predictions about its behavior, and, eventually, control its activity.

While he was producing his initial theoretical essays, Mitchell was also working on the first of the factual studies that led him to his work on business cycles. Laughlin had interested Mitchell in the history of greenbacks, and Mitchell decided to examine the period 1862–65 for his doctoral dissertation. According to Mitchell, Laughlin expected him to produce a fairly standard economic volume demonstrating the "silliness" and economic folly of the government's issuing of paper money, but Mitchell quickly departed from his adviser's expectations. By examining the historical material in detail, Mitchell was able to see how the policy had evolved out of peculiar historical circumstances and did not reflect anyone's real desires. The important issues for him became how exactly paper money policy affected such factors as the price of gold, various commodities, and wages, and what explained the violent price fluctuations of these goods.[17]

Mitchell perceived his first task as obtaining facts, specifically the prices of the various goods during the period. The only way to make these facts meaningful was to collect them into statistical tables. Careful examination of his tables uncovered unexpected findings. Although Mitchell retained his dislike of the greenback policy and the economic chaos it engendered, his reason was different from Laughlin's. One of the chief criticisms previously leveled against paper money was that manufacturers and merchants suffered from the inflationary nature of wages and relatively set prices. In fact, Mitchell discovered that prices rose much faster than wages and that the average worker's relative wages were much lower after the Civil War than before it. As for the effect of the amount of money in circulation, he discovered that the key factor in the increasing cost of gold and other commodities was not the number of greenbacks issued by the government but the relative fortunes of the Union cause. Gold prices showed a quick and definite reaction to news from the front; the worse it looked for the Union Army, the higher the price of gold rose and the higher the inflationary pressures.[18]

Reviewers universally applauded Mitchell's achievement; even a supporter of the quantity theory of money admitted that it was the most complete statistical study in existence of prices during a period of violent price fluctuations. But to regard the study as a mere statistical exercise was to do it a serious injustice. While Laughlin continued his fulminations against free silver and the quantity theory of money without noticeable success, Mitchell had grabbed the "phenomena by their handles" and demonstrated at least one case where the policy had been a disaster. Mitchell did not need to rely on abstract logic or unverifiable assertions; he could point to specific facts and challenge his opponents to disprove them. Moreover, he could show the workers, to whom much of the free silver propaganda was addressed, that their interests were those most likely to suffer. Such an ability to persuade represented Mitchell's goal for his economic research. In a 1909 letter to his wife-to-be, Mitchell declared: "I want to *prove* things as nearly as may be and proof means usually an appeal to the facts—facts recorded in the best cases in statistical form. To write books of assertion, or books of shrewd observation won't convince people who have been in the habit of asserting other things or seeing things in a different perspective. But when one can point to quantitative determinators then others must close their eyes or accept one's results."[19]

Mitchell became so committed to the utility of quantitative facts that his second book consisted of little more than statistical tables. He had originally planned to continue his study of greenbacks to include the years up to 1879, but he found his interests shifting to other areas. He therefore decided to publish the factual material he had already gathered and essentially let the facts speak for themselves. Of the 627 pages of *Gold Prices and Wages under the Greenback Standard*, the last 344 are statistical appendixes without comment, and at least half of the first 283 pages are tables. Mitchell himself admitted that the book was merely the "statistical apparatus" for the study originally proposed.[20]

More and more, Mitchell began to perceive facts in terms of quantification. He continued to believe that the key to understanding the money economy was through the business enterprise, but that could best be studied through the "collection and analysis of elaborate records of business experience in quantitative form." He saw the progress of economics following a path toward quantitative economics; objective analysis of economic reality would replace abstract theorizing about motives and utilities. Statistics provided economists with the tools to describe reality objectively and to recognize the correlations and interconnections among the various aspects of the economic system. Most economists distrusted statistics. John Stuart Mill had advocated them in his *Logic* but refused to use them because they might disprove his earlier hypotheses. Commonsense philosopher Francis Bowen of Harvard supported the use of statistics but attacked a statistical work with conclusions different from his own for denying the "testimony of consciousness." Mitchell, on the other hand, relied on statistics to prove or disprove hypotheses.[21]

The work that did the most to create a positive attitude toward quantitative research was Mitchell's own 1913 *Business Cycles*. The theorist John Maurice Clark stated bluntly that "if a single study can be selected as the 'formative type' of the present movement of quantitative research in American economics, this distinction undoubtedly belongs to Wesley C. Mitchell's study of business cycles." This work demonstrated for the first time what quantitative research could do. Mitchell temporarily dismissed all the previous hypotheses concerning business cycles and offered an analytic description of the continual process of business prosperity, crisis, depression, and revival. He countered criticism of his book as mindless empiricism by showing it to be the first systematic investigation of the subject that permitted the measurement of several factors at work simultaneously. Mitchell pointed out that all of the various theories about business cycles were logically reasonable. The only way to test them was through their conformity to quantifiable data. Then Mitchell went on to suggest the unthinkable: all or almost all of the theories might be correct. Excess savings, political uncertainty, tight money, overproduction, decrease in construction, weather, and even sunspots might all "cause" a decrease in business prosperity. The only way to determine the interconnections of this incredibly complex process was through careful statistical techniques, which had proved to be the most complete and accurate description and which more and more economists were coming to regard as the key to understanding the functioning of the present system. With *Business Cycles*, the methodology of quantification began to prove its value.[22]

Although Mitchell certainly admired statistics, his actual use of them was quite limited. Unlike his fellow service intellectual William Ogburn, he never taught statistics or had any desire to do so. He often commented not only on his lack of training but also on his lack of mathematical ability. To fully appreciate Mitchell's role, one must recognize the two different meanings of the word *statistics*. On the one hand, statistics is the compilation of accurate physical data—the "vital" and "moral" statistics popularized by the Belgian Adolphe Quetelet and championed in the United States by the American Statistical Association under the leadership of Edward Jarvis. On the other hand, statistics is statistical theory and comparisons of data. Beginning in the late nineteenth century, the British eugenics movement and the genetic research it generated led Francis Galton and Karl Pearson beyond Quetelet's determination of averages and margins of error to the invention of such statistical devices as distribution curves, regression, and correlation coefficients. Coefficients were especially necessary if researchers were to compare and correlate two or more variables.[23]

Clearly, the statistical revolution engendered by the eugenics movement was absolutely necessary before researchers like Mitchell could begin to research such complicated phenomena as business cycles. Mitchell's goal in *Business Cycles*, as it was in *A History of Greenbacks*, was to discover how various aspects of the economic system were connected over time. Yet, despite the obvious relevance of determining comparisons and correlations, Mitchell's primary statistical concern throughout his career was what he called "the quality and quantity of economic statistics." Although he admitted that American economic statistics were superior to those of any other country because of the importance of economic issues in American politics and the early standardization of many products, he constantly noted their limitations. In many ways Mitchell more closely resembled the nineteenth-century vital statisticians in his concern about inadequate data. His primary contribution in *Greenbacks* was his development of new, more accurate tables and time series. His major contribution to statistical research was a 1915 work which showed how to overcome such problems as lack of uniform qualities and seasonal variations in devising accurate index numbers for time series. Mitchell often seemed to regard himself as a pioneer devoted to locating and correcting data which later, better-trained statisticians would use to explain and predict business cycles.[24]

Mitchell seemed relatively unconcerned with his inability to achieve a testable empirical theory of business cycles. He was confident that such a theory was inevitable once adequate data were obtained. Mitchell shared the Progressives' adulation of the almighty fact. As James Bryce, the English political observer of America, declared, "It is Facts that are needed: Facts, Facts, Facts. When facts have been supplied, each of us can try to reason from them." Certainly Mitchell's business cycle research covered myriad facts. He investigated thousands of records, ranging from production, exchange, transportation, and distribution of hundreds of commodities to death rates. For the United States alone, more than eight hundred quarterly and monthly series existed, and some of these covered as many as twenty specific cycles. As Mitchell himself pointed out, simply determining the turning points of American business cycles would require literally millions of comparisons. Geoffrey Moore, a later director of the NBER noted that no current model of business cycles deals with even a fraction of those considered by Mitchell. Yet Mitchell, with his inductive approach to knowledge, regarded anything less as "superficial" work. Only extensive accumulation of detail could lead to a *provable* theory, and as he had noted in his 1909 letter to his beloved Lucy, he would accept nothing less.[25]

By the early 1920s Mitchell was the most prominent member of a large group of economists who were attempting to transform American economics into an inductive and quantitative science. They hoped their empirical studies would finish the overthrow of laissez-faire theory that the critiques of Veblen and the reform Darwinists had begun. Even classical sympathizer Allyn Young admitted that economists had to test the theory of marginal utility with facts and readily agreed that the profession most needed small-scale, empirical monographs. When the Young Turks of the profession prepared a volume on the new economics in the early 1920s, they chose Mitchell to write the first essay, "The Prospects of Economics." In it, he regarded the prospects as quite good. Economists were proving their utility daily through the collection and analysis of data directly relevant to the problems of the postwar world. Even more significant for the state of American economics was the volume's second essay, "On Measurement in Economics," written by Mitchell's prize student Frederick Mills, who boldly declared that economics had reached the "inductive era." Facts has won general acceptance in economics through the increased use and proven utility of quantitative methods. In 1923, Mills regarded Mitchell's vision of an empirical, quantitative economics as the accepted goal of the profession as a whole.[26]

As Mitchell noted in "The Prospects of Economics," one reason that he and other economists believed in the validity of their empirical, quantitative approach was that it had succeeded in World War I. Before America's entrance into the war, information on the functioning of the economy was almost nonexistent. Scholars lacked comprehensive figures on employment, retail trade and prices, credit, construction, and almost everything else. Many practical men regarded even the determination of a gross national product as impossible. Consequently, when the declaration of war necessitated a national mobilization of physical and individual resources, the individuals placed in charge of the process had little idea of what resources were there to mobilize. Bernard Baruch, chairman of the War Industries Board (WIB), declared that "the greatest deterrent to effective action was the lack of facts." The lack of information about basic aspects of the economic system, the absence of a central agency for utilizing even those facts available, and the consequent administrative chaos seriously hindered the war effort.[27]

Baruch quickly began to appoint economists, statisticians, engineers, businessmen, and other experts to the WIB. The board regarded the economists as necessary not so much for their special knowledge of specific areas, since they too were woefully uninformed, but for their trained ability to see the economy as a whole. Baruch chose Edwin Gay, a Harvard economic historian of limited scholarly production and great administrative ability, to direct the Central Bureau of Planning and Statistics. The bureau's task was to collect statistical information from all the government agencies, including the armed services, and organize it into a comprehensive form for the policymakers. Gay and his right-hand man, Mitchell, had already achieved a great wartime success in their previous positions within the Division of Planning and Statistics of the U.S. Shipping Board. Using statistics gathered by Mitchell and his group, the Shipping Board was able to demonstrate conclusively that the head of another agency was withholding ships from use as military carriers in order to strengthen national and personal postwar trade interests in Latin America. Mitchell became head of the Price Division of the War Industries Board and prepared a massive study of the wholesale prices of more than fifteen hundred commodities for the years 1917–18.[28]

Mitchell was not entirely unprepared for the confusion he found in Washington. He had worked for the Census Bureau in 1899–1900, and he left government employment angry at the servile incompetence and lack of foresight he had encountered. He thus expected the lack of information and quickly set out to correct the situation as best he could. Mitchell recounted the needs of the WIB as the following: (1) the need to know how many men and how much war materiél were required and when and where they would be needed; (2) the need to know how many men and how much materiél could be obtained and how they could be delivered to where they were required; (3) the need to know the effect on civilian morale this would create; and, finally, (4) the need to put all these facts into monetary terms. But the board did not have the information on which to make such informed judgments. During wartime, the questions asked of an economist did not deal with general tendencies but with "how much and how soon."[29]

For all the confusion, frustration, and long hours of war work, Mitchell, like many social scientists working for the government, was excited and enthusiastic. Even before joining the government full time, he had recognized the social potential of the war experience. The war might demonstrate that a society under sufficient pressure could change rapidly and could use intelligent planning. Mitchell wistfully hoped that nations would devote the same kind of hard work and common effort to reconstructing their societies after the war as they had applied to killing people during it. After the war Mitchell repeatedly referred to his experiences on the War Industries Board as proof of man's ability to plan and mold society for the common good. Production, especially of socially desirable goods, had increased, and workers had benefited from improved economic and psychological treatment. Like so many other progressives, Mitchell often looked back on the war as a golden age of expectations, a time when it seemed that economists and other social scientists would soon assume their rightful roles in an intelligently planned society.[30]

The lesson Mitchell drew from his wartime experiences was that both the economics profession and American society desperately needed to encourage economic research. Mitchell stood before the American Statistical Association in 1918 and advocated a new, intelligent method of solving social problems through social research to replace the "jerky way" of reform. He would emphasize this throughout his career, and even during the first days of World War II he insisted that economists should continue their training during the emergency so they could help to solve the problems of the postwar world.[31]

Mitchell's most important contribution to furthering empirical social science research was his role in the founding of the National Bureau of Economic Research with Gay and Malcolm Rorty, an electrical engineer and the chief statistician for American Telephone and Telegraph. The roots of the bureau lay in the prewar era. In 1913, Jerome Greene, the first director of the Rockefeller Foundation, approached Gay, his former supervisor and at that time dean of Harvard's Business School, and Frank Taussig, chairman of Harvard's economics department, for advice on establishing an independent economics research institute. Taussig, who favored aiding research within the universities, adamantly opposed the entire concept, but the enthusiastic Gay quickly established a committee to propose plans for such an organization. Gay suggested the collection of data on prices, wages, and rents as the institute's first projects and insisted that Mitchell be appointed the director. Greene's proposal, however, lost out to a combination of Rockefeller adviser Frederick Gates's opposition and MacKenzie King's propagandistic version of social science research.[32]

Two years after Greene's proposal, Rorty came to Gay with an idea for a large-scale study of the volume and distribution of American income. Rorty believed that this would be an excellent beginning to the accumulation of the economic data necessary for business and industrial stability, and he offered to provide with Harvard's Bureau of Business Research the funds for the study. Gay protested that the Harvard institute, which he headed, was too small to engage in such ambitious research and suggested that they establish an independent organization, under Mitchell's direction, to undertake the project. Mitchell agreed to direct such an agency if Rorty first raised the funds and arranged for a supervisory committee of social scientists, businessmen, and trade unionists to oversee it. Rorty agreed, but before serious work could begin, the United States entered the war and Rorty, Gay, and Mitchell went into government service.[33]

With much of the organizational work already in place, then, Rorty, Gay, and Mitchell were ready to take advantage of Woodrow Wilson's abolition of the Central Bureau of Planning and Statistics and business's desire for the continuation of statistical research. All of the individuals involved, but especially Mitchell, recognized the absolute need for total objectivity in the bureau's research in order to gain foundation support. Charles Merriam, who had worked cordially with Mitchell in establishing the Social Science Research Council and on many governmental commissions, described him as "modest looking but machiavellian." Early in his business cycle research, Mitchell recognized the enormity of his and his fellow analytical economists' task and the need for substantial funds to achieve their goals. As early as 1903, Mitchell had dedicated his *History of Greenbacks* "to the Men and Women of our time and country who by wise and generous giving have encouraged the search after truth in all departments of knowledge." Now that he was director of the bureau, Mitchell developed certain policies in an effort to ensure financial support from philanthropies and private businesses.[34]

The first of these policies was that all research must have public relevance and must be practical not just in terms of the overall goals of understanding the economy as a whole and eventually achieving a strong economy but also for the day-to-day needs of the businessmen who directly or indirectly funded the research. The bureau's first released study, *Income in the United States: Its Amount and Distribution 1909–1914,* met Mitchell's goals well. The book's extensive tables and charts gave businessmen and civil servants a good idea of where the nation's income actually went and allowed them to plan production and programs to meet projected needs. The quick sale of thousands of copies of the volume attested to the public relevance of the bureau's approach and shocked even so firm a believer in the practicality of quantitative economics as Mitchell. National income and its fluctuations served as the focus for the bureau's research for the next two decades.[35]

Connected to this insistence on practicality was the bureau's official declaration of its goal to present economic facts in a scientific fashion, free from all bias and propaganda. Mitchell insisted that research be objective both in appearance and reality. In the income study, Mitchell was so careful about objectivity that he had his two principal researchers use entirely different sources to determine the national income. The first used figures on production, and the second used income figures. Only when the two researchers arrived independently at essentially the same results would Mitchell accept the results. Such care reassured the worried foundations of the objectivity and noncontroversiality of the research they were funding. As a final proof of the bureau's lack of bias, Mitchell insisted that all reports forgo policy recommendations. As the director of research, he repeatedly informed both his coworkers and his audience of the bureau's self-enforced rule against advice concerning what ought to be done. The bureau, as a research organization, possessed absolutely no opinions on social issues.[36]

Mitchell was unwilling to allow foundations or businesses to control the bureau. The Rockefeller Foundation had tried to co-opt the fledgling bureau in 1914 and 1915 to "independently" approve King's "scientific" report on the Colorado Coal War. In 1919 a frustrated Rorty suggested accepting funding from the United Americans, a group of New York bankers and professionals opposed to communism who were looking for "facts" to use in a massive publicity campaign. Mitchell and Gay opposed all such alliances, recognizing that these type of affiliations would destroy their claims of objectivity. Mitchell further ensured the bureau's objectivity by creating an executive board composed of representatives from various interests such as Harry Laidler of the socialist League for Industrial Democracy and George Soule of the Labor Bureau on the left, and Dwight Morrow and representatives from a leading Wall Street firm on the right. The board had a final veto over all research topics and reports. The bureau's regulations stipulated that researchers had to submit all proposals to the board and its executive committee for approval. After receiving initial acceptance, the researcher next furnished the board with a statement of principles and methods, which had to be endorsed. Finally, each member of the executive committee had to approve the completed project before the bureau would accept and publish it. This elaborate procedure effectively weeded out all opinions and recommendations; only a completely factual study could survive such scrutiny. Moreover, as Mitchell would admit by 1939, although he and Gay had established its particular board of trustees to protect the bureau from foundation interference, it met the foundations' later demands for noncontroversiality and objectivity perfectly and significantly aided the bureau's ability to raise funds.[37]

Throughout Mitchell's work for the government and for the NBER his reformist goals remained implicit, if covert. He insisted that all scientists had a "moral" duty toward society and should try to direct their research into areas where they could contribute most to the common welfare. He felt that social scientists' experiences in World War I had demonstrated that it was exactly this type of quantitative work that could do the most to reform society. For example, in his introduction to *Income in the United States* Mitchell identified the key questions of the study as whether the American national income was adequate to provide a decent living for all members of the society, whether the income was increasing with the population, and whether its distribution was becoming more or less equal. Such questions had been the basis of endless debates in the late nineteenth and early twentieth centuries and had resulted in several national commissions. Without all these facts, any move to redistribute income would founder in endless debate about actual conditions. Mitchell made no secret of his personal belief in the utility and even necessity of such a redistribution of income. As he recounted in a personal letter, however, "there may be instances in which the investigator is most likely to contribute to welfare by saying nothing of his preferences." If economists really wished their results to be acted on, they must assure policymakers of their objectivity. Seen from this perspective, the NBER's rule against publishing recommendations served as a practical device for actually increasing the social utility of economic research. For Mitchell, one of the chief attractions of empiricism was its effectiveness as a political strategy.[38]

Mitchell's primary reason for choosing business cycles as his area of research was his desire to alleviate the periodic depressions and the personal suffering they caused. Business instability led directly to adversity for employees and consumers as well as for capitalists. Mitchell estimated that incomes shrank by as much as 25 percent during periods of severe depression. "The amount of money it is wise to spend on efforts to control the business cycle depends on the gains in national welfare which can be served. The most definite of these prospective gains consists in diminishing the economic losses we now suffer from the waste of booms, the forced liquidation of crises, and the involuntary idleness of depressions." What caused Mitchell particular anguish was his conviction that adequate information could prevent all this suffering. He fervently believed that the accumulation of information would lead to an empirical theory of the causes of business cycles. Once economists definitely understood these causes, they could predict and check the rampages of cyclical behavior, especially by controlling overexpansion during boom periods. Mitchell felt so strongly about the need for such control that he contributed a series of popular articles on the subject to the *New York Evening Post* and from 1920 to 1923 provided readers with scientific year-end forecasts of future business activity with the hope that informed readers would adjust their consumption and thus help moderate the cyclical swings.[39]

Much of the appeal of an empirical quantitative methodology for Mitchell stemmed from its applicability to practical affairs. Speaking to the American Statistical Association in 1918, Mitchell assured his colleagues that no executive would turn away an expert possessing a quantitative statement of his problems. The chief difficulty for statisticians able to produce such material lay not in convincing practical men of the utility of their research but rather in meeting their constant requests for more statistics. Mitchell believed that one of the areas of greatest progress in social thought in the past several decades was the employment of economists and statisticians by industries and financial institutions. Economists had to become involved in practical affairs in order to understand how the system really functioned; meanwhile, their training in seeing the economy as a whole certainly aided their employers. Furthermore, once economists began to think in this "realistic" manner, they proceeded necessarily to empirical and quantitative verification. Like users of statistics as diverse as Quetelet, Pearson, Charles Booth, Florence Nightingale, and Henry Carter Adams, Mitchell's desire to measure was motivated by his determination to reform unacceptable conditions and meet, in his words, "social needs." He revealed his philosophy in an autobiographical letter to Lucy: "My world is the world of thought, but the world of thought has a realm of action and I live there."[40]

Mitchell was both an advocate for practicality and a practical man himself. His treatise on the use and determination of index numbers was essential for the construction of price series during both world wars, and his technical and administrative skills won him the respect of "practical" men in the War Industries Board as well as his professional colleagues. Foremost among these was War Food Administrator Herbert Hoover. When Hoover became secretary of commerce under Warren G. Harding in 1921, he pleaded with Mitchell to become the official adviser to the department on all economic issues and take charge of the collection and transmittal of economic information to the public. Mitchell sadly turned down the job to fulfill his previous commitments to the NBER and the New School for Social Research—not to mention to his four children under the age of six and his exasperated wife. He did allow Hoover to appoint him to chair a group of twenty-one eminent economists who produced a report investigating various plans for controlling unemployment during a depression. Later in the decade, Mitchell led a distinguished group of economists who published a comprehensive two-volume study of the American economy entitled *Recent Economic Changes*. This book supplied, for the first time, basic factual foundations for intelligent determination of economic policy. Unfortunately, its release during the first days of the Great Depression, which it did not predict, caused reviewers to overlook its very real accomplishments.[41]

For all of Mitchell's reform sympathies and activist perspective, however, the central focus for his work remained his vision of an empirical, predictive science based on quantitative research. Without such a science, Mitchell insisted, no real reform or useful activism could take place. While the experience of World War I raised questions in the minds of individuals like Dewey and Beard as to the ultimate utility of the scientific perspective, Mitchell's war work only strengthened his conviction that a quantitative, inductive approach was the correct method for understanding society. One can recognize some of the implications of Mitchell's approach by comparing his immediate postwar actions with those of the rest of the Big Four of the New School. Veblen, Beard, and James Harvey Robinson increasingly began to stress educational reforms and write popular tracts designed to create an educated mass audience who could use the knowledge to create a better society. With the exception of the *New York Post* series on business cycles, Mitchell concentrated on writing for and training a technical elite. When the New School failed to attract students sufficiently committed to the patient fact collecting required by the new sciences, Mitchell returned to Columbia, where he continued to preach the scientific gospel whenever possible. He gave frequent addresses to scientific and engineering societies and became a prominent member, and later president, of the American Association for the Advancement of Science. Characteristically, in 1932 Mitchell spent his year as visiting professor at Oxford encouraging postgraduate students and tutors to pursue statistical and scientific research.[42]

Mitchell's inductive view of science reflected his age's dominant theory of science. He underplayed the importance of hypotheses and theoretical revolutions and saw the development of science as an ongoing process of logical rationality. Mitchell believed that economists had to emulate chemists and physicists, who had built their respective sciences through careful observation and complete testing of hypotheses. Social scientists could and should conduct experiments just as natural and physical scientists did. He admitted that social scientists could never match the precision of their colleagues in the hard sciences, but they could carefully observe the "purposeful" social experiments already set in progress. Mitchell posited six prerequisites for the transformation of contemporary economics into a true science: (1) far more reliance on empirical data, (2) detailed statistical studies of mass economic activities, (3) more thorough use of statistical methods and inferences, (4) dismissal of empirically untestable hypotheses, (5) complete dependence on testing, and (6) operationalization of all theoretical concepts and constructs.[43]

Thus, quantification was the key. In a discussion of Frederick Mills's *Behavior of Prices* during an SSRC meeting, economist and statistician Raymond Bye noted that all sciences become increasingly mathematical as they progress, and he used Einstein's theory of relativity as an example. Mitchell, who had consistently disagreed with Bye throughout the conference, quickly concurred and stated that contemporary economists found themselves in exactly that position. Statistics was the one tool an analyst could use to test and prove hypotheses. Economists could build a science on accumulated, verified hypotheses, and quantifying observations ensured the possibility of such testing. Revealingly, in his response Mitchell equated mathematics with statistics.[44]

The NBER's refusal to make policy recommendations also conformed to Mitchell's view of science. Mitchell insisted that scientists should not make ethical or practical judgments. Scientists did not concern themselves with what was good or what ought to be done. Their sole concern was with interrelationships among various aspects of the social system. One of the great weaknesses of the economic thought of such men as Adam Smith and the philosophical radicals, according to Mitchell, was their attempted combination of theory and action. They believed that theorists should become policymakers because of their superior economic and social knowledge. Mitchell rejected this view, maintaining that thinkers usually lacked the ability to deal with social crises. More important, Mitchell believed that social thinkers who became ensnared in the trap of practical utility often found themselves altering their ideas to meet the needs of their opinions. Mitchell seemed to suggest that a social thinker with preconceived opinions could not produce scientific material. Since scientific economics was the only useful economics, reformers and "propagandists" could accomplish very little. Objectivity was not merely a political strategy but a necessity.[45]

By the mid-1920s Mitchell found himself caught between the two sides of his personality. He was a deeply compassionate individual who hated the personal injustices of society and felt it necessary to work to alleviate them. Yet the method he believed could best accomplish this goal called for dispassionate objectivity and the accumulation of quantitative data without hypotheses. Either position without the other was unsatisfactory. He could not accept a mindless empiricism without ethical goals, but he also maintained that their visions of what ought to be often caused analysts to tamper with their own data. Although ideally the two sides should have been able to juxtapose in harmony, the outbreak of the Great Depression prevented this. The activist in Mitchell called for him to become involved and make recommendations that might help bring an early end to the tragedy. The quantitative empiricist side calmly answered that economists lacked sufficient information to accomplish that and must continue their patient collection of quantitative data. Mitchell could not do both, although at first he tried. The best illustration of his attempted resolution of this conflict was his work for the President's Committee on Social Trends.

The Committee on Social Trends represented the apex of Hoover's numerous fact-finding commissions. First as secretary of commerce and then as president, Hoover instituted blue-ribbon committees of dignitaries and experts to investigate such central problems of the day as unemployment, enforcement of Prohibition, and the troubled soft coal industry. Hoover, "the Great Engineer," approached the study of society as he would a geological problem. The central need in such studies was to gather all the facts about a certain situation so that the "engineer" could make intelligent decisions. Hoover fervently believed that adequate data by itself would, literally, provide solutions to social ills. While Mitchell and most of his objectivist colleagues moderated their commitment to empiricism by pointing out that social policies must depend on the goal sought, Hoover dismissed such issues as irrelevant. His experiences as an engineer and food administrator never involved debatable goals. The sole task was to get the minerals out of the ground or to feed as many people as possible. It seems never to have occurred to him that well-informed, well-intentioned people might differ in their ultimate goals. Technical expertise buttressed by sufficient information would solve the nation's economic and social problems.

Hoover's Committee on Recent Economic Changes finished its survey of the economic system in early 1929. Next, Hoover proposed a similar but more ambitious study of American society. His assistant French Strother explained that Hoover wanted a new committee to produce a balanced, analytical view of American society with enough facts and statistics to provide social thinkers and policymakers with a firm foundation for new ideas and actions. A group of experts from the social sciences served Hoover's needs admirably. From the beginning of his involvement in social affairs as head of an international mining firm based in London, Hoover had preferred to work behind the scenes, use the most competent technicians, and rely on publicity as a catalyst for future action. He perceived the chief role of politics and especially of the presidency as educating the public. By definition, the public could not develop new ideas or approaches to problems; they depended on experts to do that for them. By bringing the best social thinkers together for a comprehensive study of American society as a whole, Hoover hoped to create the factual basis for a scientific reform movement that he could lead during his second term in office.[46]

In 1929, Hoover had the firm support of a great majority of the social scientists, especially those associated with such politically connected organizations as the NBER, the SSRC, and the Brookings Institute. Hoover was the one figure in the federal government during the 1920s who maintained a belief in the utility of social science. During his tenure as secretary of commerce he incorporated into his department the indexes on prices, wages, and income begun during the war. He was also interested in such developments as scientific management and city planning, and he advocated government-funded social research and cooperation between industry and science. Most important, Hoover actively intervened with the foundations to obtain funding for his preferred institutes. Rather than utilize experts within government as the Agriculture Department did with the Bureau of Agricultural Economics, Hoover preferred to have allegedly nonpartisan experts funded by independent foundations do the work. The Carnegie and Rockefeller foundations sponsored *Recent Economic Changes* and the business cycles and unemployment studies at the direct request of Hoover. Hoover responded positively to these studies and praised social scientists for their commitment to civic duty. When Hoover asked for their aid, they were happy to give it.[47]

Once Hoover conceived the idea for the study and discussed it with Strother and E. E. Hunt, his two aides most knowledgeable in the social sciences, he turned to the social scientist he respected and trusted most, Wesley Mitchell. Mitchell had served Hoover well in both the unemployment and recent economic changes studies and had excellent academic contacts through Columbia, the NBER, and the SSRC. He was also one of the few academics who had proved successful as both a scholar and an administrator. Most important, the two men knew and respected one another.

Strother first called the prospective key members of the committee together in September 1929 to draw up plans for the investigation. Besides Mitchell, Strother invited Secretary of the Interior Ray Wilbur, University of Chicago political scientist Charles Merriam, Shelby Harrison of the Russell Sage Foundation, and sociologists William Ogburn of Chicago and Howard Odum of the University of North Carolina. This group, minus Wilbur and with the later politically motivated addition of Dr. Alice Hamilton of Harvard Medical School, became the President's Committee on Social Trends. Hoover appointed Mitchell chairman, Merriam vice chairman, and Ogburn and Odum director and assistant director, respectively, of research. Although Ogburn and Odum invested the most time in the project and had control over day-to-day matters, Mitchell and Merriam set the tone and, with Harrison and Hamilton, possessed final veto power over all work.[48]

Hoover himself seems not to have had a very clear idea concerning the specifics of the investigation. He was quite willing to leave that up to the committee. Although Strother suggested the central significance of the issues of immigration restriction, the "purity" of racial stock, and the evils of intermarriage among different races, Hoover calmly placed his faith in the power of the almighty fact. Outside of an insistence on objectivity, Hoover saw no reason to interfere. He assumed that the accumulation of factual data would lead directly to sane and progressive social programs which would quickly cure social evils. Objective, factual social research would necessarily prove utilitarian.[49]

Although Ogburn and Odum shared Hoover's faith, Mitchell and Merriam were not so certain. Merriam's extensive experience in organizing and operating social science institutes had taught him that true social and political objectivity was difficult to obtain. He doubted whether the reports could avoid political issues. Mitchell added his concern over the inadequacy of the time allowed for the study. Although he continued to believe that enough facts would produce a true science of society, Mitchell did not believe that researchers had yet collected a sufficient number. Even if they had, three years was not enough time to assemble them. Mitchell was so unenthusiastic about the prospects of the study that at the second committee meeting he asked for permission to resign as chairman. The committee reluctantly agreed but asked him to serve until they could find a successor. They never found one, and Mitchell remained chairman throughout the life of the commission.[50]

The ardor of Ogburn and Odum more than compensated for Mitchell's and Merriam's doubts. After the board of directors suggested possible topics and authors, they left the functioning of the committee in their hands. Ogburn and Odum had attended Columbia graduate school together and shared an extremely empirical and quantitative methodology. Ogburn, like Mitchell, had served the government during World War I and came away with a similar commitment to facts and statistics. A student of the statistically oriented Franklin Giddings, he taught statistics at Barnard and Columbia after the war. The University of Chicago hired him in 1927 to add the quantitative approach, and he took an extreme position, often seeming to deny the validity of case studies and other methodologies despite his personal interest in psychoanalysis and theory. At the time of his appointment to the committee, Ogburn was president of the American Sociological Society, and his presidential address, delivered the previous December, was extreme in its support of quantitative science. Ogburn's methodological position conformed to Hoover's engineering perspective, and he set out to produce an empirical study that complied with Hoover's wishes in all ways.[51]

Ogburn carefully emphasized the factual nature of the project to all the contributors. He chose only topics susceptible to statistical measurement and insisted that authors limit themselves to collecting and describing facts. He also insisted on the absence of recommendations and suggestions. As the reports began to trickle in during 1931, however, the outraged Ogburn and Odum found numerous examples of "unscientific" procedure. Robert Lynd, the author of the consumption study, even went so far as to criticize the Bureau of Standards, a government agency. Ogburn angrily composed a memorandum to all the investigators that very specifically laid down the parameters of acceptable research. The central purpose of the enterprise was to make a *factual* study of social trends, it said. The chapters were to be mere records, collections of basic empirical materials which the executive and legislative branches could use to formulate policy. Opinion, according to Ogburn, was the very antithesis of fact. Opinion depended on values, past experiences, taste, and intuition. Equally well-informed individuals might come to have different opinions, and such a possibility destroyed the scientific reputation of social science. Ogburn threatened to block the inclusion of any report that contained opinions or recommendations. He considered his memorandum and its message so important that he wished to include it as an appendix to the finished study.[52]

But Ogburn had overlooked one major factor. Although he effectively controlled the project during its research phase, the board of directors—Mitchell, Merriam, Harrison, and Hamilton—had the last word on the final reports. Moreover, the committee was beginning to demonstrate a decided lack of sympathy for Ogburn's pure empiricism. During a June 1932 meeting of the committee, the executive members criticized exactly those selections which Ogburn believed did the best job of reporting the data without comment or conclusions. Not surprisingly, the readers found them ponderous and dull. Merriam, who could match anyone in recognizing the advantages of objectivity, protested against Ogburn's version of it, which he believed consisted solely of disembodied facts which were meaningless without scholarly interpretation.[53]

The key incident that pushed the latent conflict into the open was Ogburn's negative response to Merriam's own chapter, "Government and Society." Ogburn, as a faculty member at Chicago and longtime member of the SSRC, certainly recognized Merriam's power in social science institutions, and he tactfully suggested that Merriam's contribution lacked factual verification. He began by praising Merriam's ability to integrate the massive amount of material but added, almost offhandedly, that the chapter seemed to lack an "equivalent" amount of evidence to support the observations. Ogburn supporter and Hoover's unofficial observer on the committee, E. E. Hunt, was much more blunt: "I think the statement of problems seems to rest upon your authority rather than on the data." Actually, Ogburn and Hunt were quite correct in this assessment. Although the essay was well written and intelligently conceived, Merriam, characteristically, did not bother to cite specific facts to prove his points. Even his longtime collaborator Harold Gosnell agreed that the chapter lacked sufficient evidence. Despite the validity of the criticism, Merriam, already unhappy with the direction of the report, began to oppose what he perceived as Ogburn's excessive emphasis on quantification.[54]

Mitchell, who was at Oxford proselytizing for the quantitative approach during much of this clash, found himself in a dilemma on his return. As author of the all-important introductory "Review of Findings," Mitchell had to provide the tone for *Recent Social Trends*. Indeed, given the more than fifteen hundred pages of text and the highly technical character of much of the material, Mitchell's summary would probably be the only section read by most of the audience. Ogburn wrote to Mitchell warning him about members of the committee who wanted him to use his introduction to point out some of the conclusions that might be derived from the data. Ogburn wanted Mitchell to reemphasize the fact-finding nature of the study and leave all conclusions to the readers. Mitchell certainly respected Ogburn's viewpoint; yet he also privately shared Merriam's boredom and dissatisfaction with the purely factual nature of many of the essays. The ultimate purpose of social science was to help individuals build better lives for themselves, and Ogburn's editorial policy did everything possible to obscure the social implications of much of the research.[55]

Mitchell's introductory chapter demonstrated his consistent movement away from normative concerns toward a purely empirical approach. He began his summary of the findings by emphasizing the interrelatedness of the social organization and the key factor of social change. From this central thesis he temporarily acceded to Merriam's perspective and called for the solution of America's social problems through the use of the combined intelligence of the nation, the development of new social and technical inventions, and greater control of social and economic life. Still, these recommendations were exceedingly vague. His only specific proposal was the creation of a national advisory council, which amounted to a permanent institutionalization of the research committee, dedicated to accumulating factual data in the service of policymakers. In other words, the solution to the problems of the Great Depression was more research. Moreover, Mitchell concluded his summary by noting that the purpose of the project was to determine past social trends and predict their probable tendency, not to offer final solutions to the problems of society. He even allowed Ogburn to include a short summary of his infamous memorandum on method in a prefatory note.[56]

Although many reviewers poured lavish praise on *Recent Social Trends*, others were not so certain. An English reviewer regarded the findings as "disappointingly vague," platitudinous, and lacking specific recommendations. Columbia economist Adolf Berle, soon to become a member of Franklin Roosevelt's brain trust, criticized the committee's reliance on "barren" quantitative theory, statistical measurements, and facts. He believed that the contributors should have done more than just note social trends. An analyst should not stop with noting that the use of the automobile had led to an increasingly mobile society; he or she should also determine whether society should encourage or discourage this mobility. In two powerful and influential reviews, Charles Beard saw *Recent Social Trends* as reflecting the essential sterility of quantitative, empirical social science.[57]

The response and number of such purposivist reviewers as Berle and

Beard reflected the changing political and ideological environment of the 1930s. During the 1920s, social scientists like Mitchell were allowed the luxury of proceeding slowly toward their utopia of a perfect social science, and few criticized them. The Great Depression destroyed this idyllic framework. Critics from without and within the profession and even the foundations argued that social scientists must use their knowledge, however limited, *now* and quit preparing for the distant future. A trustee of the Carnegie Foundation wrote to its chairman that the NBER had "disgraced itself and the Carnegie Corporation" by failing to predict the coming depression in *Recent Economic Trends* because of "political pressure" and worked successfully to cut off further Carnegie support for the bureau. These critics and others like them saw the careful accumulation of empirical facts as evidenced in Mitchell's business cycle research and *Recent Social Trends* as an extravagance American society could no longer afford.[58]

Despite all the pressures pushing him toward activism in the 1930s, Mitchell retained and even strengthened his commitment to quantitative empiricism. The breakdown of the economic system and the experts' lack of success at reviving it only further convinced him of the inadequacy of present knowledge. The scarcity of reliable information doomed any attempted reconstruction of the American economy. Only large-scale, quantitative economic and social research would give politicians and administrators the data they needed to make intelligent decisions. He maintained that the only true progress made in the social sciences between 1900 and 1930 was the collection of more complete and accurate records of social information. At a 1933 dinner celebrating the tenth anniversary of the Social Science Research Council, Mitchell declared that the depression had most affected social scientists by increasing their belief in the central importance of developing an empirical science.[59]

Mitchell's caution derived in part from the public's perception of him as *the* expert on business cycles. The work of Mitchell and the NBER in the early 1920s, especially the 1923 *Business Cycles and Unemployment*, first brought the central importance of cycles to public attention. Businessmen experiencing the sharp contraction in prosperity that seemed inevitable after every war found an explanation in Mitchell's description of the business cycle, and journalists quickly popularized the term. As the postwar downturn proved of short duration and the economy entered the boom of the 1920s, however, the widespread interest in business cycles faded, to reemerge suddenly with the stock market crash and the economy's plunge into a severe depression. Mitchell again became the man of the hour, and government, industry, and civic groups begged for his advice. But Mitchell had no easy answers. He hoped researchers would eventually know enough to be able to control business fluctuations, but that remained far in the future. He could suggest certain short-term reforms such as the regulation of the stock market and the banking industry and the creation of a planning agency to help prevent future depressions, but he possessed no secret cure for the present situation. What he wanted, more than anything else, was to be relieved of public pressures so that he could concentrate on his quantitative research. As he grew older, Mitchell became ever more dedicated to finishing his ambitious project. He believed that if he could do anything to help society, it would be this. When George Soule of the *New Republic* asked him as "a public duty" to write a popular essay on ways to end the depression, Mitchell politely declined, saying he considered his real public duty to be the completion of his business cycle research.[60]

Mitchell did not refuse to aid the federal government in its attempt to hasten the end of the depression. Indeed, the New Deal appealed to his belief in government intervention and regulation of the economy. But his commitment to gathering facts and more facts prevented him from providing the government with specific solutions. For example, an unspecified government agency, hoping to anticipate the upturn and accelerate it, sponsored research by Mitchell and Arthur Burns to determine which aspect of the economy improved just before a cyclical upswing. Mitchell and Burns obviously welcomed the opportunity for public service; they began their report by stating that "what we have to offer is a digest of past experience, which we take on the whole to be the best teacher of what to expect in the future." But then they immediately drew back and noted the "peculiar" nature of each business cycle. Their final conclusion was that no particular trends were infallible predictors of a business upswing. They could not even determine if a particular upswing would continue into permanent business prosperity or relapse into stagnation. Thus, even though they ended their analysis with the assertion that knowledge of past cycles could help to predict future situations, their own study demonstrated its extreme limitations. Mitchell's insistence, here and elsewhere, on the distinct empirical differences of each business cycle effectively checked a more activist approach to the situation.[61]

Mitchell did not abandon his role as adviser or as a member of government and independent commissions in his later years. Although he seemed to begrudge his time more, he continued to serve as a consultant and expert when asked. Indeed, he and Merriam were two of the few social scientists consulted by Hoover to whom Roosevelt later turned for advice. Mitchell was consistent in his belief that the purpose of economics was to serve the practical needs of society. Nevertheless, a definite change occurred in his thought. While he continued to insist on the utility of economics, he increasingly postponed the date when the science would become of real value. More and more he emphasized the tentative nature of present economic knowledge and discouraged too great a reliance on it. The present applicability of economic knowledge became increasingly secondary to the accumulation of the basic economic data needed for a complete science. In spite of Mitchell's humanitarianism and theoretical sophistication, quantification and empiricism came to override the need for action. In the 1930s, they became the central foci for all his work.

Mitchell's activity on Columbia University's Butler Commission on the Depression provides an example of how his attitude worked in practice. The commission, appointed in December 1932, consisted of sixteen eminent New York social scientists, including Berle, Soule, John Maurice Clark, Robert MacIver, Alvin Hansen, Alvin Johnson, Joseph Schumpeter, Jacob Viner, Leo Wolman, and Mitchell. Its purpose was to investigate the current economic situation and propose recommendations that might alleviate the suffering. Despite the great ideological differences among its members, the commission agreed on a well-financed program of public works concentrating on slum clearance and city planning projects; it also favored national economic planning as the only rational approach to solving the problem on a national scale. Although Mitchell had supported such policies as early as 1913, in 1934 he qualified his approval. He signed the report but added that he thought such policies, like all others offered at that time, were "fallible." The portions of the report he especially commended were those that emphasized the need for more and better research.[62]

This report provides an additional illuminating perspective on Mitchell's thinking at that time. Mitchell joined a Columbia professor of engineering and the president of the Taylor Society in submitting an appendix calling for greater reliance on technical experts to meet current problems. Mitchell and his coauthors argued that the "engineering technique" could produce a more efficient and healthy economic system. By engineering technique they meant concentrating on the factual basis of the problem and then determining the best technical means of meeting it. From this perspective, ideological and ethical issues were no more than obstacles blocking the most efficient solution. Mitchell and his coauthors maintained that the engineering approach coupled with sufficient information could lead to full production, and hence end the depression. Solving social problems thus became merely a technical exercise of obtaining enough facts and then turning the social engineers loose.[63]

Mitchell's admired teacher Veblen had advanced a similar pretechnocratic argument that only the technicians—or, as Veblen called them, the engineers—could eliminate the wasteful nature of the present economic system. They alone were dedicated to the production of goods rather than the making of money, and only they could establish an economy of abundance. Although Mitchell and Veblen had met with some of the leaders of the Taylor Society, including Howard Scott, before World War I, at that time Mitchell had shown no particular support for such beliefs. Indeed, he clearly regarded Hoover's identification of social science with engineering as naive and wrong. Yet, as early as 1931, the chaos of the depression caused Mitchell to more closely investigate the technocratic approach. In an address before the American Society of Mechanical Engineers, Mitchell contrasted the economic wasteland of contemporary America with the "open secret" that production experts, if given complete freedom, could increase production by anywhere from 300 to 1,200 percent and solve the problems of distribution. He even quoted a recent *Forum* article in which the author stated that an "omniscient dictator" with the support of the engineers could produce enough to "flood, bury, and smother the population." Mitchell called on engineers to use their special talent for improving economic mechanisms to rescue America in her hour of desperation. By the 1930s, Mitchell had at least temporarily come to espouse technical expertise guided by sufficient facts as the solution.[64]

In the late 1930s, however, Mitchell found himself increasingly under attack for his purely empiricist views. Nazi Germany under Hitler was demonstrating what a society without ethical values could become, and many objectivist social scientists, shaken by this spectacle, began to question some of their previous assumptions and to adopt a more purposive stance. Values and goals, which had once seemed irrelevant to their discussions, now became of central importance. Mitchell, who had never denied that economic value and welfare were the ultimate goals of economics, clearly recognized that the amoral relativism of fascism represented a serious challenge to objectivist social science and attempted to address the issue.[65]

He remained consistent in his claim that quantitative research was the best means for achieving meaningful social reform, but his tone changed considerably. In his 1931 summary in *Recent Social Trends* he had noted the volume's emphasis on facts and the absence of specific suggestions somewhat apologetically while calmly asserting the greater utility of this approach for social change. In 1940, in his defense of twenty years of NBER research, Mitchell was both more apologetic and more dogmatic. He first expressed his sympathy and understanding of the critics of the bureau who advocated that it concentrate on solving America's many urgent problems. Mitchell countered that the bureau was committed to such issues but that successful practical action was impossible without adequate data, and contemporary economists simply lacked sufficient knowledge. "The National Bureau tries to serve society by laying the foundations for a more useful type of economics. . . . The gradual accumulation of economic data enables men to observe phenomena about which their predecessors could only speculate." Mitchell went on to defend the bureau at great length against claims that it lacked concern for social welfare and reform. Mitchell's report was completely out of proportion to the few criticisms actually leveled at the body. Indeed, Mitchell seemed to be trying to convince himself that he and the bureau were doing the most useful and practical thing for the welfare of society.[66]

Mitchell's defensiveness came to the fore during a 1940 discussion of his student Frederick Mills's book *Behavior of Prices*. When an opponent accused him and Mills of rejecting all a priori theory, the usually serene Mitchell angrily denied it. When his adversary persisted in this claim, Mitchell testily retorted that he certainly knew what he actually believed. During this conference and throughout the World War II years, Mitchell unwaveringly defended statisticians and quantitative economists against claims that they lacked theoretical knowledge and humanitarian goals. But he could never demonstrate how they necessarily relied on normative ends.[67]

Mitchell felt the tension between his humanitarian sentiments and his firm belief in empirical, inductive science more during these years than ever before. He sincerely desired values and ideals for economics but knew of no scientific way to determine the correct ones. He expressed his dual allegiance in a semiautobiographical 1940 essay revealingly entitled "Feeling and Thinking in Scientific Work." Mitchell believed that "feeling" plays an important and useful role in the investigation of social issues. In the final analysis, however, "a warm heart is not indispensable to scientific work and a cool head is." Mitchell regarded feeling and thinking as antagonistic forces. Although emotion and individual commitment should influence a researcher's choice of topic, they should be kept in close check during the actual research. Mitchell greatly feared the possibility of wish fulfillment in social research. Investigators should never confuse what they wanted to see with what actually happened. For social scientists to fulfill their potential, he thought, they must rely on rational thinking rather than emotional feelings.[68]

That perspective reinforced Mitchell's conviction that the social scientist qua social scientist should not make normative decisions. As a private citizen, one had the right and even the responsibility to make value judgments, but in one's role as a technical expert one had to refrain. Science could not make ethical or aesthetic choices; these remained personal decisions. As individuals, social scientists were no more free from bias and prejudice than the average man on the street.

As scientists, social investigators could predict the consequences of certain acts. Whether society would welcome these results, however, was not a question the social scientists were equipped to answer. As more and more social scientists entered positions of power within the government, first with the New Deal and later during World War II, Mitchell became even more critical of the trend. These thinkers might correctly claim to possess superior knowledge concerning how people behave, but that did not necessarily make them good policymakers. Too often specialists lacked administrative experience and plain common sense. In addition, the recruitment of able research personnel into government positions detracted from the ultimate goal of obtaining enough verifiable data to achieve a true science of society. The social scientist was more properly a technician than a decision maker.[69]

World War II reaffirmed Mitchell's faith in the quantitative approach. His 1941 annual report as director of research of the NBER proudly listed the bureau staff engaged in government war work and emphasized the essential nature of the bureau's type of work during emergencies. He testified before a 1945 congressional hearing that the relatively smooth functioning of the war effort was due to the substantial amount of information placed in the hands of well-trained experts. Where he and his World War I colleagues had often relied on blind hunches, the technicians of the 1940s possessed the data on which to base wise and speedy decisions. Mitchell rejoiced in this situation and urged the congressmen to continue federal support of empirical research.[70]

In talks before the Columbia Economics Club in 1944 and 1945,

Mitchell noted his "cherished" goal for a quantitative economics that would explain and predict behavior. A testable science such as this would have extensive applications and could eventually provide a valid guide to the intelligent reconstruction of economic life. When he looked back on his fifty-year career, Mitchell regarded the accumulation of economic data and sophisticated methodological techniques as by far the most important developments within the profession. He had consistently placed his faith for progress in scientific techniques and now reiterated his belief in empirical quantification for the future. He faced the postwar world with hope and optimism. Perhaps this time ideological quarrels would disappear and the engineers would have the opportunity to create a society of plenty for the public welfare rather than for private profit.[71]

Mitchell ended his career espousing much the same empirical methodology he had championed consistently from the beginning of the century. The quantitative empiricism he had used so adeptly to oppose the theoretical do-nothingism of the laissez-faire economists survived to combat the call during the 1930s for greater activism in the social sciences. During Mitchell's career, a methodological approach designed to provide practical men with the information necessary to make policy decisions became concerned solely with accumulation of economic information. A theory greatly influenced by Veblen's critique of contemporary economic life and his emphasis on economic change developed into an effort to create a detailed, noncritical description of the present system. An individual who expressed and demonstrated his personal commitment to substantial change in the social structure throughout his lifetime concluded that social scientists could not make ethical judgments in their professional capacities. The young theorist who at first appeared to be Veblen's heir insisted by the 1920s that any worthwhile theory would have to wait for the completion of thousands of limited, detailed research projects. Facts and their quantification, which had seemed to represent the best means toward Mitchell's ethical goal, slowly became the ends themselves.

The irony of Mitchell's career demonstrates the inner logic that so many empirically oriented objectivists followed. No one can criticize their rejection of the armchair theories of their predecessors. Their initial task was necessarily to gain knowledge about as many aspects of the largely unstudied society as possible. Moreover, insights and recommendations based on empirical evidence proved far superior to the hunches and guesses of the theorists. As their research progressed and social scientists began to recognize the amazing complexity of society, the demands of their empirical work almost inevitably swallowed up their time and their activist commitments. The situation was not as simple as it initially appeared. Probably none of the first generation of objectivist social scientists suspected the existence of so many relevant social facts or recognized the far-reaching implications of the organic philosophy of society. Yet they were unwilling to reject the scientific model that had brought them such early success. They turned almost inevitably to an emphasis on factual research; the application of the knowledge gained and the construction of explanatory theories would have to await the accumulation of enough data to establish a predictive science. Quantification, with its proven success in the physical sciences and its susceptibility to testing, seemed the perfect type of empiricism. Even such an excellent critic and historian of economic thought as Mitchell succumbed to the pressure. Facts became his obsessive concern, and he and many of his colleagues sacrificed the ethical ideals that had first motivated them in their emulation of the scientific model and their search for adequate research funds.

Tragically, objectivist social scientists who had pleaded for an opportunity to prove their utility in social reconstruction retreated when given a chance in the 1930s, believing that they did not possess enough information to make verifiable and unqualified predictions. Moreover, they insisted that as scientists they could not tell policymakers what they ought to do. Social scientists became expert technicians, unquestioning servants of the decision makers of society, providing policymakers with available information and leaving all decisions to them. The social scientist who did the most to put this viewpoint into effect was Mitchell's associate from the Social Science Research Council, the Recent Social Trends study, and the National Planning Board, Charles Merriam.

3

CHARLES MERRIAM AND TECHNICAL

EXPERTISE

If Wesley Mitchell's career was ironic because his desire for social reform led him to an extreme empiricism unrelated to and sometimes even opposing such reform, then the experiences of his fellow service intellectual Charles Merriam were even more ironic. Charles Merriam was a political theorist who denied the utility of theory, a champion of quantitative social science who could not do the most elementary calculations, a lifelong Republican who became a close aide to Franklin Roosevelt, and, strangest of all, a politician who insisted that social scientists must be completely apolitical. Merriam's goal of a practical science of politics that could lead to the achievement of a harmonious society led him to develop an extremely comprehensive and successful system of organizations to guide and fund the development of the social sciences. Moreover, the financial and political demands of those organizations caused Merriam to deny the political activism of his early years and champion the vision of social scientists as technical advisers to society's political leaders.

Merriam was undeniably the most important social science entrepreneur of his day. If Merriam could call Mitchell machiavellian for his success in obtaining funds for social science organizations, one could hardly conceive of an appropriate adjective for Merriam's activity in the same cause. Merriam developed a political science department at the University of Chicago that dominated the discipline for thirty years. After that he was the leading figure in the creation of the first interdisciplinary social science research institute, Chicago's Local Community Research Council, and he obtained first local and later national funding for its increasingly ambitious work. Through the American Political Science Association Committee on Political Research, Merriam led the movement to establish an organization to coordinate the research of the various social sciences and serve as a clearinghouse for the latest developments in the fields. Moreover, Merriam succeeded in obtaining sufficient funds from philanthropic foundations for this new institution, the Social Science Research Council (SSRC), to develop from a relatively innocuous fraternal body into the chief dispenser of funds for social research in the nation, and consequently the dominant force in contemporary social science. Other entrepreneurial successes included the building of Eleven Twenty-six and the consolidation of the headquarters of the nation's leading administrative and municipal organizations in a common building on the University of Chicago campus. He also served on the Committee on Recent Social Trends, the National Planning Board, the President's Committee on Administrative Management, and several other national commissions. The organizational structure of contemporary American social science and its interrelationships with government, private industries, and foundations owe more to Charles Merriam than to any other individual.[1]

Merriam's ambivalence with regard to social science as activism or technique stemmed directly from his progressive background. Certainly he shared his rural midwestern and strongly Protestant background with many other Progressives. Born in Iowa to a Civil War veteran and his devout Presbyterian schoolteacher wife, Merriam remembered his home as being equally devoted to a Calvinist God and the Republican party. His later books and articles are liberally sprinkled with biblical quotes and metaphors, and he remained a member of the Republican party even during his service with the New Deal. Again like many other Progressives, Merriam rejected the traditional professional options of the ministry and the law to enter one of the newly emerging professions. As a young professor at the University of Chicago he became involved in local politics, served on several local commissions, and was elected a Chicago alderman in 1909. In 1911 he was the Republican candidate for mayor and narrowly lost a bitterly fought election to the popular Carter Harrison, Jr. In 1912 he supported Theodore Roosevelt and the Progressive party and tried to keep the Illinois branch of the party alive after Roosevelt's defeat. In the words of his former campaign manager and fellow Bull Moose Harold Ickes, Merriam was "the most consistent liberal of them all" and the last of the "old Progressive movement."[2]

The University of Chicago was strongly associated with local reform movements, and in an autobiographical essay Merriam noted the influence of philosophers John Dewey, George Herbert Mead, and James Tufts and political scientist Ernst Freund on his political activism. Merriam, who was one of the first political scientists to reject the formalistic exegesis of the ideal forms of government and call for examination of actual political institutions, quickly became a protégé of Walter Fisher, leader of the Civic Federation and the so-called reform boss of Chicago. Merriam produced scholarly studies on Chicago's municipal revenue system and its primary elections and directed investigations of public utilities, police, and municipal services. As head of an aldermen's commission investigating Chicago's finances, he authored a critical report and was able to get the Chicago City Council to establish a reform-controlled "bureau of efficiency" concerned with standards and civil service reform.[3]

Merriam's reformism was a particular type of reform, however; one devoted to efficiency and control by technical experts. The group of reformers to which he belonged, associated with Fisher, the Civic Federation, and the City Club, had long considered themselves *the* reform movement of Chicago. However, many individuals allied with labor and ethnic groups accepted the need for substantial civic reform while disagreeing with the solutions proposed by Merriam and his associates. Conflict erupted in the years 1903–6 during the attempt to obtain a new city charter for Chicago. The charter then in effect allowed control by the state government and created a decentralized, weak mayor and a strong council. The charter commission, efficiency-oriented progressives chosen by the powerful Union League, bypassed those issues for the most part to concentrate on their own priorities. They wanted a centralized method of controlling and disbursing revenues, a centralized school board composed of experts free from local control, and the ability to enforce temperance and Sunday closing laws. At least one member of the commission opposed the whole concept of home rule because he feared Chicago's lower-class immigrant population more than the distant state government. The opposition, led by the Chicago Federation of Labor and the ethnic United Societies for Local Self-Government, proposed an entirely different system of reform. They were relatively unconcerned with financial reform; instead they wanted a strong central government under a mayor with real power and at-large aldermen. They pointed out that the voters had already overwhelmingly passed a referendum calling for local teacher and citizen control of the school board, and they opposed the threat to civil liberties represented by such "reforms" as Prohibition. Their successful defeat of the proposed charter was due not to the "anti-reformism" attributed to them by Merriam and most historians but to their rejection of control by "experts."[4]

Merriam's political views reflected his lifelong approach to the study of politics and society. In his scholarly works he consistently argued that the primary goal of politics was to eliminate wasteful activities such as war, revolution, and class and ethnic conflict. "Improper adjustments" such as these could be eliminated by technical experts and their professional skills. Merriam shared this attachment to technology, social control, and, as the historian Robert Wiebe aptly put it, "the search for order" with the progressive movement in general. Since Progressives did not accept the possibility of conflict, they were convinced that everyone would agree on policies once technical experts obtained sufficient information and devised specific techniques. In Merriam's confident words, "the future is a problem of social engineering"; only incorrect "social attitudes" could prevent the coming utopia. The only possible rationale for opposing such expert-based reform was self-interested biased thinking based on the conflicts that were the very basis of all the world's problems.[5]

The emphasis on the need to abolish conflict in politics was central to Merriam's conception of a good society. In his 1925 presidential address he informed the assembled members of the American Political Science Association that the basic function of politics was "fundamental readjustment" and compromise and coordination of various groups. On other occasions he harked back to Aristotle, Confucius, and other classical theorists who similarly proclaimed the purpose of politics to be "to render change as little wasteful as possible under the conditions." Even during his years as a New Dealer Merriam never accepted its theory of a politics based on group interests. He insisted on consensus: "the striking thing in America is not the clash of economic objectives but the unity of political objectives." Most of the time Merriam stubbornly refused to admit that real group and economic differences did exist. On the infrequent occasions when he did admit their existence, he complacently stated that the clashes would naturally work out for the common good.[6]

Merriam believed that politics would reach acceptable compromises because he believed in the human ability to reason and to use knowledge gained through careful research to solve problems. Merriam firmly maintained that any problem could be solved by relying on intelligence and reasoning capacity. In an autobiographical essay he grandly declared, "What is difficulty? A mere notice of the necessity for exertion." Reason by itself would solve all the evils of society, and Merriam would not accept any limitations on human rationality.[7]

Since humans were rational and could rise above their class and economic interests, the sole factor standing in the way of a satisfactory society was lack of knowledge. Merriam stated that social scientists could solve the tricky problem of Prohibition if they conducted enough scientific studies on the effects of alcohol use and alternative practices. Merriam cheerfully reported that "in the long run it is inevitable that the intelligent ordering of society will make its way." Such optimism and faith in human reason was a basic tenet of progressive belief. As the Progressive Frederic Howe stated in his autobiography, "It was mind that would save the world, the mind of my class aroused from indifference, from money-making, from party loyalty, and coming out into the clear light of reason."[8]

Merriam based his social thought on the belief that individuals could consciously control their social environment. The books that most influenced him during his graduate years were by reform Darwinists such as Edward Ross, Lester Frank Ward, and Henry Carter Adams, and Merriam maintained throughout his career that their hypothesis of man's possible control over the environment represented "the greatest of all revolutions in the history of mankind." This idea literally transformed the individual's attitude toward life. No longer did the dictates of blind chance bind one. Each person was free to control life and choose goals for oneself and society. Control of the environment also freed one from the violence and coercion of the past. It was possible to achieve social control through knowledge and reason rather than by power alone. Such rational action was necessary to counter the theories of the hated socialists and anarchists, who argued that naked power was the very basis of the state. As early as his graduate years Merriam criticized Marxism for failing to recognize the constant progress of society and the possibility of good men renouncing their economic interests without coercion. Control became instead a matter of cooperation and an appeal to human rationality.[9]

By 1931, Merriam's belief in the power of social science was so great that he could proudly declare: "A quiet revolution is going on, the results of which are likely to be far more eventful for mankind than the noisier and more dramatic social and political demonstrations that have occupied the attention of the race." This new "higher type of political and social science" would surely change the entire perspective of society in twenty to thirty years.[10]

Nevertheless, Merriam's personal political experiences prevented him from calling for an end to politics and its substitution by "good government" or for turning to a soviet of technocratic engineers as Mitchell had seemed to do in the early 1930s. Indeed, in his APSA presidential address he contemptuously dismissed such proposals as illusory and even counterproductive. Merriam was an able politician and an even more astute observer of Chicago politics. He recognized that the political machine often accurately represented the legitimate needs and desires of its constituents and that such demands could only arise in a full-fledged democracy. Unlike many of his colleagues, Merriam honestly liked politicians and the rough-and-tumble of democratic politics, and he appreciated the contributions of individuals involved in and knowledgeable about politics.[11]

Merriam's dual allegiance placed him in a painful dilemma. Social scientists skilled in techniques possessed the necessary knowledge to create a just and harmonious society; yet, they had no right to do so, nor had they any expertise in choosing the proper ends for a society. On the other hand, the politicians chosen by the citizens to make such decisions lacked the education and perspective to use the new tools. They did not even recognize the possibilities open to them. Merriam himself blanched at the thought of placing the supposed power of modern eugenics in the hands of "old-time" politicians. If this were done, "well, God help us, that is all." Where would the leadership capable of making such decisions come from? One could point to the schools and speak of the need for a vastly improved scientific and civic education, but this begged the question of who would design such educational facilities. The basic question of who would regulate social control remained unresolved.[12]

Merriam never answered or even asked this question. Consistent with his refusal to admit disagreement and conflict, Merriam simply did not admit that a problem existed. As a former politician, he believed in the correctness of democratically elected representatives making decisions. As a social scientist, he recognized the superior knowledge and skill of the men and women the graduate schools of social science were producing. His compromise was that the decision makers would rely on the expertise of the social scientists, who would become their technicians. The social scientists would provide enough data to enable social leaders to make intelligent decisions and then, after the decisions were made, would suggest the most efficient means of putting them into effect. Merriam ignored the possibility that the technician's advice and the decision maker's action might conflict, since his optimistic progressivism maintained that the two would always coincide.

Until the 1920s Merriam had not really decided how to bring service intellectuals and practical politicians together. From the period 1910–19, it appeared that *he* would be the practical politician with social science expertise. He lost the mayoral election in 1911 by a narrow margin, was a leader in the Illinois Progressive party in 1912, and was once again a leading reform alderman by 1915. But the mayoral election of machine Republican William Hale Thompson in 1914 and Thompson's success at destroying Merriam as a party rival ended Merriam's career as an elected official. From 1917 to 1919 he was again involved directly in politics as director of American propaganda in wartime Italy. By 1920, however, it had become increasingly clear to Merriam that his role would be to use his political experience to champion a technical social science directly related to the practical needs of elected officials.

Merriam began his campaign for a practical, empirical social science in 1921 with "A Survey of the Present State of the Study of Politics," in which he emphasized the need to develop new techniques and methods for the study of politics. At his initiative and urging the APSA established the Committee on the Organization of Political Research and appointed Merriam its chairman. The committee instituted a 1923 conference on the "science of politics" where leaders from various fields within political science came to exchange information on the most recent developments in their specialties. Merriam argued for the utility of such techniques as psychology and statistics in comprehending political life and the development of a scientific approach to politics.

Merriam was hardly the first political scientist to call for a scientific study of politics; however, none of his predecessors ever organized so thorough a campaign. Previously, researchers would point to a particular area in which progress was possible and then undertake a case study. Merriam, however, went beyond this limited approach and published several articles suggesting hundreds of different research topics in political science. Eventually he collected these essays in a 1925 manifesto, *New Aspects of Politics.* The purpose of *New Aspects* was not to develop a new method but "to suggest certain possibilities of approach to a method in the hope that others may take up the task and through reflection and experiment eventually introduce more intelligent and scientific technique into the study and practice of government." In the preface to the second edition in 1931 he freely admitted the poor quality of many of the scientific studies conducted in the intervening years but insisted that the important factor was their direction and method—the important thing was to do scientific research. Merriam never claimed to be a methodological innovator himself; his own primary research was in political theory and the history of political thought. His goal was to provide fruitful suggestions for future generations of political scientists.[13]

Merriam advocated small-scale, empirical studies that would employ quantitative methods. Of all social scientists, political scientists were most ignorant of statistical techniques, and Merriam insisted that they must begin to use techniques from all the other sciences to modernize the profession. Merriam himself found the area of quantitative psychology especially promising for the study of politics. Its initial attraction for him stemmed from his Italian propaganda efforts. In Italy, Merriam used such devices as visits by Italo-American labor leaders, gifts of miniature American flags, and letters from Italian emigrants to combat Austria's "insidious efforts" to question America's commitment to the war. At times, Merriam's inability to admit conflict caused him to call his own work "publicity" while he condemned the "poison gas" of his Austrian counterparts. At other times, however, he clearly recognized the potential of propaganda and psychological control. Its increasing sophistication as well as the great successes in psychological testing of American military recruits caused Merriam to praise the rapid progress of psychology "from a speculative philosophy to an experimental science, from introspection to objective measurement." A science such as this could provide techniques on which to build the study of politics and perhaps even make political behavior somewhat predictable.[14]

Merriam's political psychology did not focus on political participants. Despite his occasional mention of the need to conduct intensive interviews with individual voters or even to study abnormal political types, Merriam was never interested in the individual political actor. For him, as for the original developers of social statistics, statistics was a way of studying mass phenomena without becoming bogged down in specifics. Nor, despite his respect and admiration for the English Fabian and political psychologist Graham Wallas, did he follow Wallas's insistence on the "philosophical implications" of political psychology. Rather, he was concerned with an intensive study of psychological traits which could aid in the determination of such issues as how and why voters acted as they did. The study would include administering psychological tests to civil service and police applicants to correlate political attitudes and electoral behavior with intelligence and temperament. All the research would be quantitative, and Merriam proclaimed himself concerned solely with "net results."[15]

Nor did Merriam limit his admiration of statistics to psychological studies. A year before the publication of *New Aspects,* Merriam and his Chicago colleague and frequent collaborator Harold Gosnell completed *Non-Voting,* a statistical analysis of the reasons given by individuals for not voting. Merriam and Gosnell attempted to correlate these reasons with categories of citizens. This was the first political science study to use the techniques of sampling and the statistics of attributes. The authors' approach attested to their concern with scientific methodology. They made up a careful questionnaire, chose 5,310 nonvoters through the use of a random sample, and polled them. The authors noted that their major concern in the study was with the methodology and that the results were definitely secondary to the testing of the applicability of statistical methods. Although Merriam did little of the quantitative work and, according to Gosnell, understood even less of it, his active participation in the organization of the research and the writing attested to his strong commitment to the approach.[16]

In *New Aspects,* Merriam called for many more such small-scale empirical studies: "The real obstacle [to progress in the social sciences] is found chiefly in the lack of minute inquiry patiently carried out on a small scale, the absence of microscopic studies of the political process carried on in an objective manner." Merriam wanted to establish statistical standards for all types of political behavior and institutions so that such issues as the quality of different cities, relative merits of democracy and communism, and the utility of the League of Nations could be examined. Like Mitchell, Merriam believed statistics were essential because they proved things. No longer would society have to rely on opinion and tradition for its decisions. Statistics would replace the armchair philosopher and the "man of hunches" with the scientist. Moreover, statistics were immensely practical. One of Merriam's favorite anecdotes involved an unlettered police chief who attended one of the University of Chicago's joint conferences of social scientists and law enforcement officials. After Merriam delivered an address advocating the use of traffic statistics by police departments, the chief rose in the back and declared, "The prof is right; statistics is great; I use 'em to explain, and they can't answer me back, because I've got the dope."[17]

His appreciation of the practical utility of statistics caused Merriam to overlook many of his doubts about its extremist advocates. Although he had clashed with objectivist William Ogburn over both the Eleven Twenty-six inscription and his contribution to *Recent Social Trends,* he refused to go along with the complaints of SSRC Executive Secretary Robert Lynd concerning Ogburn's overemphasis on statistics. He calmly told Lynd that he felt the state of the discipline justified Ogburn's position. Or, as he explained with a characteristically religious metaphor in a letter to another detractor, the first step was to get the "sinners" to the "mourner's bench." Overreliance on numbers could be discouraged later; at present, one should encourage rather than discourage statistics.[18]

Merriam's admiration of quantitative psychology and statistics came from his intense belief in the supremacy of science and the scientific method. The development of a science of politics was the key to Merriam's thought, and the very word *science* came to have a magical quality for him. As early as 1897 he had inscribed on the inside of his notebook for E. R. A. Seligman's course in the history of political economy the quotation, "There is about the same distance between the scientific and theological mind as that between a clever person and that of a gorilla." The core of his APSA presidential address was the statement that "more and more it appears that the last word in human behavior is to be scientific." Anything scientific was necessarily helpful to the achievement of a better society. For instance, in 1946 Merriam wrote that "intimate" cooperation between political and atomic scientists would immeasurably aid society, even though he demonstrated a total lack of knowledge of atomic physics or any substantive idea of what atomic physicists could offer social science. That they were scientists, and the most "advanced" scientists, was enough.[19]

Merriam was able to place so much faith in science because of his particular theory of science. Personally, he never defined science beyond a simplistic "intelligence in human affairs." Rather, he referred to the works of his older brother, John, a paleontologist and president of the National Research Council and the Carnegie Institute. John Merriam studied under the famous geologist and popularizer Joseph LeConte at the University of California and became his friend and ideological successor. LeConte was an "evolutionary theist" who saw God's presence in nature and assumed, along with his close friend and frequent hiking companion John Muir, an almost Emersonian attitude. John Merriam retained much of the optimism and many of the ethical beliefs of his mentor, and his brother Charles shared these beliefs. In his speeches John Merriam talked of God's immanence in nature and quoted liberally from such romantic poets as Wordsworth and Tennyson. Science was "a sure approach to knowledge" whose purpose was "to strengthen our belief in the orderliness and law-abiding nature of the universe" and show the interconnectedness of all life. Consequently, a Baconian approach—accumulating as much data as possible and then correlating it with other data—would provide an accurate view of a world that was by its very nature orderly, rational, and even moral.[20]

This view of science led Charles Merriam to two important conclusions. First, the sole need for a complete understanding of society was empirical, quantitative facts. Consequently, in *New Aspects of Politics*

Merriam championed quantitative approaches to the study of society almost exclusively. In anthropology, he ignored Boas and the American historical school in favor of biometry and anthropometry. He found eugenics far more promising than education for developing good citizens. Second, his brother's emphasis on "sure approaches to knowledge" led Charles to call for a virtual reproduction of the approaches of the physical and natural sciences in the social sciences. In *New Aspects* Merriam declared that predicting future political activity would soon be more accurate than weather forecasting. Like Mitchell, Merriam hungered for certainty and the ideal of a harmonious society, and he believed that the scientific method alone could provide them. Only the achievement of such certainty and consequent effective social control would satisfy Merriam's ambitions for social science.[21]

Merriam saw the chief obstacle to the attainment of such a science of society as the traditional reform bias of American social scientists and their lack of objectivity. He believed that the major difference between scientists and social scientists was their relation to their data. Blissfully ignorant of the work of skeptical scientists and philosophers of science, Merriam maintained that natural and physical scientists possessed no preferences as to the outcome of their experiments. They remained totally objective and simply tabulated their results. If social scientists wished to match the accomplishments of other scientists, they must imitate this example and reject normative goals. They must become practitioners of an apolitical, amoral technique concerned solely with the discovery of factual knowledge. Not only did bias prevent a truly objective study of the subject and consequently a trustworthy science, it made potential funders of social science research nervous. Merriam, like Mitchell, clearly recognized the immense cost of quantitative research and the potential availability of research funds from foundations and private businesses. Objectivity was the sine qua non for Merriam's ambitious goals and hopes for social science.

William Archibald Dunning, Merriam's principal professor at Columbia, was an exponent of the absolute importance of objectivity. Although he worked in the field of political theory, Dunning's approach was far different from that of such formalist predecessors as John Burgess. In fact, Dunning's work was quite similar to Dewey's in the history of philosophy and Mitchell's in the history of economic theory. Political theory was primarily a function of its time and environment, and it represented the attempts of individuals to grapple with their immediate social and political problems. Like Mitchell and unlike Dewey, Dunning concluded from this that since true objectivity was impossible, no political theory was valid or even especially useful. Dunning became so obsessed with the issue of objectivity that he once confided to Merriam that he regretted ever publishing anything.[22]

Merriam's early work in political theory accurately reflected Dunning's attitude. The conclusion to his dissertation set the mood for all his work in political theory. In it, he noted that his work was simply a survey of the various concepts of sovereignty. While a "dogmatist" would provide the correct point of view, scientific historians should limit themselves to describing the various approaches to the subject. He followed this approach throughout his many studies of American political thought; each objectively described the different theories without analysis of any sort. Although he began by referring to his subject as political "theory," he soon started referring to it as political "thought," and by the time of *New Aspects* had downgraded it to political "thinking." Since political theories were no more than justifications and rationalizations of particular special interest groups and "more or less thinly veiled propaganda," any attempt to view them as anything else would destroy the scientific standing of political science. By 1944, when Merriam was preparing a second edition of his classic *American Political Theories*, even the terms *thought* and *thinking* seemed too "scientific" for his taste, and he planned to replace them with either *doctrines* or *hypotheses*.[23]

The issue of objectivity was especially acute for political science. The American Political Science Association, formed in 1903, deliberately tried to disassociate itself from the ethical orientation of some earlier social science organizations by including in its constitution a specific clause prohibiting the discussion of partisan political issues at its meetings. The founders of the organization had done this primarily to protect their positions within the universities, but Merriam soon recognized the applicability of the issue of objectivity for the post–World War I funding crisis. Even as the emerging foundations began to grant considerable sums to natural and physical scientists, anthropologists, psychologists, and even economists and sociologists, they ignored students of politics. Donors were fearful of being considered partisan in their gift giving and conceived of political questions as inherently biased. In addition, most benefactors possessed significant vested interests and did not wish to spend their money tampering with the established political and social order. On top of all this, political science researchers required access to political institutions to conduct their work. To gain this entrance, they needed to convince government officials of their objectivity. Unless political scientists could convince conservative foundations and governments of their lack of reformist objectives and their commitment to scientific research, they could never achieve their goal. The future of political science seemed to depend almost wholly on its winning a reputation as an objective science.

No one did more to attain this goal than Merriam. He devoted a large portion of his career to establishing institutions dedicated to objective social science research, and he was a master at organizing these agencies and raising funds for their work. By establishing strict control over the type of research encouraged by these organizations, Merriam succeeded in convincing the foundations that researchers would follow strict guidelines in the conduct of their inquiries. The key to obtaining funds lay in the organization of social science. As he explained it in "The Present State of the Study of Politics" (1921), "the success of the expedition is conditioned upon some general plan of organization. Least of all can there be anarchy in social science."[24]

Merriam succeeded in allaying the fears of foundations because he was able to present them with an image of general agreement among social scientists. Merriam convinced many of his colleagues, traditionally opinionated and diverse, that they could not proceed toward a science of society without agreeing on certain fundamental principles. Merriam sought consensus through a wide variety of conciliatory measures. He championed the conference method, in which experts could assemble, share their knowledge and opinions, and attempt to arrive at common positions. He also used his control over the research fellowships given by the Social Science Research Council to encourage certain types of noncontroversial research and build a network throughout the country. Merriam's insistence on conformity had the dangerous results that technique became the only problem in social science and genuine disagreements and problems were pushed aside. Yet, something of this sort was probably necessary to convince foundations, government, and business to accept social science as a tool for the solution of their problems. Merriam's great importance in this regard lay in his encouragement of the creation of a social science that achieved acceptance through proving its utility.

Merriam's first experience with raising funds came in 1905, one of his first years at the University of Chicago. A group of prominent local businessmen and professionals associated with the Commercial and City clubs wished to encourage research leading to the improvement of municipal conditions. They turned for advice to Merriam, whom they knew through shared civic and political activities. Merriam suggested and instituted a particularly appropriate project, a comparative study of eight municipal revenue systems. The selection of this topic demonstrated Merriam's considerable political savvy. The project was practical, providing information on a subject then under discussion in Chicago, but it was also politically safe, using "objective" statistics to compare the various arrangements and steering well clear of the corrupt Chicago system.

Encouraged by the continuing interest of community groups, Merriam and several other University of Chicago professors officially founded the Local Community Research Committee (LCRC) in 1923. This organization offered the expertise of the university's social scientists on any local project for which a Chicago group was willing to contribute half the funds. The committee conducted research for the Real Estate Board, the meat-packing industry, different social settlement houses, the International Advertising Association, and the League of Women Voters. Merriam did all he could to assure Chicago's economic elite of the committee's lack of radicalism and probusiness beliefs. Above all else, the committee stressed its objectivity. In a 1929 volume celebrating the achievements of Chicago social science, two of the committee's directors insisted that "much of the research conducted under the auspices of the LCRC is not immediately concerned with any proposal for reform or change, but is directed solely toward the better understanding of the conditions of life in an urban community. . . . [It] has no immediate reformist end." The committee wanted to meet the needs of the community—but only to the extent of providing knowledge. Its members' expertise lay in describing current situations and suggesting means to achieve policies already determined. Its self-assumed role did not involve giving advice on policy. Merriam proudly declared that the committee and institutions like it were scientific bodies composed of well-educated technical experts, and that it differed completely from the "propaganda agencies" of the previous municipal research organizations with their staffs of untrained reformers.[25]

Merriam was active both in organizing the committee and, more important, in raising the necessary funds for its existence. In 1923 he approached Beardsley Ruml, the new director of the Laura Spelman Rockefeller Fund, with a plea to provide the nonlocal half of the funds for the committee. Ruml, who received his doctorate from the University of Chicago, consented, and the two men began a long and mutually profitable relationship. Merriam cultivated Ruml and his associates assiduously. He regularly informed them of the progress of the various research projects and reported on the state of social science in general. Merriam shrewdly wrote to them as equals in knowledge, asked their advice as fellow experts rather than as holders of the purse strings, and confided to them his plans for the future of social science. Nor did Merriam neglect the Rockefellers themselves. By the 1930s he was well acquainted with the family and on a first-name basis with the younger generation. Although Merriam's organizations obtained grants from the Carnegie Foundation, the Commonwealth Fund, the Rosenwald Fund, and the Russell Sage Foundation as well, the various Rockefeller foundations provided the financial base for his entrepreneurial empire. By 1952 they had contributed over eight million dollars to the SSRC alone. They also provided the majority of the funding for the LCRC, the Public Administration Clearing House, the Social Science Research Building at Chicago, the President's Research Committee on Recent Social Trends, and the commissions of inquiry of the SSRC.[26]

Merriam's most successful social science organization was the Social Science Research Council. Ever since its founding in 1923 the council has served as the chief communication body for the social sciences. Also, until the end of World War II and the rush of funding by the federal government and private industry, the SSRC was the major disseminator of grants for social science research. Over the years it has proved to be the most important social science organization in American history.

Merriam had more to do with the institutionalization of the SSRC than any other individual. He and his APSA Committee on Political Research developed the idea for the organization to aid in the production of more sophisticated scientific research and provide communication among the various social sciences. The frequent disputes between the various disciplines over areas of specialization and the bitter competition for scarce research funds endemic in social science in the early 1900s convinced many individuals that an interdisciplinary organization would prove beneficial for all the social sciences. Before Merriam, however, their discussions remained theoretical. Despite considerable indifference and even hostility from the historians and his general lack of clarity about his overall purpose, Merriam—with the aid of a few powerful allies such as Mitchell—was able to form a skeleton organization. Although the SSRC lay relatively dormant for its first few years, Merriam remained confident of its potential and worked tirelessly to obtain the funding necessary for it to live up to its potential. As Merriam's biographer, Barry Karl, put it, "While the degree to which his writings establish[ed] the intellectual base for that organization is open to debate, the fact that he established the economic organization is beyond debate." Moreover, while the other founding members served out their terms on the executive council and gave up their positions to younger members of their disciplines, Merriam was constantly renominated and continued to serve through the 1940s.[27]

The council sustained Merriam's commitment to total objectivity. In its early conferences and annual reports, the SSRC consistently insisted that it was not an "action body"; its primary purpose was to serve as a clearinghouse for research techniques and findings within the social sciences. The Council itself did not do research; it encouraged and coordinated social research and chose specific social scientists and projects for funding. In its early years the council was careful to avoid partisan political issues. Its first projects were a survey and analysis of social research in progress, a survey of social science methods, and an annual index and digest of state laws. It turned down several well-endowed and prestigious proposals because of their political nature. At the suggestion of John Merriam, E. E. Hunt, Herbert Hoover's specialist on the social sciences, approached the council in 1923 with proposals for studies of national unemployment and the basis of justifiable settlements in labor disputes. Although some members of the council welcomed the opportunity, the leadership, influenced by Merriam's and Mitchell's strong opposition, refused the offer, arguing that the unemployment study was too large for a beginning organization and carried too early a due date to be completed in a scientific manner. As for the "proper" settlement of wage disputes, the council considered this a political rather than a scientific issue. Ever since the 1900s, arbitration boards had pleaded with economists to provide some theoretical basis for the determination of justifiable wage settlements. Economists had so far failed to agree on any acceptable scheme, and the SSRC did not wish to be sucked into that type of dispute.[28]

An example of the Council's justifiable fears of politicization took place in 1926. In 1925, the SSRC began a preliminary survey of the operation of Prohibition with the implicit goal of establishing a national commission to devise a solution to the problem. Merriam's and the others' enthusiasm quickly cooled once they recognized the lack of hard data and the controversiality of the issue, and the council quickly backed out of its commitment to the study. Merriam wished to husband carefully the accumulated goodwill due the organization, because he believed that "if we bungle the situation, the kind of opportunities we now have will not come again at least during our lifetime."[29]

As the SSRC expanded in the 1920s, with more money and more research projects, its leaders began to fear that they had lost control of the work done under the council's auspices. If foundations lost their faith in its ability to keep social science objective, the SSRC might lose all the gains, not to mention funding, it had so carefully accrued. Consequently, the council undertook an internal reorganization in 1929 and established a permanent supreme committee, the Problems and Policy Committee, to oversee ongoing research, encourage new areas of study, and choose new projects. Revealingly, this committee included members not on the executive council who were apparently selected by the foundations themselves. The official historian of the council admitted that the committee was created to protect the SSRC from radical shifts within the disciplinary bodies which might alienate grantors of funds. The council recognized that its financial well-being depended on foundations' impression of its objectivity.[30]

This is not to say that the council's and especially Merriam's position on objectivity stemmed merely from a desire to obtain research money. Merriam believed deeply in the supremacy of democratic politics. Although society needed expertise in social trends and technique to meet the rapid changes caused by developing technology, it did not necessarily follow that the experts should become the decision makers. Merriam laid out the ground rules clearly in *New Aspects of Politics:* the social scientists—or, as he consistently began to refer to them, the technicians—could create a new social system within twenty years *"if it is desired to do so."* Quoting from his brother's mentor LeConte, Merriam argued that the scientist's proper role is always advising, never "controlling." Scientists should gather information and disseminate it to the society at large but never take positions. He adhered to this position so strongly that on one occasion he even stated that these technical advisers would be of equal use to totalitarian or democratic states: "They are not primarily dependent upon any special value system. They may be appropriated by whoever wishes to take them . . . to utilize in whatever undertaking may be at hand."[31]

Unlike Mitchell, Merriam was not personally content with complete reliance on empirical studies. Perhaps it was because, again unlike Mitchell, he lacked the talent or skills to do the type of quantitative research he so ably championed. Or perhaps his discontent stemmed from his recognition as a former politician that his fellow academics lacked an adequate concern for practicality. In his autobiographical essay he referred to himself as a split personality, with the practical "Carlo" of his Italian propaganda days looking with disdain on the professorial Merriam. In fact, Merriam never totally rejected Carlo. Still, as a commentator acutely observed, "A life which combined an active involvement in politics with the 'apolitical' study of politics was a triumph in the maintenance of a very delicate balance."[32]

Early in the 1930s Merriam believed he had found the answer to his dilemma in the form of social technicians who devoted themselves to the practical work of society: political administrators. Only they seemed to fulfill Merriam's goal of being both inside and outside politics. Merriam became increasingly interested in and supportive of their work and became their most influential publicist within the structure of organized social science, and later in the New Deal. The 1930s became, in his own words, the period in which he "entered the school of Public Administration."[33]

Merriam's burgeoning interest in public administration during the 1930s was not completely accidental. As the Great Depression put incredible strain on governmental agencies, Merriam's cherished consensus dissolved in a chaos of conflicting interest groups and ideological alternatives. Merriam recognized and even welcomed gradual social change, but he desperately feared rapid, ill-conceived changes. He hoped that a sound administrative system would stabilize the situation and make transitions as smooth and moderate as possible. "In a time of clashing social policies without a very clear directive upon which there is general agreement, the importance of sound administration is exceptionally great. If beneath the storm of the surface of public opinion, there is a solid basis of administrative efficiency, the shocks of strife are less dangerous in their influence upon social relations."[34]

Like his views on political theory, Merriam's approach to public administration came directly from his Columbia teachers. Frank Goodnow was a central figure in the history of public administration for his rebellion against the study of administration as purely legal rules. Instead he emphasized practical politics, improved administrative services, and the necessity of centralized administration. In his best-known work, *Politics and Administration*, Goodnow rigidly separated government into the will of the state (politics) and its execution (administration). Merriam consistently followed Goodnow's ideas throughout his scholarly and practical work.

Merriam began to study public administration at Columbia because of his interest in urban reform. Municipal ownership of city utilities, improved sanitation and health, and more efficient control over municipal services were some of the key goals and accomplishments of the progressive crusade. Merriam was deeply involved with this movement in New York and Chicago, and, like many of his fellow Progressives, saw the smoothly functioning German municipal system with its highly trained, capable personnel as the best answer to the cities' problems. Merriam did more research in municipal government than in any other field except political theory, kept abreast of current work in the field, and taught an annual graduate seminar on urban government throughout the 1920s. He continued this concern throughout the 1930s by serving on the Urbanism Committee on the National Resources Committee and choosing that topic for his address at the 1939 symposium celebrating the tenth anniversary of Eleven Twenty-six. In line with his progressive background and commitment to social control, Merriam perceived disorganization to be the root of the problems of the city. Hundreds of different governmental bodies and agencies were responsible for the same areas; city, regional, state, and federal jurisdictions overlapped; and the body politic itself was in a constant state of flux and turmoil. Merriam's goal was to achieve a centralized and rational control over the city through the introduction of specialists and sophisticated methodological techniques.[35]

Merriam's greatest hopes for the realization of this goal rested on the nonpolitical municipal officers who were beginning to form professional organizations and attempting to establish standards of professionalization for their occupations. He himself participated actively in such groups as the International City Managers' Association, the National City Secretaries, the Municipal Finance Officers' Association, and the National Association of Police Chiefs, and he aided these groups in whatever way he could. He wrote articles for their publications, addressed their conventions, served on their executive boards, advised them concerning funding, and even had the university appoint some of their leaders as research professors. Most of all, Merriam was able to use his connections and access to Rockefeller money to establish the Public Administration Clearing House (PACH) and finance a building on the Chicago campus to house it. This building, at 1313 East 60th Street, soon to be known as Thirteen-Thirteen, became the headquarters of fifteen of the leading public and municipal administration societies. Merriam hoped that their proximity would encourage the societies to share their knowledge and experiences. To ensure this cooperation, the Rockefeller Fund established PACH under Louis Brownlow, formerly of the City Managers' Association, to serve as the formal disseminator of information on public administration to any organization or governmental body that requested it.

Merriam both admired and relied on the city managers, whom he referred to as the "type par excellence in public administration" and a model all technicians should emulate. Merriam told of attending a joint conference of mayors and city managers and quickly identifying the respective members of each group. The mayors were loud, hearty, and reminiscent of favorite fishing companions. The city managers were coolly competent and knowledgeable, combining their technical expertise with political wisdom. He reported to his foundation contacts that the International City Managers' Association under the direction of Brownlow, soon to become one of his closest friends, was "the most promising group" connected with government because of its dedicated attempts to professionalize its members and conduct basic research in the field. Merriam began associating with this group more and more in the late 1920s and early 1930s. The city managers met Merriam's ideal: technical experts, divorced from political decisions, engaged in practical work and using scientific knowledge from many different fields. Upon being made an honorary member of the association, Merriam, apparently in all sincerity, effusively thanked them by declaring, "Coming from a group of men such as the managers, this is a very real tribute which I prize more highly than any academic degree I have received."[36]

As his sponsorship of Thirteen-Thirteen and the PACH indicates, Merriam believed that he could do the most for his new infatuation through his extensive contacts with foundations and existing social science organizations. He had done this earlier for the social sciences at large, and he was equally committed to do the same for public administration. He believed that the most important need of the field was for well-trained administrators, so he focused on the issue of education. In 1928 he formed an advisory SSRC committee to encourage research in the field. When the Rockefeller Fund came under criticism for not funding "practical" research in the late 1920s, Merriam and the fund's treasurer, Raymond Fosdick, successfully lobbied for the field of public administration. Soon after, the fund gave a $125,000 grant to the University of Chicago for training and research in the area and a similar sum for research to the SSRC Committee on Public Administration.[37]

Merriam perhaps best demonstrated his commitment to public administration in 1933 when he coaxed his beloved Social Science Research Council out of its fear of direct investigations. Although ten years earlier Merriam had been among the strongest opponents of the proposed investigations into unemployment and wage arbitration, in 1933 he urged the council to establish three commissions of inquiry to study specific areas of pressing political and social concern, one of which was public administration. These commissions differed considerably from normal council research activities. Whereas the SSRC traditionally insisted on original and fundamental research, the goal of these commissions was to examine as quickly as possible all available data on the problem, analyze and interpret it, and then advance recommendations for its solution. Although many prominent members of the council, including its president, Robert Crane, opposed the commissions as departures from the traditional objectivity of the organization, Merriam successfully argued that exactly this objectivity permitted the SSRC, and the SSRC alone, to undertake these studies. According to Merriam, the council already possessed the confidence of the public because of its nonpartisan approach. This hard-won reputation ensured careful attention to its recommendations, while critics would immediately accuse a nonaffiliated body with political bias and favoritism.[38]

If Merriam wished for these commissions to have an effect on public policy, as he most fervently did, some official sanction was needed from the government. Indeed, without that, even access to information was not assured. Upon the advice and intervention of Merriam's former campaign manager and now Secretary of the Interior, Harold Ickes, and Secretary of Agriculture Henry Wallace, who had served on the council's Committee on Agricultural Economics, Crane petitioned FDR to request officially that the Social Science Research Council undertake a study on public administration. Roosevelt, a consummate politician, was unwilling to blindly approve a commission over which he had no final control. He wished to use social scientists, not for them to use him. He shrewdly gave the council his "approval" and ordered government officials to cooperate while retaining his own freedom of action.[39]

Significantly, as soon as the Commission of Inquiry on Public Service Personnel received official support and cooperation from Roosevelt, it again retreated to an insistence on total objectivity. The preface to its final report declared that after the government and the SSRC established it, the commission was no longer responsible to them. Its sole concern was with the truth. Merriam wanted it both ways. He wished to serve the government, have his recommendations taken seriously, and have a practical effect. Yet, he also clung to his insistence on the absolute objectivity of the social scientist.[40]

Merriam was able to maintain this claim of objectivity because he adhered to Goodnow's strict compartmentalization of the political and administrative functions. Administrators were to enforce the rules formulated by policymakers; hire, fire, and supervise personnel; prepare budgets; collect material for planning; and run public services. Administrators were technical experts wholly reliant on broad, general policies instituted by the legislature. They used their special knowledge to implement these policies and attempted to bring the predetermined objectives into effect. Merriam consistently stressed that administrators were technicians, "the means by which the people's ends are reached." Their function was to be "on tap, not on top."[41]

This did not mean, however, that administrators should have no influence on policy decisions. Policymakers who wished to make good decisions would make use of their technicians' special knowledge. Merriam did everything he could to bring the two groups together. The Public Administration Clearing House often deluged elected officials with advice, solicited or not. Moreover, he used his fundraising skills to encourage organizations that sought to integrate elected and appointed officials. The American City Planning Institute (ACPI) based at Harvard was a small, self-proclaimed "technical society" with strict membership qualifications and a paramount interest in professionalizing the discipline. In the 1920s, Brownlow founded the rival American Society of Planning Officials (ASPO) as a service group designed to educate and exchange information and open to all public officials, elected or appointed. Merriam quickly included the ASPO in Thirteen-Thirteen, helped it obtain Spelman funds, and included its officials on governmental commissions. By the late 1930s the ASPO had far surpassed the older ACPI in political influence and membership.[42]

Merriam pointed out administrators must realize that politicians would often ignore technical advice for reasons of their own. This should not concern them. Their task was to gather and present the relevant data and make recommendations without reference to political exigencies. Whether the correct decisions were then actually made was the responsibility of the politicians, not the administrators. In one of his last series of lectures, the 1947 Maxwell Lectures at Syracuse University, Merriam demarcated the "boundary lines" between politics and administration in great detail.[43]

Merriam believed that most of his administrator acquaintances understood the need for objectivity and followed it completely. Yet, as the Public Service Personnel Inquiry itself demonstrates, public administration was not per se objective. The line between politics and administration was never as clear-cut as Goodnow and Merriam insisted. Merriam and his coinvestigators began their survey with very little doubt about their eventual findings or recommendations. They represented a continuation of the battles fought by American civil service reformers against the spoils system and for hiring and promoting on the basis of merit. Indeed, many Washington observers initially questioned the utility of the study since everyone already knew the weaknesses of the present civil service system. The commission recognized this and concentrated on bringing the facts before the public. They hired the well-known publicist Edward Bernays as their public relations counsel and arranged to hear a large number of witnesses from many different occupations, organizations, states, and nations. The hearings provided good publicity and gained the influential support of such civic and reform groups as the League of Women Voters. Merriam and his fellow committee members consciously perceived the study as a case of public education rather than an attempt to discover new knowledge.[44]

The commission's final report predictably mirrored the accepted scholarly opinion about the American civil service. It recommended that Congress establish a career service open to advancement on the basis of personal merit and free from political interference. The commission adopted much of the British model, including that system's distinctive compartmentalization of different classes of administrators. It also insisted that administrators be dispassionate technicians kept separate from policy decisions and engaged solely in carrying out the decisions of the electorate and their representatives.[45]

Yet, for all its vaunted objectivity, the report departed from a scientific basis on several key political points. The commission recognized that if it expected politicians to notice its recommendations, it must take certain political actualities into account. For instance, although the commission unanimously agreed in principle that congressmen should not recommend applicants for civil service positions, Merriam and his Chicago colleague Leonard White successfully argued that the inclusion of such a naive and idealistic position would make the entire report appear ridiculous. The members of the commission found themselves compelled to mold not only the topics but the results of their research to the needs of the sponsoring agency.[46]

As such instances began to multiply, the majority of the SSRC Executive Committee began to regret their agreement to turn to an activist approach. Although the commissions into public service personnel and the redistribution of population resulted in significant legislative and administrative action, Crane, Ogburn, and others strove to reassert the traditional pattern of funded research. The annual report for 1934–35 emphasized that the year's research consisted of work "of more immediate public utility" than the usual projects of the organization and carried the clear implication that the situation was temporary. Two years later, the report announced the ssRC's return to long-term research and studies of social science technique. In another two years, the council would emphasize the creation of new techniques as the most important need of contemporary social thought.[47]

Merriam did not follow the council in this action. He continued to lobby for the commission of inquiry method and suggested that the ssRC investigate such issues as freedom of speech, teaching, and research; stimulation of industry; currency and banking; and the effect of the National Recovery Act on American labor. He even suggested that he and the ssRC had been wrong not to undertake the Prohibition study back in the 1920s. But Merriam was not crushed by the direction the ssRC had chosen. In the meantime he had helped develop another organization that would meet his ambitions for social science much better. Merriam became a prominent national planner and one of the three members of the National Planning Board.[48]

Planning represented Merriam's final and best dream for social science, especially in a society mired in an economic depression. It was the most widely advocated measure to meet the social chaos of the depression. At least one historian of the period has argued that planning constituted the core of 1930s liberalism. Many conservatives and business interests desired a type of planning in which trade associations would control production and prices and eliminate the cutthroat competition which they identified as the chief cause of the depression. The most popular proposals were those advanced by the United States Chamber of Commerce and General Electric's Gerard Swope. The group of planners associated with the technocracy movement advocated total control of society by trained engineers possessing all available information on every aspect of American social and economic life. A large number of social scientists, most notably George Soule, Rexford Tugwell, and Stuart Chase, used the Veblenian idea of a technical elite more moderately. They envisioned a national planning board staffed by technical experts appointed by the federal government. Other planners believed that effective national planning could arise only through control of crucial areas of the economy such as public works. In addition, the Communist party attracted widespread support among intellectuals with its call for a totally controlled and socialized society and an American five-year plan. Different groups seeking different goals according to their respective personal visions all turned to planning as the technique that would provide the key to the kingdom. A commentator wrote in 1942: "We are at the end of a decade in which planning has been something of a magic word. It has been on everybody's tongue; it has been the fad to use it everywhere; and the result is that the vogue has produced word-magic. Planning has meant a thousand things—including nothing—depending upon who was talking."[49]

Planning as a field arose from the bureaucratic orientation of progressivism that so influenced Merriam. The New Nationalism of Herbert Croly and Theodore Roosevelt advocated business regulation and sufficient control of social and economic life by the national government to ensure the welfare and "increasing liberty" of the majority. Movements for urban planning, conservation, and scientific public administration that arose during the Progressive Era formed the basis on which the national planners of the 1930s built their theories and expectations.

One of the many individuals whose commitment to national planning began with the limited planning favored by progressivism was Franklin Roosevelt. His initial attraction to planning came when his uncle Frederic Delano, one of the designers of the Burnham Plan for the growth of Chicago, pointed out the purposes and possibilities of the approach to his young nephew. During his early post—World War I political career, Roosevelt followed the example of his distant cousin and his wife's uncle Theodore and became involved in the issue of conservation of national resources. He emphasized this area upon his election as governor of New York in 1928, and he extended his earlier interest in city planning to include state planning. In a speech before the 1931 Conference of Governors, Roosevelt declared that if, as everyone agreed, city and county plans were absolutely essential, then comprehensive state programs must be even more important. Upon his election as president he used the same logic to justify national planning and further emphasized the organic nature of the national interest. His chief advisers in the brain trust were all planners, albeit of very different types, and much of the early legislation of the New Deal such as the NIRA, the AAA, and the TWA attested to Roosevelt's confidence in the utility of planning. Roosevelt believed that a national planning board that could provide information about the present state of society and predict its probable direction was fundamental to the achievement of successful national planning. Such an organization could plan and attempt to control the future and break the pattern of government merely responding to crises as they occurred. Merriam was to become an important part of Roosevelt's plan for this board.[50]

The legislative mood of the early 1930s was highly receptive to the idea of a limited national planning agency. In 1931, almost against President Hoover's wishes, Congress passed the Federal Employment Stabilization Act, which gave the executive branch authority and funds to gather the economic information necessary to anticipate economic trends and combat downturns in the business cycle. The initial occasion for the formation of a New Deal planning institution came when Ickes, head of the Public Works Administration as well as secretary of the interior, requested expert advice on determining the relative merits of proposed public work projects. Ickes, who was honest to a fault, demanded factual material on which to make his decisions. For several decades economists had been calling for a listing of public work projects that the national government could institute in the event of a depression, but no list existed at the time. Roosevelt formed the National Planning Board (NPB) to advise Ickes on the relative merits of specific projects, investigate the importance of the entire subject of public works, and gather relevant information for a national plan.

The three members chosen by Roosevelt to sit on the board represented the best of American expertise and knowledge. The chairman of the committee was Delano, the dean of American urban planners. Shortly after World War I, Delano had left a highly successful career as a railroad executive to devote himself to his interest in planning. During his illustrious career he helped formulate the Chicago plan, actively participated in the conservation movement, served in the Transportation Corps during World War I, directed a huge regional study of New York City and its suburbs, managed the first large-scale survey of the nation's land resources, propagandized for a master plan for land use, and served as chairman of the District of Columbia Board of Supervisors. Delano was very cautious about his personal relationship with his nephew and refused to use his family connections for the advantage of the board.

The second and third members of the NPB were Mitchell and Merriam. Mitchell possessed a deep commitment to and an extensive knowledge of planning, and his appointment was unanimously praised by economists and planners alike. Merriam too was an obvious choice, for both intellectual and personal reasons. Not only did he have a strong interest in planning and superb connections in the social sciences and foundations, but he also had personal contacts with all the principal actors. He and Mitchell had worked closely together in establishing the SSRC, on the Recent Social Trends survey, and on numerous social science conferences and commissions. Merriam first met Delano in the early 1900s when he was serving as secretary of the Chicago Harbor Commission and Delano and Charles Wacker were developing plans for the harbor area. Although Merriam and Roosevelt did not know each other personally, Merriam was a close friend of brain truster Raymond Moley. Moreover, Roosevelt knew and admired Merriam's work in establishing the Public Administration Clearing House. The key to Merriam's selection, however, lay in his friendship with Ickes. It had taken Ickes very little time to win a reputation within the New Deal as someone who refused advice. One of the few individuals whom the prickly Ickes did trust was his old friend and fellow Chicago reformer Merriam. Various New Deal acquaintances deluged Merriam, even before his appointment to the NPB, with requests for advice on how to deal with the irascible Ickes. This rare ability to work with Ickes combined with all his other contacts and his commitment to planning made Merriam an excellent selection as an authority on government planning.[51]

Merriam quickly became the dominant member of the board. Delano's advanced age and his worries about charges of nepotism caused him to abrogate many of his responsibilities as chairman. Mitchell, who had chaired many earlier commissions, was submerged in the quantitative facts of his business cycle research and had little time for the work of the NPB. Charles Eliot III, the executive secretary of the board and Delano's longtime personal secretary, was too young and had too few connections within the circles of organized science and social science; his early attempts at leadership further won him the lasting distrust of Merriam. Staff members of the National Planning Board and its successor organizations agree that Merriam established the general outline for the type and direction of the research the board would undertake. He also supplied a majority of the researchers through his connections with the SSRC and his brother's National Science Association.[52]

Despite his keen interest in planning, Merriam never provided a specific definition of it. To him, *planning* was a "good American word" involving the "laying out as carefully as possible the day's work or the season's work or the year's work . . . in the home, in the farm, [or] in the factory." Anything involving any kind of control over the present or the future was a plan. Using this definition, Merriam pointed out a long series of American plans and planners beginning with the Constitution and the Founding Fathers. Since the Constitution established a particular institutional framework for the American government, it was a plan and the United States became the world's first planned government.[53]

If Merriam's definition of planning was somewhat all-encompassing, his goal for planning was very specific and required a differentiation between American and European planning. According to Merriam, where European programs concentrated on economics, American plans devoted primary attention to national resources. American planning was democratic and flexible, not a "fixed and unchangeable system which might be clamped down like a steel frame upon soft flesh" like the European models. The American public itself chose the goals and limits of planning through democratic means and, Merriam was sure, would leave the vast majority of social life untouched. Indeed, Merriam viewed planning as a preventive measure against the social chaos or totalitarianism that unplanned systems were sure to create. The planners would remain technicians offering possibilities and alternatives for public choice.[54]

Merriam believed that the democratic nature of American planning could best be ensured by keeping it as much as possible on the local level. Throughout the 1920s he advocated and helped in the establishment of city, regional, and state planning commissions. Upon his urging, one of the first acts of the National Planning Board was to establish a program to provide expert planning and administrative assistance to local planning agencies. Local planning appealed to Merriam's progressive instincts. It permitted small-scale experimentation of specific reform measures which, if successful, national planners could adopt. It also relied on local support and participation. Merriam became so enraptured with the merits of decentralization that he later tried to argue, despite overwhelming evidence to the contrary, that the process was continuing during World War II.[55]

Merriam made it quite clear that the chief function of the NPB was to provide information to local planning organizations, federal departments, and, most important, the president. Without sufficient data, planning of any type was impossible, and at the time planners lacked sufficient information to generate comprehensive programs. Merriam perceived his proper role in the planning movement to be helping to create organizations that could collect this necessary data. At this stage, all one could do was devise a "plan for planning."[56]

Skilled technicians were needed to gather and analyze the information. Poorly educated investigators failed to recognize the significance of certain data and were unable to translate it into a form susceptible of easy utilization. The board experimented with using WPA employees to assemble simple data on certain projects, but this proved a total failure. Apparently at Merriam's instigation, a committee of the SSRC wrote a report for the board outlining "The Aid Which the Social Sciences Have

Rendered and Can Render to National Planning." The committee began the report by noting the central importance of data collection and insisted that only specialists could do that task correctly. They believed it particularly necessary for social knowledge to be expressed in statistical form. Such exactitude would, the committee believed, rescue public policy from its previous vagueness. In the report's conclusion the committee noted the SSRC's ten years of experience and its superior wisdom in planning research and volunteered the council as coordinator of social research for the NPB.[57]

The SSRC committee advocated using social scientists in national planning because of their dispassionate objectivity. According to the report, social scientists saw their duty as simply to provide all available information to policymakers. They would never try to interfere in the process of policymaking. This certainly conformed to the position of Merriam and the NPB regarding the role of the planner. Merriam solemnly informed an international conference that "the separation of the function of study and advice from that of execution and administration is fundamental to the American planning organization." Indeed, planners' detachment from political pressures and decisions accounted for their ability to provide governmental officials with unbiased advice. The sole purpose of a planning board was advisory; it had no real power of its own, and neither Merriam nor his colleagues believed it should have. Merriam and Delano even opposed legislation that would have given the NPB more power. Delano called one such bill "dictatorial" and urged his nephew to prevent its enactment.[58]

In all of its actions the NPB followed Merriam's emphasis on decentralized planning and the dissemination of information and continued to stress its advisory role. In its first informal report to Ickes, the board noted its stimulation of city, regional, and state planning and its role in establishing standards for new governmental planning commissions. Later, the board collected inventories of basic data and established uniform standards that would permit the easy communication among different governmental and planning bodies necessary to eventually develop a national plan. Throughout, the board insisted on its objectivity and its technical role. In its final report the NPB proposed a permanent planning board dependent on executive support for its very existence. It argued that a planning board should be helpless without the backing of the executive and legislative branches. A planning board composed of experts must remain a purely advisory body controlled by the people and their representatives. In all its reports and replies to requests for information and advice, the board carefully emphasized words like *suggest* and

recommend. Planning, like administration, was a neutral technique conducted by objective technicians.[59]

Despite the board's insistence on its own neutrality and purely technical service, it did serve a definite political purpose. Indeed, if it had not,
Roosevelt would certainly not have gone to the trouble of finding another governmental agency to house it after the Supreme Court declared
the National Industrial Recovery Act unconstitutional. Recognizing the
hostility that the very concept of national planning aroused among many
congressional conservatives, Roosevelt removed the word *planning* from
its title and replaced it with the allegedly uncontroversial *natural resources.* Roosevelt emphasized the physical aspects of planning by ordering the new Natural Resources Committee to prepare a comprehensive
study of land and water use as its first task. Roosevelt and the committee
apparently believed that such a study would be purely technical, avoid
political issues, and receive unanimous support. This reflected a very
naive view of what was politically controversial, especially in the western states. As a final concession to his congressional opponents, Roosevelt placed the newly designated National Resources Committee under
the official direction of a cabinet commission headed by Ickes.[60]

The initial hostility from Congress should have warned Merriam and
his colleagues that the NPB was not a nonpolitical instrument. Indeed,
its very nature represented a political stand in the context of the 1930s.
The chief political disagreements of the decade centered on the issue of
whether the federal government should intervene in the private sector of
the economy, and a planning board, no matter how conservative, represented an interventionist position. Moreover, the board's reports were
not purely technical studies of factual data. The authors often used their
data to recommend specific policies or at least to imply the advisability
of certain actions over others. Although the board and its experts never
lobbied for their recommendations or offered their conclusions as anything but suggestions, their advice still carried the weight of the national
government and the active support of the president behind it. The NPB's
recommendations influenced numerous projects and affected the allocation of significant government resources. Groups and individuals who
had benefited economically from previous control of such decisions by
local groups or the Army Corps of Engineers complained bitterly of their
tax money being spent for purposes opposed to their interests. They were
joined in this by business and industrial organizations who considered
the entire concept of national planning as socialistic and opposed to their
cherished ideology of free enterprise.

The board did struggle to keep its political opinions to a minimum.

First of all, it refused to take responsibility for the recommendations of its technical committees. Even after this prior denial of accountability, the board members edited these documents carefully and removed what they considered controversial suggestions. Merriam once lambasted a report from the Water Committee for "slipping" from engineering questions to those of economic and social policy, despite Delano's protests that the two were often inseparable. Another case in point involved a study of the NRA and AAA which the board had authorized its chief researchers, Lewis Lorwin and H. R. Hinricks, to undertake. In the first draft of their report, Lorwin and Hinricks criticized the domination of the NRA by self-chosen industrial and labor boards and the exclusion of consumer interests. Moreover, they went on to note how large and medium-sized farmers represented by the Farm Bureau had reaped great benefits from the AAA while its policies actually forced many small farmers and renters off the land. The National Resources Committee reacted with horror to the disclosure of these open secrets, attacked the report for its "controversial expressions of personal opinion," and canceled the entire project.[61]

For all of its attempts to remain a technical, purely advisory body, the National Planning Board was deeply involved in political and social issues. Moreover, these areas included many in which powerful groups and individuals possessed strong personal interests. While natural resources and conservation may have seemed uncontroversial to easterners, they were the most important and divisive political issues in many western states. Many livelihoods and considerable money depended on government policies with regard to grazing rights, forests, and minerals on federal land. Western congressmen, especially those from the Rocky Mountain states, reflected the viewpoint of their constituents dependent on the extraction and use of natural resources when they chided eastern interests for having exploited their own natural resources first and then trying to prevent westerners from following suit. Although the allocation of water for irrigation appeared to be a purely technical problem from the vantage point of either of the Hyde Parks, it took on an entirely different aspect on the arid plains of eastern Colorado, where water meant the difference between wealth and starvation. Even within the executive branch the board faced political challenges. Secretary of War George Dern worked against the board's attempt to establish an overall water resources plan because he felt this prerogative belonged to his own Army Corps of Engineers. The corps was more responsive to private interests than the Water Resources Committee promised to be, and Dern organized the corps's many congressional friends into a voting bloc opposed to the board. Nor could the board and its successors reasonably expect to investigate such contentious matters as industrial capacity, consumption and advertising, housing, and health care without creating political waves.[62]

In 1939 a coalition of conservative, western, and pro–Army Corps of Engineers congressmen joined to cut off the NRC's funds. Roosevelt quickly changed its name again, this time to National Resources Planning Board, and transformed it into an executive agency. Upon the outbreak of World War II it became FDR's agency for postwar planning and began to assume a more open ideological position, with Roosevelt's blessing. Finally, in 1943, a resurgent Congress, determined to check executive power on the domestic front, cut off future appropriations over Roosevelt's angry protests.

The evolution of the National Planning Board into an executive agency indicated its exact political nature. For all its emphasis on local and regional planning, the board finally depended on strong executive leadership, and even protection. Merriam recognized quite early that national planning in the present American context would have to rely on the executive branch. As he began to recognize the complexities and conflicts involved in the formulation of a national plan, he realized that the simple correctness of factual data would not necessarily lead to a society planned in the interests of the majority. Again he was faced with the central dilemma of social science during the interwar years: the continuing conflict of the role of the social scientist with regard to knowledge. Merriam saw that planning must have a direction and goal, but he also believed strongly that social experts had neither the power nor the right to create them. The answer to Merriam's problem was the presidency, which had the power, the democratic right, and, in Roosevelt's case, the desire to use planning to achieve a just society. Merriam became an ardent supporter and admirer of FDR and used his skills in an attempt to make the presidency an even stronger instrument for this purpose.

Merriam had always recognized the importance of leadership for political activity. He began a series of lectures in 1926 with the statement, "Leadership is one of the basic factors in the organization of life, and its implications are everywhere of profound significance." As he became more involved in planning during the 1930s, Merriam began to stress leadership even more. In his major theoretical work of the period, *Political Power: Its Composition and Incidence,* Merriam accentuated the need to choose good political leaders even more than the need for education and technical skills for citizens. A society might select its leaders successfully in different ways, but, Merriam insisted, no factor was more important to its health than its political leadership.[63]

Certainly Merriam came to feel a strong allegiance to Roosevelt. Although he had taken the lead in denying Hoover's attempt to influence *Recent Social Trends*, Merriam kept FDR informed of the progress of ongoing NPB research and edited out unflattering comments about New Deal programs. Once the board came under Roosevelt's official supervision in 1939, the president even selected its topics for research. For instance, in September 1939 the board proposed to the president that it undertake a study of the tax system and offer recommendations for a more just system. Roosevelt agreed that the question was important but ordered the board not to do the study as Congress was not in a mood to handle the issue satisfactorily. Merriam increasingly began to regard himself, and to be regarded by Roosevelt, as an adviser and member of the unofficial brain trust. Merriam served as one of FDR's principal speechwriters on such issues as planning and interstate cooperation and increasingly sought to guide research within the planning agencies and social science organizations in directions useful to the New Deal.[64]

The best example of Merriam's commitment to strengthening Roosevelt's position specifically, and the power of the central government in general, was his participation on the President's Committee on Administrative Management. In early 1936 Roosevelt appointed a blue-ribbon committee to advise him on how to modernize the executive branch of government and make it more effective. He chose as its members Merriam, Merriam's friend and confidante Louis Brownlow, and Luther Gulick, director of the New York Bureau of Municipal Research. Although the committee was ostensibly free to make any recommendations for executive reorganization, in actuality Roosevelt controlled the situation. From the very beginning Roosevelt indicated that he had considered the subject at great length and had definite opinions on the needs of the executive. He also implied that he would not have appointed a committee that might recommend policy contradictory to his own desires. Merriam assured him that the committee would keep him informed of its progress, hear his positions on their recommendations, and investigate only those areas chosen by him.[65]

The committee interviewed authorities on the subject and many present and past members of the executive branch of government, and its twenty-six-member staff completed more than a dozen technical studies. Yet these were clearly secondary; Merriam even referred to them as "non-supporting documents." The primary consideration was the president's desires and needs. Merriam informed the staff that the report was for Roosevelt's use, and his alone. If he wished to read it and simply forget it, that was his right.[66]

The central thesis of the final report of the Committee on Administrative Management reflected Roosevelt's belief that many of the congressionally authorized agencies were out of control, and this prevented the executive branch from fulfilling its duty of running the government effectively. Using some of the most recent scholarship on business management, the committee argued that the presidency had to have some control over the heretofore independent agencies, who were exercising "power without responsibility." The committee asserted that its recommendations for a larger presidential staff, plenary authority over the commissions, and total control over delegated funds were merely "better tools of management," and not political machinations. Merriam again was attempting to transform a political act into simply another case of technical experts arriving at a well-documented, universally accepted conclusion.[67]

Unfortunately for Merriam, his committee colleagues, and Roosevelt, not all social scientists were committed to FDR's leadership. Harold Moulton, executive director of the Brookings Institute, had originally supported the New Deal and helped draft the original proposal for the NRA. However, his belief in the free market and an almost pathological reaction to Keynesian economics had turned him into Roosevelt's bitter enemy, and he used his position, despite Frederic Delano's chairmanship of the institute's board, to drive out all New Deal sympathizers. Recognizing this situation, conservative Senator Harry Byrd hired the institute to undertake a competing executive reorganization study for Congress. Although the Brookings Institute's resident administration specialists, W. F. Willoughby and Lewis Merriam, had always supported executive control over administrative agencies, they reversed their traditional position to argue that the presidency was the real political branch of government and would dominate independent commissions if given the opportunity. The Constitution had wisely given administrative power to Congress, and the true efficiency of the independent commissions lay exactly in the lack of political control over them.[68]

The opposing study drove the usually diplomatic Merriam into an uncharacteristic rage. Despite Willoughby's and Lewis Merriam's reputation as well-respected scholars in the field, he accused them of manipulating their data and of consciously writing a report that selfish interest groups could use to oppose the public interest. More tactfully, Brownlow pleaded with the Brookings group to try and reach a consensus with Roosevelt's committee on the subject. "In this situation, it seems to me of the utmost importance that the 'doctors' do not disagree on technical matters, as the disagreement will be used by opponents of any reform to confuse the issue. . . . It may be that the reputation of government research . . . for scientific impartiality is at stake." Brownlow did not say how two diametrically opposed views could reach such a consensus. In the end, the Brookings report coupled with Roosevelt's recent defeat on the Supreme Court bill led a rebellious Congress to defeat the reorganization bill, much to Merriam's anger and surprise.[69]

As with Wesley Mitchell, the central theme behind Merriam's approach to social science was his desire to make it a practical technique that established authorities could use for beneficial ends. What made Merriam's path more circuitous than Mitchell's was the combination of his discipline, his experiences as an elected official, and the man of action in his personality. Like Mitchell, Merriam recognized that the popular identification of social science with social reform prevented it from having influence in the corridors of power and also from obtaining the funding from philanthropic foundations necessary for large-scale empirical research. Consequently, Merriam championed the evolution of a technical, nonnormative variety of social science which could provide necessary data for decision makers. Yet Merriam, unlike Mitchell, was much more a man of action than a scholar. His chief contributions to objectivist social science were organizational rather than intellectual. Moreover, as the specter of dreaded social chaos loomed ever larger during the late 1920s and 1930s, he turned to technical men of action such as city managers and national planners to provide the scientific unifying answers for society. Despite his adamant insistence that politics and administration were completely separate, however, Merriam's work and actions were clearly political—as, indeed, was Mitchell's refusal to commit himself on public issues. For all its claims to neutrality, the social science of technique represented a clearly biased approach to the study of society.

The individual who perhaps focused most strongly on the limitations of objectivist, technical social science was a friend and ssrc colleague of both Mitchell and Merriam, Robert Lynd. Mitchell had personally lobbied for Lynd's appointment as executive secretary of the ssrc, and Merriam publicly mourned his later departure to Columbia's Department of Sociology. Yet, in his administrative work within organizational social science and his original community and consumer research, Lynd became increasingly convinced of the fatal deficiencies of a social science of technique. In both his trenchant critique of mainstream social science and his subsequent inability to develop a strong alternative, Lynd represents well the strengths and weaknesses of purposive social science.

4

Robert Lynd and Knowledge

for What?

Despite being a generation younger than Mitchell and Merriam, Robert Lynd was a self-conscious throwback to the founders of normative social science. Like so many of his nineteenth-century predecessors, he was trained as a clergyman and came to the social sciences only when he concluded that they offered a better opportunity for the achievement of his ethical social goals than did religion. Lynd, who had an extremely varied social science career as a researcher for a Rockefeller-funded organization, executive secretary of the Social Science Research Council, Columbia professor, and contributor and adviser to several governmental commissions and agencies, invariably insisted on the normative function of social science and an activist role for the social scientist. In his work, culminating in the manifesto of the purposive movement, *Knowledge for What?*, Lynd had three major goals. First, he developed a sophisticated and effective attack on the assumptions and implications of social science as technique. Second, through his studies of Muncie, Indiana, consumer activities and a Wyoming oil-mining camp, he attempted to demonstrate the didactic and normative purposes that a purposively conceived, empirical social scientist could achieve. Finally, and ultimately unsuccessfully, Lynd sought to fulfill John Dewey's plea for a means–end continuum in the social sciences by determining scientifically based normative goals toward which empirical social scientists could scientifically and ethically strive.

Although he had written the most telling indictment of the objectivist manifesto, *The Folklore of Capitalism*, and probably had been Merriam's and Ogburn's most incisive and successful critic within the research institutions, by the late 1930s Lynd felt that a public challenge of the best technical social science was necessary in order to convince its adherents of their fallacy. As a symbol of the unfulfilled promise and ultimate failure of mainstream social science he sadly chose Wesley Mitchell, his former teacher, present colleague, and personal friend. Lynd believed that if he could show that Mitchell, with his great technical and theoretical sophistication and honest commitment to meaningful social change, was guilty of transgressions against the proper role of social science, then he might fairly extend his criticism to all of technical social science.

Lynd felt bad about selecting Mitchell as the representative culprit of American social science, since Mitchell's early theoretical essays had provided him with the basis for his lifelong criticism of economics. Lynd both publicly and privately noted his indebtedness to Mitchell and rated him with Veblen and Dewey as the chief influences on his thinking. Mitchell hired Lynd as executive secretary of the SSRC and was one of the few members within the upper echelon of the council sympathetic to Lynd's constructive criticism of the organization. As director of the President's Research Committee on Recent Social Trends, Mitchell had helped to choose Lynd to do the section on consumerism. During the 1930s Lynd enlisted Mitchell's aid and name in such causes as the collection of money and aid for the Spanish Republic and the defense of academic freedom against the Dies Committee. When Mitchell retired in 1944, Lynd sent him an eloquent note praising him as the best of the Columbia social scientists and "the fairest, humanly most wise man I have ever known." Even after Mitchell's death, Lynd consistently referred to him as one of the few truly great men of the century.[1]

Lynd's critique of Mitchell came as part of his 1938 Stafford Little Lectures at Princeton. He chose this prestigious forum as the best way to publicize his increasing dissatisfaction with the preconceptions and pretensions of objectivist social science and to suggest a new approach to social research. But first he needed to clear away the detritus of technical social science, as Veblen and Mitchell had earlier helped dispose of nineteenth-century formalism. He began his critique by complimenting Mitchell and his chief disciple, Frederick Mills, on their careful empirical research, which Lynd called "current economic research at its best." Furthermore, he argued, their emphasis on empiricism was absolutely necessary. Yet Lynd found disturbing implications within their approach. Empirical investigators had to immerse themselves totally in the institutions and standards of the existing system. In some sciences this presented no problem. The method was quite safe for anthropologists, for example, because they always retained the knowledge and usually the values of an alternative culture. An economist studying the economic system of his or her own culture did not possess this advantage, however, and could become so totally wrapped up in the facts of the situation as to accept completely the prevailing definition of the system. In the United States, this meant accepting business's view. The economist usually did not consciously choose such a position. Rather, the need to gather data and chart related trends increasingly became the sole focus of attention. The description and analysis of "what is" turned into a lifetime proposition, and the social scientist never got around to asking what Lynd perceived as *the* basic question of social science: Where are our institutions taking us, and where do we want them to take us? Although Mitchell's name was never specifically mentioned in this context, the resemblance of his work on business cycles to Lynd's description of endless empirical research would have been obvious to Lynd's audience of social scientists.[2]

Lynd perceived objectivist social science as based on two unstated assumptions: (1) facts automatically provided answers to problems without the intercession of hypotheses, and (2) the existing institutional system was correct and adequate, or at least adequate enough that moderate reform would correct its minor deficiencies. In economics these preconceptions had rationalized a fait accompli, accepting capitalism as the best system for American society. Economists unquestioningly accepted prices, production, and distribution as the significant areas to be investigated without recognizing that such research tied them inextricably to the status quo. Lynd believed that American economists should also study subjects outside of economic systems controlled by prices and alleged economic equilibrium. Without knowing the alternatives, how could one judge the true benefits of the present system adequately? "The social scientist who steps within a given institutional area and accepts *its* statement of the problem as *his* may be largely surrendering that objectivity which makes science potentially useful to man in confronting his dilemmas." In anthropological terms, current economic research, as symbolized by the work of the National Bureau of Economic Research, was simply accepting the economic folkways and mores of American culture. Arguing from *within* the perspective of scientific theory, Lynd simply stated that this was neither true objectivity nor science.[3]

Lynd quickly went beyond this criticism to deny the validity of value objectivity itself. Rather than consciously avoiding issues such as the merits and demerits of trade unions, as the NBER had done in a 1924 monograph on trade unions, social scientists should address exactly these problems. Facts and data by themselves solved nothing, and American social scientists' "failure of nerve" in dealing with what Lynd considered the truly important questions of American society had resulted in less knowledgeable and altruistic individuals assuming control. Mitchell and others like him abstained from opinions on such issues as the optimum use of natural and social resources by pleading lack of scientific data and calling for more time. Lynd bitterly likened such action to "lecturing on navigation while the ship is going down."[4]

Ironically, the model Lynd postulated for economics was derived from the "early" Mitchell, the one who wrote "The Backward Art of Spending Money" and "Human Behavior and Economics." Lynd postulated the existence of two Mitchells: the economic theorist of the early essays, who had clear ethical goals, and the present-day quantitative economist, whose employment in Washington during the crisis-filled days of World War I converted him to empiricism. Lynd alternately argued and pleaded with Mitchell to return to his early analysis and use his wisdom and experience to comment on contemporary economic issues and institutions. Lynd believed strongly that if Mitchell returned to his earlier Veblenian perspective, he would soon reject his empirical shortsightedness for "a more forthright recognition of the really large institutional shortcomings of our culture."[5]

Mitchell was not indifferent to Lynd's criticisms. A request by the Columbia Economics Club to review Lynd's lectures, published in 1939 as *Knowledge for What?*, gave Mitchell an opportunity to defend himself publicly against Lynd's strictures. Mitchell, always a civilized and rational person, refused to take the criticism personally, unlike some of his followers, including future Federal Reserve Board chairman Arthur Burns, who publicly called Lynd an idiot and a fool. Like Lynd, Mitchell began his review graciously. He noted Lynd's exceptional gifts as both a scholar and as an individual, and further prefaced his remarks by explaining that Lynd had "very tactfully, more in sorrow than anger . . . used me at times as an example of how an economist can misdirect his efforts." He agreed with Lynd that the fundamental aim of social science should be to improve culture so as to better meet the needs of individual personalities, but he disagreed over the most effective way of making social science serve that end. While Lynd believed that social scientists should concentrate on changes that ought to be made in society, Mitchell argued that social scientists should first learn all they could about the system they wanted to improve:

> I personally think we err, not by giving too much attention to the workings of our present culture, but in not making our studies sufficiently realistic, detailed, and precise. Inspirational reforms we have in

abundance, and most of them are disappointing. If social scientists can do a better job, it will be because they have deeper insight into the behavior of people whose culture is being changed—the ways in which they will react to new institutions. In short, our peculiar contribution to the great task of creating a better world is to provide deeper and fuller knowledge to guide action.

Then, in a clever and good-natured response to Lynd's description of the two Mitchells, Mitchell called for a return to the earlier empirical Lynd of the Middletown studies; the man who concentrated on concrete, solvable problems rather than on the empty generalizations of *Knowledge for What?*[6]

The debate generated many letters between the two men. Mitchell simply did not believe that social scientists possessed enough knowledge to assume a policymaking role at that time. More significantly, Mitchell, like many of his objectivist colleagues, honestly failed to recognize the real differences between the two viewpoints. As long as he and Lynd agreed on the ultimate goal of social science, their disagreement was a mere matter of "tactics." When Lynd insisted on the central importance of change, Mitchell maintained that "workers ought to understand the functioning of the organization they wish to better." Mitchell apparently could not conceive that true reform might lie in establishing an entirely different institution rather than engaging in piecemeal reform of the present organization. Mitchell wrote in another letter to Lynd, "I do not see any important distinction between the close analysis of business cycles in which I am engaged and the study of human behavior under the cultural conditions characteristic of the United States or western Europe since the Civil War." This, Lynd might have replied, was exactly the point. The business cycle was a product of the capitalist economic structure endemic to these cultures since the 1860s. Mitchell and his associates assumed that business cycles were a permanent institution of Western society and could be controlled and manipulated once enough was known about them. Lynd hoped that research could discover an economic system that could replace business cycles with a manifestation more beneficial to the needs and desires of individuals in Western society.[7]

Despite his constant references to the depression and fascism in his Stafford Little Lectures, Lynd's commitment to an activist role for social science and social scientists clearly predated the crises of the 1930s. Even before he decided to become a social scientist Lynd had focused his thinking on the purposive aspects of thought and action. Throughout his varied career his consistent goal was to effect meaningful social change through his dual efforts as man of knowledge and man of action. Nowhere is this more evident than in Lynd's pre–social science career.

Robert Staughton Lynd was born in 1892, in New Albany, Indiana, directly across the river from Louisville, Kentucky, where he would grow up. His parents were both devout Presbyterians with long traditions of ministerial service in their families, and church was an important part of young Robert's life. His father, Staughton, a self-made banker who rose to become the president of Manufacturers' Bank of New York City, was in many ways his son's role model. Staughton Lynd was the embodiment of the complex personality type of the Puritan. Tightfisted and laconic, Staughton championed small-town values. He sent his son to Princeton only after arranging for him to have a minister's son for a roommate, and he was consistently offended by the cultural mores of New York City. Yet, he was also extremely competent, honest, and committed to individual and communal responsibility for helping the less fortunate. His final advice to his son when he left for Princeton was "ride and shoot straight and tell the truth." In a 1954 note, Lynd claimed that this had remained his guiding philosophy throughout his life.[8]

Such advice was not helpful for gaining popularity at Princeton, and, as Robert's wife and son independently attested, the snobbery he encountered there left lasting scars. Upon graduation, he used his father's New York connections to enter the publishing industry, where his competence and prodigious work habits quickly propelled him to the position of managing editor of *Publisher's Weekly*, the trade publication of the book industry, and, later, to head of advertising for Charles Scribner's Sons. Still, neither his obvious success nor the offer of a five-thousand-dollar-a-year job from the Hearst publishing interests met his need for self-fulfillment. When he questioned his father's powerful New York friends, he discovered a disturbingly large number that expressed the view of one famous corporation lawyer who admitted he had never experienced much "of this happiness stuff."[9]

Ironically enough, Lynd found his answer in the army. In 1918 he spent five months as a private in the Field Artillery, most of it apparently in an army hospital recovering from influenza. There Lynd discovered personal joy in being able to help his fellow patients with such simple tasks as writing letters and talking about their personal problems. He tentatively concluded that the key to life was not "quantitative" but the "texture of the thing as it passes through one's hands." Lynd's reading of the English economist John Hobson's *Work and Wealth: A Human Valuation* at this time solidified this determination. Although Veblen, Dewey, and Mitchell were more influential for Lynd's later work, Hobson provided the initial spark. When the editors of the *New Republic* asked Lynd in the 1930s to list the books he considered central in his intellectual development, he headed his list of nineteen with *Work and Wealth*. In it, Hobson adamantly denied that the pecuniary calculus of capitalist society satisfactorily reflected true human valuation and insisted that one could determine economic valuation in terms of human welfare. Using John Ruskin's humanistic *Unto This Last*, Hobson condemned English economic life as unconcerned with the good of the majority.[10]

Bolstered by these personal and intellectual experiences, Lynd quit his position at Scribner's and joined the small avant-garde publishing firm of B. W. Huebsch. Huebsch was a cultural and political radical who had put out the first American edition of James Joyce's *Portrait of the Artist as a Young Man* and began publishing the radical journal *Freeman* in 1920. Under the editorship of Francis Neilson and Albert Jay Nock, the *Freeman* championed single-tax theory and experimental literature and quickly won a reputation as one of the most intellectually stimulating periodicals of the 1920s. Lynd soon became virtually its managing editor. Nevertheless, he remained dissatisfied with the profit orientation of publishing and called for its transformation into a "public utility" providing quality publications at the lowest possible rates.[11]

Given Lynd's strong religious upbringing, his turn to the ministry as an answer to his normative goals for society was a natural one—except for two factors. First, he readily admitted that he shared the conventional distaste of the practical man for "preachers." Second, he also conceded that he lacked real theological beliefs and that even his concept of God was extremely "rudimentary." When compelled to note a religious affiliation, he declared himself either a member of a local independent pacifist congregation or of Felix Adler's Ethical Culture Society. Even during his one three-month stint as a minister, Lynd publicly denounced all doctrinal questions as irrelevant.[12]

Yet Lynd came to believe that religion, despite these limitations, was the only agency in American society devoted wholly to fostering the spiritual values that individuals need to develop as human beings. Religion constantly reasserted the higher values of life above the mundane concerns of everyday existence that seemed to dominate life, and throughout his career Lynd noted the need for cultures to possess such institutions as the locus of the emotional values of their people. Even in

Middletown, whose "irreligious" attitude was criticized by the study's sponsoring religious agency, the Lynds praised religion for providing Middletowners with a tradition of value and worth in a society whose rootlessness and lack of standards seriously threatened their self-worth. In an important 1922 note to himself, Lynd stated his creed:

> My religion is that quantitatively every man is bound to fall short of his dreams, but that qualitatively *any* man can make his life exquisitely satisfying. Every conscious moment of a life gives off a kind of a spiritual electricity—positive or negative according to personal, not objective, standards, an energy which is bumping against each of our lives thru the medium of people in all sorts of places, books, the spoken word, music, etc. Experience has shown that it is apparently the experience of giving off this energy in the form of socially productive activity which reacts upon the giver in the sense of the satisfyingness of life upon the receiver in an impulse to respond in kind. The whole job of the preacher as I grope it out is to re-mind [*sic*] people of the ways in which men have found they can give off this energy.[13]

Except for his lack of theological belief, Lynd's decision to enter the seminary possessed all the characteristics of a religious conversion. He later recounted a weeklong canoe trip in which he continually asked himself why, even if he were correct about religion, *he* should become a minister. Whenever his opposing feelings drove him into a "hot-box," he would dive overboard to cool down. He faced every step of the decision in this manner and emerged from his wilderness experience with the conviction that he would "bet" his life on the ministry.[14]

Lynd "bet" on religion by entering Union Theological Seminary, by far the most liberal American theological institution of its time. Headed by one of the first Americans to apply historical criticism to the New Testament, the faculty included such prominent liberals as Harry Ward, Harry Emerson Fosdick, and Henry Sloane Coffin. Lynd's first Union contact was its professor of Hebrew, *Freeman* supporter Charles Prospero Fagnani, "a wise jolly soul" who regularly outraged conventional fellow members of the Madison Avenue Presbyterian Church by challenging Presbyterian dogma. When Lynd told Fagnani that he was entering Union, Fagnani was startled that anyone would ever conceive of leaving the *Freeman* "to become a parish priest." Lynd himself was shocked when during an interview the professor of comparative religion got down on his knees to pray for Lynd's deliverance into the true faith of Presbyterianism.[15]

At Union, Lynd soon began to concentrate on how to use religion for his social goals. In "Has Preaching a Function in Adult Re-education?" one of the few of Lynd's seminary papers that have survived, one sees the first of Lynd's many adaptations of Dewey's thought to his normative goals. The paper seeks to demonstrate how Dewey's theory of the process of thought and the dominance of habitual thinking can be used to make preaching serve an important function. Lynd postulated that since individuals act out of habit, the only way to reeducate them is through a demonstration of the inadequacy of that habit. The minister had the awesome task of causing people to question habits conditioned by their competitive and acquisitive culture and then to offer alternative modes of behavior. Although one could never hope to succeed fully at that task, a minister might serve as a precipitating agent to help individuals see things more clearly and begin to think more rationally.[16]

This paper is in many ways an articulation of Lynd's experiences of the previous summer. In the spring of 1922, still uncertain about his decision to become a minister, he approached the Presbyterian Board of Home Missions to inquire about a possible summer position. They assigned him as a home missionary to the isolated oil camp of Elk Basin in northwestern Wyoming, where he dispelled the men's initial suspicions of him by hiring on as a pick-and-shovel man. He quickly formed a nondenominational church of Protestants, Catholics, and Mormons and told his parishioners that the real purpose of religion was to help them face their problems of poor wages and living conditions. Religion was not a list of prohibitions but a vision of what an individual's life could and should become. Lynd saw himself as a resource specialist in the building of a true community. Hoping to crystalize the group's inherent desire for communal responsibility and stability, Lynd organized the building of a combination church and community center; instituted Boy and Girl Scout troops, a sewing club, and other organizations; and used his professionally trained voice to begin Wednesday night sing-alongs. He saw the role of the minister as a man of action who possessed the requisite "spiritual" information needed by individuals to achieve their own goals and potential.[17]

Lynd was outraged at the living conditions in Elk Basin. The work week was seven days, with twelve-hour shifts of difficult, boring tasks. Most families lived in rickety shacks or floorless tents, had to purchase all their water at high cost, and lacked a common meeting place. Claiming that this experience represented his "awakening to the facts of life," Lynd wrote to Union professor William Adams Brown asking if Brown's friend John D. Rockefeller, Jr., was aware of the conditions at Elk Basin. When Rockefeller blandly denied the existence of Standard Oil at Elk Basin, Lynd composed a coldly factual, heavily documented report for *Survey* magazine, a journal so heavily subsidized by the charity-oriented Russell Sage Foundation that it was relatively immune to Rockefeller pressure. Using photographs and statistics, Lynd drew a graphic portrayal of the material and emotional deprivation of the isolated camp's inhabitants. Relying on advance knowledge of Rockefeller's tactics, Lynd turned to official government documents to prove that Standard Oil of Indiana controlled the Elk Basin fields and was making a 300 percent annual profit on its investment. Lynd sought to publicize the issue so extensively that the Rockefeller interests would have to correct the situation. Even if they did not, a portion of the public at least would be made aware of the facts.[18]

Rockefeller was in a position where such publicity could do him a large amount of damage. Publicly embarrassed by his company's involvement in the 1913–14 Colorado Coal War and his later censure by the congressional Committee on Industrial Relations, Rockefeller had assumed a prominent posture of Christian stewardship. He supported the six-day work week and the eight-hour day, aided organizations such as the Pittsburgh YMCA, which had supported the 1919 steel strike, and established a shop committee plan for his companies. Lynd's article embarrassed Rockefeller considerably, but his threats to sue were silenced when his chagrined lawyers informed him that all the facts were correct. Then, trying a different tack, Rockefeller's chief lawyer, Raymond Fosdick, summoned Lynd to his office and promised a Carnegie library for Elk Basin if Lynd would withdraw the article. When Lynd refused, Rockefeller submitted an article to follow Lynd's in which he insisted that Standard Oil was a "minority stockholder" in Elk Basin but promised to do everything in his power to alleviate the bad conditions. He reasserted his belief in the six-day work week and eight-hour day, agreed completely with Lynd that decent housing was a matter of "common justice," and praised Lynd for bringing the matter to the attention of the public.[19]

By his own standards, Lynd's Elk Basin experiences were among the most productive of his life; for once he seemed to succeed simultaneously at both of his goals. As a man of action he had helped people overcome their inertia and take a direct role in defeating the spiritual poverty of their lives. He had guided these individuals in achieving the goal, later expressed eloquently by Dewey in such works as *Liberalism and Social Action,* of going beyond individual needs to a communal liberation of potential. Yet he had also served as a man of knowledge, using the facts of a particular situation to educate others about American social and economic life, an activity that he hoped would lead to lasting individual and institutional changes. Later in his life he spoke of his Elk Basin experiences frequently and clearly regarded them as a key influence on his life.

For all Lynd's remarkable success in Elk Basin, it probably had a negative impact on him in the long run. The quick results strengthened some of Lynd's least desirable traits. All his life Lynd would refer to himself as "one of them urgent boys." His wife simply called him "impatient" and claimed his favorite phrase was "You can't skin a tiger one paw at a time." In general, Lynd saw the American situation as so desperate that things had to change immediately. In Elk Basin this actually seemed to happen. But Lynd would never again face the unlikely combination of Elk Basin's isolated homogeneity and Rockefeller's public vulnerability. Change would never again come so easily, even in the small city of Muncie, Indiana, and this led Lynd, who often seemed to disbelieve in his very real abilities and accomplishments, into ever more frequent periods of depression and desperation.[20]

His Elk Basin work did have immediate positive effects on Lynd's career. Although he had decided to bet on religion, the movement away from the social gospel within 1920s Protestantism convinced him that an "experimental thinker" would find no place in the ministry. He hoped that social science might provide a better base for his social activism, and he turned to his friend, Lawrence Frank, a Laura Spelman Rockefeller Fund official. Frank was one of the key figures in American social science, both because of the organizational positions he held and for the fertility of his mind in charting and encouraging new developments in the social sciences. Trained as an economist, Frank went to work at the Spelman Fund in the early 1920s and became a central figure in the evolution of both the child development movement and the culture and personality school. He and Lynd had become very good friends as young businessmen in prewar New York, and Lynd told Mitchell that "Veblen, Dewey, you, and Larry Frank are the four people who have influenced my thinking the most." The Lynds were frequent visitors to Frank's rambling New Hampshire summer home, and their friend and Middletown research assistant Dorothea Davis would later become the widower Frank's second wife. In the spring of 1923 Frank began searching for a position for his friend in Rockefeller or other foundation circles.[21]

The appointment of a muckraker who had attached Rockefeller interests to such a position was not as absurd as it sounds. Lynd had impressed Rockefeller and Fosdick with the thoroughness of his research, and Fosdick later informed Lynd that his information had allowed Rockefeller to identify a dishonest business associate. Moreover, the *Survey* piece had reaped unexpected good publicity. A month after its publication, *Survey* praised itself in an advertisement by noting that 287 newspapers with a circulation of more than sixteen million readers had reprinted parts of the Lynd-Rockefeller exchange and printed excerpts of several. Every one ignored the Elk Basin situation to applaud Rockefeller for his announcement of an enlightened labor policy. None criticized him for allowing the original abuse to occur or even pointed out his past similar promises. Given such results, neither Rockefeller nor Fosdick would have harbored lasting resentment against the relatively restrained Lynd.[22]

Finally, Fosdick believed he had found the perfect position for someone of Lynd's talents. At the end of World War I, Rockefeller had become heavily involved in the Interchurch movement, an ill-advised nondenominational effort to consolidate and modernize American Protestantism. When the movement collapsed, many ongoing studies of the role of the church were left unfinished, and Rockefeller founded the Institute of Social and Religious Research to continue the largely statistical research and appointed Fosdick and other associates to its board. Among the subjects being investigated were income and expenditures of churches, training of ministers, church schools, and the role of the rural church. The institute had become disenchanted with the author of a study on the role of religion in the everyday life of a small city, and Lynd, with his ministerial training, proven administrative ability, composition skills, and small-town midwestern background, seemed a far preferable alternative. Also, the institute could refute criticism of the dismissal of the previous author by noting Lynd's earlier critical attitude toward Rockefeller interests.[23]

Methodologically, the institute was split along the traditional lines of dispute of late nineteenth- and early twentieth-century social science. One group, dominant in the board of trustees and best represented by Shelby Harrison of the Russell Sage Foundation, continued to see social science and morality as interconnected. They were convinced that the mere collection of sufficient data would lead to automatic conclusions, which would, of course, validate traditional Christian morality. The staff officers of the New York office, especially its statistical experts, Luther Fry and Stanley Went, sided with expert advisers such as Mitchell, Frank, and economist L. C. Marshall in calling for the use and testing of scientific hypotheses before pronouncing conclusions. Executive Secretary Galen Fisher, a longtime YMCA secretary in Japan, who had been appointed for his devoutness and administrative skills, had few personal opinions on the subject and tried to serve as a mediator between the two groups. Lynd's study, which would eventually become *Middletown*, seemed to possess elements of both perspectives. Only after it was completed did the two sides recognize that it represented an entirely new approach to social science.[24]

At first, Lynd appeared to be allied with the Harrison group. He shared their ministerial background and their beliefs in the need for normative concerns and a survey approach. In one of his seminary papers Lynd noted his attraction to the ministry because it included so many different approaches to problems. As soon as Lynd began the research, he widened its scope. Although the institute traditionally insisted that its researchers study the church in relation to the community and its other organizations, Lynd went further. He argued that one could not understand the true meaning of an institution like the church by considering it in isolation. The study had to be an inclusive view of the whole community, with the study of the church only one topic in the larger framework. Even later in his career, when he began to criticize surveys, including his own, for not focusing sufficiently on specific problems, Lynd constantly maintained that getting a "general picture" was absolutely essential.[25]

But Lynd's views departed from those of the survey supporters in several significant areas. He did not share their goal of traditional Christian morals. Nor did he possess their optimistic progressive faith in the absolute and immediate efficacy of facts to achieve reforms. Finally, their concepts of science differed greatly from his own. For Harrison and his group, science constituted a careful use of the scientific method to collect facts. Lynd, who had taken graduate courses with Dewey and Mitchell while at Union, recognized the inadequacy of this simplistic approach and developed a more sophisticated theoretical perspective. An adept politician, Lynd also recognized the dominance of the central office and its commitment to a purely scientific approach. Since their religious connection seemed to imply reformism, the administrators emphasized the scientific character of the institute's work and, like the Bureau of Economic Research, insisted on their unanimous consent before any research could be published. Lynd's initial progress reports to the institute emphasized his scientific leanings by disparaging the earlier "efficiency surveys" and promising a "straight fact-finding study." Throughout their work, Lynd and his coauthor and wife, Helen, insisted on their objectivity and dedication to scientific research.[26]

Certainly *Middletown* was a very sophisticated piece of research for its day. Although Lynd often spoke of his inadequacies as a researcher, two important historians of sociology independently selected the Middletown books as worthy of special mention for their methodological competence. The Lynds' research was meticulous. They carefully established a representative sample of Middletowners, and they and their assistants engaged in intensive personal interviews conducted with the aid of long, carefully designed questionnaires. The interviewers recorded not only the respondents' answers but their own reactions as well. Each social club in the town completed a four-page questionnaire, and Lynd personally interviewed each minister. In a major methodological contribution, Helen wrote a much-praised appendix which described how they obtained their material and gave critics the opportunity to judge for themselves the validity of the facts.[27]

Yet, as presaged by his previous career, Lynd was unwilling to settle for pure fact finding. He needed to discover a method that could describe the situation analytically while simultaneously providing at least implicit criticism. Contemporary American sociological thought failed Lynd on two accounts. First of all, as the analysis of American Sociological Society presidential addresses in chapter 1 notes, sociology was seeking to catch up with the other social sciences in prestige by denouncing its earlier reformism and attachment to a general theory of society. Second, the dominant Chicago school of sociology founded on George Simmel's theory of group conflict emphasized the specificity of different groups and the pluralism of the American scene, especially the city. Lynd insisted on the need to see American society as a continuum and had abandoned the study's original site, South Bend, Indiana, because of its cultural and religious heterogeneity. Very early in the project, Robert Lynd, by all accounts the theoretician of the two, adopted what the anthropologist Alfred Kroeber called "the anthropological attitude": studying a modern society objectively as one might view a primitive society. That perspective seemed to satisfy Lynd's scientific and critical needs.

The original model for his approach was clearly the work of Veblen. Veblen's adoption of the perspective of the cold, detached observer allowed him to rip into the idiocies and inconsistencies of Western civilization while maintaining a reputation as a scientific expert. Lynd repeatedly noted his indebtedness to Veblen. The list of influential books Lynd prepared for the *New Republic* included all of Veblen's. *Middletown*, indeed all of Lynd's work, relies on such Veblenian insights as pecuniary culture, conspicuous consumption, and the instinct of workmanship. According to both Lynd's and his wife's accounts, he was initially attracted to her when she mentioned Veblen's *Theory of the Leisure Class* during a chance encounter on a Mount Washington hiking trail. As late as the 1950s, Lynd continued to preach the gospel according to Veblen, much to the bemusement of his sophisticated graduate students.[28]

Although American anthropologists such as Clark Wissler, Edward Sapir, and Melville Herskovitz quickly acclaimed *Middletown* as a successful application of anthropological methods to contemporary life and a necessary liberation of community studies from statistics collecting, American anthropology had provided little aid in Lynd's search for a developmental hypothesis. Under the leadership of Franz Boas the field had, at least temporarily, adopted particularism and was engaged in intensive studies of rapidly disappearing cultures. Although Boas's personal interest in culture and personality, developed by his students Ruth Benedict and Margaret Mead, would be highly influential for Lynd's later work, American anthropology in the 1920s had little to offer in the way of explanatory theories. Lynd had conspicuously "adapted" Wissler's concept of a "universal cultural pattern" to the particular circumstances of modern society. Wissler's cultural schema consisted of speech, material traits, religion, art, mythology and scientific knowledge, society, property, government, and war. Lynd, relying on the work of the British anthropologist W. H. R. Rivers, transformed this pattern into "six main-trunk activities": getting a living, making a home, training the young, using leisure, engaging in religious activities, and acting within the community. These six activities served as the Lynds' means of investigating the organization of Muncie.[29]

As the lack of close conformity between Wissler's and the Lynds' list demonstrates, however, even this use of American anthropology was tangential. Wissler was a key player in Lynd's ongoing battle within the institute; he was its anthropological adviser, a curator of the American Museum of Natural History, and a native of a small town twenty miles from Muncie. Lynd's reference to Wissler seems to have been largely political flattery.

Lynd's primary debt in the area of anthropology was to the British school of functional anthropology, Rivers, and Rivers's best student, A. R. Radcliffe-Brown. When the Lynds wished to demonstrate that modern American culture shared many characteristics with "primitive" cultures, they usually turned to Rivers's study of the Todas of India. Although Rivers wandered widely in his later work, experimenting with Freudian psychology and accepting an extreme diffusionism, the basic insight the Lynds gained from his work was that each social activity and ceremony has a specific meaning in relation to the cultural whole. Nothing is circumstantial or meaningless. The best illustration of this approach is Radcliffe-Brown's *The Andaman Islanders*, a book the Lynds knew and respected greatly. Radcliffe-Brown, uninterested in the history or origins of social customs, rebelled when Rivers suggested a historical study of the islanders. Instead he wanted to discover the "meaning" of customs in relation to the interrelated organism. For example, he noted the prevalence of weeping at Andaman ceremonies and casual meetings and traced the meaning of this custom to the central importance of the social community in the hostile environment and the needs of the community to reaffirm the social bond at every opportunity. The emotion displayed on these occasions demonstrated objectively the ties felt by the community's members. Later in his career, Radcliffe-Brown would criticize Rivers's emphasis on "empirical generalizations" and insist on the centrality of "explanations." Radcliffe-Brown's functionalism provided the Lynds with the perspective they needed to recognize the meaning of Middletown's customs in relation to the culture as a whole.[30]

Lynd's clear goal in adopting the functionalist perspective was to transcend mere description and actually explain American society. The Lynds began their study of Muncie with the social aspect of work because they believed that earning a living dominated the culture. Work and the money it brought overshadowed all other areas of life. Newspapers editorialized on "Your Bank Account Your Best Friend," and leisure time activities were means for status climbing. Money was the sole determinant of status. Working-class high school students, ashamed of their lack of money and stylish clothes, dropped out of school. Even religion, which Lynd viewed as the repository of the higher values of the culture, followed the pecuniary pattern. Churches competed for the richest parishioners, and Baptists and Methodists became Episcopalians so as to associate with a "better" (i.e., richer) group of people. Church members praised religion because it "paid"; one man rose during prayer meeting to tell an enraptured audience how prayer had led him to take a successful gamble on a particular stock. The churches themselves determined their success solely by their financial standing. In short, Muncie appeared to be a culture stripped of its traditional values and institutions by the pellmell drive to get rich. The social theorist Edward Shils, who was largely uncharitable toward the work, lauded *Middletown* as "the first work of academic sociology which came forward to meet the growing desire for the self-understanding of society."[31]

Lynd's chief criticism of Radcliffe-Brown's functionalism was its decidedly ahistorical and even antihistorical perspective. In *Middletown* the Lynds constantly compared the present situation with the preindustrial village of Muncie in 1890, by relying on newspapers and the diary of a socially active baker. Their historical information was admittedly sketchy and often intruded into the clearer functional focus. Still, the historical viewpoint contributed significantly to Lynd's didactic purposes. The Lynds compared 1920s pecuniary society and its harried, unhappy workers with an idyllic vision of the harmonious 1890s, a time of genuine intellectual endeavors and viable social organizations for the working class as well as the business class. According to the Lynds, 1890s culture represented a coherent blend of material and spiritual needs. In contrast, the inhabitants of the 1920s suffered from an extreme cultural lag in which social and intellectual life was far outdistanced by material life. Lynd's use of history was designed purely to criticize contemporary American society and demonstrate the existence of a healthier alternative.[32]

His adulation of preindustrial Muncie demonstrates several important facets of Lynd's personal value system. Although H. L. Mencken gleefully entitled his review of *Middletown* "A City in Moronia" and praised the book lavishly for confirming his views on the stupidity of rural America, the Lynds did not share his or others' condemnation of small towns. Muncie's problem was not its bucolic provinciality but rather its attempts to imitate the customs of the sophisticated city. Robert Lynd truly liked Muncie. On several occasions Helen remarked with equal wonder and horror that her husband would have been quite willing to live his entire life there. In Muncie, he joined organizations, became a featured soloist in the Presbyterian choir, and made strong friendships. Indeed, the friendships he formed with the three other members of "the Sewing Club," who met weekly to talk about local, cultural, and international affairs, were, according to his wife, deeper than any he formed with later academic colleagues. Lynd honestly liked and empathized with the people of Muncie; one moving passage in *Middletown in Transition* describes how he spent an evening shortly after he began his follow-up study in 1935 strolling through the darkened streets of the town thinking sadly about how the depression had affected the lives of people he had known ten years before.[33]

What Lynd clearly liked about Muncie was its small-town heritage. In the 1930s he advised Roy Stryker, a former Columbia colleague and at that time director of the Farm Security Administration's photography section, on the kinds of shots his photographers should take of small-town America to capture its spirit before it vanished altogether. His detailed memorandum to Stryker leaves no doubt of his belief that its disappearance would make the nation much poorer. Moreover, he despised large urban areas and specifically criticized New York City as an inhuman boomtown devoid of the social ties and organizations necessary for human happiness.[34]

In his idolization of small-town America, Lynd ignored the fictional perspectives of such writers as E. W. Howe, Harold Frederic, Edgar Masters, Sherwood Anderson, and Sinclair Lewis as well as that of his hero Veblen, who had only recently denounced the country town as "the perfect flower of self-help and cupidity standardized on the American plan," parasitically living off farmers' labor and the anticipated rise in real estate values and engaging in extravagantly conspicuous consumption. Historical research conducted in the 1970s points out that each town had its "Shacktown" or "Back of the Tracks" section of immigrants, blacks, and "grotesques" and notes the large degree of anomie and geographical and psychological rootlessness in these supposed paradises. Moreover, the Lynds' evidence to the contrary was itself painfully shallow. They contradictorily accepted 1890s newspaper reports at face value while constantly demonstrating the half-truths and outright lies of the 1925 versions. Also, they relied heavily on one individual's personal diary for their historical conclusions while insisting on representative samples and intensive interviewing for their contemporary data. Neither the representativeness nor the accuracy of this diary is verifiable, and certainly it cannot be fairly compared with material obtained in an entirely different manner.[35]

Despite its drawbacks and weaknesses, however, Lynd insisted on the necessity of the historical perspective. People needed reachable goals, and Lynd's happy small-town childhood seemed worlds away from Princeton, New York, Elk Basin, and even Muncie. Like Charles Beard and James Harvey Robinson, Lynd was searching for a "usable past" that might offer values and goals for an unhappy society. Lynd's apotheosis of the small town was an earlier version of the widespread movement espoused by even such erstwhile critics as Anderson and Lewis in the 1930s to find the soul of America in its small-town and rural values. As with his use of functional anthropology, Lynd wished not only to explain but to do so in a way that would promote and encourage change.[36]

Despite its careful methodology and the Lynds' attempt to mollify the institute's staff, *Middletown* was not objective according to the social technicians' meaning of the word, nor was it meant to be. In a 1938 lecture, Lynd admitted that he went to Muncie with certain assumptions and values. In opposition to the optimism of the people of Muncie, he believed that individuals were confused, socially illiterate, and conditioned by habit. Middletowners resisted social reform and wanted all change to be slow, while Lynd considered the proper role of the social scientist to be to work for rapid social change. Chief among the positive reforms he desired were collective bargaining for labor and a planned economy to control wasteful capitalism. Lynd acknowledged that those views shaped *Middletown* and that it was "research with a point of view." Nor did he apologize for this since he believed that social scientists should take an active role in improving life.[37]

The reflection of the Lynds' values was revealed not only through their anthropological and historical perspectives but also through their connotative words and phrases. For instance, when they wished to voice their disapproval of the increasing emphasis on athletics and social clubs in Muncie's schools, they compared it to the camel who had already put his hump as well as his head into the tent. In other cases they abandoned all pretense at objectivity, as when they complained of the recent surge of local boosterism: "Another type of social illiteracy is being bred by the stifling of self-appraisal and self-criticism under the heavily diffused habit of social solidarity."[38]

Another method the Lynds used surreptitiously to present their views was to use quotations from social analysts and personal interviews juxtaposed with a simple description of the social situation. For instance, they concluded their chapter on the inadequate social welfare facilities of Muncie with R. H. Tawney's statement that "there is no touchstone, except the treatment of childhood, which reveals the true character of a social philosophy more clearly than the spirit in which it regards the misfortunes of those of its members who fall by the way." After a long discussion of Muncie's extensive unemployment, including the frank admission of businessmen that they encouraged an "easy labor market," the Lynds simply placed the statement of the wife of a "prominent" businessman who summarily stated, "People come to the house a good deal and tell me they can't get work. Of course, I don't really believe that. I believe that anyone who tries can get work of some kind." Although the Lynds themselves did not make unobjective statements, it is clear that theirs was only a formal objectivity.[39]

One of the Lynds' more successful ways of interjecting their own positions into the book was through their colorful additions to generally factual descriptions of events. In the middle of what purported to be the transcription of a hate-filled speech of a Ku Klux Klan leader comes the statement, "At this point a shuddering 'Yes, yes' went up from the crowd like the fervently breathed ejaculations one hears punctuating many working class services." But the Klan speaker did not say this. And who said it was a "shuddering" reaction to his remarks on miscegenation? Another effective scene occurred in the local court when the judge threatened a young father of four with jail unless he displayed repentance for passing bad checks. When he and his wife protested that they had to feed their children some way, the judge angrily threatened to send him to jail and the couple begged forgiveness. The point was well made already without the added picture of the family leaving the courtroom with the "tow-headed baby looking back with wide, uncomprehending eyes." It was excellent drama, good writing, and effective persuasion, but it was not objective.[40]

Lynd's departure from the traits of objectivist, technical social science caused problems with the institute. Fosdick, who was largely responsible for hiring Lynd, had apparently quickly changed his mind about him. In a closed meeting a year later he accused Lynd or someone identifying himself as Lynd of making incoherent and obscene attacks on him during a telephone conversation. Only the disbelief of board member William Faunce, president of Brown University, and Lynd's impassioned denial of any calls to Fosdick saved Lynd's job. A year later, Fosdick wrote to Fisher complaining of Lynd's reliance on "predetermined theories and principles." The staff soon officially transmitted its unhappiness and warned Lynd that "he should not lose sight for a minute of the facts, and he should be careful to guard against the presentation of his own theories in any guise and should confine himself strictly to the available material." Staff official Luther Fry, author of a study on the rural church that presented a quantitative scale for measuring the vitality of individual congregations, continued to criticize ongoing revisions as "incoherent" and lacking sufficient statistical data. Again and again the staff objected to Lynd's separation of Muncie into business and working classes and asked unabashedly about material on the "middle" class. They further claimed that Lynd's "natural sympathy" for the working class biased his work and blinded him to the problems of "the bosses." After Lynd's three years of work, Fisher blandly thanked him for his time and effort and informed him that the institute would not publish the work but would retain control of it. The decision not to publish *Middletown* was more political than methodological.[41]

Lynd fought the decision. He deluged Fosdick and Fisher with glowing reviews of the manuscript by Frank, Harrison, social psychologist Gardner Murphy, and, much to Fosdick's surprise and anger, L. C. Marshall. Interestingly, Lynd focused his anger not on Fry or Went, or even Fosdick, but on Fisher, whom he accused of toadying to Rockefeller. Later in his career, he would use his position on the SSRC to malign Fisher and blackball his attempt to write the religion chapter for the Recent Social Trends study. Lynd hated Fisher so much that he successfully promoted Fisher's former subordinate and his own statistically oriented opponent, Fry. Finally, with the strong intercession of Wissler and the staff's certainty that Lynd would be unable to locate a publisher for such an "uninteresting" work, Fisher was convinced to release the manuscript. Thirty-six hours later, Lynd's old publishing acquaintance Alfred Harcourt enthusiastically accepted *Middletown* for publication, and the book received glowing reviews and quickly became a bestseller.[42]

While the debate over *Middletown*'s publication continued, Lynd again needed employment. As before, Larry Frank sought out foundation positions for his friend and quickly found him one as an adviser to the Commonwealth Fund. In his eighteen months there and his following two years as executive secretary of the SSRC, Lynd continued to emphasize the implicit questions of both the Middletown and Elk Basin studies: the didactic role of social research and the social function of the researcher. In memoranda to the Commonwealth directors he constantly advocated abandoning the fund's "opportunistic" small-scale research to attack such fundamental questions as how children learn and adjust to their environment. In *Middletown* the Lynds had demonstrated how the Muncie school system used social studies to indoctrinate students into accepting the status quo and economic laissez-faire. Lynd argued that the Commonwealth Fund should spearhead a revitalization of social science education based on Dewey's educational theories. Traditional social studies with its emphasis on "impersonal" facts was more interested in what was best for education than in what was best for those being educated.[43]

Frank continued to push his friend's career. Shortly after Lynd's appointment to the Commonwealth Fund, Frank wrote Merriam, then president of the Social Science Research Council, asking him to invite Lynd to the council's Hanover Conference because Lynd's position at the fund could be useful to the council. A year later, the SSRC, suffering from the lack of a permanent staff, offered Lynd the position of assistant to the officers of the council. Mitchell, the new president, rejoiced in the selection of his former student, an individual with administrative experience and skills who possessed research and intellectual interests in the field and was not a "mere paper-shuffler." Lynd's initial duties were to establish a central office and to sort out the complex and neglected administrative affairs of the council. He obviously accomplished this task well, as the council the following year designated him, much to his and Helen's bemusement, "permanent" executive secretary. The position was an important one. Until 1929 the presidency of the council was a part-time, largely symbolic position, and many of the day-to-day decisions were left to Lynd. When the council sought a full-time permanent president in 1929, Lynd was seriously considered for the job and was rejected only because of his lack of status with foundations and academicians. When Lynd left the council after the publication of *Middletown* to become a professor of sociology at Columbia, Merriam wailed to council president Robert Woodworth, "This is a heavy blow to the Council, and I do not know how we are going to find a successor for him."[44]

Lynd was certainly not a "mere paper-shuffler" at the ssrc. He served on several committees, chaired the Committee on the Family, and successfully encouraged the institutionalization of several interdisciplinary research areas. Most important, he served as an intellectual gadfly, constantly challenging the council to question the direction and purpose of its funded research. For example, at the same time that Lynd was helping Stuart Rice edit the council's heavily statistical casebook *Methods in Social Sciences*, he invited the neo-Thomist Mortimer Adler to comment on the book at the 1930 ssrc Hanover meeting. In his address Adler called the entire conception of current social science "misdirected and methodologically ill-advised because of erroneous conceptions of the nature of science which comprise the raw empiricism characteristic of contemporary social science." Although Lynd was hardly willing to embrace neo-Thomism, he did wish to make his complacent colleagues at least think about their approach to research. He frequently questioned the relationship of government and industry to social research and appealed for an overall strategy before "promptly putting [our] noses into the feed bag." Lynd even bypassed his superiors to write directly to the various professional organizations, encouraging them to appoint new people to the council and replace the self-perpetuating group of eastern professors.[45]

The best example of Lynd's approach was his 1929 "Confidential Notes for the Committee on Problems and Policy for a Discussion of the Program and Policy of the Social Science Research Council." In it, Lynd dispensed with praise and blame and immediately stated the theme:

"How can the work of the Social Science Research Council be made even more effective?" After presenting a summary of recent developments in the social sciences, he turned to a long list of basic questions that needed answers. Although the council's charter said that the ssRC was concerned with "any scientific work or investigation or research," it did not define *scientific* or even *social sciences*. Lynd believed the council must decide what type of research it wished to encourage. On the most elementary level, the ssRC needed to choose between funding as much soundly conceived research as possible or concentrating on strategic overall problems no other agency could afford to fund. Throughout the fifty-page memorandum Lynd demanded that the Problems and Policy Committee decide exactly what it wished the council to accomplish.[46]

One of the areas Lynd believed the council should explore was consumerism, a relatively unstudied field that touched directly on individuals' lives and one where social research could help change people's lives for the better. In *Middletown* Lynd had noted the central importance of mass consumption for American pecuniary society, and especially the role of American business in encouraging and directing consumption habits. Within the council, Lynd had a powerful ally in Mitchell, whose pioneering 1912 essay "The Backward Art of Spending Money" advocated disseminating information so that consumers could spend their money wisely and rationally. The two arranged to establish a council committee to encourage research in this still "well-nigh virgin field," and Lynd became its secretary. Soon he was one of the most prominent researchers in the area.[47]

Ogburn, the director of research on the President's Committee on Recent Social Trends, solidified Lynd's burgeoning reputation as an expert in consumer matters when he chose him to write the commission's chapter on consumption habits. Given Ogburn's extreme advocacy of a technical social science, as revealed in his presidential address and his and Lynd's past disputes, his selection of Lynd is somewhat surprising. During the review process of *Middletown,* Ogburn had criticized it as "too interesting to be science," and later, within the ssRC, opposed Lynd's and Frank's encouragement of social science textbooks as detrimental to the factual documentation and scientific standards of social science. Ogburn truly believed that the scientific method consisted solely of gathering facts, and in the late 1920s he opposed all interpretation of data. Science was purely a "pile of knowledge" to be pursued for its own sake. Lynd, on the other hand, bluntly stated that " 'knowledge for its own sake' is not science" and in 1929 called on the ssRC to block the path down which Ogburn was leading the American Sociological Society.[48]

Lynd's selection was due at least partly to Ogburn's contradictory nature. Ogburn demanded that social scientists keep their research separate from their personal interests, but he also believed, at least early in his career, that empiricism led inexorably to political and social change. He called for a "wholly colorless" social science free from interpretation and theory but was best known for his own theoretical work *Social Change*, with its influential concept of cultural lag, and he knew as much about psychoanalysis as any American social scientist of the time. After disparaging *Middletown* as "too interesting," he worked for its publication as a popular work and received an acknowledgment in its preface. Ogburn liked and respected Lynd and immediately accepted Lynd's self-deprecatory offer to do the consumerism study. Ogburn had originally not wanted to include such a chapter because he feared it would be impossible to ensure its absolute objectivity. Still, when Mitchell, the chairman of the commission, insisted on its inclusion, Ogburn demanded someone with enough "imagination" to produce something worthwhile. He recognized Lynd's lack of statistical training but insisted that "one of the safe and sane statisticians would not be exploratory enough." Ogburn, like his fellow objectivist social scientists Mitchell and Merriam, found himself torn between the demands of a technical social science and his desire for a more humane social order. In Lynd, he hoped he had found someone who could integrate the two.[49]

Ogburn's hopes were not realized; he and Lynd clashed from the outset. Whereas Ogburn wanted to call the chapter "Consumption Habits," Lynd held out for "The People as Consumers." This difference represented much more than just a title. Ogburn originally conceived the study as concentrating on shifts in consumption habits as reflected in the biennial census of manufacturing and changing standards of living. Lynd's interests, however, centered on the causes of these shifts and "the conditioning factors out of which our American pattern of consumption emerges." He was relatively unconcerned with indexes. Rather, he wished to understand the consumer, how advertising and other business techniques affected him or her, and what all this meant in terms of individual lives. Lynd perceived making money and its corollary, "buying a living," as dominating American life. He and his research associate, Alice Hanson, undertook an extensive study of advertising to determine the shifts in the products advertised, the amount expended, and the types of advertising used. This study provided the evidence for Lynd's call for a need to balance increased advertising pressure with government sponsorship of consumer literacy. While business was well organized and possessed strong lobbies, consumers lacked a voice in public affairs. Consequently, Lynd advocated the establishment of a department of the consumer to play roughly the role that the Department of Commerce had assumed for businessmen.[50]

Lynd's chapter appeared over the protests of Ogburn. Even before seeing the first draft, Ogburn wrote to Lynd emphasizing the need to make the study "as pure and scientific as statements in the social sciences will permit" and to avoid all recommendations. He simultaneously told the directors of the committee that he believed Lynd's chapter would require extensive revision. When the chapter came in, Ogburn's worst fears were realized. True, the work was factual, and with it Lynd had submitted a fifty-two-page annotated list of the various publications and newsletters he and Hanson had consulted to reach their conclusions. But it did contain recommendations, and even worse, it criticized a government agency, the Bureau of Standards, for its lack of interest in consumer problems. Worse still, the Bureau of Standards was under the jurisdiction of Hoover's cherished Commerce Department. Hoover himself had reorganized the bureau during his tenure as secretary of commerce, and he lavished numerous positive press releases on its activities. E. E. Hunt, secretary of the committee and Hoover's longtime personal aide and unofficial representative on the committee, was outraged and threatened to exclude the chapter completely. Ogburn angrily wrote to Lynd that "commenting upon the administration of a law is different from commenting on the law itself."[51]

Just at that time an unlikely savior arose. As Ogburn began to introduce his complaints about Lynd's chapter during the executive meeting of the committee, Dr. Alice Hamilton interrupted him to express her strong support for the chapter as it presently stood. In a canny political move, Hoover had appointed Hamilton, a professor at Harvard Medical School and an expert in industrial medicine and worker safety, to the committee at the last minute as a token woman representative. Except for the chapters on women, labor, and health care, she had not taken an active role in the proceedings. On this occasion, however, she very actively insisted on the validity of Lynd's statements. She criticized the chapter only for not condemning the Bureau of Standards more strongly. At this, Hunt exploded. He defended the bureau, insisted that Lynd lacked expertise, and censured Lynd's conclusions for their lack of statistical foundation. The meek-looking but strong-willed Hamilton chidingly reproved, "Don't you believe anything except what is backed up with tables of figures? I think they [Lynd's conclusions] are evident." This, in turn, angered Ogburn, who did *not* believe anything not backed up by statistics, and he testily insisted that he had taken opinions out of the preceding chapters and did not intend to stop now. At this point, Merriam, who was serving as chairman while Mitchell was away in England, informed Ogburn that he could "communicate" his opinions to Lynd but that refusal of the chapter was out of the question. The chapter remained essentially unchanged and was one of the few to escape Ogburn's pure empiricism. Indeed, one of the reviewers pointed to Lynd's chapters as the one contribution that met the potential of the study by going beyond merely describing the situation to offering a positive approach to solving the problem itself.[52]

Lynd's criticism of consumerism was part of his increasingly radical critique of America's pecuniary culture, in which people made money rather than things and accumulated property through the manipulation of pecuniary institutions rather than through actual work. Lynd saw Western society as increasingly spiritually impoverished. Individuals were burdened with new "necessary" ways to spend their money until they became little more than the sum of their purchases. The constant pressure to purchase goods for individual consumption acted as "a kind of Gresham's law in which superficial values tended to drive out values expressing deeper and subtler ways of viewing human experience." Traditional institutions and habits broke down in the face of the promise of happiness in the form of mass consumption. Nor was Lynd overly optimistic about the future. He felt that social factors such as increased urbanization and new techniques of production and consumption were complicating the problems of consumers more rapidly than government, education, and science could solve them. Lynd viewed "this modern kingdom of Consumption" as antithetical to the real needs of the individual.[53]

Lynd went beyond rejecting the goals of consumer society; he challenged its very assumptions as outdated and culturally biased. Scarcity was not inevitable; in many societies scarcity and the consequent competition for goods were unknown. In fact, America's industrial plant could easily meet all the desires of its population if only society would regard consumption rather than production as the ultimate goal. More important, consumers were not rational. Dewey had recognized that human beings are largely creatures of habit and that the repetition of emotional issues could drive rational considerations out of the decision-making process. Even if consumers possessed adequate information to make rational decisions (which they did not), skilled advertising could prevent them from doing so. Lynd argued that advertising seemed to create a psychological consumption to buy. The consumer was not free to buy what he or she actually desired, and consumers' wants had little, if any, impact on production.[54]

Lynd recognized that his condemnation of pecuniary America was neither original nor sufficient in itself. Despite the ssrc's and Ogburn's claims that consumer research was nonexistent, a number of individuals and organizations had begun to provide consumer information and to lobby for consumer interests in the mid-1920s. Frederick Schlink and Stuart Chase had written a bestselling exposé in 1927 of the dangers and inefficiency of consumer goods, and Schlink's organization, Consumers' Research, worked actively for government testing of consumer goods and publication of results. Many of these activists far surpassed Lynd in their condemnation of America's "business civilization" and their call for the creation of a true consumer society.[55]

Yet none of these organizations possessed solutions for the problem. While moderate groups such as the American Home Economics Association, the General Federation of Women's Clubs, and the American Association of University Women called for increased consumer information and mandatory labeling of canned goods, Consumers' Research demanded a powerful federal department of the consumer. Lynd insisted that both solutions were shortsighted and overlooked the central power of business in American society. He had begun to study consumer issues at the time of the Great Crash, and the information he had accumulated on consumer manipulation combined with the extreme economic deprivation of the times convinced him that big business and its organizations had almost total control of American society. Business and advertising interests infiltrated consumer organizations or formed their own to preach the common interests of producers and consumers. Lynd contemptuously dismissed this argument and warned consumers to form their own pressure groups to force decision makers to listen to their needs. From this period onward, Lynd would concentrate on the issue of power and seek ways for social scientists to aid consumer, labor, and other middle- and lower-class groups in overcoming business's dominance of American society.[56]

The central difficulty Lynd faced was a lack of consumer consciousness. Unlike the residents of Elk Basin, who clearly recognized their common identity versus Standard Oil, most individuals did not perceive themselves as consumers. Certainly members of the General Federation of Women's Clubs saw their roles as consumers as secondary to their positions as middle- and upper-class women. Consumers' Research, the one organization striving to form such an identity, had grown to 42,000 members by 1932 but was torn by internal dissension when its director, Schlink, became convinced that communist labor groups were trying to take over the organization. Although cofounder and frequent Schlink coauthor Arthur Kallett led an eventually successful walkout to found the much more politically active and prolabor Consumers Union, the immediate impact was to weaken the consumer movement.[57]

Given the lack of public education and identification, Lynd searched for other ways of using his expertise and knowledge to effect change. His reluctant choice was to ally himself with the admittedly "meagerly powered" Consumers Advisory Board (CAB) of the National Recovery Administration (NRA). The NRA was an early New Deal effort to end the nation's industrial stagnation that, like much of Roosevelt's early legislation, promised to be all things to all people. Since the legal establishment of production levels and minimum prices strongly attracted business groups, they were willing to accept labor representation, collective bargaining, and even the addition of consumer representatives to the various code-writing authorities. Nevertheless, under the dynamic and headstrong leadership of General Hugh Johnson, the NRA concentrated on making and implementing industrial codes, and neglected labor and consumer interests. Johnson, a former executive of a farm machinery company, had little sympathy for consumers. He recognized their relative lack of strength compared with business and labor groups and considered the CAB a hindrance to the effective functioning of the code-making process. Johnson represented an extreme example of the businessman who refused to recognize even the existence of consumer interests and once actually snapped, "Who is the consumer? Show me the consumer."[58]

Lynd clearly recognized the limitations of the CAB but, unlike Schlink and his followers, who attacked the New Deal as a "sinister" business-controlled conspiracy to "deliberately neglect" consumer interests, he perceived the CAB as a significant symbol of the government's emerging recognition of the importance of the consumer as an economic and political factor. Also, Lynd respected the ability and power of the head of the CAB, Mary Harriman Rumsey, the liberal socialite daughter of E. H. Harriman and a personal friend of the Roosevelts. Although political insiders initially snickered at the appointment, Rumsey proved to be a tough and capable administrator who ruthlessly used her business and Roosevelt connections to advance the board's interests. Lynd joined such well-known social scientists as Ogburn, Paul Douglas, Leon Henderson, Walton Hamilton, Gardiner Means, and George Stocking on the research staff and in 1935 became a member of the CAB's first executive committee.[59]

The CAB faced two essential tasks. Although consumer advocates were allowed to participate in the meetings in which codes were developed, they lacked the firsthand knowledge possessed by industry and labor representatives directly involved in the various industries. To offset this advantage, the CAB's able staff began to turn out the secondary research necessary to oppose both specific code provisions and such general issues as price fixing. Second, in 1933 the CAB formed the Committee on Consumer Standards, chaired by Lynd. Ever since *Your Money's Worth*, consumer advocates had pointed to the advantage derived by the federal government and large companies from requiring certain standards for their goods, and they demanded the same policy for individual consumers. The committee's report, "A Proposal to Develop Standards for Consumer Goods by Establishing a Consumer Standards Board and Funds for Basic Testing," commonly known as the Lynd Report, followed and extended this line of reasoning. It called for the federal government to set up a board with its own director and technical staff to establish and test standards and grades for all products sold to consumers. Although the Bureau of Standards would play a leading role in the testing of standards, the report specifically called for administrative independence for this new board because of the bureau's previous close ties to business. In this report and elsewhere, Lynd insisted that consumer education was impossible without government standardization and its enforcement.[60]

Despite such excellent and important work, the CAB remained largely impotent due to its lack of vocal public supporters. Whereas industry and labor could turn to their constituencies to provide political pressure and publicity, the CAB often could not even find consumers willing to testify at public hearings. Lynd had noted as early as 1930 that while consumers were quite interested in research and exposés, they seldom banded together to actually do something themselves; this conflicted directly with Lynd's insistence on individual participation and choice in social change. Lynd consequently advocated primary concentration on the "building up of constructive and vocal data" on consumer wants and the establishment of active consumer organizations. First Paul Douglas and then Dexter Keezer worked with some success to establish local consumer organizations on a countywide basis to provide political support and information on local conditions. After the demise of the NRA and CAB, Lynd joined Douglas, Keezer, and others in attempting to transform these local groups into permanent private operations. In 1937 he helped found and became vice chairman of the Consumers National Federation, an umbrella organization comprising the Consumers Union, the National Federation of Settlements, and about twenty-five local associations across the country, which hoped to serve as a national coordinator and clearinghouse for consumer information and action.[61]

As Lynd finished his consumer research in 1931 for *Recent Social Trends*, Columbia University unexpectedly offered him a position as a graduate professor of sociology in recognition of *Middletown* and his activities in organizational social science. Although Lynd and his friends rejoiced in this apparent good fortune, it would have significant negative consequences for his later life and career. First, the Columbia position and, later, Helen's position at Sarah Lawrence rooted him in New York City, an environment completely foreign to his goals of community involvement and solidarity. Second, and more important, he found himself constantly embroiled in departmental feuds centering on the uses of social science research. Sociology at Columbia bore the stamp of its first professor, Franklin Giddings, who had placed the department within the Faculty of Political Science to distance it from social work and social charities. Giddings championed a pronounced objectivist version of social science and produced in such students as Ogburn, Odum, and Stuart Chapin some of the leaders of the new technical social science. After Giddings retired in 1928, Columbia brought in Robert MacIver, who shared many of Giddings's interests in the theory of social structure but was uninterested in and at times even actively hostile to empirical research. Lynd was supposed to continue the Giddings tradition of empirical research, an expectation whose obvious weakness was demonstrated by the search committee's insistence that Lynd complete a graduate statistics course before he started teaching. Lynd did wish to encourage empirical research, but he lacked sufficient training and, unlike both Giddings and MacIver, emphasized social problems instead. MacIver, also a reformer in his personal views, argued that "a science must first exist before it can solve problems." The pair's constant debates culminated in MacIver's vicious review of *Knowledge for What?*, after which the two men and sometimes even their students refused to talk to one another.[62]

The 1940 appointments of Robert K. Merton and Lynd's friend Paul Lazarsfeld to conduct the empirical mid-level analysis that Lynd had failed to produce further exacerbated the situation. On the one hand, Lynd had feelings of inferiority about his inability to do their type of statistical research. On the other, he was infuriated by the willingness of especially Lazarsfeld, an Austrian socialist and activist who had only barely escaped Hitler, to produce research for corporations and the military. According to Lazarsfeld, his "great colleague" Lynd consistently demanded to know where his social conscience was, and his admittedly weak answer was, "Well, that begins after five o'clock." More and more Lynd felt a pressure to formulate an empirically grounded social theory that would be both sociologically relevant and politically useful. Further, Lynd's didactic role as a professor, popular speaker, and essayist required enormous amounts of time, and despite frequent plans and false starts he did little of the empirical investigation of communities and individuals necessary, in his own conception, of a viable social science. Mitchell's gentle gibe about "the two Lynds" was quite appropriate and stung more than Mitchell perhaps appreciated. Like Beard, Robinson, Harry Elmer Barnes, and other purposive social scientists, Lynd found the political and professional strictures of traditional academic settings detrimental to real work, especially normatively oriented research. Unlike many others, however, he remained in academia.[63]

The one empirical study Lynd did complete after his Columbia appointment was his 1935 restudy of Muncie, published as *Middletown in Transition*. Lynd's reasons for returning to Muncie reflected normative concerns strengthened by the suffering of the depression and the results of his consumer research. Lynd was never content solely with statistics on the amount of advertising or consumer indexes. He always wanted to know what this meant for the individual. He was concerned with how advertising affected individuals, what installment buying represented to buyers and how it would change their lives, and how the cravings created by a mass consumer society compared with real needs. The study of such topics was part of Lynd's research model. Moreover, despite his unhappiness at disturbing Muncie again, it provided him with the unparalleled opportunity for a case study of social change in a particular community over ten years, "something analogous to an experimental situation." Where the Lynds had been forced to rely on inadequate 1890 data for comparisons in their first study, they could now use their own extensive scientifically gathered data to get an accurate picture of historical change.[64]

A second reason for a restudy of Muncie was Lynd's discovery of the centrality of the issues of social structure and power during his work on consumerism. During their original research, the Lynds had quickly recognized the Ball family's pervasive influence in Muncie's financial, political, and social affairs. Lynd, however, had chosen Muncie in order to study *the* typical American community, and no existing works of American sociology even addressed the issue of power. When Park and Burgess defined sociology as social process, they ignored not only class and power but even social structure. One can thus excuse Lynd for trying to overlook this apparent anomaly. By the 1930s, however, Lynd was convinced that this "exception" was closer to the norm, and he wished to provide a more accurate view of Muncie. In *Transition,* the Lynds noted how the "X" (Ball) family dominated Muncie society through their ownership of its major industry, department store, both banks, distillery, and dairy; their leadership positions within both political parties; and their philanthropic donations to churches, charities, and civic organizations. During the depression, the Balls had even used the increased profits resulting from the growing demand for the home canning jars they manufactured to buy up failing local businesses and further strengthen their economic control.[65]

As the title suggests, Lynd's paramount interest was in the changes in Muncie. While *Middletown* concluded with a short seven-page summary of findings, *Middletown in Transition* led up to two lengthy concluding chapters that describe the changes and lack of them in Muncie and the reasons for this state of affairs. Life for the average individual had, in fact, changed little over the intervening ten years. Work remained the key to Middletown's existence. Who one was, whom one knew, how one lived, and what one hoped to be all depended on one's occupation. Indeed, Muncie's social structure had even ossified slightly during the decade. With the advent of industrial experts, factories hired fewer foremen and ended the policy of taking lower management personnel from the ranks of labor. Larger businesses forced their smaller and weaker competitors out of business. The major change in Muncie appeared to be the increased resistance to change. The Lynds recognized that "Middletown in Transition" was not an accurate title; *transition* implied change, and Muncie had not changed despite the crises of the 1930s. The values of 1925 remained dominant, and no new symbols or ideologies had developed to challenge the ruling consensus. The Lynds maintained that a Rip Van Winkle who had fallen asleep while giving an address to the Rotary Club in 1925 could have finished it in 1935 without changing a word.[66]

In their preface to *Transition* the Lynds stated that since total objectivity was impossible, they would openly note their own desires for social reform and change; and throughout the book they criticized the local inhabitants' desire to avoid change. They noted the economic and psychological stress engendered by high unemployment and lack of economic and social opportunity and pointed out how this could easily fuel a native American fascism masquerading as patriotism. Muncie had a heritage of activities by the Ku Klux Klan and other xenophobic organizations, often covertly encouraged by the city's business interests. The Lynds were convinced that all the elements of a fascist movement were present both in Muncie and in the United States in general and needed only a precipitating incident.[67]

The increasing danger of the situation coupled with the relative lack of institutional, ideological, and individual change forced Lynd into a difficult dilemma. What happens in Elk Basin when the Rockefellers don't budge and the inhabitants either don't recognize the difficulties or at least show any commitment to do anything about them? The only glimmers of hope in *Transition* were the changes forced on Muncie by federal planning and outside intervention. What was the role of the social scientist faced with such inertia in a time of crisis? Did one select a powerful organization and try to effect changes through it, as Merriam and Arnold had advocated and Lynd had actually attempted with the Consumers Advisory Board? Yet how would outside control by experts differ from the type "that will manhandle life deliberately and coercively" which Lynd opposed so completely as fascism? These questions, precipitated by the conclusions of his Muncie research, helped crystalize Lynd's thinking about the role of the social scientist and his work. The result was a series of 1938 lectures published as *Knowledge for What? The Place of Social Science in American Culture*, by all accounts the most thorough statement of the purposive movement in American social science and the most revealing example of both its strengths and weaknesses.[68]

In the lectures Lynd began with his activist definition of social science as "an organized part of the culture which exists to help man in continually understanding and rebuilding his culture . . . an instrument for furthering man's purposes." He noted Ogburn's and others' conception of social science as the disinterested pursuit of knowledge but maintained that from the time of Adam Smith the dominant and correct characteristic of social science had been its "*interested* desire to know." As he noted in his criticism of Mitchell and the National Bureau of Economic Research, American social scientists by engaging in small-scale, empirical research and insisting on the necessity of value neutrality, had retreated from a society desperately in need of its aid and had, in fact, supported the status quo. Instead, social scientists must become involved, formulate values and goals, and assume an active part in breaking down established institutional habits. Since change was inevitable, especially in the present crisis, the issue was to select the changes that would best permit the continuation of basic human values. In his concluding paragraph Lynd summed up what had been the implicit belief behind all his previous research and would subsequently be explicit: "But what is it that we human beings want, and what things would have to be done, in what ways and in what sequence, in order to change the present so as to achieve it."[69]

Before he could develop such a social science, Lynd had to dispose of his objectivist opponents. His criticism of technical social science was threefold. First, as his critique of Mitchell made clear, Lynd thought the role of the social scientist as a technician contradicted the very basis of social science. To accept a retainer from a private company while supplying information on how to manipulate individuals or the social system for private advantage was to abnegate the ethical role of the social scientist. To turn social science into an instrument for sale to the highest bidder "actively invites the Hitler-type of open control over science by whittling away the crucial claim of science that it is objective and cannot be bought." Lynd's high standards led him, unlike most of his Columbia colleagues, to refuse to accept fees or research money from commercial sources.[70]

Second, again seen in his critique of Mitchell, Lynd believed that American social scientists had overemphasized quantification. Although he firmly believed in the need for empirical data and precise measurement for the continued growth of social science, he felt that many researchers chose their subjects purely on the basis of their quantifiability. This in turn modified the experimental design and the way subjects were studied. For instance, students of investment finance perceived their task to be to determine the amount of money expended in the market rather than to investigate why specific investors entered or left the market. The concept of process was ignored in the quest for quantifiable data. Since only existing institutions could be quantified, a permanent link was forged between social science and the status quo, and the possibility of creating alternatives was ignored. Lynd insisted that the question for quantified data, as for every other area of social knowledge, remained "What are they worth for what?"[71]

Third, and related to the second point, Lynd criticized the consequent weakness of social theory. Although empiricism represented a clear advance over the armchair generalizations of the social Darwinists and Lynd's Columbia adversary MacIver, it could not provide the hypotheses necessary for the growth of any true science. Without hypotheses, one could not even know what information one should collect. "Science without hypotheses is sterile, however beautifully 'objective,' . . . and becomes the ditty bag of an idiot, filled with bits of pebbles, straw, feathers, and other random hoardings." Lynd felt that current social science theory did not lead to anything beyond the haphazard collection of facts.[72]

Lynd thereupon set out to create a social science theory based equally on empirically determined facts and normative goals. The greatest difficulty lay in determining empirically derived normative standards. Much of the progress in twentieth-century social science had consisted of movement away from the culturally biased views of early evolutionists who proclaimed Western civilization the permanent apex of cultural development and derided all other cultures for their inability to match those standards. Arguing that this demonstrated the inadequacy of all value-oriented social thought, objectivists turned to a cultural relativism that accepted all cultures and their mores and institutions as equal. Like so many others during the late 1930s, Lynd pointed to the rise of fascism as a telling criticism of absolute cultural relativism. A cultural analyst must always retain an overview that compared cultures and institutions.[73]

Lynd noted that contemporary Western society did not measure up to the only acceptable criteria for judgment of cultures: the degree to which they permitted the maximum growth of individuals and their potentials. The strict physical and emotional limitations constraining the lives of the people of Elk Basin had provided the first impetus for Lynd's turn to social science, and his Middletown studies first implicitly and later explicitly criticized American society for its reliance on pecuniary standards and the consequent spiritual deprivation of the individual. His work on consumerism further demonstrated the pervasive and pernicious manipulation of individuals by capitalism and its standards. Lynd now concluded that Western society "does not now operate, and probably cannot be made to operate, to assure the amount of general welfare to which the present stage of our technological skills and intelligence entitle us." Echoing neo-Freudian psychiatrist Karen Horney, Lynd asserted that the emphasis on competition and the consequent alienation of one individual from another had created a society of neurotic personalities.[74]

Lynd's rejection of cultural relativism and contemporary Western culture as acceptable models provided no answer to his question of "What it is that we human beings want?" He needed to identify human needs and desires endemic to all societies, and he turned to recent psychological research to locate them. Given the importance of this search for a viable theory of social science, Lynd argued, the reintroduction of psychology to the study of society was potentially the most rewarding avenue for contemporary social science. Social scientists should shift their emphasis from institutions to "where it basically belongs—upon people . . . as the active carriers, perpetuators, and movers of culture."[75]

Lynd thought to speak about the individual "in society" was a tautology. To talk about individuals was to deal with "something living and interacting with other individuals." In return, though, one could not study a society without investigating the individuals who composed it. Individuals interacted with their culture to produce unique personalities, and different personalities existed in every culture. Individuals were deeply influenced by their cultures, but their personalities were not culturally determined. This perspective freed social scientists from a blind acceptance of the status quo and allowed them to attempt to develop cultural institutions that encouraged the greatest possible growth in individuals. Through Helen, who taught social philosophy and psychology at Sarah Lawrence and would soon begin a lengthy analysis with Erich Fromm, Lynd became well versed in social psychology, psychiatry, and especially the ideas of the child development movement, which demonstrated how culture and personality interacted to form behavior patterns in the preschool child.[76]

Lynd also needed information about psychological development in non-Western cultures. The burgeoning culture and personality school of American anthropology fit this need perfectly. As early as 1923, with Ruth Benedict's "The Concept of the Guardian Spirit in North America," American anthropology began to reemphasize its traditional interest in the interaction between individuals and society. Lynd had become interested in this research during the late 1920s and, as SSRC executive secretary, had actively, if not always successfully, pushed for extensive funding of the field. He also was a charter member of the council's Committee on Culture and Personality, which, despite relative neglect by the council hierarchy, proved to be the SSRC's most important and innovative research committee during the 1930s. In *Knowledge for What?* Lynd called culture and personality "*the field of all the social sciences.*"[77]

Although Lynd knew and used the work of Mead and Benedict extensively and was one of Benedict's few friends and supporters among the Columbia faculty, two more important influences were Lynd's longtime friend Larry Frank and the anthropological linguist Edward Sapir. Frank argued that cultures do not develop classic types of personalities, as Benedict suggested, and are little more than a congeries of random individuals. An early proponent of the child development movement, Frank composed a list of fundamental needs for all children the same year Lynd delivered his *Knowledge* lectures. In this and other essays, Frank argued that social and economic analyses were inconsequential and even futile without preconceived goals. Sapir, chair of the Committee on Culture and Personality, was even more extreme and always referred to the field as "personality and culture" rather than "culture and personality." In a 1934 article, quoted approvingly by Lynd in his lectures, Sapir stated that the concept of culture as used by most anthropologists was dangerous because it assumed that individuals were nothing but products of culture and could not change their environment. To Sapir, every individual had his or her own individual culture. Simple categorization of individuals locked objectivist social scientists into an acceptance of the status quo and prevented the liberation of the individual from the cultural constraints that hindered his or her growth. Benedict once remarked that her friend Sapir seemed compelled to prove that cultures did not really matter that much.[78]

Considering its impressive grounding in social psychology and cultural anthropology, Lynd's determination of human needs was painfully disappointing. Adopting a variation of W. I. Thomas's "four wishes," Lynd constructed a list of nine human "cravings," things all normal individuals supposedly desired and required for a fulfilling life: (1) a need for a tempo of life in conformity to the body's natural rhythms, (2) a sense of growth and realization of personal potential, (3) a need for meaningful experience, (4) a certain amount of psychological and physical security, (5) a certain amount of novelty, (6) a limited degree of competition, (7) shared experience and communication with others, (8) coherence and stability in the direction of one's life, and (9) a feeling of freedom and diversity within certain limits of security. As his references to "cravings" and Thomas's four wishes attest, Lynd seems to have based his normative goals largely on a vague form of instinct psychology, a physical behaviorism far removed from a determination of normative goals. To the extent that the nine cravings did not rest on behavioral needs, they simply reflected Lynd's personal small-town values. For all of his emphasis on the need for universal human values, Lynd, at least in *Knowledge for What?*, equated values with those he had learned from his father.[79]

Lynd's consequent plan for remodeling the social sciences also reflected his inability to divorce himself from his own cultural values. Turning to anthropology again, Lynd insisted on the need to see culture

as an integrated, functioning whole. Extensive specialization in the social sciences had prevented social thinkers from recognizing the interrelationships between different problems and thus stood in the way of
viable solutions. Social scientists should recognize the lessons of anthropology and see contemporary life as "interacting parts in a single whole."
Then, social scientists from various disciplines could use their expertise
cooperatively in such "problem areas" as labor economics, political behavior, and the family. For instance, economists, anthropologists, and
psychiatrists, as well as sociologists, would study the institution of the
family. The problem areas, however, were themselves products of the
ongoing social system. Like business cycles and investment finance,
constructs such as the family depended on the definitions of society.
Replacing sociologists with family experts would lead inevitably to the
same type of specialization.[80]

Lynd's turn to a social science of problem areas and social problems
reflected his consistent desire for an activist social science. The ultimate
goal of his projected interdisciplinary social science was the development of institutions that would allow individuals to fulfill their human
cravings. Since individuals must express their own desires, this could
happen only in a political, economic, and social democracy. American
society in the 1930s was not such a democracy. The decision-making
bodies of government, business, and the like had become so powerful
that ordinary individuals believed they had no influence. Lynd advocated
the creation of organizations, especially for unorganized workers and
the middle class, to fill the gaps between the individual and large institutions. Social scientists should help develop such organizations and
then through such works as Harold Lasswell's *Politics: Who Gets What,
When, How* help them recognize the central function of power and teach
them to manipulate the system to meet their needs. Ethical social scientists working with these organizations could establish social and economic plans designed to achieve individually based goals and could even
use "propaganda" for democratic purposes in opposition to that of dictatorial forces. Ultimately, purposive social scientists, as portrayed in
Knowledge for What?, also became technical experts. The only difference lay in their active role in choosing the normative goals of their
research and in their service to middle- and lower-class majoritarian organizations rather than established economic and political institutions.
In Thurman Arnold's words, they simply chose other organizations.[81]

As World War II loomed on the horizon, Lynd began to develop institutions among social scientists that would attempt to ensure the continued

consideration of human needs. Lynd remembered the situation of World War I and the social scientists' willing and even eager participation in the attack on civil liberties. In the summer of 1939, he and Alfred Bingham, editor of the radical journal *Common Sense*, proposed an institute for integrated research in economics and the social sciences. A year later, Lynd wrote a confidential report proposing an independent watchdog agency to monitor wartime mobilization activities to ensure their conformance with individual rights and democratic decision making. Most of all, Lynd wished to guarantee the integrity of the universities during the coming war. In what his son Staughton identified as one of his father's favorite pieces, Lynd expressed, in Columbia's official 1939 opening address, his fears of the power of intolerance and dictatorial control during wartime. Certainly Columbia itself had failed in its responsibilities twenty years earlier, and only determination and hard work could ensure the university's continued intellectual integrity.[82]

In his search for fellow members of these organizations, he turned to his old contacts at the Social Science Research Council. Although Frank, as usual, shared Lynd's views and positions, a more common response was that of Merriam, who huffily rejected Lynd's proposed watchdog agency as "immature and impractical"—and unnecessary under a truly democratic administration like that of the New Deal. As the 1930s ended, Lynd frequently found his closest ally in such endeavors to be the hero of his Columbia address, the man who had fought so bravely for Columbia's academic freedom during World War I—historian and political scientist Charles Beard.[83]

5

CHARLES BEARD AND ACTIVIST SOCIAL

SCIENCE

Robert Lynd was certainly not alone in looking to Beard for guidance. By all accounts, including those of his many powerful enemies, Beard was, for good or bad, the most influential historian and one of the most important political scientists of his day. Indeed, he was the only individual of his generation to be honored with the presidency of both the American Political Science Association and the American Historical Association. At the time of his death in 1948 he had published forty-nine books which had sold over eleven million copies. The two-volume history *Rise of American Civilization* that he wrote with Mary, his wife, was by far the best survey of American history to date in both scope and coherence. John Higham, the preeminent student of the American historical profession, stated flatly that Beard "came close to dominating the study of history."[1]

More important to Beard, his influence was not limited to academics. In the *New Republic* symposium "Books That Changed Our Mind," his *Economic Interpretation of the Constitution* tied Veblen's *Theory of the Leisure Class* as the most cited work. Contributors mentioned him as an intellectual influence second only to Veblen and far more often than Dewey and Freud. Even the inveterate anti-intellectual Thurman Arnold, who used the occasion to praise newspapers, noted that Beard was second in importance only to Freud for his personal intellectual development. Many of the young intellectuals and activists of the 1930s respected Beard as an individual who conducted important social and historical research that was consistently relevant to existing needs. Beard did this, as Lynd did, by constantly demanding answers to what he perceived as the central questions of American society. Just as Lynd asked Knowledge for what? and Consumerism for what?, so did Beard question the ultimate purposes of efficient public administration, civic education, American foreign policy, and the study of history and society. An unassuming man who delighted in his generic nickname "Uncle

Charlie," he half jokingly referred to himself as "a kind of peripatetic philosopher . . . [who] is always finding out less and less about more and more." Yet, according to his frequent collaborator George H. E. Smith, Beard's "unruffled surface" hid "an unlimited depth of human emotions." Unlike Mitchell, who shared these personal characteristics, Beard believed intensely that the social scientist–historian had a responsibility to bring about ideals—in his wife and coworker's words, "to help the human race to realize its true potential." The social scientist *must* become "the thinker who is also a doer." Throughout his career, but especially after World War I, Beard directed his work toward previously determined moral goals. His success at uncovering and publicizing the ethical vacuum at the core of the objectivist argument was matched only by his complete failure to validate those personal values central to his own purposive approach.[2]

One can see Beard's consciously activist and even moralistic perspective reflected in the fact that, unlike Mitchell, Merriam, and Lasswell—and even more than Lynd—he consciously wrote for a mass audience. He saw himself as a teacher—not primarily of college students or even fellow academics, but of an interested, informed, and, eventually, articulate public. Beard believed intensely, almost religiously, in human rationality. Yet he also agreed with Dewey that habits control individual behavior. Consequently, change, if it were to occur, had to be formulated "realistically and with such ethical power" that the educated class would be convinced and act on it. His and his fellow social scientists' proper role was to develop the plans for positive social change.[3]

Somewhat ironically, Beard's greatest skills as a mass educator were ones he developed in his relatively short career as a college professor. From 1907, when he founded the program, until 1917, when he left the university, Beard practically *was* the undergraduate government department at Columbia, teaching almost all its courses. Such breadth gave him a holistic view of the political system and enabled him to put knowledge into an everyday context for his audience. Further, despite his self-professed preference for seminars and his constant praise of the Socratic method, Beard with his "enormous voice" lectured primarily to huge classes. He had begun to grow deaf at a very young age and both literally and figuratively had difficulty hearing others' points of view. His lectures and books further reflected his experiences as a champion debater in high school and college and a sponsor of Columbia's debate team. All his life he retained the habit of italicizing the key word in print to replicate the speaker's emphasis. Then, arguing from a clear and coherent thesis,

Beard would marshal myriad specific facts, tied together by a mixture of eloquence and midwestern home-style metaphors, to prove his point. To Beard, "power of style [was] power of mind." No wonder an awed young Max Lerner would refer to his professor as "half farmer and half Roman philosopher," while the great chronicler of the 1920s and 1930s Matthew Josephson would refer to his neighbor as "one of the great talkers of the day."[4]

The other characteristic of Beard's work that derived from his lecture and debate background was the belief, quoted from his beloved John Ruskin, that "a good teacher must exaggerate." Beard sought to compel his audience to question all accepted truths from new perspectives. In 1916 he informed his Columbia colleague Raymond Moley that "the thing to do is lay a mine, store it with nitro, and then let it off in such a fashion that it rips the bowels out of something important, making it impossible for the fools to travel that way anymore." Admittedly, such an accomplishment required some exaggeration of facts. Beard's open acknowledgment of this would later give his enemies a powerful weapon.[5]

Of the five men who are the subjects of this work, Beard took his didactic role the most seriously. He was an enormously popular teacher at Columbia and was also the director of training for the New York Bureau of Municipal Research. One of the principal founders of the labor college Ruskin Hall in England, he served U.S. adult education through his connections with the New School for Social Research, the Rand School of Social Science, and the Workers' Educational Bureau. His textbooks of American government and history were the most widely used in colleges and universities, and he and Mary wrote a series of popular history texts for secondary schools. Beard also addressed public school teachers on numerous occasions and consistently insisted on the centrality of their profession in creating a better society. Yet, in 1917, during World War I, he became convinced that university regulations and the shrinking parameters of objectivist social science conflicted with his purposive and activist conception of the role of the scholar. He resigned from Columbia, never to return to regular academic teaching. From that time forward, Beard would direct his stinging criticism of objectivist social science from outside its strongholds in the universities, foundations, and government agencies, and he would do so on the basis of the need for a truly purposive approach. This combination of independence and professional prestige provided him with a superb platform from which to launch his vocal and thoroughgoing critique of mainstream social science.

Very much like Lynd, Beard acquired many of the beliefs and values he incorporated into his scholarship from his Indiana childhood and his father. Beard's father had honored his own Quaker father's opposition to slavery by moving from North Carolina during the Civil War and serving in the Union Army. Later, he became a prosperous farmer, contractor, real estate speculator, and, in Charles's words, "about as solid a citizen as Indiana ever produced." Yet he remained fiercely independent, championing Robert Ingersoll's intellectual brand of agnosticism while sending his two sons to a nearby Quaker academy. Beard said that the Quaker-run Spiceland Academy first opened his eyes to the injustices of the world and inculcated his commitment to change. Despite his own later lack of specific religious membership, he associated personally to a remarkable degree with Quakers, looked them up in his travels, and lapsed into Quaker phrases in private.[6]

Beard combined these ethical concerns with two of his father's other characteristics, a recognition of the importance of economics and a confident individualism. Despite the innumerable accounts of Beard's supposed sneering references to individuals acting on the basis of their economic interests, his hard-headed realism simply assumed that any intelligent individual would consider economic factors in his or her decisions. Certainly Beard himself did. He was able to walk away from Columbia because he made money from his books, especially his textbooks. Moreover, during the early 1930s he bought and ran a large dairy farm in Connecticut and made a profit on it every year. Beard noted this significant difference between himself and other reformers and attributed it to his eager attendance at his father's and fellow Republican leaders' informal political caucuses. His father's name, as he often noted with arched eyebrows, was William Henry Harrison Beard.[7]

Moreover, Beard, like his father and grandfather before him, was willing to take an independent stand against the majority. He said that both men had belonged to one-man churches and that he followed in their tradition. This was true even in his youth. When Beard was sixteen, he and his older brother wrote and printed a broadside critical of the faculty and administration of the University of Indiana. Not only was brother Clarence expelled from the university, but Charles was thrown out of Spiceland as well. Such actions could hardly have pleased their politically conservative father, but within a year he had bought them a country weekly newspaper to run. Charles learned that independence had its price but often its rewards as well.[8]

Beard, again like Lynd, sincerely admired rural and small-town America and its traditions. Critics noting Beard's thesis of worldwide industrial and technological development have assumed his scorn for agricultural society. On the contrary, he praised its communal spirit of thoughtfulness and mutual aid, specifically rejecting Turner's individualistic interpretation of the frontier. Beard's retreat to a dairy farm was not accidental; according to his grandson, he believed that "somebody cut off from the soil was no longer safe and secure." Beard throughout his career was positive and even nostalgic about his rural heritage, and after her husband's death Mary raged about posthumous characterizations that emphasized his family's wealth and supposed business orientation.[9]

After several years as a small-town editor, Beard's love of public speaking led him to consider a ministerial career. Through the encouragement of a local Methodist minister, he entered DePauw University, an academically and socially prestigious church-supported school in nearby Greencastle. At DePauw, Beard continued his interests in such social activities of the church as the YMCA and the temperance movement but concentrated on his studies, especially history and political science. One of his main professors, trained at Johns Hopkins, emphasized original documents research; another, a former diplomat, combined correct political views with extensive reading in classical political and social thought and sympathetic treatments of Marx and the reform Darwinists. From these and previous experiences Beard developed a new ideal career for himself: activist scholar. As he proclaimed in a college newspaper editorial, "The true scholar does not seek truth for truth's sake, but that he may pour it out into life's great current to uplift and inspire a burden stricken humanity."[10]

In his graduate career Beard continued to follow his independent course by rejecting the career paths of most of his contemporaries who enrolled in the new graduate programs at places like Johns Hopkins, Columbia, and the University of Chicago. Instead, supported by his father, Beard studied at Oxford. Although some critics have interpreted this as reflecting Beard's belief in the Teutonic origins of democracy, his son-in-law, Alfred Vagts, asserted that Beard told him that he went to England to study its changing political structure and ideology for its applicability to the American situation. That is, Beard's goals for his graduate education followed his long-term ambition of combining activism and scholarship.[11]

Although Beard did succeed in doing the original research for his eventual Columbia dissertation, "Office of the Justice of Peace in England," during these years, his major interests were Ruskin Hall, the Labour party, and English social reform in general. On the very day he arrived at Oxford, Beard met the wandering American social reformer Walter Vrooman, whose belief in his own importance was matched only by the size of his wife's fortune. Vrooman had a vague plan for a working-class college that would train new leaders loyal to their class and its interests. While Vrooman supplied the enthusiasm, rhetoric, and seed money, Beard used his own quieter powers of persuasion to win the support of the local trade union councils and several Oxford dons. Although Vrooman's simplistic vision of the college consisted of creating political agitators and opposing "brain-cramming," Beard developed an educational philosophy based on John Ruskin's call in *Unto This Last* for the creation of intellectually wealthy individuals that he retained throughout his life. Ruskin stated, "There is no wealth but life. . . . That country is richest which nourishes the greatest number of noble and happy human beings." In the college publication *Young Oxford*, Beard stated that "mere acquisition of knowledge [was] worthless" by itself and achieved significance only "in relation to human needs."[12]

Unlike Vrooman, who soon moved on, Beard remained active at Ruskin Hall. He helped establish the rules, arranged the first series of public lectures, gave the first official course, and traveled throughout the area lecturing on the ethical bankruptcy of the industrial revolution and its product, capitalism, but also noting the potential of industrialism to liberate humankind industrially and intellectually. The key figures along this path to the good society would be scholars (like Beard) who would "analyze present conditions and state clearly the industrial problem, regardless of class privileges [and] vested interests . . . to show us 'what ought to be' and how we can build on 'what is' to attain it." As at DePauw and throughout his career, Beard envisioned the social scientist–historian as *the* central figure not only in executing but also in determining policy.[13]

In 1902 Beard found himself faced with another career choice similar to his earlier turns from journalism and the ministry. On the one hand, if he was ever to secure a university teaching position, he must return to the United States and obtain an appropriate degree. On the other hand, he was liked and respected by the Labour party, and he had become one of its leading advisers on educational policy and was expected to be named a member of its shadow cabinet. In 1900 he had married his college sweetheart, Mary Ritter, with whom he would have a long and fruitful personal and intellectual partnership. Although she shared her husband's economic and political interests and became active in English labor and feminist circles, the birth of their first child combined with Beard's father's decreasing financial support complicated matters. Probably the key factor in his return, and an ironic case of historical foreshadowing, was Beard's conviction that the "respectable" faculty at Ruskin Hall had become focused on administrative and "official" matters and were bent on eliminating him and his idealistic vision from the college.[14]

Beard's study at Oxford made his choice of Columbia's School of Political Science a natural one. At Oxford, Beard had studied under Frederick York Powell, the eccentric Regius Professor of History who noted Americans as first among his many active dislikes but adored Beard, "the nicest American I have ever met." Powell had studied under Bishop Stubbs and had been a friend of E. A. Freeman, two of the intellectual idols of Columbia's John Burgess, dean and founder of the School of Political Science. Burgess had adopted an extreme version of their Anglo-Saxon–Teutonic theory of racialism, which portrayed all positive governmental and social institutions as arising from the innate genius of the Germanic people. Although Powell himself focused more on social and economic topics, and Beard later claimed to have always opposed the Teutonic theory as, "one of the weirdest delusions . . . of American intellectual life," Beard's training in medieval original sources fit the Burgess model well. Certainly Burgess saw Beard as a fellow believer. During Beard's first year, Burgess helped him to rewrite a prizewinning master's essay, and after his completion of the doctorate a year later he appointed Beard a lecturer.[15]

More important to Beard's success at Columbia—and more problematic for his later career—was Powell's and Columbia's shared emphasis on the empirical study of society using the methods of the physical sciences. Powell argued strongly that "History is an absolute science, as much as, for example, Botany," and that historians should never "pass judgments" or engage in "special pleading." Powell saw this, and not the theory of racialism, as Stubbs's and Freeman's greatest contribution to scholarship. Although Burgess's praise of empiricism and the scientific method was mere lip service, Columbia professors Herbert Levi Osgood in colonial history, Frank Goodnow in public law and municipal government, William Dunning in American history and political thought, and E. R. A. Seligman in political economy were deeply involved in attempting to create a truly scientific and empirical study of society. Indeed, Charles Merriam had used his training under these very same individuals a few years earlier as the basis for his objectivist model of social science.[16]

Certainly Beard in his first years at Columbia appeared to subscribe to Powell's empiricism. In a 1907 address "Politics" for a prestigious lecture series, he dismissed previous definitions of politics as utopian and meaningless. Politics was always changing due to environmental pressures, and one could say only what politics is, never what it should be. Beard contended that it was necessary to downgrade theories and legislative rules and to study specific historical experiences and facts. For example, one should study how Joe Cannon had used the speakership of the House of Representatives, not how the office was supposed to work under ideal circumstances. "It is not the function of the student of politics to praise or condemn institutions or theories, but understand and expound them; and thus for scientific purposes it is separated from theology, ethics, and patriotism."[17]

Beard's historical training under Powell and his Columbia teachers emphasized the profession's current concern for empiricism and fear of ethical generalizations. To be scientific meant to avoid generalization, interpretation, and grand theories, to concentrate only on the relation of facts to one another. This represented the model of German historian Leopold von Ranke, who spoke of writing "*Geschichte wie es eigentlich gewesen* [history as it actually was]. Although von Ranke was actually a romantic idealist who sought comprehension of the ideal and universal through facts, most historians overlooked this aspect, instead emphasizing his concern for documents and their authenticity. European historiography came to see historical truth as residing completely in the collection and "scientific" analysis of documents. The French historians Charles Langlois and Charles Seignobos asserted that once all documents had been discovered and analyzed, then "the work of critical scholarship will be finished."[18]

The first generation of professional American historians matched their European counterparts in their adulation of documents. The AHA was the first social science organization to break away from the American Social Science Association, and it did so because of the ASSA's conscious moralism. From its inception the American Historical Association championed "scientific history," the collection of all the facts and their listing in chronological order. At the second annual meeting the AHA elected von Ranke as the association's first and only honorary member. Scientific analogies and metaphors were repeated like mantras, with history seminars becoming "laboratories" and books and documents "literary, political, and historical apparatus." The historian Herbert Baxter Adams sought to portray American history as "an organism of historic growth, developing from minute germs . . . the very protoplasm of state life." J. Franklin Jameson, editor of the *American Historical Review* and self-appointed conscience of the AHA, called for historians to concentrate on "improvement in technical process" and consequent acceptance of unimaginative, admittedly "second-class work," which would provide the empirical basis for the important work to follow. American historians saw science as rigidly inductive and assumed that the truth would emerge once enough facts had been collected.[19]

Although at this stage in his career Beard did seem to concur in this faith in empiricism, he never agreed to its corollary of a value-free, "useless history." Even as he proclaimed the gospel of ethical neutrality in his lecture "Politics," he asserted his conviction that the future would "not be hideous . . . but beautiful and magnificent" because of the work of scholars like those in his audience. Two years later, he insisted that one could be detached and still serve "the practical interests of humanity." Beard could not conceive of the bifurcation of scholarship and action. Indeed, positive social change was the sine qua non for the existence of Beard's work: "A word, an article, a pamphlet, a speech or a book may set in motion forces of incalculable moment."[20]

As Beard began to do more and more original research in history during the 1910s, he also began to recognize the conservative implications of the approved purely empirical approach. Historians had traditionally come from aristocratic and conservative backgrounds; those who did not, Woodrow Wilson and Albion Small, for example, usually transferred to other academic disciplines. While calling themselves politically neutral, American historians attacked immigrants and urban politics and championed white supremacy. Osgood, Andrews, and other members of the "imperial school" of colonial historians were so conservative that they criticized even the American Revolution. Throughout his career Beard remained uncomfortable in the AHA, which he once accused of being "as regular as Louis XVI's court scribes."[21]

His critics' attempts to separate Beard's career into periods of complete attachment to scientific objectivism and purposive activism is misguided. Beard, unlike some true historical relativists, never denied the utility and even the necessity of the scientific method. On the other hand, he also never abdicated his original activist goals, and these would become even stronger in response to greater social needs during the Great Depression. For example, during the same year that he delivered "Politics," he and a coauthor cheerily admitted "consistently subordinating the past to the present . . . to enable the reader to catch up with his own times." He made the point even clearer in an address a year later to high school teachers in which he pleaded with them to design their courses to deal with current events. Failure to do this made history "sterile" and useless.[22]

Beard owed his recognition of the limitations of scientific history primarily to his two daily luncheon companions, the historian James Harvey Robinson and John Dewey. Robinson began teaching his famous graduate course "Intellectual Development of Modern Europe" in 1900, and Beard was one of his first students. The two later coauthored several books, and the Robinson connection would have considerable intellectual consequences for Beard's consequent criticism of conventional history. B. T. Wilkins put it quite well: "Never has there been in the history of American scholarship a historian more critical of historians." While Beard's "Politics" advocated pure empiricism for the study of politics, Robinson's address on history in the same series denied the possibility of a true science of history because of the complexity of the data and the inability to establish a true experimental situation. In a classic series of essays published four years later, Robinson noted the failure of scientific history and called for a "New History," which would consciously subordinate the past to the present by emphasizing material relevant to contemporary issues, examine social and intellectual as well as political topics, and integrate the insights and methods of the other social sciences into the study of history. Robinson's view of history was clearly activist: "The present has hitherto been the willing victim of the past," but the past possesses "overwhelming value" and should be "wrest[ed] from the hands of the conservatives . . . and exploit[ed] in the interests of advance." What, he asked sourly, was objective history except history without an object?[23]

Like the other social scientists of his day, especially those committed to an activist role for their disciplines, Beard saw Dewey's thought as the key. Although Beard lacked philosophical sophistication, he insisted that Dewey and James were "the two outstanding thinkers of the generation," and he respected instrumentalism for its championing of openness and freedom of inquiry. The social determinants of knowledge destroyed the concept of universal truth and allowed thinkers to create solutions adapted to changing circumstances. To Beard, Dewey and his fellow pragmatists avoided the classic philosophical error of separating thought from action and making theoretical thinking an end in itself. Moreover, Beard came to share Dewey's ambivalent views on science. Although science was the best method for solving problems in an unbiased way, the scientific method could not determine the moral and aesthetic values necessary for the creation of the good society. Throughout the 1920s and 1930s the two men grappled independently with the problem of determining values and devising ways of justifying these values in a democracy. Beard, despite his constant references to Dewey's work, clearly did not understand the intricacies of Dewey's logic, and this confusion led to fatal inadequacies in Beard's later attempts at a theory of valuation.[24]

Beard's Oxford training in the origins of political institutions had led him to emphasize the history of American political institutions and behavior in his American government class and the accompanying text. In 1912, as he began work on *Contemporary American History*, a companion to his and Robinson's earlier *Development of Modern Europe*, he perceived such contemporary issues as the tariff, free silver, Granger laws, and the income tax as rooted in economic conflicts. But if contemporary issues and institutions had their origins in economic conflicts, wasn't that true also of historical institutions? If one could not understand the Supreme Court's repeal of the income tax without understanding the historical roots of judicial review, then one also needed to understand the economic origins of other such cherished American institutions.

Historical issues like these gained additional importance in light of Beard's conversion to the New History. Beard admitted the "impressionistic" nature of *Contemporary American History* and his primary goal of helping the average citizen understand the present better. As for the belief that one could not truly know recent history, that was a "pernicious" error. He admitted to his chief researcher, Lewis Mayers, that such an attitude "may not be scholarly. Scholarship as such has no interest for me. The important thing is that college students should not go out without some understanding of the new economic forces which are transforming the very world under our eyes and rendering obsolete old moralities and 'principles.' " Beard put aside *Contemporary American History* to write about his new insights in three revolutionary and extremely influential books: *The Supreme Court and the Constitution* (1912), *An Economic Interpretation of the Constitution of the United States* (1914), and *Economic Origins of Jeffersonian Democracy* (1915).[25]

The Supreme Court and the Constitution addresses the specific question of the Founding Fathers' intentions concerning judicial review. Judicial review was an important political issue at the time because the conservative-controlled Supreme Court was using a questionable interpretation of the due process clause of the Fourteenth Amendment to overturn progressive state and federal laws. Several reformers—including ex-president and current presidential candidate Theodore Roosevelt—argued that judicial review was not mentioned in the Constitution, was, in fact, "rank usurpation" by the judicial branch, and Congress should officially abolish it. The situation was an open invitation to Beard's purposive conception of history. Beard examined records of the national and state constitutional conventions and found little historical evidence to justify the reformers' position. Whenever the issue of judicial review had come up during those meetings, it was almost invariably met with silence. Some reformers contended that the majority's silence signified disapproval, but Beard found that argument highly questionable. He noted that one might very well assert the harmful and undemocratic nature of judicial review and call for its abolition, but that did not alter the Founding Fathers' original acceptance of it.[26]

While many conservatives nodded sagely at Beard's conclusions, they overlooked an aside that was probably the key point of the book: "It is an ancient and honorable rule of construction, laid down by Blackstone, that any instrument should be interpreted 'by considering the reason and spirit of it; or the cause which moved the legislator to enact it.' . . . The underlying purpose of the Constitution, therefore, is to be revealed only by a study of the conditions and events which led to its formation and adoption." Beard's research into the state and national constitutional conventions and his examination of recently discovered documents in the Treasury Department coupled with his Hamiltonian perspective and study of recent American history convinced him that the Constitution reflects specific economic interests, including those of its framers. He began *An Economic Interpretation of the Constitution* by arbitrarily separating economic interests into real property, or land, and personal property, consisting of money, public securities, manufacturing, shipping, and western land speculation. The Articles of Confederation adversely affected personal property owners, a group later disproportionately represented among the supporters and framers of the Constitution. Beard somewhat disingenuously made the disclaimer that his goal was "not, of course, to show that the Constitution was made for the personal benefit of the members of the Convention." Rather the question was, according to Beard, whether the framers represented certain economic interests and, like Madison, consciously recognized this fact.[27]

Economic Interpretation was assuredly not the first book to note the economic conflicts behind the ratification of the Constitution. Several popular conservative historians, including John Fiske and J. B. McMasters, had interpreted it in a similar way in their standard texts, and socialists Algie Simons and Gustavus Myers had point-blank accused the Founding Fathers of acting out of simple greed. J. Allen Smith, in his popular *The Spirit of American Government* (1907), entitled his chapter on the writing of the Constitution "The Constitution as a Reactionary Document." Beard himself cited Frederick Jackson Turner and Columbia's own Seligman as forerunners in the economic interpretation of politics. Several years later, Beard gave a series of lectures tracing the idea of the economic basis of politics through such political theorists as Aristotle, John Locke, Madison, and Daniel Webster. As for individuals acting to further their economic interests, Beard, his father's son, saw no necessary shame in that.[28]

Beard's work had a far greater impact than the earlier interpretations had had because he directly challenged the traditional myth of the Constitution as "founded on broad general principles of liberty and government entertained . . . by the whole people and having no reference to the interest or advantage of any particular group or class." Conservatives had portrayed the Constitution "as a type of holy book conceived by virgin birth" which the courts could interpret in only one way. Beard successfully challenged this perspective by pointing out the Constitution's origins in specific historical events and economic interests. In doing so he produced perhaps the key historical work of the sociological jurisprudence movement. Moreover, his detailed facts, dispassionate tone, and reputation as a hardheaded empiricist made his work far more difficult to refute than that of Simons or Myers. This was especially true since many of his would-be critics had lauded *The Supreme Court and the Constitution* only a year earlier for exactly the same reasons.[29]

The conservatives' heated response when the book was published demonstrated Beard's success. President William Howard Taft fulminated against the book and called Beard a "fool." Senator and future president Warren G. Harding's newspaper, the *Marion Gazette*, called *Economic Interpretation* "libelous, vicious, and damnable in its influence" and Beard the nation's "Chief Hyena." The New York Bar Association appointed a special committee to investigate the book and peremptorily summoned Beard to appear. The private response was even more telling. Taft supposedly admitted to a friend that "the facts seem right enough, but why did the damn fool have to print it?"[30]

This was exactly the point, and Beard's consistent activism provides an answer to this question. When he heard of Taft's public response, he noted sarcastically to Mayers that "Taft has read my book on the Constitution and said it deeply wounded his patriotic sensibilities. Too bad."

He admitted to a positive reviewer that he had overemphasized certain points of the book to get attention and generate public debate. He saw the conventional interpretation of the Constitution as a major obstacle to the creation of the good society and stated, "I believe (from the numerous reviews I already have) that I have hit the tradition a body blow with the truth for a sword."[31]

Although Beard blandly informed the infuriated New York Bar Association that they had no authority over nonlawyers and refused to attend their star chamber proceedings, he could not dismiss another powerful institution quite as easily. Columbia's president, Nicholas Butler, and its conservative board of regents were among those incensed at *Economic Interpretation.* They became angrier still when he continued his thesis in *Economic Origins of Jeffersonian Democracy.* During World War I, their anger and Beard's insistence on the absolute independence of scholarship clashed in one of the most celebrated academic freedom cases in American history, a case that would permanently affect Beard's career and views of social science.

From the time he chose scholarship as a career, Beard had demonstrated a deep commitment to academic freedom. If social scientists were to fulfill their potential and create a truly good society, the university would have to become a bastion of freedom of inquiry and tolerance. "At bottom and forever the question of academic freedom is the question of intellectual and spiritual leadership in American democracy. Those who lead and teach, are they free, fearless, and worthy of trust?" One can perhaps judge the depth of Beard's emotions by examining the contents of the Beard Manuscript Collection. Late in his life, Beard asked his wife to burn his papers after his death. Mary, who, ironically, had spent many years gathering manuscript collections for a proposed women's studies archive, complied—with two exceptions. The two sections of his papers that remain, almost certainly at his own request, are material on his Indiana childhood and files on academic freedom cases, including his own.[32]

World War I represented one of the low points for academic freedom in the United States. The war was unpopular, especially among intellectuals, although established institutions such as universities and professional associations tended to support it blindly and sometimes even hysterically. A historian of the subject documented twenty-four academic dismissals at major universities alone on the basis of opposition to the war. Beard's anger and eventual resignation came about only partly because of war hysteria, though. He was actually an eager and vocal supporter of America's entry into the war. He attacked the Central Powers so strongly in a speech at City College in 1914 that the college forbade him to speak on the subject again. He also gave many prowar speeches throughout the West and Midwest. Once the war began, he contributed an anonymous article on atrocities to the *War Cyclopedia* of the Committee on Public Information in which he recited the standard Allied propaganda of Hun barbarisms. He noted that he had "never belonged to Mr. Wilson's sweet morality band" and had voted for Hughes over Wilson in 1916 because of the latter's reluctance to enter the war. In his resignation notice, he even accused Columbia of blocking his prowar activities.[33]

Beard's resignation stemmed from a series of events that occurred both before and after the war and through which he became convinced that Columbia and probably American universities in general would not protect academic freedom and were becoming increasingly dominated by the wealthy interests who controlled their boards of trustees. In April 1916 the *New York World* misquoted Beard on his response to an antiwar speaker's cry of "To hell with the flag!" Beard was able to correct the error, get an official apology from the *World*, and apparently straighten out the matter personally with President Butler. When he called on trustee William Parsons, chairman of the Committee on Education, Parsons accepted his explanation but asked him to attend a "friendly conference" to protect the university's name. Once he had explained his position at that meeting, several trustees harangued him for his "disrespectful" scholarship and ordered him to tell members of his department to avoid such teaching and research. Neither Butler nor the two faculty representatives at this meeting, Seligman and Graduate Dean Frederick Woodbridge, supported Beard or mentioned academic freedom.[34]

An incensed Beard aroused the faculty and tried to establish a committee to oppose such inquisitions. The trustees responded by appointing their own advisory committee of five deans and four trustee-appointed faculty members. A year later, the board went against the recommendation of their own committee and decided not to reappoint Leon Fraser, a pacifist lecturer in Beard's Department of Political Science. Ironically, the previously pacifistic Butler had hired Fraser, his protégé, over Chairman Beard's objections several years before and then abandoned him when Fraser refused to surrender his convictions. The trustees also fired Assistant Professor of English H. L. Dana for his antiwar activities and psychologist James McKeen Cattell for his opposition to their governance. Beard, who had a universitywide reputation for supporting his

fellow faculty members—to the extent of teaching the classes of a habitual drunkard whom he detested—could not accept this. According to
Mary, his frustrations suddenly "surged into speech," and he determined
to resign.[35]

In retrospect, the war hysteria played a rather insignificant role in
Beard's decision. He found fault with the way universities were run during both peace and war. Twenty years later, he spoke of awakening to
his "abysmal ignorance" of Columbia's suppression of men and ideas.
Adapting the ideas and title of Veblen's *Higher Learning in America: A
Memorandum on the Conduct of Universities by Business Men,* Beard
began consistently to refer to universities as "Hire Learning," institutions where professors "became a kind of hired man to be fired without
notice by his employers—the president and trustees—if he said anything
extraordinary, either wise or foolish." Beard's public letter of resignation
emphasized exactly this point. In it, he stated that Columbia was under
the control of a few trustees "who have no standing in the world of education, who are reactionary and visionless in politics, narrow and medieval
in religion," and had dropped the status of professors "lower than that of
the manual laborer who, through his union, has at least some voice in the
terms and conditions of his employment." Beard simply could not accept
a situation in which a president could publicly proclaim that "a university teacher owes a decent respect to the opinions of mankind" and "common loyalty . . . to the institution which maintains him." When the
nationally prominent Cattell criticized trustee policies and called for his
colleagues to be "gentlemen" rather than subservient "clerks" and oppose them, he was fired. How could scholars engage in critical scholarship and be "free, fearless, and worthy of trust" under such conditions?
The situation threatened not only Beard's conception of himself as a
social scientist, intellectual, and policymaker but also as a man. In one of
his last Columbia lectures, Beard proclaimed that "as long as there is
corn in Indiana and hogs to eat the corn, Charlie Beard will bow to no
man." In a letter to economist Henry Mussey, who followed him out of
Columbia, he declared, "If we are wrong, then it matters little anyway,
for you and I are not interested in keeping a nicely feathered cot in a doll's
house." Beard proposed to do "emancipated thinking"; the universities
were no longer the place for that.[36]

Beard did not abandon the ideal of academic freedom and his hopes for
the universities. He recognized that his personal liberation depended on
the financial success of his textbooks and a significant inheritance. Intellectual progress depended on freeing scholars from interference by

trustees and special interest groups. During the 1920s and 1930s Beard played an active role in academic freedom fights at the universities of Wisconsin and Minnesota, Yale Divinity School, and numerous other institutions and incurred the enmity of the Hearst newspaper chain when he attacked William Randolph Hearst for trying to impose his prejudices on American education.

Personally, Beard never regretted his decision to leave academia. Indeed, he increasingly came to see control by businessmen trustees as only part of the problem. The deeper issue was faculty and students who willingly accepted this control. In a 1928 lecture Beard listed the problems of the university: "too many charming friends who must not be offended; too many temporal negotiations that call for discrete management; . . . too many promotions requiring emphasis on the amenities of life rather than on its thinking process; . . . too much calm, not enough passion; too many sacred traditions that must be preserved; . . . too many students, not enough seekers." In short, the university, and implicitly his colleagues in political science and history, had become too safe, too conservative, and too dependent on the status quo. When Alfred Jay Nock, editor of the free-thinking *Freeman*, wrote an editorial praising Beard for resigning and advocating a return to student- and faculty-controlled medieval universities, Beard replied with a mildly critical letter. Nock's vision, he said, was inspiring but impractical. Certainly most of the Columbia faculty had not supported either Cattell or himself in their fight for faculty control. Still, the ever-optimistic Beard ended on a positive note: "For the true teacher, the restless searcher-out of all things, there is a greater forum than the narrow schoolroom with its handful of students. If he has anything to say, he can clothe it in type, release it in a lightning's flash, and send it to all climes and all ages. . . . Has not the printing press made the university obsolete?" In leaving university teaching, Beard assumed his true role as educator to the masses.[37]

Actually, Beard's departure from academic life was not as clear-cut as it first appeared. Almost immediately after his resignation from Columbia, the New York Bureau of Municipal Research appointed him its director. Beard had been an adviser to the bureau since its inception in 1907, and since 1912 he had served as one of the three directors of its new Training School for Public Service. For years Seligman had publicly worried that the bureau would entice Beard away from Columbia by offering a full-time job and a reasonable salary. Revealingly, Beard never denied this.[38]

The lure of public administration and municipal research for Beard derived from its apparent ability, unlike the fields of history and political science, to combine the elements of social reform and empirical research. He sincerely believed that contemporary practitioners of public administration were inept and that "a great society that cannot administer cannot endure." In typical hyperbole Beard proclaimed in his revised *American Government* textbook (1924) that administration had become the "heart" of government and "the destiny of the state." Even after later experiences convinced him that empiricism and reform were not necessarily connected, he continued to insist that "no subject [was] more important . . . [for] the future of civilized government and, I think, of civilization itself."[39]

Beard's belief in the efficacy of a strictly empirical approach to problems of public administration originally came out of his study with Frank Goodnow. Like Merriam, Beard had rebelled against Goodnow's legalistic approach to the subject and had helped redirect the field to the study of social and political processes. Again like Merriam, Beard remained complimentary of Goodnow as the founder of the systematic study of American public administration and early in his career accepted Goodnow's classic distinction between administration and politics. For example, in 1915 Beard said that "the function of politics is to determine what should be done," while "the function of the trained expert [is] to carry out the public will with all the instruments and methods which modern science . . . can command." One could achieve this through "facts, facts, and more facts verified and tested." As late as 1925, Beard returned from studying Tokyo's administrative problems convinced of the value of science as the "best hope for mankind struggling to conquer itself and the world."[40]

Beard's connection with the New York Bureau of Municipal Research demonstrated that it was possible to weave activism and research into a seamless whole. While many of the early municipal research institutes succumbed to the pressures of their financial supporters within the business community and came to concentrate solely on such business-oriented measures as eliminating graft, establishing "good government," and lowering taxes, the New York bureau aggressively fought that viewpoint. Founded in 1907 by the so-called ABC Triumvirate of Philadelphia social worker William Allen, socialist lawyer Henry Bruere, and municipal accounting specialist Frederick Cleveland, the bureau reflected not only Cleveland's fiscally oriented examination of municipal institutions but also Allen's social work approach. As early as 1908 Allen identified the bureau's goal as "not to stop graft, not to head off the politician, and not to get good men into office, but rather to keep the public informed of what public officials are doing." Its overall aim was social, not fiscal, efficiency. The bureau defined social efficiency in terms of providing the most benefits to the most individuals and called for the establishment of such social welfare programs as free medical examinations in the schools and a bureau of child hygiene.[41]

As Bruere gradually withdrew from daily participation in the bureau, Beard increasingly became the B of the triumvirate and mediator of the increasingly heated debates between Cleveland and Allen. Beard and Cleveland respected one another and worked well together, and Beard strongly supported Cleveland's plan for a nonscholarly training school. The two coauthored the bureau-sponsored *Government of the State of New York*, which advocated, in the tradition of Goodnow and objectivist administration, a strong executive branch and the separation of state government into political and administrative functions. Nevertheless, in final decisions Beard always took Allen's side. Luther Gulick, Beard's student and later an ally of Merriam who succeeded his teacher first as director of the training school and finally as head of the bureau, stated that all of Beard's written and practical work in public administration reflected, "the dreams of the crusader and the passion of the reformer."[42]

If Beard hoped that he had left behind the interference of powerful economic interests across town at Columbia, he was soon disappointed. The bureau's major project during Beard's tenure as director was a study of New York's municipal transit system. Beard authored the final report, which criticized the private traction companies for their huge profits and lack of service and suggested municipal ownership. The traction interests, supported from within by some of the bureau's board of trustees, counterattacked by calling the report biased and socialistic. After a long and bitter dispute, the board, under the leadership of its chairman, praised the empirical character of the report and officially accepted it.[43]

This experience drove home two lessons for Beard. First, it strengthened his predisposition to base his hypotheses on as much factual material as could be gathered. Even when Beard adopted a so-called relativistic theory of history, his work was always empirical, sometimes, as in *The Idea of a National Interest*, excessively so. Second, the closeness of the decision and the decreased private funding that resulted, especially from the bureau's chief contributor, the Carnegie Foundation, demonstrated the limitations of activist scholarship in this setting as well. Out of devotion to the bureau and its staff, Beard resigned in 1921. He still loved the work but recognized that he lacked the required skills at fund-raising. On

Beard's recommendation the board chose the more objectivist Gulick as his successor. Revealingly, under Gulick the board changed its name to the more professional and prestigious-sounding National Institute of Public Administration and appointed a figurehead board of directors that included Robert Brookings, Newton Baker, Herbert Hoover, and the omnipresent Merriam to attract funds. Although Beard never publicly voiced his anger, as he had at Columbia, the entire episode could have only increased his bitterness at the power of vested interests over scholarship and the researchers and academics who accepted the situation.[44]

Once again Beard's retreat on one front masked a rapid advance on another. Almost simultaneously with Beard's resignation from the bureau, Shimpei Goto, veteran Japanese statesman and new mayor of Tokyo, invited his friend Beard to Japan to help organize a full-scale study to generate a long-term plan for Tokyo. Beard jumped at the opportunity to do truly activist research. Revealingly, he refused to accept any payment, even for travel expenses. His experiences of the past several years had convinced him that accepting funds would give others control over his work. He wished to be absolutely free to make any recommendations for Tokyo he thought necessary.

The Administration and Politics of Tokyo, the results of Beard's year-long research, was by far Beard's most important work in the field of public administration, and it reflects Beard's independence and willingness to go beyond technical problems. Beginning with the survey approach, *Tokyo,* like most of Beard's work in the field, revels in such technical details as soil samples, building regulations, and traction routes. Moreover, Beard was extremely complimentary of Japanese expertise and dedication. Throughout, he fought against any image of himself as the all-knowing foreigner riding in to solve all the problems of the ignorant natives. Despite an occasional ethnocentric slip, such as recommending sidewalks and baby carriages "to relieve mothers' backs," and suggesting large-scale buying without recognizing Tokyo's shortage of space, Beard succeeded at surveying the overall situation while at the same time deferring to local administrators' greater knowledge of specific situations. Beard concluded that increased public education, interdisciplinary expert teams, centralization of government authority and responsibility, and, above all, planning would do much to meet Tokyo's needs.[45]

Beard recognized that these recommendations were fundamentally political rather than technical issues. Moreover, he noted very early in *Tokyo* that the problems there did not signify lack of knowledge or appropriate techniques. Beard used his mandate to speak "freely and without reserve" to place the blame squarely on the imperial government and local large landowners who controlled the government for their own economic and political ends. Beard disdainfully pointed out Tokyo's "disintegration of functions and dismemberment of administrative organs" and cited numerous patent absurdities such as huge areas of the city remaining exempt from taxation and private gas companies tearing up public streets without municipal control or regulation.[46]

In *Tokyo* Beard adopted his long-advocated interdisciplinary, systemic perspective. This approach made it evident that public administration questions were not merely technical; they reflected ongoing political, historical, cultural, and economic issues. Beard had previously noted the need to integrate economic analysis into the study of history; now he viewed it as but one of many different facets. One point became especially clear: it was impossible to separate politics and administration into Goodnow's separate, impermeable spheres.

Despite Beard's potent faith in public education's ability to transform the situation, *Tokyo* remains a pessimistic book. Huge obstacles lay between accumulating the necessary knowledge and successfully resolving the city's problems. Yet the editor's enthusiastic preface contradicted Beard's discouraged tone. As the book was being set in type, a terrible earthquake leveled two-thirds of the city. The editor explained breathlessly that Beard could not write the preface himself since "the first official news dispatched from Japan with regard to the disaster" was Goto's summons for Beard. He went on to assure the readers that the disaster had "clear[ed] the field of old . . . and entrenched prejudices" and permitted the construction of a new city designed by enlightened statesmen like Goto and Beard.[47]

Originally, Beard shared much of this enthusiasm. His original reply to Goto's request for advice was, "Lay out new streets, forbid building within city lines, unify railroad stations." Once he arrived in Japan, however, his observations coupled with his knowledge of history and past personal experiences lowered his expectations. Speaking to an appreciative audience shortly after his arrival, he half humorously remarked: "If the Imperial authorities rise to the great opportunities now presented to them, the whole world will applaud and take heart. If the Imperial authorities in this crisis fail to rise to great heights the world will say, 'Well, the Japanese are very much like other people.'" Six months later, he would explain Tokyo's return to the old patterns to an American audience by noting that the city had been "only superficially cleared"; it retained its old economic, political, and cultural structure. Beard's immersion in the practical obstacles of the world increasingly led him to characterize the objectivist faith in the absolute autonomy of facts as shortsighted and naive. These experiences and a later, even more pessimistic study of public administration in Yugoslavia, a state torn apart by ethnic factions, significantly influenced not only his work in public administration but in history, government, and foreign policy as well.[48]

Beard's response to his international experience was to join fellow pioneers Ordway Tead and Marshall Dimock in developing an approach to public administration based on a refutation of Goodnow's separation of politics and administration and insisting upon a need for public administration to consider ethical decisions, supposedly the exclusive province of politics. Dwight Waldo, the preeminent historian of public administration, asserted that by the 1930s this purposive group represented a serious challenge to the accepted objectivist paradigm best represented by the Chicago group of Merriam, Brownlow, and Leonard White. As early as 1926, Beard specifically applied his new conclusions to American regional and urban planning, neither of which had achieved very much, despite beautifully conceived, logical plans because of planners' concentration on technical concerns and domination by special interest groups. Many administrators did not even recognize that no plan could ever possibly satisfy every interest. This limited city planning to "mere decorative work, making it easy for business men to drive rapidly from their offices to their country clubs."[49]

Beard perceived the nearsighted concentration on technical problems as symptomatic of a deeper problem which affected not only students of public administration but all social scientists. As he noted in Tokyo, "It is impossible for the coldest 'efficiency expert' in administration to stop with a study of 'what is.' He must inevitably ask 'what ought to be.'" As he stood before the annual conference of the National Government Association in 1926, Beard shared his anguish at the recent direction of American society. It appeared "as if George F. Babbitt were rich, all dressed up . . . and with no place to go—efficient, fed, and poverty stricken." Social scientists had failed in their duty to provide Americans with direction because their ends were "merely material and numerical," and these could never "kindle human work with divine fire." All political and social research must turn to "the higher realm of the spirit—the imagination." More and more, Beard turned away from technical concerns in public administration. Although he never disparaged such work by itself, he insisted that it could not stand alone. As he entitled one of his articles,

"Life Is Not a Table of Logarithms." Administration was "a means, not an end, an instrument for accomplishing great public purposes, not a chart to hang on 'the chief's wall.' " Administrators must start by determining ethical goals and then use their administrative skills to achieve them.[50]

Beard soon extended his critique of the study of public administration to all political institutions and behavior. Beginning with his talk before the National Government Association and his APSA presidential address a month later, Beard delivered a series of lectures designed to force his fellow social scientists to question their basic assumptions about such issues as the conflict between knowledge and opinion. Beard's biographer Ellen Nore openly wondered why Beard, who disliked professional institutions and administrative constraints upon his time, finally acceded to the requests of Raymond Moley and other former students and colleagues to accept the presidency of the APSA. The answer lies in the various special committees, especially those on public policy, that were established during Beard's tenure, and in his presidential address itself. Beard seemed convinced, especially after Merriam's address the year before, that the APSA was emphasizing all the negative aspects of objectivist social science and leading the discipline into an intellectual dead end.[51]

Charles Merriam came to symbolize for Beard the weakness of American social science. Beard and Merriam came from similar backgrounds, had roughly the same graduate education at Columbia, shared many research interests, were committed to political and social reform, and above all believed intensely in human rationality. Indeed, in 1909 Beard departed from the usual acerbic book reviews of his youth and gave Merriam's *Primary Elections* the ultimate accolade of having successfully combined scholarship and activism. By 1920, however, he would criticize Merriam's book on American thought as wasting time on "a great deal of talk"—this from an individual who would soon trace the intellectual bankruptcy of American political science to the neglect of classic political philosophies. Beard's sourness clearly derived from his jealousy and anger at Merriam's successful entrepreneurship. Lack of foundation support had pushed Beard out of his beloved New York Bureau of Municipal Research, and Merriam and his political allies had come in immediately to take control of the executive board. By 1926 Merriam had so much foundation money that he was trying to copy the American model of organized social science in Europe. Beard's correspondence, on the other hand, was filled with unsuccessful requests for funds for his researchers. In 1924 he told Merriam that his proposed research plans "have been filed by gentlemen of means in the waste basket so I am out of the game." He admitted that he was "simply no good at raising money. Contact with people of cash gives me no special respect for them or their talents and nothing that I write or say seems to give them any respect for me. So frankly I am out of the begging game." The tone of Beard's letter indicates his increasing personalization of the issue. Beard found Merriam's objectivism wrong from a philosophical standpoint, and such phrases as "the begging game" seemed to question Merriam's lack of integrity as well. After all, wasn't Merriam good exactly at that? What did that say about him and the value of his research?[52]

If Merriam retained any doubts about Beard's attitude toward him, Beard's presidential address dispelled them. In contrast with Merriam's adulation of past and future empirical research in his speech the previous year, Beard emphasized the effects of time and technology on society. Researchers who failed to recognize these influences and the changing nature of social reality were left behind, conducting "myopic research into the unimportant." Beard asserted that most contemporary political research consisted of exactly such shortsighted work—statistical studies of minute, unimportant topics and narrow specialization. If anyone had somehow missed the inferences of his criticism for objectivist social science and Merriam's address in particular, he made it specific by characterizing such research as "generally praised and patronized."[53]

Although this and Beard's American Historical Association presidential address of 1934 are his best-known critiques of objectivist social science, they are not the only or even the most thorough ones. As Merriam consolidated his hold on organized political science through his control of research funds and the production of new doctorates and became the preferred political scientist representative on federal commissions, it must have infuriated him to see Beard's continued higher esteem among the general public. Through the late 1920s and 1930s Beard was selected to present the position of political science at various distinguished conferences. Beard, in turn, used these platforms to attack Merriam's objectivist paradigm of social science.

He presented probably the most important of these addresses at a symposium honoring the establishment of the Institute for Research in the Social Sciences at the University of Virginia in 1927. He began by denying any intention of criticizing the scientific method itself. It had proven of immense benefit in dealing with "inorganic substances," and the whole goal of a science of society was noble and in many ways appealing. Nevertheless, it was not possible to achieve a science of society similar to that of the physical sciences. Individuals naturally possess prejudices, convictions, and "hunches," which preclude the objectivity demanded by the model of the physical sciences. Indeed, in a theme that would become stronger throughout the 1930s, Beard maintained that a true science of society was undesirable in several ways. First of all, objectivity in political issues was not necessarily good. None of the great political thinkers ever "professed to be a disinterested seeker of truth, without ulterior ends, indifferent to consequences," and many such as Locke, Hobbes, Rousseau, and Jefferson owed their greatness to a courageous grappling with ethical issues. Second, unthinking reliance on the scientific model had led researchers to concentrate on "minutia [rather than] great causes and ideas." Most of the "great" questions did not fit neatly into any of the disciplines and thus remained unstudied. Finally, Beard opposed the scientific model on the basis of free will and choice. If a true science of society were achieved, everything would be predictable and humankind would no longer need to make choices. "We should imprison ourselves in an iron web of our own making." For an individual committed to rationality and independence, this was unacceptable.[54]

If Merriam could shrug off Beard's invitation to this symposium by noting the responsibility of the individual Virginia departments for the selection of the speakers, he could not do the same for a series of lectures offered by the Brookings Institute in 1930. The Brookings Institute was very much a part of Merriam's world of organized social science. Its board of trustees included such friends and allies as Raymond Fosdick, Frederic Delano, and his own brother John, and the invited speakers included such objectivists as Ogburn, Thomas, and the psychologist Madison Bentley. Most important, the theme of the addresses was problems of method in the social sciences. Yet again, Beard rather than Merriam represented political science.

Beard, moreover, was not overwhelmed by his audience. He began by referring to the whole topic of method as "cabalistic." As in the APSA and Virginia speeches, he savaged the objectivist model, especially attacking its emphasis on collecting "all" the data. No matter how much a topic is limited, it can never be isolated from the surrounding environment, he said. Since one "can scarcely expect to command the omniscience necessary to understand the omnibus," the researcher cannot achieve true predictability and is left with an interpretation. Rather than despairing at this state of affairs, Beard called on his listeners to accept it and to recognize that such admitted interpretations as Rousseau's *Social Contract*, despite its historical inaccuracies, succeeded at capturing the necessary "higher generalizations" of a society far better than any work of the scientific model. For Merriam, who had characterized such writing as "rationalizations," such talk, especially at a research institute, was heresy.[55]

Beard appeared at times to dominate even Merriam's beloved APSA. During Beard's presidency, the organization established a committee to survey the discipline of political science, analyze the role of the association, and make recommendations for increasing the relevance of its work for public welfare. Beard's vision was prophetic; the committee reported just as the Great Depression struck. Merriam, who headed the research subcommittee, continued the theme of his presidential address by listing and praising the discipline's key empirical and statistical works, but Beard negated it by preceding it with his own report, which ridiculed such work. The scientific approach, he stated, "has not added a single concept of any importance to the science of human government." While Merriam based his vision of social science on shared assumptions that would produce incremental work and ensure potential funders of the practicality of their support, Beard's report questioned these very beliefs and suggested beginning anew with a strong infusion of personal ethics and morality.[56]

Poor Merriam could not seem to find refuge even in his work for the federal government. Understandably proud of his work as vice chairman and entrepreneurial organizer of the largest work of social science research in North American history, Merriam saw his authorship of the concluding essay of *Recent Social Trends*, "Government and Society," as sure to guarantee his preeminence within the field of political science. Yet even here Beard remained an influential negative force. In two separate reviews of *Recent Social Trends* Beard questioned its methodological and philosophical bases and became for the book's organizers the very symbol of wrongheaded opposition to "true" social science. He began both reviews civilly by noting the exciting scope of the work and the deserved reputation of its contributors. He even cited Merriam by name and stated that no one alive could have bettered his contribution. The work as a whole was "an epoch in the history of social thought, but also an end to this epoch" and represented "the coming crisis in the empirical method." He noted correctly that President Hoover was willing to fund the study because he assumed that once all the facts were known, policy conclusions would inevitably follow. Beard quickly noted that this overlooked both the impossibility of ever obtaining all the facts and the inevitable biases of the observers. More important, however, was the cruel juxtaposition of arguably the greatest moment in objectivist social science with a time when Americans were pleading for answers to the ongoing crisis. For all their facts, however, the report's directors denied an activist role for themselves and their knowledge. From Beard's purposive perspective, this indicated the intellectual and spiritual bankruptcy at the core of objectivist social science. Its time had passed; "the next great survey undertaken in the name of the social sciences may begin boldly with a statement of values agreed upon, and then utilize science to demonstrate the conditions, limitations, inventions, and methods involved in their realization."[57]

Beard's constant writing and speaking on the purposive role of social science, especially given his active dislike of public addresses and organizational activity because of their demands on his time, indicates his commitment to its significance. In fact, as the suffering caused by the Great Depression grew, and the original promise of the New Deal was followed by Beard's perception of its potentially disastrous foreign policy, he became even more obsessed with the topic. The first two chapters of *The Open Door at Home*, the manifesto of Beard's foreign policy work and probably his key work of the 1930s, deal exclusively with the roles and limitations of the social sciences, including history. All of Beard's substantial writing and organizing work for the Commission of the American Historical Association on the Social Studies in the Schools focused on the same subject. His criticism of social science stemmed not, like Robert Hutchins's criticism, from derision of its importance but rather from his belief in its absolute centrality. By the 1930s Beard believed even more than at the time he wrote "Politics" in the importance of the social scientist for the creation of a positive society. Even after the "omniscience of determinism is discarded," its service to society remained "enormous." In response to objectivists such as Mitchell who insisted that they possessed insufficient information to make predictions, Beard bluntly asserted that the nature of social reality ensured that "if those who know more will not attempt it, those who know less will attack the problem."[58]

The underlying theme behind all of Beard's writing on the social science crisis was the need for an agreed-upon set of values and goals on which to base social science. "An ostentatious expulsion of great philosophy at the front door usually means that a poor little vulgar philosophy of prejudices and passions is smuggled in at the back door." Yet, after denying the utility of both science and theology in determining such a philosophy, Beard simply stopped. He seemed to have little conception of either these values or their origins. Even Dewey's unclear reference to the scientific determination of values and Lynd's half-hearted reliance on

Thomas's four wishes seem substantial in comparison. Beard's values seem to have revolved around what he termed "the good life" and individuals' actual choices. These values, like Lynd's, would lead to such specific goals as equal rights, economic security, and right of employment, and such abstractions as cooperation and democracy. But exactly what were these values, and how was it possible to obtain universal acceptance of something one could not even define? Indeed, Beard's emphasis on individual biases, cultural and historical influences, preliminary assumptions, and conscious and unconscious goals would seem to have made the determination of such moral standards even more difficult. Even if such a Sisyphean task were somehow accomplished, Beard remained silent on how to formulate specific research projects guaranteed to aid these moral goals while remaining committed to the scientific method and free inquiry.[59]

Even Beard, who could be maddeningly oblivious to inadequacies in his thinking, acknowledged the vacuum in his philosophy. Although he noted the need for "something *new* . . . [which] does not exist on land or sea . . . [but] only in the realm of the ideal, the imagination," he turned to the past, to history, for guidance. In the search for new values, Beard paradoxically proclaimed, "We have only the lamp of experience to guide us—our own experience and the records of history." Beard claimed to find in American history exactly the values that could provide direction and goals to social scientists.[60]

For all of Beard's deserved reputation as a historian, his activist perspective ensured that his history would always depend on contemporary society and politics. As his series of books on the economic aspects of early American institutions and history in the early 1910s was related to ongoing political conflict, so would his work on the philosophy of history in the 1930s be connected to his desire for a purposive social science. Beard was well aware that the logic of his critique could lead to total subjectivism, and he feared this greatly. In his view, however, the experience of history prevented this. One could never truly know the present because of its unfolding and ever-changing complexity, and the future was surely unknowable. The most certain things came from the past. Indeed, everything that affected present reality came from the past. Beard stated bluntly that the historical perspective "is the *only approach* open to the human mind." Sociological knowledge *was* historical knowledge. History had become "the crown of all studies" by examining everything and providing a truly integrated and holistic perspective on social reality. Beard openly resisted the public's turn to mathematicians and physicists as somehow the culture's wisest individuals and thus proper social critics and prophets. Even physics, he said, "is relatively simple as compared to a subject [i.e., history] which includes physicists and physics and everything else." Because of their perspective historians were the best choices for such social leaders. "History so conceived furnishes such guides to grand public policy as are vouchsafed to the human mind. They may not be final guides, but what else have we?" Rather than being useless antiquarianism, then, history was the most practical and activist of all the disciplines.[61]

This perspective required Beard to critique contemporary historiography as he had the study of public administration and politics. To do this he turned to European philosophers of history and away from the antiphilosophical animus of American historiography. Ephraim Emerton, an American historian, fulminated against "the ghost of our ancient enemy, the philosophy of history" before an appreciate audience at one of the first AHA conventions, and John Higham has asserted bluntly that "the special bête noire of American academic historians was philosophy of history." Beard, on the other hand, decided in 1927 that "we have too much noise in this country and too little quiet thinking," and he went to Germany with his son-in-law, the historian Alfred Vagts, to study continental philosophers of history. Key influences on Beard's emerging philosophy of relativism were the Italian historian Benedetto Croce and the German school of Historismus, especially Hans Vaihinger and Karl Heussi. What Beard drew from them as well as from such sociologists of knowledge as Karl Mannheim was their pervasive questioning of every commonly accepted aspect of the historical method.[62]

Although some of Beard's historical relativism was relevant purely to the discipline of history, much of it was remarkably similar to his overall approach to the social sciences. His one concise definition of historical relativism shows the resemblance clearly: "No historian can describe the past as it actually was and every historian's work—that is, his selection of facts, his emphasis, his omissions, his organization, and his method of presentation—bears a relation to his own personality and the age and circumstances in which he lives." As in his earlier scoldings of political scientists, he demanded an end to pseudoscientific analogies and metaphors and pointed out the inevitable limitations of the social observer. Indeed, historical sources limited historians even more than other social scientists. Sources do not and cannot exist for every topic, and one can never create extra information. The writing of history consequently involves a constant organization and selection of facts from an incomplete and inaccurate database. Moreover, the integrated perspective that gives history its central significance further restricts the possibility of any certainty. Social causation is so incredibly complicated that no human can ever possess enough skills to determine all the factors that could influence a situation.[63]

The goal of historical relativism, in Beard's eyes, was the destruction of the self-centered smugness of his fellow historians. Late in his life, Beard explained to an interviewer, "Long ago I found out that I was not God. Such a discovery is, in my opinion, good for anybody who thinks he can encompass the history of the world in any set of formulas." His friend and fellow historical relativist Carl Becker agreed: "What they can't forgive you for is for saying . . . that history is an act of faith. . . . You are casting doubt on the absolute value and truth of their studies—that's why they call you a defeatist." Although some critics might legitimately consider Becker's work defeatist, exemplified by his AHA presidential address "Everyman His Own Historian," Beard's work was in many ways its opposite. Like Becker, Beard clearly recognized the necessary limitations on the discovery of historical "truth," but he went beyond this to insist that historians come to specific conclusions and use them to justify public policy. Ironically, one can best see this in what his critics saw as the epitome of his defeatist "treason," his AHA presidential address "Written History as an Act of Faith."[64]

Beard began his address by repeating his rejection of the possibility of absolute neutrality. The writing of all history involves selection and arrangement, he said, "an act of choice, conviction and interpretation respecting values." Facts by themselves do not prescribe one interpretation over another; that depends on the perspective and selection process of the historian. Beard then spent the rest of his address restricting his relativism: "Contemporary criticism shows that the apostle of relativity is destined to be destroyed by the child of his own brain. If all historical conceptions are merely relative to passing events, . . . then the conception of relativity is itself relative." Unlike true relativists such as Croce and Becker, Beard never denied the independent existence of facts. Croce and Becker believed that facts existed only in the individual's mind, and thus no one could be wrong; every man *was* his own historian. This represented extreme subjectivism and was, in Beard's activist vision, truly defeatist treason. In his speech Beard insisted on retaining the scientific method and demanded honest and critical use of facts and sources.[65]

The second limitation on neutrality was central not only for his historical relativism but for his entire activist perception of social science. While noting that each historian had a "frame of reference" or perspective derived from personal experiences, Beard denied Becker's contention that these frames were infinite. Beard saw a finite number and devoted most of "Written History" to detailing them. He defined three frames of reference as possible viewpoints on the nature and direction of historical events in general: the world as chaos, a collection of unrelated events; world history as cyclical, with events occurring in repetitive, never-ending circles; and history as moving in an ascertainable positive or negative direction. The historian's true act of faith lay not so much in selecting and arranging historical data as in choosing one of these three points of view. "The historian who writes history consciously or unconsciously performs an act of faith, . . . a conviction that something true can be known about the movement of history and his conviction is a subjective decision, not a purely objective discovery." Beard's choice, "founded on the study of long trends and on a faith in the indomitable spirit of mankind," was movement toward a "collectivist democracy."[66]

Beard's belief that historians needed to work according to a philosophy of the direction of history stemmed from his earlier activism and preceded his immersion in European thought. As early as 1919 he asserted that historians' "highest function" was the determination of the main currents of history. A year later, Beard made his purposive intent even clearer by remarking that the true historian should not only discover future trends in the present but also should "seek thoughtfully to direct it rather than to oppose blindly the inevitable and be overwhelmed by it." Revealingly, the first book Beard cited in the *New Republic* symposium on "Books That Changed Our Mind" was neither Mannheim's *Ideology and Utopia* nor Croce's *History: Its Theory and Practice* but rather Brooks Adams's *Law of Civilization and Decay*, with its search for the direction and purpose of history.[67]

Although Beard claimed that the choice of a philosophy was up to each individual, he reacted violently to historians who chose either chaos or cycles. This was hardly surprising. To choose chaos was to deny the role of the intellectual in explaining the world to others and constituted abdicating one's personal responsibility. He reacted even more angrily to cyclical theories and furiously denied their use by Aristotle and other classical thinkers. No individual, not even the wartime Franklin Roosevelt, could make Beard as angry as Oswald Spengler. Not only had Spengler refused to assume an activist role, but, according to Beard, he had also manipulated facts to reach his pessimistic conclusions.[68]

In his search for an antidote to Spenglerian despair, Beard found a kindred spirit in the English historian J. B. Bury and his *Idea of Progress*. Bury, an extreme optimist who dedicated his book to such believers in preordained progress as Condorcet, Comte, and Spencer, conceived of progress as one of the central ideas of humankind. Moreover, like Fate or personal immortality, one had to believe or disbelieve as an act of faith. Such things simply could not be proved or disproved. Still, "the world is largely ruled by ideas, true and false." Belief in progress seemed almost to ensure its continuation. The concept of progress had not emerged until the sixteenth century, and Beard attributed much of the subsequent actual progress to belief in its existence. Coupled with "immense efforts of will and intelligence" such beliefs "may [allow] mankind [to] rise above necessity into the kingdom of freedom, subduing material things to humane and rational purposes."[69]

But this reliance on self-fulfilling prophecy contradicted Beard's life-long commitment to rationality. He desperately needed an empirical basis for his choice of progress as the true direction of history. This became doubly important as he came to locate his specific values and goals for social science within the continuum of progress itself. Beard would find both empirical and ethical validity for his choice in the American past.

Despite numerous attacks on him as unpatriotic, Beard was intensely American. For all his travels, interests, and respect for other nations and nationalities, Beard retained throughout his life the values of his rural Indiana childhood. Indeed, his experiences in Japan, China, and especially Yugoslavia combined with his original research in European archives heightened his mistrust of foreign places and values. Although European intellectuals might provide positive insights for viewing social reality, European history represented an incantation of what *not* to do. In 1935 Beard would declare bluntly, "If there is a promise of any kind for the future of America, that promise inheres in the past and present of American history." He came to believe in the social, political, and even moral uniqueness and exceptionalism of the United States. If the nation was ever to achieve its potential moral and material greatness, its intellectual leaders must focus, in his words, on "the promise of America rather than upon the 50 century-old quarrels of Europe." The United States could and must continue on the path of progress; Beard had less faith in the fate of the rest of the world, especially Europe. Throughout the 1930s he increasingly came to see America as John Winthrop's "citie upon a hill," a sanctuary for the good society and a model for the rest of humankind after its recovery from chaos.[70]

Beard's positive model was rooted in past American events and values. Like the critic Van Wyck Brooks, Beard consciously sought to create a "usable past" that could employ past events and people's attitudes toward them to help direct the future toward positive outcomes. The past and perceptions of it had important consequences, especially in such an inward-looking nation as the United States. The Beards consciously wrote *The Rise of American Civilization* as a way to help intelligent citizens know enough about their history and its direction to work for a "social democracy." At the time of his reflections on Bury in 1932, Beard believed that one could both find and create values through a study of the American past. "Many historical theories now exploded by critical scholars have exerted a powerful influence on the course of history. Every nation is inspired and given direction by what it thinks its past to be.... If the past as interpreted has been unsatisfactory, it may be reinterpreted in such a way as to help shape the ages to come."[71]

Beard's reinterpretation of American history revolved around what he and Mary called the idea of civilization, "a body of professed values appropriate and indispensable to a new policy—values abundant in literature and faith, and realized here and there in practice." This concept filled in many of the philosophical and ethical gaps of Beard's social science methodology. Early in his career he had noted the domination of economic interests and the inability of theology, idealism, or even science to check them. That state of affairs made Beard's belief in the possibility of conscious direction of society toward valued ends problematic. Yet the idea of civilization represented a collection of desired and desirable values, which had proven their ongoing existence and influence empirically and provided a central activist role for the intellectual. These values not only provided guidance in devising new and reframing old policies, they also led to rejection of actions based on such allegedly un-American social and economic philosophies as laissez-faire capitalism.[72]

The Beards' chief problem was their inability to state their values in any explicit fashion. They attempted to list the values and trace them through American history in the fourth and final volume of their *Rise of American Civilization* series, *The American Spirit*. While the first three volumes explore the United States' "exterior" history, *Spirit* examines the unique "interior," or intellectual, qualities of American history. Unfortunately, the Beards could arrive at nothing more specific than "a composite formulation" which spoke vaguely of Americans' respect for human life and rights. Indeed, *The American Spirit* is frankly embarrassing, an endless string of unconnected note cards cobbled together. Beard would later note the lack of sophistication and coherence of their framework but somehow failed to recognize that universal values demanded at least this. In the final analysis, Beard failed to uncover the values needed for the implementation of his philosophy of history.[73]

Although several historians and philosophers opposed Beard's relativistic history, they did so not on the basis of its painfully inadequate values but because it questioned the possibility of absolute objectivity. Throughout the 1920s and 1930s, the old guard historians sought to increase the detachment and specialization of the discipline. They wanted to copy objectivist social science rather than provide an alternative model to it. The historian Theodore Clarke Smith responded to "Written History as an Act of Faith" by turning a historical survey of the AHA into an attack on Beard's work as "non-professional . . . unfair . . . muckraking" which led directly to fascistic-type history. According to Smith, all progress in history derived from von Ranke's vision of scientific history, and the AHA should literally disband rather than allow Beard's sort of history to be written under its auspices. Smith was one of only a few who opposed Beard openly; Beard remained simply too powerful in the public mind, and even within the profession. Strong allies within the AHA such as Arthur Schlesinger, Sr., of Columbia and Roy Nichols and William Lingelbach of the University of Pennsylvania largely accepted his critique and provided invaluable organizational help. As late as the 1940s Beard and Nichols succeeded in convincing the Social Science Research Council to fund a commission of inquiry into the state of contemporary American historiography. In a classic piece written for this study, John Randall and George Haines, two emerging leaders of the profession, asserted that most of the new generation of historians "employ principles of selection and interpretation of which [they] are clearly conscious" and seek to direct their research toward helping solve ongoing social problems.[74]

The most open debate over Beard's views on the social sciences—including history—involved public education, and his chief opponent was Charles Merriam. In his writing of textbooks, his personal involvement in adult education in England and the United States, his activism on behalf of academic freedom, and his conscious instruction of the general citizenry through books, speeches, and public activities, Beard demonstrated his intense concern for education. Public school teachers were his favorite audience, and it was to them that he made important announcements such as his conversion to New History. As early as 1915 Beard had labeled the neglect of history, government, and civics education in the public schools as "nothing short of a disgrace to the republic."

Almost alone among public figures, Beard opposed professional educators' emphasis on social utilitarianism and proposed intellectual liberation as the true purpose of education.[75]

Beard's interest in public school teachers and education represented a conscious throwback to his predecessors' activities. From the start of professionalization, historians and social scientists had attempted to increase their already strong influence on teaching in the public schools. Between 1892 and 1923, more than a dozen different commissions from various professional organizations worked on the issue. Probably the most influential was the American Historical Association Commission of Seven for the Secondary Schools of 1899, which laid out specific programs of study, established sequences of courses, and provided definitions for various courses. Problems arose when other commissions recommended entirely different programs and goals. In 1923–24, the AHA History Inquiry under Edgar Dawson investigated social studies in the schools and found total "chaos." For example, the curriculum for required senior-year "civics" classes could be economics, government, sociology, or history.[76]

In response the AHA formed a committee in 1924 with representatives from the education and social science professions. Chaired by medieval historian A. C. Krey of the University of Minnesota, protégé and golf partner of AHA and SSRC power broker Guy Stanton Ford, the commission included four historians, three professors of education, an economist, and the political scientist Charles Merriam. Krey delivered the group's preliminary report during the AHA convention of 1926. In the report he noted two reasons why the subject of social sciences was significant. First, Americans generally agreed on the necessity of social studies courses for developing "effective social membership." In addition, secondary schools in the United States had expanded to include all social classes and groups. The classic Greek philosophers dreamed of institutions capable of providing societywide citizenship training; Americans now possessed them. The commission requested more time and funding to conduct intensive studies on the schools themselves, methods of instruction, testing, teacher training, and international civic education. Most important, Krey called for the determination of specific objectives for the social sciences. In reply to a later critic of the commission, Krey insisted that all the participants of the original study, but especially Merriam, advocated transcending technical and professional issues to concentrate on "the most profound considerations of the history and policy of the nation." Although the Rockefeller Foundation turned down the commission's financial request in order to fund Merriam's series on international civic education, the Carnegie Foundation provided grants totaling half a million dollars.[77]

In this call for specific objectives, the Krey Commission took a major step away from its predecessors. Krey's report specifically warned about the dangers of the American Legion and similarly untrained groups trying to impose their views on public education. The Committee of Seven, on the other hand, had specifically stated its absolute objectivity and acquiescence to local control. In 1918, the official historian of the state of New York defined propaganda as anything that questioned the present system or its institutions; anything that supported them was by definition not propaganda. Even as the committee began work on its special reports, an editorial in the *Mississippi Valley Historical Review* declared, "The public which controls the schools will dictate . . . the history that is taught in them. . . . The historian who will be read must win the good will and esteem of his readers. To do this he must consult their sensibilities and prejudices."[78]

Krey noted in his preliminary report that his greatest fear was turning the further work of the commission over to untrained personnel rather than to "persons of ability, maturity, and experience." Much to Krey's delight, Beard accepted his nomination to the commission and agreed to be the temporary director of research as well. In addition to Beard, the commission added a geographer, a sociologist, two more education professors, an educational administrator, a foundation representative, and a university president. Beard's reason for involvement, as he cheerfully admitted to Krey, was his perception of social science as a "mess" and his desire to "clean up the situation." Although Beard relinquished the research directorship to his friend and ally George Counts in 1931, he served on numerous subcommittees, wrote two of the commission's volumes, and was the principal author of the original draft of the study's conclusions. Moreover, despite his lack of an official title and the opposition of Merriam, Beard's strong personality, reputation, and clearly perceived goals quickly overwhelmed Krey and made Beard the group's central figure.[79]

Beard soon assumed responsibility for what Krey had perceived as the chief function of the commission, the determination of objectives for the social sciences. Of the commission's sixteen volumes, five deal primarily with those issues. Beard wrote two of these: the first volume, *A Charter for the Social Sciences*, and *The Nature of the Social Sciences;* Counts composed a third, *The Social Foundations of Education;* the two coauthored *Conclusions and Recommendations of the Commission*, with its summary of objectives; and Merriam wrote the fifth, *Civic Education in the United States*. Beard immediately made his position clear. Within a year of his appointment he sent out a rough draft of *Charter* to the Committee on Objectives. In it, Beard portrayed the commission's task as a philosophical one. The root issue was the choice between either acceptance of a predetermined fate or belief in human control over events. If predetermination was rejected, then social scientists should devote themselves to helping individuals make good choices in order to achieve desirable ends. The rapidly changing nature of society and consequent range of choices made it necessary to teach decision-making tools such as the scientific method, imagination, aesthetic appreciation, toleration, and, above all, ethics. Without ethics, the choice of good things, social science would become "inert scholasticism without direction and . . . [lacking] a dynamic quality." To be successful, a teacher must go beyond facts and make personal decisions. "Every statesman, every judge, every informed citizen, who acts on something more than prejudice has in mind a more or less logical picture of an ideal social order to be preserved or realized. . . . The teacher of social science can only escape presenting the necessity of choice by fleeing from the world of reality to a land of abstraction. . . . Then civic instruction might as well be taken out of the schools."[80]

Beard's invaluable ally in establishing objectives and providing contacts with educators, inside and outside the commission, was his successor as director of research, George Counts, a professor of education at Columbia's Teachers College. Counts stood out in the field of education for the intensity of his belief in the social origins of education and his political radicalism. Although he received his doctorate in education at the University of Chicago under Charles Judd, a leader in the scientific and statistical study of education, at Teachers College his official title was professor of social foundations of education. Counts himself made it clear that his research interests, which ranged from American school boards to education in the Soviet Union and the Philippines, always revolved around the social and cultural foundations of education. During the 1920s Counts had taken the statistical skills he acquired under Judd and turned them on American educational institutions to demonstrate their biased and class-centered nature. His first book, *The Selective Character of American Secondary Education* (1922), demonstrates the perpetuation of social, ethnic, and racial inequalities by public secondary schools. *The Social Composition of Boards of Education* (1927) notes how school board members came almost exclusively from the upper class and controlled local educational policies for their own economic and political purposes. *School and Society in Chicago* (1928) is a case study of how Chicago elites used their power to remove a popular superintendent of schools. For Counts, as for Beard, time, place, and culture always conditioned education as they did every social institution. Since education was such a powerful influence on American life and so dominated by the status quo, its reformation was absolutely necessary for any real social change to take place.[81]

Counts represented a new generation of progressive educators who criticized the cultural aspects of the education movement. Although he always praised Dewey for providing the central insight—the need in public education for a unifying purpose—he bitterly opposed child-centered progressive education because it assumed that children would automatically make good choices by themselves. Counts argued that such romanticism allowed professional educators to ignore issues of power, control, and values and concentrate on transforming themselves into a new technical elite eagerly serving the existing power structure.[82]

Like Beard, Counts viewed objectivity as a chimera and all knowledge as reflecting some point of view. The question was "not whether imposition will take place but rather from what source it will come." Since indoctrination was an inevitable part of the educational process, Counts called for teachers to become activists and impose their own views rather than those of conservative school boards. As much as anyone in the profession, Counts recognized the power of business interests, their control of school boards, and their willingness to use their power brutally, especially in times of economic and social crisis. He also recognized the limitations of teacher training and commitment to social change. Nevertheless, given the lack of positive leadership from other sources and the manipulation of education by selfish special interests, teachers had to assume an activist role. After all, they did represent a positive moral force in the community as guardians of children, bearers of culture, and servants of the people as a whole. No other group in American society came close to matching their intellectual, experiential, and moral qualities in formulating educational policies and social goals.[83]

After meeting through their joint commission membership, Beard and Counts formed a strong partnership and alliance, serving on the editorial boards of each other's journals and coauthoring books. Counts accepted Beard, unlike Dewey, as his mentor. In a Christmas 1933 letter, Beard referred to Counts humorously but affectionately as "my beloved son." Thirty years later, Counts remembered that compliment literally, and his biographer referred to it as "no mere figure of speech." Actually, Beard, who often referred to himself as "Uncle Charlie," did not bestow the term lightly, but it also was not applied exclusively to Counts. Still, he respected Counts greatly, and the two constantly encouraged one another to remain true to their strong beliefs and make the commission produce "fighting document[s]." For once, Beard found himself working with someone more radical and activist than himself. Counts wrote frequently about the need for revolution, praised the accomplishments of the Soviet Union, and chastised Beard for his flirtation with the New Deal. An exasperated Beard once wrote to his friend, "You put on a red coat, jump up on the ramparts and say to the American Legion, the D.A.R., and every school board in America: 'Here I am, a good Red: shoot me!' . . . Your idea . . . tells the enemy exactly where and when to shoot at sunrise. Dead men do no work."[84]

As finished studies on such topics as the history of civic education, testing, and teacher training began to arrive, the need for a summary volume to integrate all the material for a wider audience became clear. The commission ensured the strongly philosophic and activist nature of this work by selecting Beard, Counts, and Krey as coauthors. The commission members probably hoped that Krey would have a moderating influence, but unfortunately he had an apparent nervous breakdown and turned total control over to Beard and Counts. Privately, Beard admitted his bewilderment at the task and the propriety of their committing the commission to a particular viewpoint. Indeed, he very much doubted the possibility of winning the diverse members' approval for any document. Publicly, however, he told Krey that he wanted the commission to be courageous and "place all of its cards on the table."[85]

Certainly the *Conclusions and Recommendations of the Commission* laid Beard's and Counts's cards on the table. Although Krey's preface stated that the commission based its conclusions on the sponsored factual documents, this was clearly not always the case. For example, the conclusions reflected Beard's personal obsession against testing as "all hokum, pretense, and a sham" and "an enemy of teaching" rather than Truman Kelley's detailed volume on the subject. The report was equally critical of Ernest Horn's specialities of instruction and curriculum making. Interest in methods separate "from knowledge, thought, and purpose" was "sterile," "a gross neglect of duty," and "the besotting sin of pedagogy in the United States." The criticism at times occasionally passed over into sarcasm: "It [*Conclusions*] makes no effort to reach those who seek relief, through reliance on particular methods, from the pain of acquiring knowledge."[86]

Conclusions reflects Beard's and Counts's shared views on social science methodology, the objectives of social studies in the schools, and, most of all, the role of the educator. It begins by repeating Beard's position on the scientific method as necessary but limited by its inability to determine ethical and aesthetic goals. Ethical values must come from a personal frame of reference and are essential for the process of education, especially during periods of crisis and transition like the 1930s. An informed frame of reference must recognize the emerging new age of "collectivism" and the passing of the time based on individualism. This development was not necessarily the wish of the commission but "a fact established by empirical inquiry." Once one acknowledged this trend, then the goal of education became to "ease the strains of transition" by preparing students for the new age. One could do this by encouraging cooperative work, providing equal and universal education, requiring more work in the social studies, and trying to create well-rounded individuals. As with Beard's and Counts's earlier work, the responsibility for such actions was placed on the teachers. *Conclusions* specifically calls for removal of educational decisions from school boards and administrators. Teachers, unlike other groups, possessed special competence as "servants of the community as a whole and . . . [were] trained to think in terms of the more abiding interests of mankind." To ensure teachers' ability to address such sensitive issues, *Conclusions* makes a number of specific recommendations, including the establishment of a strong national teachers' union to guarantee academic freedom and better working conditions and benefits.[87]

Perhaps nowhere else in Beard's works are his conclusions, their applicability to society, and their limitations more clear. All of Beard's conclusions depended on his belief in the special knowledge, both empirical and ethical, of the social scientist–educator. The empirical validity of the historical trend toward collectivism plus the ethical justification of such an outcome relied essentially, as Beard himself admitted elsewhere, on a leap of faith. The question then became, What makes the choice of the social scientist–historian more credible than that of the elected official or the average citizen? Beard maintained that social scientists had more knowledge and skills for making such judgments. Even if this were so, it does not justify Beard's and Counts's attempt to place public school teachers in a similar elevated position. As the commission studies themselves make painfully clear, teachers lacked adequate training. Beard and

Counts may have rhapsodized on public esteem for teachers, but teachers' salaries, as noted by the Lynds in *Middletown*, did not reflect this regard. Nor had teachers as a whole shown any great commitment to the spirit of free inquiry, especially with regard to citizenship education. A study conducted under Counts's supervision at Teachers College found that more than one-third of American teachers believed that their job in teaching citizenship was to impose accepted viewpoints so strongly that students would never modify them. In many ways, Beard's and Counts's objectives for education appear to be the equivalent of Beard's re-creation of a usable past, designed to convince the American public of a useful and needed empirical and ethical tradition in education which could be used as a guide in the present.[88]

Obviously, *Conclusions* is not only activist but socially and politically radical in a fundamental way. Not surprisingly, many of the commission members immediately criticized the report. Jesse Newlon, Counts's Teachers College colleague and the only commission member perhaps even more radical than either Counts or Beard, estimated that only seven of the sixteen members would sign. Significantly, its opponents did not attack it for its unquestioned faith in teachers as unerring guides to knowledge but rather for its frank discussion of education as social control.[89]

Unsurprisingly, Merriam soon emerged as the leading opponent of *Conclusions* within the commission. At first he claimed to accept the ideas themselves but wanted them "softened" and such controversial words as *collectivist* eliminated. Eventual signers Guy Stanton Ford and economist L. C. Marshall agreed with him on this. According to Horn, a fellow Beard opponent and ally of Merriam, Merriam was the only commission member personally hostile to Beard. Eighteen months after the publication of *Conclusions*, Krey sighed to a friend that a political scientist had warned him years earlier of the impossibility of getting Beard and Merriam to agree on anything. Merriam, who had helped arrange Counts's appointment as director of research, did not extend his enmity to his former student, whom he believed was manipulated by Beard, and Counts joined Krey in unsuccessful attempts to mediate the conflict. Counts anticipated Merriam's opposition and rushed an early copy of the draft to him, confessing that he would probably find it "a bit radical" but offering to make adjustments. Neither this offer nor any other would make any difference.[90]

In many ways, Merriam's opposition is difficult to understand since he never specifically articulated his disagreements. In three separate letters written during 1934 he did state that his divergent opinions were evident in his commission work *Civic Education in the United States* and in his contribution to his own series *The Making of Citizens,* but the differences are not really that apparent. In his preface to *Civic* he advocated the establishment of objectives as the primary need for civic education. Merriam's wartime work in Italy had made him very aware of the existence of propaganda in educational systems, and he had even specifically praised the Chicago system for its successful Americanization of immigrants.[91]

Merriam's disagreement derived from his unwillingness to openly oppose traditional bases of power. His problems lay not so much with having objectives as with who should decide them. He viewed educators–social scientists–administrators as technicians only. The ethical decisions and choices of a society were not their concern. Indeed, at times Merriam blithely seemed to ignore the possibility of disagreement about such choices. For example, immediately after agreeing on the need for objectives in education, Merriam insisted that "the obstacles that stand between us and the realization of men's dreams are those of social attitudes and social and political management"—technical, not political questions. Teachers cannot and should not oppose community wishes. Years earlier, Merriam had gone so far as to defend, privately, William Jennings Bryan and the state of Tennessee in the John Scopes trial. The people had expressed their wishes electorally, and Scopes should have honored their desires. Indeed, in *Civic Education* Merriam would make perhaps his strongest assertion about the nonactivist function of the social scientist–educator. His or her role is "to indicate the special methods by which there may be accomplished through political channels what it is desired to accomplish." He or she could be "a technical adviser to a fascist state, or an oriental or an occidental system, or a capitalist or a communist regime . . . [since] aptitudes, skills, tricks, . . . have a definite value in any system of organization. . . . The object is given and he proceeds on that assumption, as an engineer builds a bridge."[92]

Merriam's grumblings and the more open complaints of several other committee members, especially Horn, led Krey to schedule a series of meetings in Chicago in early October 1933. The meetings became extremely heated when Merriam took the lead in calling for a less aggressive document that reflected "openness of minds . . . [and] more friendly discussions." Beard responded by quoting Lord Salisbury that this would lead to a manuscript that was "perfectly fitting, perfectly true, perfectly meaningless." Beard and Counts complained that other commission members criticized their ideas but were never willing to specifically state their own positions. If they believed something different, then they should say so in their own drafts. Even when, as in the case of Kelley and Horn, they were given an opportunity, they failed to meet reasonable deadlines. Beard and Counts suspected that many of the members, and especially Merriam, wished to avoid the entire controversy by not meeting the January 1, 1934, deadline imposed by the AHA. The deadlock continued, and Krey was forced to call another meeting shortly before Christmas at Princeton. This proved even more acrimonious with the physically exhausted Beard storming out of the first session only to return after turning off his hearing aid. The discussions resulted in a quick revision by Beard's old Columbia colleague Carlton J. H. Hayes, with the "help" of Krey, Counts, Newlon, and Teachers College professor and commission moderate Henry Johnson. The final draft reflected this uneasy compromise by moderating the overall view while retaining the original activist language. A furious Merriam, ignoring all peace entreaties from Krey and Counts, continued to assert the report's overemphasis on "a special point of view peculiar in part to Counts and part to Beard," demanded a "more balanced, judicious, and statesmanlike" report, refused to sign, and claimed to represent at least ten other members.[93]

Despite Merriam's boasts of influence on the commission, Counts's and Krey's active lobbying quickly undermined his support. By early January, the Columbia group of Hayes, Newlon, and Johnson had joined the sociologist Jesse Steiner and, with reservations, the geographer Isiah Bowman to side with Beard, Krey, and Counts. It soon became clear that Krey's old mentor Ford would have the key vote on the committee, and Krey pleaded with Counts to keep his "truculent" friend Newlon under control so as not to alienate Ford. Ford did agree to sign, as, surprisingly, did Merriam's friend and Rockefeller Foundation Director for the Social Studies Edmund Day. In the end, only three of the other fifteen members followed Merriam's lead and refused to sign, although Bowman did file a dissenting report regarding the work's implications for his discipline. It must have been a bitter blow for Merriam, who owed his prominence largely to his skills in forming coalitions, to lose so badly and so publicly to his old enemy Beard.[94]

The reasons behind the other three dissenters are equally relevant to the underlying issue of objectivity versus activism. Ernest Horn, a self-proclaimed technocrat, correctly felt attacked by many of the conclusions, and his dissent was foreordained. Even the diplomatic and gentle Krey could find little personal sympathy for Horn, who had savaged

Counts incessantly and constantly complained about financial and personal arrangements. In retrospect, the refusal of Frank Ballou, superintendent of the Washington, D.C., public schools, was equally expected. Like his self-professed mentor Horn, he criticized the material on testing and teacher education and the absence of specifics on instruction and curriculum. A deeper problem, which he never publicly addressed, involved his personal political situation. Both local and congressional politicians kept Ballou, as superintendent of D.C. schools, under intense scrutiny. Indeed, three years later, in an official hearing, a congressman would claim that Ballou's participation on the commission proved his communist beliefs, despite his vocal dissent to its findings. Finally, Merriam's friend and Rockefeller contact Day withdrew his signature. Everyone recognized Day's precarious position. Very early, Newlon had pointed out Day's predecessor and patron Beardsley Ruml's attack on Beard's *A Charter for the Social Sciences* as "indoctrination" and noted its necessary impact on Day's actions. The report's criticism of many Rockefeller-supported projects along with what Krey saw as Day's "natural conservatism" made his position very difficult. Finally, the potential loss of face for his longtime friend and foundation ally Merriam made Day's approval personally impossible. Interestingly, Day never noted any actual disagreements but simply declared that his previous approval had been "essentially unwise."[95]

Beard and Counts succeeded in gaining approval for their report from the American Historical Association as well. The review of *Conclusions* in the *American Historical Review* complimented its "bold and fearless view"; the AHA agreed to assume sponsorship of the commission's journal, *Historical Outlook*, in order to continue its activist interest in the secondary schools; and *Conclusions* and the other volumes of the commission were regularly praised at annual meetings as among the most important recent work of the association.[96]

Most important to Beard, *Conclusions and Recommendations* received a great deal of public attention and numerous reviews. About half of the reviews were extremely positive, and the negative remainder were split into a few critiques from radicals who accused the commission of bolstering the status quo and numerous furious attacks from the technocratic perspective. Few, if any, were lukewarm about the book. Since Beard's goal, as always, was to precipitate discussion and force individuals to rethink their assumptions, this in itself represented a major accomplishment.[97]

With the publication of *Conclusions* in 1934, Beard had achieved many of his goals. His gamble at leaving Columbia had succeeded beyond his wildest hopes. He still retained the respect of his fellow professionals, as attested by his directorship of the New York Bureau of Municipal Research, his election to the presidencies of both the American Political Science Association and the American Historical Association, and invitations to speak at numerous special occasions. Indeed, his departure from Columbia gave him a reputation of altruism and moral integrity and made him even more respected. He used the time once used for teaching to become an educator on a national scale through his enormously successful textbooks and innumerable articles and letters in popular journals like the *New Republic* and *Nation*. Moreover, his methodological critiques of the various disciplines had important effects. Although they precipitated strong counterattacks from more traditionally oriented individuals, they led numerous people in public administration, political science, and especially history to consciously alter their research approach. Beard's work and influence were major reasons for the growth of the purposive school among the social sciences during the 1930s. Finally, his victory within the AHA commission demonstrated the appeal of his perspective at the grass-roots level and at least held out the hope that a purposive institutional structure for education might still be developed.

Having seemingly conquered the provinces of academic social science, Beard in the 1930s set his sights on his ultimate target for social scientists: effective impact on and eventual control of policymaking. Perhaps his recent successes, the Great Depression, his advancing years, or some combination of these caused him to bypass his traditional caution and ignore the power of his entrenched opposition. For whatever reasons, beginning in the mid-1930s Charles Beard launched a frontal assault on American policy, especially in the area of foreign affairs. As his attack splintered against his own private Russia of World War II and Franklin Roosevelt's role in it, revolts against him and his purposive vision broke out throughout the provinces.

Initially, despite private reservations about Roosevelt, Beard had eagerly welcomed and supported the New Deal. He and George H. E. Smith quickly wrote a book praising it with the adulatory title *The Future Comes*. This was doubly complimentary because a year earlier Beard had entitled an edited book of possible blueprints for economic and political change *America Faces the Future*. Beard actively participated in pressing for New Deal reforms such as the National Recovery Administration, the Civilian Conservation Corps, and the Supreme Court reorganization plan. The Beards met and had dinner with the Roosevelts twice, and Beard planned the publication dates of his books to influence Roosevelt personally and the political process in general. Unlike such objectivists as James Harvey Rogers and Mitchell, Beard did not plead for more time; he immediately advocated specific policies in a number of areas.[98]

Beard reacted most positively to the New Deal's interest in planning. Long before the 1930s he had noted the necessity of planning, especially in administration. By the early 1930s Beard, like many others, was viewing the Soviet Union's Five-Year Plan with interest and trying to adapt it to American circumstances. In his view, planning represented the only possible solution to the Great Depression: "The cold truth is that the individualistic creed of everybody for himself and the devil take the hindmost is principally responsible for the distress in which western civilization finds itself." In a Fourth of July letter of 1931 he asserted bluntly, "I think that planning is the secret of the hope. Money plans nothing." During the 1932 election and after, he defended national planning as part of the national tradition both historically and ethically. In phrases similar to those he and Counts had used to write about indoctrination in the public schools, Beard declared that the question was not planning itself but "how much planning, by whom, under whose auspices, and to what ends?" Especially important was planning that considered the overall goals of society.[99]

While Beard applauded Roosevelt's development of the NRA and similar planning agencies, he became progressively more worried about the direction of the administration's foreign policy. As he began to develop his idea of American civilization in the late 1920s, he came to see American history as being split into a virtuous internal heritage and an antidemocratic foreign policy that constantly intervened in foreign nations and threatened native traditions. Beard came to believe, like his Enlightenment heroes, that one could guarantee progress at certain periods in a nation's history only by concentrating on domestic issues. Publicly, Beard lauded Roosevelt for possessing exactly this recognition of the centrality of domestic affairs. Again and again he pointed to FDR's actions at the London Economic Conference, where he sabotaged an international plan to stabilize the gold standard and instead emphasized the need for strong independent national economies.[100]

Privately, Beard reacted quite differently. As early as 1933 he told Smith, "I agree with you on Roosevelt. I think he is a dangerous man in foreign affairs; he has no headlands for guidance as he is moving as swiftly as he can, whatever his idea, into a war with Japan. . . . There is something admirable about his freedom from old claptrap, but where he is drifting, God only knows. . . . The London Conference showed up his muddle-headedness from the start. No policy, backing and falling, jumping and snorting." This comment shows Beard's central difficulty with New Deal foreign policy: it had no plan, no clearly conceived purpose. Lack of direction had traditionally been the central weakness of American foreign policy, and Roosevelt seemed to be repeating it during a period of extreme danger.[101]

The key concept in foreign policy, Beard thought, should be the idea of national interest, the concept of the existence of a common best interest within a nation. This was the central thesis of all of his foreign policy writings and the subject of his most important 1930s books, *The Idea of National Interest* and *The Open Door at Home*. These companion volumes fit the twin goals of Beard's activism. They established ethical goals and standards for the direction of policy and research and simultaneously attempted to create an informed citizenry. Beard was reading works by European thinkers and developing his relativistic history at this time, and he came to view foreign policy the same way he viewed other social subjects. Facts by themselves meant nothing and did not lead to any necessary conclusions; "facts do not command anyone to do anything." Designers of adequate foreign policy must keep in mind overall desirable goods. "Since foreign policy is directed toward action, it must include in its image things deemed necessary, things deemed possible, and things deemed desirable."[102]

American foreign policy had almost never done this, according to Beard. Politicians had based foreign policy on abstract and unclear conceptions of moral obligation, which too often led to colonial expansion or wars fought on behalf of special interest groups. As early as 1922 Beard rejected "this loving and hating business [as] dangerous to the intelligent pursuit of our national interests." A true national interest would begin with the recognition that foreign policy is inextricably linked with domestic politics. Not only are they connected, but foreign affairs follow domestic needs and are nothing but "a reflection of public interest in the domestic field." Since Beard had previously defined politics as having an economic basis and reflecting the needs of specific interest groups, foreign policy must reflect such groups' desires and actions. Indeed, at one point Beard, with characteristic overstatement, asserted that "foreign affairs . . . strictly speaking is a department of industry and marketing." Much of the criticism of Beard's condemnation of America's entry into World War II involved his apparent inability to see foreign policy as influenced by anything other than domestic needs.[103]

Beard split his study of the national interest into two volumes. The first, *The Idea of National Interest*, researched and cowritten with Smith, a thorough but plodding Yale-based lawyer and researcher, provides a "cold summary" of the "confusions and contradictions" of past policy. Although Beard was determined to remain purely empirical in the first book, it contains a clear, if implicit, criticism. The record of the past documented the failure of past policy to meet national needs. In the second, *The Open Door at Home*, Beard began by "frankly confess[ing] in advance [that] this is my interpretation of history and policy, my presentation of a policy." Since any policy must begin with desired values, Beard began his by noting that his personal "ideal concept" centered on a high standard of living for all Americans and an economic system designed to provide individual security. Like his idol Ruskin, Beard also included such "intangibles" as education, scientific advancement, music, art, and recreational facilities. The goal was, in Beard's phrase, "a more promising way of life for the people of the United States." All of this would occur, he said, in a point that would become increasingly important during the 1930s, "within the frame of national security" in "their present geographic home."[104]

In Beard's view, the fatal flaw of American policy rested on agricultural overproduction and the consequent dependence on foreign markets. This resulted in the allocation of an increasing amount of the nation's resources to finance a larger military, especially a navy, to protect American investments and markets abroad. Beard argued that the United States could increase its domestic consumption sufficiently to consume all of its own products. Smith had pointed out in *The Idea of National Interest* that exports never exceeded 10 percent of domestic production except during wartime. Exports simply were not that important. Meanwhile, much of the exports consisted of production machinery, which in effect created competition and lowered prices and wages in the United States. Military intervention escalated the national cost astronomically without even ensuring viable outlets.[105]

Beard's conclusions were quite clear. Existing American foreign policy did not reflect a true national interest. Instead it represented the special interests of particular economic groups—overseas investors, the military and its suppliers, exporters and importers, international bankers, and investors in foreign securities. Their desires worked against the true national interest. Beard portrayed this interest in a series of admitted clichés: "Let us keep out of the next war; mind our own business; till our own garden; create the wealth; establish a sound and efficient domestic economy; make America a work of art."[106]

Beard's choice of "let us keep out of war" as his first "commonplace phrase" was indicative of his thinking. Economic and foreign involvement led naturally to greater potential for war, and the United States was increasing both during a period of imminent explosion. All nations were seeking new markets to offset their depressed internal consumption and bolster their national economies. Beard concluded that: "The degree of probability that the United States will become involved in any war . . . bears a direct relation to the extent of economic interests possessed by American nationals in the affected area, and in the fortunes of the respective belligerents."[107]

The specter of World War I haunted Beard. He had never retracted his early support for the war, arguing that American interests were at stake and that intervention had represented the true American interest. Looking back on the war's affect on the domestic front, however, Beard reacted with dismay at the "drastic" and even "savage" actions of the national government. As early as 1925 Beard was opposing a potential Pacific war because he felt domestic repression and destruction of constitutional government was sure to result. In 1937 he told an English audience that he was very enthusiastic about America's democratic heritage except for the possibility of a war. "If it [the United States] participates in another general European war, no matter what the alleged pretexts or the alignment of powers may be, that participation will mark the end of democratic institutions in the United States."[108]

Beard's belief in the inevitability of an impending conflict haunted him. In 1917, while still teaching at Columbia and fully supporting the Allies, he worried that another war would soon follow if the Allies achieved total victory and imposed a draconian peace. Shortly after the Treaty of Versailles, he began to refer to the past conflict as "World War One." His travels during the 1920s further convinced him of the international tinderbox and the great potential for both Asian and European wars. Except for his years in England, Beard had had very little foreign experience before the 1920s. Several biographers quoted Beard's letters to Merle Curti in which he stated that "after a trip to the Orient an Occidental is never the same, if he is sensitive." "I became a changed person [and] . . . have never been the same again." What they did not note was exactly *how* Beard changed. He became increasingly pessimistic, not just of public administration but of a world future in which a Japan run by a self-centered, greedy, economic elite was expanding into a Pacific dominated by American economic interests.[109]

Beard's experiences in Yugoslavia in 1928–29 solidified this belief.

Called on to develop a national administration that would lessen the hostilities among the feuding nationalities, he found himself faced with ethnic-based political machines far more powerful, self-centered, and venal than anything ever dreamed of in New York or Chicago and fueled by centuries of atrocities and hatred. Beard found some hope in the truly national attitude of the Croatian leader Stephen Radich. A few days after Beard's interview with him, however, a Montenegrin political opponent assassinated Radich. Moreover, Yugoslavia was, as the title of Beard's book stated, the *pivot* of Europe and the birthplace of World War I.[110]

Not surprisingly, Beard returned to the United States convinced, as he told an interviewer later, that he would "center my efforts on the promise of America." As he later told a House committee, the American people's integrity and intelligence could not match the problems created by the "blood rust of fifty centuries of warfare." Significantly, *The Balkan Pivot* appears to have been written for an American audience, despite its avowed purpose of creating an administrative organization for Yugoslavia. It contains a long and detailed history of ethnic conflicts already well known to people in Yugoslavia and certainly no aid to the goal of diminishing hostilities. Moreover, it is full of comparisons with examples from the American past such as the Articles of Confederation, which would be known to a literate American audience but not a Yugoslavian one. Even in this work, Beard was concentrating on trying to save American society by pointing out the endless potential for a European war.[111]

Beard possessed a final reason for fearing an aggressive international policy during a period of extreme potential for war. He maintained as early as 1910 and consistently throughout his career that despite myths to the contrary, the American people have a definite warlike streak and "enjoy war beyond measure, if the plain facts of history are allowed to speak." In 1936 he put together a slim volume "refuting the devil theory of war" as the work of an outside "demon" and recounting numerous examples of popular instigation of war in the United States. Beard had two reasons for pointing out this trend. First and most obviously, the American people needed to recognize their inherited cultural tendencies in order to protect themselves from making similar mistakes in the future. Second, certain special interest groups that recognized this hidden desire for war had manipulated the country into war in the past in order to further their own interests and block rising American reform movements. Although Beard at times seemed to imply a continuing pattern of powerful economic interests consciously using war hysteria to block reform, he never specifically stated this until 1934, in his article "Historical Approaches to the New Deal." As the title indicates, he had come to believe that the New Deal was now equally at risk.[112]

Beard devoted most of the remainder of the decade to trying to identify the groups that might seek to imitate Shakespeare's Prince Hal and "busy giddy minds with foreign quarrels." Although the American people had often taken an active role in the initiation of war, "most of us sit blindfold at the preparation." Beard was determined not to let this happen again. According to his son-in-law, Beard perceived the manipulation of historians and social scientists by the federal government during World War I as the central threat to the integrity of the profession, and by connection to his own as well. Social scientists' function was to inform the public, yet they themselves had taken an active part in misinforming it. He was determined he would not be "had" again.[113]

Beard's combination of purposive philosophy and public popularity allowed him to assume a position that objectivist social scientists could not and would not take. He participated in policy debates through articles and letters in popular journals and newspapers, books directed specifically to a popular audience, and even frequent testimony before congressional committees, all made possible by his popularity and public recognition. The few objectivists, such as Mitchell, who could have assumed such a role rejected it as unprofessional. After years of gathering data, they believed that they still possessed insufficient information to offer recommendations on policy; further, they saw themselves as addressing a different audience. Beard viewed his primary role as the education of an informed citizenry, who would then choose and direct policymakers. Adherents of social science as technique such as Merriam perceived their function as directly influencing the decision makers by being local advisers.

Indeed, Beard increasingly distanced himself from his objectivist colleagues. Although he had earlier given personal advice to Roosevelt, he progressively took a public oppositional role. His position on the indeterminacy of final truths paradoxically led him to assume an even stronger belief in the superiority of his own conclusions. As Beard became convinced that the government's conduct of foreign policy was inimical to the larger good of a collectivist democracy, he took a more activist and public role, challenging elected and appointed officials and claiming to represent the true democratic spirit.

Beard's greatest fear was the growth of the navy and its consequent expansion into the Pacific. In a series of three muckraking *New Republic* articles in the early 1930s he attacked the navy and its lobbying group, the Navy League, for its goals of expansion, its connection to the steel industry, and for the league's hiring of a convicted felon as its primary publicity agent. In these articles he bluntly asserted that "armaments make war possible," since certain groups whose economic interests lay in actual conflict always exist. In 1938 Beard would straightforwardly affirm before the House Commission on Naval Affairs that increased naval expenditures were part of plans for "aggressive warfare in the Far Pacific or Far Atlantic."[114]

Beard's fear of naval expansion, his vocal support for the Nye Committee's investigation of the armaments industry and its impact on American entry into World War I—despite his private reservations concerning the sensationalistic approach—and his support of the Neutrality Acts all reflected the American public's fear of the outbreak of war and a belief in the necessity of avoiding foreign entanglements. According to a poll conducted by George Gallup's American Institute of Public Opinion in 1936, 95 percent of the American public opposed intervention in any European war for any reason. A year later, in a similar poll, 70 percent of Americans called the United States's entrance into World War I a definite mistake. Although most isolationists were conservatives like William Randolph Hearst and Charles Lindberg, Beard joined a substantial group of so-called liberal isolationists that included Harry Elmer Barnes, Stuart Chase, George Soule, George Norris, Hiram Johnson, William Borah, and Gerald Nye, who saw foreign involvement and the war that might result as the greatest threat to domestic reform.[115]

As a historian, Beard became absorbed in the reasons behind America's drift toward war. Were the bankers and manufacturing interests repeating their actions of twenty years before? Or had Franklin Roosevelt become Henry IV seeking to conceal his failure to solve domestic problems behind the melodramatics of an aggressive foreign policy? From the beginning, Beard had demonstrated his wariness of Roosevelt's foreign policy. He had successively alternated praise for FDR with implicit warnings about past political leaders' use of war to retain power. In 1935 Beard more explicitly noted that "President Roosevelt has given no indication that this alternative will be rejected." In October 1937, when FDR followed his defeat on Supreme Court reorganization with an appeal in a Chicago speech to "quarantine the aggressors," Beard became convinced that Roosevelt had made his choice.[116]

Beard's opposition to American involvement in European affairs was based on his belief that the United States had no achievable goals there.

He never opposed European or Asian military responses to fascism; in fact, he saw their national interest as requiring action to prevent German and Japanese domination. He wrote many articles critical of fascism, helped both the New School exiles and the Frankfurt school at Columbia, and even opposed applying the Neutrality Act to Republican Spain. Yet he insisted that Washington's Farewell Address correctly attributed different interests to Europe and the United States. Like most isolationists, Beard denied any military threat to the continental United States from either Germany or Japan and considered the existing military sufficient for defense. He agreed with his friend and fellow isolationist Stuart Chase that discussion of a possible invasion was an utter waste of time and "an admirable topic for a debate in an insane asylum." The United States had begun its history in a world filled with despotism and, if necessary, could again survive in such a world. Its best hope for preserving its own unique culture of freedom resided in correcting its domestic weaknesses and staying out of the war. This was the true national interest, a true purpose for action. An anguished Beard pleaded, "If we go to war, let us go to war for some grand and national advantage openly discussed and deliberately arrived at, and not to bail out farmers, bankers, and capitalists or to save politicians from the pain of dealing with a domestic crisis."[117]

As the external and internal pressures for war mounted, Beard became uncharacteristically bitter. His vision of progress toward a cooperative, collectivist democracy depended on a rational citizenry, social scientists' freedom of inquiry, and articulation of empirically based, ethical alternatives to the status quo. War hysteria under the domination of entrenched business interests would destroy this, perhaps forever. In May 1940 he confided to fellow rebel and isolationist Harry Barnes, "The mad dogs are off again with foam flying. My experience with 'men of science' in 1917 prepared me for the run but I am not as young and strong as I was then." Despite this, Beard would continue his work and purposive vision throughout the war years.[118]

6

Harold D. Lasswell and the Lost

Opportunity of the Purposive School

The career of Harold Lasswell in the 1920s and 1930s reflects both the enormous promise of the purposive school and its simultaneous weaknesses. A prodigious worker, Lasswell nearly equaled Beard in his output and surpassed him in the range of his interdisciplinary perspective. A favorite student of both Merriam and Robert Park, he mastered the empirical techniques they had only championed and which purposive thinkers like Lynd recognized as essential for the creation of a truly useful science of society. Unlike either Lynd or Beard, Lasswell developed a sophisticated and consistent individual and social psychology that promised to actually locate universal human values. Yet, despite a consistent and apparently deeply felt commitment during this period to create a social science firmly based on normative goals, by the early 1940s he had adopted a value-free empiricism which accepted established political elites and abandoned advocacy of public education and criticism.

One cannot attribute Lasswell's failure to any lack of interest in a normative, purposive social science. He studied with George Herbert Mead as well as Merriam and Park at the University of Chicago and possessed a clear conception of pragmatism as directed toward specific goals. In a 1928 review he noted that the conventional view of pragmatism as merely a "convenient method of burning over the ground and ridding it of old underbrush" was totally insufficient. Late in his life, Lasswell noted his consistent indebtedness to Dewey, whom he had met while still a high school student, and he described his own approach to social policy as "a contemporary adaptation of the general approach . . . recommended by John Dewey and his colleagues in the development of American pragmatism." Throughout his career he consistently maintained that "the problem of politics is the advancement of the good life," and he felt that the proper role of the social scientist was to aid in this advancement. The social sciences became, in Lasswell's words, "comparative history with a public purpose," and social scientists the individuals responsible for the determination of this purpose. Lasswell wrote probably the most laudatory of all the reviews of *Knowledge for What?*, praising it as "brave" and completely correct in its identification of the major problems of social science. His one criticism was that the book was not activist and specific enough in its call for an increased role for social scientists in the creation of a better and more humane society.[1]

Like Lynd and Beard, Lasswell insisted that quantitative and qualitative work were not antithetical. One did not have to sacrifice objectivity in order to achieve a purposive social science. One should use an ethical perspective in choosing research projects and in determining the best uses of the results of such work, but in the actual research one should utilize maximum objectivity and the most sophisticated methods available. Lasswell described much of the empirical research of the times as similar to "the acquisitive reflexes of the magpie." He derided Ogburn's choice for the Eleven Twenty-six inscription as indicative of the pervasive and mindless "lure of measurement" and of a time when individuals had won renown for "writing books in which they said that social facts could be counted and [then] counting some." Lasswell perceived social scientists' role to include both a description of the functioning of society and the consequent control and manipulation of that system to achieve a harmonious social order. His ultimate goal for empirical social research was a politics of prevention in which social scientists—or, as he called them, social psychiatrists—would forestall the outbreak of wars and social violence through the alleviation of personal and collective insecurities.[2]

Yet, despite his public advocacy of a social science based on ethical goals, critics have consistently labeled Lasswell as an amoral technician absolutely unconcerned with values or social betterment. One 1935 reviewer called him "the new Machiavelli" without even Machiavelli's implicit ideals. Floyd Matson, in his scathing critique of the assumptions of modern social science, *The Broken Image*, singled out Lasswell as one of the leaders in the destruction of the normative perspective in contemporary social science. Even those sympathetic to Lasswell's claims of ethical orientation have, in what I consider a curious reversal, located its origins in the late 1930s in response to the totalitarian threat. Lasswell himself quietly but firmly insisted that he had adhered to the same value premises throughout his career.[3]

Much of the misinterpretation derives from the nature of Lasswell's "high-German style of writing," a dense, unemotional, often nearly incomprehensible prose. Part of the attraction of such language for Lasswell stemmed from his personal shyness, which he hid through playing the role of David Riesman's inside dopester and affecting an "exterior of omniscience." Political scientist and novelist Leo Rosten described his friend and mentor's actions in the following way: "Not that he is callous—far from it, he is just better at analyzing emotions than expressing them. He feels, I think, very deeply—when no one is watching." In 1941 Lasswell laughed that his own coworkers used to tune in to his radio broadcasts to see if he really could deliver a comprehensible address to a popular audience. Still, the major reason behind his adoption of such language was his desire to be objective. Lasswell agreed with Beard that absolute objectivity was impossible; unlike Beard, however, he felt that the development of new language, free from the connotations of past terms, could help eliminate some of this subjectivity. Nor did Lasswell's concern for objective methodology end with language. From the psychoanalytic interview to world politics, he attempted to apply a "configurative analysis" that would study every aspect of the subject equally and eliminate the researcher's covert biases. This scientific emphasis led many superficial readers to overlook Lasswell's normative goals.[4]

In many ways, however, the inner logic of Lasswell's quest for a more scientific methodology led him, like Mitchell, to a confirmation of Matson's critique. As Lasswell's career progressed, the abstract terminology of psychoanalysis, physiology, and content analysis replaced the simpler language of his earlier work. As his work became more abstract, Lasswell did incorporate frequent statements about the need for normative goals for social scientists into his writing, especially in nontechnical articles and book reviews. Yet the implications of his work, and especially of its audience, led Lasswell toward a technocratic social science. Unlike his earlier work and that of Lynd and Beard, which appealed to an educated citizenry as well as to fellow social scientists, Lasswell directed his later work almost exclusively to specialists within various areas of the social sciences. This made eminent sense to Lasswell, since even more than Lynd and Beard he advocated a purposive policymaking role for social scientists. In contrast with Lynd and Beard, who turned to the public to inquire what people wanted, Lasswell was certain that this was unnecessary because his perspective had located true desires. Once social psychiatrists–policy scientists attained positions of responsibility, they could relieve personal and collective insecurity and create a harmonious society. Public input was unnecessary and even dangerous. Surprisingly, for all his astute writing on the subject of power, Lasswell never questioned the cost of access to policymaking roles. In the mid-1930s he had called for social scientists to use propaganda and every other technique to aid the "middle-income skill group," possessors of the desired ethical values, in their rise to power. By the late 1930s, however, a number of career reversals had led him to place his techniques in the service of existing government and private industry. Like Mitchell, he did not question the goals of his research or the recipients of its results. Like Merriam, he accepted the government as the proper decision maker. And finally, like Thurman Arnold, Lasswell consciously used myths and untruths to manipulate the public in the service of an allegedly moral organization.

Like Merriam and Lynd, Lasswell had a strong childhood background in evangelical Protestantism. His father, a Presbyterian minister in a number of small Illinois towns, was interested in reform politics, and the family spent summer vacations at the old Salem Chautauqua, where young Harold met William Jennings Bryan and Robert LaFollette. Although Lasswell eventually forsook his Presbyterian faith, he confessed to its residual effect in his interest in preaching on a secular level. A more lasting influence was his parents' positions as local intellectuals. Brought up around books and intellectual conversation, Lasswell developed into a precocious student. After graduating as class valedictorian at the age of sixteen, Lasswell received a scholarship to the University of Chicago by winning a competitive examination in modern history. In 1918 he entered the university, beginning a twenty-year association with it.[5]

Lasswell continued his brilliant academic career at Chicago by winning awards in debating and scholarship. When he graduated with a degree in economics in 1922, Merriam convinced him to enter graduate school in the field of political science. In retrospect, Lasswell attributed his abandonment of economics for political science to the relatively untouched nature of the latter. The department's innovative faculty and their encouragement of graduate students to work in unconventional areas further impressed him. Lasswell immediately became an instructor, a position he held until he was appointed an assistant professor in 1927.[6]

From the time his first article was published in 1923, Lasswell adopted the functionalist perspective of Merriam and the Chicago political science department. In "Chicago's First Ward: A Case Study in Political Behavior," Lasswell investigated Chicago's infamous First Ward, where the corrupt political bosses "Hinky Dink" McKenna and "Bathhouse John" Coughlin effectively controlled the district's voters. Rejecting the institutionalism of John Burgess and the moralism and genteel snobbery of James Bryce and A. Lawrence Lowell, Lasswell discovered the reasons for the bosses' success in the effective functioning of the wards. McKenna and Coughlin met the basic human needs of their constituents by providing city jobs for the unemployed, food and shelter for the temporarily disadvantaged, and intercession with local authorities for those in trouble. Lasswell departed even further from the dominant perspective by openly commending McKenna for his individual decency and chiding well-to-do reformers for their lack of understanding and concern for the needs of the ward's inhabitants.[7]

Lasswell's second work, "Political Policies and the International Investment Market," added an activist orientation to this functional perspective. In it, Lasswell argued that investor nations used their financial interests to control and manipulate weaker states and that some countries blocked from legitimate investment by their lack of colonies and other nations' refusal to provide opportunities on an equal basis turned to military adventuring to gain suitable outlets. Like Beard at about roughly the same time, he demonstrated the inevitable interaction between politics and economics. Lasswell also considered it his responsibility as an expert to recommend a solution for the problem. He suggested that all nations engage in a "consortium" agreement which would guarantee equal investment opportunities to all and forbid military intervention for the collection of debts. This arrangement would benefit both investor and debtor nations by preventing the constant hostilities that so often escalated into major wars. The roots of Lasswell's later goal of a preventive politics are discernible as early as this work.[8]

The third theme found throughout Lasswell's early work was his insistence that both functional and activist perspectives required careful attention to the scientific method. This was his chief point in his many book reviews for the *American Journal of Sociology* in the 1920s. He lavishly praised Carroll Woody's *Chicago Primary of 1926* for the author's active participation in a political campaign, exploration of tactics as part of an ongoing process, and attempts at measurement, but he criticized it for failing to suggest reforms. On the other hand, he fulminated against many activist books for their lack of scientific rigor and praised others for their scientific approach despite the unimportance of their conclusions.[9]

In 1924 Lasswell coauthored his first book, a junior college textbook on labor economics. As an economics instructor at a Chicago business college, Lasswell had perceived the need for a text that concentrated on the specific environmental conditions of American workers and explained their beliefs and actions to students who had little or no contact with wage laborers. By reading about workers' labor and working conditions described from a functional perspective, students could recognize issues which abstractions like the wage fund doctrine ignored. Although the authors professed complete objectivity, they did favor collective bargaining, social insurance, and even labor's restriction of output under certain conditions. Most important, they insisted "that the factory exists for man and not man for the factory, that in the ultimate analysis all industrial conditions must be justified in terms of human welfare."[10]

Although Lasswell's early work demonstrated a wide range of interests, he soon began to concentrate on political psychology. Merriam had trumpeted the call for a scientific study of the subject several years earlier, but no one, including Merriam, had a very clear idea of how to begin. Given his current interest in measurement, Lasswell turned first to public opinion and in 1923 suggested an audit of public opinion similar to the National Bureau of Economic Research's enumeration of business cycles. Merriam patiently calmed his zealous student and suggested the less ambitious task of determining current public opinion on the issue of public utility regulation. After writing an article on the subject, Lasswell sought to expand his perspective and, with Merriam's backing, received one of the first ssRc grants in order to study "institutional attitudes" in Geneva, Berlin, and London. Throughout the year he spent abroad, but especially at the London School of Economics, experts advised him to concentrate on a specific topic in a limited historical period and study it in depth.[11]

Although Lasswell strongly resisted that advice at the time, he began to recognize that he was really not interested in the tabulation of public opinion but rather in that abstract creature "political man." Surely one could not develop a truly functional view of politics without an adequate explanation of the actions of its participants. Moreover, without this understanding one could hardly change political institutions to better meet societal and individual needs. Lasswell began his search for the motivations behind individual political activity through an examination of civic education and one of its primary agents, propaganda.

During the 1920s Merriam became the general editor of a University of Chicago series on international civic education. Lasswell became Merriam's unofficial troubleshooter for the project and undertook such thankless tasks as determining the qualifications of possible contributors, revising manuscripts, and attempting (unsuccessfully) to edit the profascist opinions out of Robert Michels's manuscript on Italian civic education. In the summer of 1925 Merriam sent Lasswell to Germany to study patriotic organizations there and to determine the possibilities and limitations of an extended study. Lasswell submitted an outline report emphasizing the psychological basis of German political attitudes and their roots in the populace's past experiences and convictions. He pointed out how such apparently secondary influences as patriotic holidays, collections for patriotic purposes, special assembly lectures by war veterans, sightseeing trips to battlefields and war museums, and teacher hiring and promotion policies had a profound effect on the context of the overall psychological attitude. Again and again he stressed that adequate comprehension of political behavior must begin with insight into the influence of such agencies on individuals. Indeed, it was at this time that Lasswell became interested in determining what factors led one member of a society to become a patriot and another a "sub-patriot," an interest that would mature into his classic *Psychopathology and Politics*.[12]

Given Lasswell's interest in international attitudes, his British professors' advice, and his purposive goals, World War I propaganda seemed an almost preordained choice for research. During the 1920s more and more Americans were beginning to recognize the pervasive influence that propaganda agencies, especially America's Committee on Public Information, had had on their conduct during the war. As the Beards described the situation, "Never before in our history had such a campaign of education been organized; never before had American citizens realized how thoroughly, how irresistibly a modern government could impose its views upon the whole nation and under a barrage of publicity stifle dissent with dedications, assertions, official reasons, and reiteration." Nor was this awareness limited to the United States. Many Germans came to regard their susceptibility to Wilsonian propaganda as the main cause of their defeat, and several German universities offered popular courses on the subject.[13]

Lasswell himself had significant interest and experience in the art of persuasion. Like Beard, he was a champion debater in high school and college. At the age of sixteen he had used his skills to become a star encyclopedia salesman, selling over six thousand dollars' worth in small Illinois towns. Lasswell could also draw on Merriam's personal experiences as "Carlo," director of American propaganda efforts in Italy during the war. Merriam had written a pioneering essay in 1919 exploring the various techniques used to convince the Italian public of the United States's commitment to the war and had advocated the study of propaganda in *New Aspects of Politics.* In the spring semester of 1926, he and Lasswell even cotaught a research course on propaganda.[14]

Despite his activist interests, Lasswell did not share German sociologists' and American revisionist historians' view of propaganda as a vicious social evil to be detected and combated. Reflecting his interests in functionalism and scientific methodology, he concentrated, as his title stated, on propaganda *technique.* He was interested in the functioning of propaganda—how it worked and influenced individuals. All governments in the age of mass communications engaged in propaganda to promote their policies, and propaganda had become a natural function of politics. By itself propaganda was no more moral or immoral than a "pump handle." In *Propaganda Technique in World War I* Lasswell described and classified technique. As he would later put it in his well-known first paragraph of *Politics: Who Gets What, When, How,* "The science of politics states conditions; the philosophy of politics justifies preferences. This book, restricted to political analysis, declares no preferences. It states conditions." Lasswell's definite preferences would come later.[15]

The question Lasswell sought to answer was which propaganda techniques the various nations had used during World War I and which had proved most effective. In an approach that fifteen years later he would condemn as too impressionistic, Lasswell intensively studied American, British, French, and German newspapers and government records and the many memoirs and analyses published since the end of the war. He did not distinguish between the Allied and Axis powers; the propaganda of both sides shared common goals, and "everybody tried to tar the other fellow with the same stick." Lasswell identified five objects for wartime propaganda: (1) to make the enemy appear satanic and completely evil, (2) to develop effective propaganda for every different group in the opposing countries, (3) to assure the civilian population of ultimate victory, (4) to preserve friendships among allies and influence neutrals, and (5) to demoralize the enemy by creating dissension. Propaganda included every possible medium from posters and billboards to assassination. Lasswell pointed out that one of the most effective propaganda instruments of the war was the English sentimental novel *Christie,* which purported to be the letters of an English girl who went to Germany to study the violin and gradually awakened to the brutality of German culture.[16]

Lasswell also stressed the psychological basis of successful propaganda. Human beings, he said, especially in times of stress and insecurity, were not rational creatures and were most effectively influenced and controlled through their emotions. In wartime, it was quite easy to arouse hatred by reporting or even fabricating an atrocity story. As Lasswell sardonically remarked, "A handy rule for arousing hate is, if at first they do not enrage, use an atrocity. It has been employed with unvarying success in every conflict known to man." In other cases, as in trying to influence a neutral country, the emotion the propagandist needed to arouse was affection, or at least identification. For this purpose, the propagandist attempted to picture the enemy as evil and his own nation as moral, and to increase identification through such activity as personal contact between the citizens of the two nations. For instance, Lasswell pointed out how Great Britain successfully swayed American public opinion by sending titled aristocrats to mingle socially with influential Americans.[17]

Although *Propaganda Technique* limits itself to stating conditions, Lasswell, in what would become an established routine, simultaneously wrote several articles in which he noted his preferences. He quickly admitted that it was obvious that propaganda "may be employed for subversive, fraudulent, libelous, and lascivious purposes." Yet to pretend that it could be wished out of existence was foolishly naive. In socially diverse, technologically complex societies, some means of ensuring social stability was necessary, especially during crises. Lasswell even suggested that nonviolent persuasion through propaganda was superior to governments' previous reliance on brute force. Since propaganda was inevitable in the modern world, social scientists should become skilled at its use and then apply it to reach normative ideals. Since the public listened to the loudest or most "entrancing" voice, the proper role of the ethical social scientist was "to outbrazen the rest." Propaganda, like Lasswell's pump handle, was a tool one could use either to draw water or to mug an innocent bystander. The function of the social scientist was to make sure that it pumped water. If social scientists truly wished to bring about a just, harmonious society, they must use all the tools at their disposal, especially such powerful ones as propaganda.[18]

In a post–World War II memorandum Lasswell noted that in the 1920s he had conceived a trilogy on propaganda—its technique, its causes and consequences, and its control. After *Propaganda Technique in World War I* was published, Lasswell turned to the first part of the second of these, the roots of propaganda within the individual personality. He explained in an article published the same year as *Propaganda Technique* that "collective attitudes" such as response to propaganda were simply a distribution of individual acts. To study collective attitudes without intensive study of individual cases was simply "a form of taxidermy." In his commitment to comprehending the political process, Lasswell turned to the study of these individual acts. This emphasis on the individual participant and his or her actions became the central theme of Lasswell's work and the basis of much of his reputation.[19]

In his concentration on the individual and individual psychology, Lasswell conformed to the position of such purposive thinkers as Dewey, Lynd, and Sapir, who insisted that ideals and goals must be based on individual needs and desires. Although purposive thinkers recognized the necessity for research on group interaction and public opinion, they argued for a constant recognition of the basis of group behavior in individual behavior and thought. American political and social thinkers had long emphasized the need to study individuals to maintain democratic society. Walter Lippmann, in his *Preface to Politics* (1913), scorned the formalistic study of institutions and analyzed politics through individual political behavior and attitudes. Political scientists such as Merriam stood before conventions and graduate seminars expounding the impending glories of political psychology. Yet no one, in either psychology or political science, possessed the techniques or knowledge for an adequate approach to such a study.

Lasswell's quest became a physical one as he traveled across the United States and Europe looking for a useful political psychology. He turned first to Lippmann in New York but found him vague and somewhat hostile to the quantitative research Lasswell was then proposing. He next stopped at the London School of Economics, where he attended the lectures of Lippmann's mentor, Graham Wallas. Lasswell was ambivalent about Wallas. He agreed with Wallas's criticism of American social science for its insistence on "all" the data and its lack of activism; yet Wallas had turned from his earlier notation of the irrational bases of political thought in *Human Nature in Politics* to didactic calls for increased rationality. Lasswell saw this as naive and dangerously superficial.[20]

Nor did Lasswell approve of Merriam's conception of political psychology. Although he readily gave Merriam credit for championing political psychology and for introducing him to the field, he did not accept Merriam's opinion on the most beneficial approach to the subject. Merriam's concern was with what the social psychologist Floyd Allport called the "common segment" aspect of psychology, which deals with the common characteristics of people in a particular group and includes such subjects as public opinion, intelligence tests, and political habits. Merriam continued to be interested in measuring political traits and in

1924, while Lasswell was studying in Europe, brought in psychologist L. L. Thurstone to develop mathematical scales for the measurement of social attitudes and opinions. Lasswell argued that the "face-to-face" perspective offered considerably more insight because it treats the individual in a holistic manner and examines political acts in context.[21]

Lasswell's and Merriam's differences over the most useful approach to political psychology were indicative of a deeper split. Their actual personal contact during these years was slight, and Lasswell obtained many of Merriam's insights secondhand from Merriam's frequent collaborator and data collector, Harold Gosnell. Lasswell gave Merriam complete credit for the permissive atmosphere of the department and, like the rest of the staff, referred to him affectionately as "the Captain." Yet, in private and in some of his later articles, Lasswell criticized Merriam for proceeding in an eclectic and haphazard manner after *New Aspects* and producing sloppy and undigested work. Lasswell maintained that the department degenerated into fact gathering, which brought in funds and political support at the price of abandoning the ethical purpose of the social sciences.[22]

Although Chicago's political scientists were unable to provide insights for Lasswell's individualistic political psychology, the university's sociologists were much more helpful. Social philosopher George Herbert Mead was a key intellectual influence on Lasswell. Mead maintained that all behavior had social origins, and consequently the individual and society were a cohesive whole. Lasswell studied under Mead as an undergraduate and was an occasional visitor at Mead's home, especially when Dewey visited his old friend and former colleague. According to Lasswell, Mead's popular advanced social psychology course provided the basis for Chicago sociology's well-known life history studies. Lasswell also took two graduate courses from Robert Park, who with Ernest Burgess encouraged this approach. Park, who bluntly declared that "social relations are finally and fundamentally personal relations," was also interested in communications and the press and was an early reader of Lasswell's propaganda manuscript. Park considered Lasswell "one of the few students that I had whom I would call brilliant . . . altogether the most stimulating, interesting, and thoroughgoing student that I have ever had," and Lasswell, who was often quite waspish about his older Chicago colleagues, had "great reverence" for the "always interesting" Park.[23]

Chicago sociologists' acceptance of Lasswell is evidenced by his many publications in their *American Journal of Sociology* and especially their invitation to him to give a paper at the central colloquium of the 1927 annual meeting of the American Sociological Society. In honor of W. I. Thomas, the society's recently elected president, a group of distinguished speakers presented a series of papers on "The Individual in Relation to His Society." Unlike most previous work, which had investigated individuals exclusively through such techniques as biometric measurements and intelligence tests, this conference viewed personality as a product of group life. Thomas set the tone in the first sentence of his opening address: "It appears that the particular behavior patterns and the total personality are overwhelmingly conditioned by the type of experience encountered by the individual in the course of his life."[24]

Lasswell's article, "Types of Political Personalities," largely agreed with Thomas's thesis. In it, Lasswell proposed the existence of three types of political personalities—the agitator, the statesman, and the boss—and demonstrated the role of each in politics. Lasswell freely admitted that social conditions were primarily responsible for the development of these types but was unsure about exactly which conditions. Although he was certain that Chicago sociology had provided a key ingredient for understanding the individual personality, Lasswell felt the task was still incomplete. For one thing, he agreed with his original teacher Mead that biological processes play a part in the development of personality. Like Thomas, Park, and many other social scientists, Lasswell turned to psychoanalysis to deepen his insights into human psychology. Unlike the others, psychoanalysis would gradually become the basis for his perspective on the individual.[25]

Although Merriam was relatively uninterested in individual behavior and scorned Freud, whom he referred to as "the great Unanalyzed," his unmatched connections within social science provided Lasswell with a superb teacher in Elton Mayo. An Australian professor of philosophy and psychology, Mayo had become involved in the treatment of neurotics, especially soldiers suffering from shell shock, during World War I. His reading of works by such neurologists as Pierre Janet and psychiatrists such as Freud and Jung convinced Mayo that the cure for neuroses was through the creation of strong social bonds. Mayo applied these ideas to contemporary events, and especially to Australia's postwar industrial unrest, arguing that workers' "fantasy compensations" arose out of the owners' disregard for them as human beings. Feeling isolated at the University of Queensland, he left and was trying to work his way across the United States and eventually to England by giving lectures when Dr. Vernon Kellogg of the National Research Council befriended him. Kellogg introduced him to Merriam, who found Mayo's emphasis on empirical techniques, the utility of psychology, and practical goals identical with his own. Kellogg and Merriam in turn brought Mayo to the equally impressed Ruml, who used his Rockefeller connections to arrange for Mayo's articles to be published in high-paying magazines, a lectureship at the University of Pennsylvania, consulting work with private industrialists, and, finally, a Rockefeller-funded research professorship at Harvard Business School.[26]

The original appeal of Mayo's psychiatric approach to Lasswell, as it had been to Merriam, was its emphasis on the effects of society on the personality. Unlike psychoanalysts and even more than the eclectic American psychiatrists Adolf Meyer and William Alanson White, Mayo regarded the social environment as the key factor in individual neuroses. In a famous study of Western Electric's Hawthorne plant in Cicero, Illinois, Mayo and his coinvestigators isolated a small experimental group and began to adjust such variables as lighting conditions, rest periods, and pay. They discovered that as a general rule, production increased with each experimental change, even when, as in the case of poorer lighting, it logically should have fallen. After much agonized theorizing, Mayo and his associates realized that the cause of the increased production was the strong interpersonal relationships among the group itself and their positive self-image as deriving from their selection as participants in the experiments. When management applied the results to other departments and began to seriously consider workers' suggestions and complaints, production shot up. Mayo pointed out that this demonstrated that the entire social environment, not just the family background of childhood, affected the individual personality.[27]

Mayo's approach further appealed to Lasswell because of its strong physiological and clinical background. Although Mayo actually flunked out of Australian medical school on three separate occasions and never came close to graduating, he used that training and his experiences as a consultant on neuroses to pose successfully as a physician in the United States. Mayo recognized the organic basis of many psychological problems and insisted on an extensive physical examination before searching for social causes through analysis. During his tenure at Harvard, Mayo maintained a small clinical practice at Boston Psychopathic Hospital. In fact, Mayo's biographer claimed that Merriam sent a psychologically unsettled Lasswell to work with Mayo more to receive psychological counseling than to study psychiatry. Mayo did analyze Lasswell, taught him basic analytic techniques, and assigned him a few mildly neurotic Harvard students to work with. Lasswell found this clinical perspective extremely rewarding and continued to do analytic work at Chicago and elsewhere throughout his long career.[28]

Finally, and less obviously, Mayo attracted Lasswell because of his concern for the individual human being. Although Mayo began the Western Electric experiments, he left it to his assistant, Fritz Roethlisberger, to supervise them and write up the conclusions. Mayo was principally concerned with the implications of the research for workers within the system. In his *Human Problems of an Industrial Civilization* Mayo eloquently asserted that industrial management had previously missed the entire point. While they had concentrated on purely economic problems, the important issues lay within the human sphere, particularly the worker's adjustment to the work situation and happiness within it.[29]

Lasswell and Mayo first met in September 1925 at the First Annual SSRC Hanover Conference. The two liked one another, and several months later Lasswell asked Merriam if he could get Mayo to take him on as an unpaid assistant. In 1926 he spent a month with Mayo in Philadelphia, ostensibly learning how to administer tests for Merriam's civic education series. A year later he joined Mayo at Harvard Business School, where the two became close friends and Lasswell submerged himself in psychopathological literature. During this time Lasswell accepted two key ideas that would permeate and redirect his purposive social science.[30]

The first of these was Mayo's emphasis on adjustment. Mayo's thought reflected his own upbringing in a rigidly moralistic upper-class family. He personally retained many Victorian beliefs and refused to accept the dominance of sexual factors over all others. He denied the omnipotence of family influences, emphasized the entire environment, and, most significantly, insisted on the possibility of total and rapid change. Mayo based his entire analytic approach on such an optimistic perspective. He was relatively unconcerned with the etiology of neuroses; his primary interest was in the cure, which, he thought, lay in the reestablishment of strong social bonds. Often, in direct opposition to Freud's theories on transference, Mayo encouraged his patients to become dependent on him and thus form links with society once again. In short, Mayo emphasized the individual's adjustment back into society.[31]

Although Lasswell described Mayo's work as "reverbalized so as not to shake up schools of business and the companies he was working for," it was more than that. Mayo not only desexualized but also deradicalized Freud. Unlike Freudian theory, which views society critically, Mayo's thought accepted industrial society and its institutions. Despite his concern for workers, Mayo, like Merriam, fervently opposed socialism and the concept of class consciousness. Once a worker adjusted to the social environment, happiness would follow. For all of his undeniable humanism, Mayo never seriously considered that workers might be unhappy because of deep structural problems within society. That approach accounted in large part for his attractiveness to the Rockefeller Foundation and progressive business interests. Lasswell's acceptance of this concept of adjustment colored much of his later thought and led him, as it had Mayo and Merriam, to an acceptance of the status quo.[32]

Although this concept would have the greatest overall impact, of more immediate utility was Mayo's borrowing of Freud's belief that a very thin line separates the abnormal from the normal and that pathological examples are excellent case studies for ordinary behavior. One can see how this belief would appeal to Lasswell, who was searching for the key to an individualistic political psychology. By examining individuals with extreme political tendencies, Lasswell hoped to determine how normal individuals act in political situations. Moreover, his emphasis on irrational behavior conformed to what he had seen on a collective basis during World War I. Although much later in his career Lasswell emphatically denied that all political behavior is neurotic, he consistently maintained the utility of using extreme cases as insight into normal behavior. Lasswell's overemphasis on irrational behavior in normal individuals caused him to scorn those like Wallas who believed that people could be taught to act in their own best interests.[33]

Mayo had thought a good deal about the implications for society of his conclusions about individual behavior. He believed that group decisions were even more irrational than individual ones and advocated the addition of courses on psychopathology to the political science curriculum. The only hope for a harmonious society, he concluded, was through control by benevolent industrial managers and psychiatrists. The whole concept of patriotism and political involvement was simply a "primitive idea" or "obsession." Under Mayo's direction, Lasswell in 1927 completed "Patriotism," a manuscript that explores exactly this undemocratic hypothesis.[34]

Lasswell began his study on patriotism with an examination of the files of Mayo and Gilbert Van Hamilton, director of the Bureau of Social Hygiene's Division of Psychobiological Research. Hamilton, a California psychiatrist and student of Adolf Meyer, was involved in a sophisticated study of sexual relations and marriage and had conducted extensive in-depth interviews. Through Mayo's intervention, Hamilton allowed Lasswell to examine his files and question some of his patients about their politics. These files and interviews, significantly not of politicians per se but of individuals with severe marital or sexual problems, provided the core data not only for "Patriotism" but also for the later *Psychopathology and Politics*.[35]

"Patriotism" followed Mayo's theories almost slavishly. Individuals began with "a sense of sin" which resulted in "obsessions" caused "by a floating burden of guilt" "swollen by a multitude of past reveries." These obsessions caused patriotic individuals to attach themselves to a social institution. By acting in conformity to the guidelines of this institution, usually the state, the individual avoided a sense of sin. This situation was extremely dangerous because it prevented the individual from looking at existence realistically. In fact, it was a potential tinderbox for unscrupulous manipulators of society. In attempting to develop a typology of political personalities, Lasswell also adopted Mayo's conception of the "agitator" from a series of 1922 articles in the *Industrial Australia Mining Standard*. Finally, Lasswell repeated Mayo's unoriginal criticism of Freud's work as unscientific and totally dependent on a few physiological impulses and drives.[36]

One must view Lasswell's imitation of Mayo in the context of his overall career. Lasswell was famous, or probably more accurately infamous, for presenting large numbers of "tentative hypotheses," most of which never saw print. Moreover, the shy Lasswell possessed many elements of the chameleon in his personality. His Chicago colleague Harold Gosnell made the excellent observation that "Merriam sent him to England and he came back with an English accent, he sent him to Vienna and he came back with a full-grown psychoanalytic vocabulary, he sent him to the Soviet Union and when he came back he showed that Marx could be reconciled with Freud." Lasswell tended to reflect elements of his major associates' thoughts in his writings throughout his career. This could only be accentuated with Mayo, who encouraged transference in his analysis and, by Lasswell's own admission, was a personal role model.[37]

Lasswell, however, was unhappy with "Patriotism." For all of his admiration for Mayo's theory, he found his etiology imprecise, unscientific, and finally unsuccessful at explaining the motivations of his interviewees. If the causes of pathological behavior remained unknown, social scientists would never be able to adjust society to eliminate the roots of the problem. Despite his unkind references to Freudian theory in "Patriotism," he used a 1928–29 SSRC research fellowship to study psychoanalysis in Europe. Lasswell had first read Freud as a precocious fourteen-year-old and had used such Freudian terminology as *inferiority complexes* and *compensatory drives* in some of his earliest published work. But it was only after European study with Freudian luminaries Edward Hirtschmann, Paul Federn, Alfred Adler, Sandor Ferenczi, and Franz Alexander and analysis with Theodor Reik that Lasswell applied orthodox Freudian thought in a systematic fashion.[38]

In *Psychopathology and Politics* Lasswell used the six case studies he had used in "Patriotism" and thirteen more from Mayo and Hamilton's files and adopted a strict Freudian perspective. He temporarily abandoned the social orientation of Chicago sociology and Mayo and accepted the physiological etiology of Freud and Karl Abraham. Lasswell's shift may have stemmed in part from the influence of his analyst, Reik, who idolized Freud and slavishly copied his thought and even his physical mannerisms. Lasswell himself stated that a more important reason was his desire to test orthodox Freudian thought. He clearly recognized the tenuous nature of the work's hypothesis and illustrative materials, but he also believed scholars had never tested Freud's insights in good faith. Thus, Lasswell offered *Psychopathology* as more hypothesis than proven conclusion.[39]

Lasswell defined *politics* in this work as the process by which the irrational bases of society come into the open. He did not say that politics itself is irrational. What he did say was that individuals displace their sexual energy onto politics in a way that has no logical connection to the satisfaction of the repressed impulses. This repression provides the energy for the conduct of politics. Lasswell even constructed a formula to describe the activity of the political personality: $p \} d \} r = P$, where p represents private motives such as repressed childhood hatred of father or siblings, } stands for transformed into, d is displacement onto a public object, r is rationalization, and P is the public man. Lasswell later summarized this as "Private Motives Displaced on Public Objects Rationalized in Terms of the Public Interest." In other words, political personalities seek to fulfill their own goals while claiming to act for the common good.[40]

Given Lasswell's difficulties with Mayo's theory, his principal goal in *Psychopathology* was to discover what part of the individual's developmental experience caused the various types of political personalities. Relying on Freud's "Character and Anal Eroticism" of 1908 and Abraham's later classification of libidinal stages into oral, phallic, and genital,

Lasswell contended that a traumatic episode during one of the childhood libidinal stages causes the adult to fixate on one bodily function like an automobile stuck in low gear. Thus, the individual's later adolescent and adult behavior manifests itself largely as a response to the original trauma. Lasswell tentatively classified the political types as agitator, administrator, and theorist. He perceived the political agitator, who responds strongly in an oral or written matter and seeks excessive popular action, as representative of Abraham's oral type. Lasswell's example of the anal personality is the political administrator whose fastidious desire for order corresponds to the anal character's original obsession with feces and their disposal. The political theorist with his or her inhibited personal rage represents the phallic character who suffers excessive guilt from his or her unsuccessful repression of Oedipal sexual desire for the mother and jealous hatred of the father. Although the insufficient data weakened Lasswell's argument considerably, the results were far superior to those of the earlier Mayo-influenced study.[41]

Many critics, including one of the leading historians of the neo-Freudian school, noted this typology and classified Lasswell as an orthodox Freudian, but this was never true, even in *Psychopathology*. Freud's thinking conflicted with Lasswell's overall purpose of using psychology to understand and control society in two crucial areas. Lasswell's initial problem with Freud's work, as it was for most American social scientists, was what Lasswell referred to "as the unhappy marriage of Freud and nineteenth century ethnology." In *Totem and Taboo* Freud relied on outmoded anthropological works such as James Frazer's *Golden Bough* to postulate the existence of a primal horde in which a dominant male monopolized all the females. The acceptance of cultural relativism and the diversity of cultural traits by contemporary anthropologists directly threatened Freud's assertion of the universality of human behavior and psychoanalytic concepts, and so he simply refused to accept them. Freud's behavior left even an apologetic Lasswell admitting that Freud's work was disappointing and "thin" from a sociological standpoint. As many previously orthodox analysts discovered when they came to the United States, Freud's claims of universal traits were difficult to take seriously amid America's cultural diversity. For Lasswell, with his training in the Chicago school of sociology, it was probably impossible.[42]

In addition to his knowledge of American and especially Chicago's diversity, Lasswell knew anthropology well and recognized its implications for refuting Freud and creating a more valid social and political psychology. In the same year that he traveled to Europe, Lasswell began an analysis of the implications of Bronislaw Malinowski's *Sex and Repression in Savage Society* for psychoanalysis. The choice of Malinowski as subject probably owed much to Mayo, whose successful career really began with Malinowski's early friendship and encouragement. In his research on the matrilineal Trobriand islanders Malinowski noted the absence of traditional Oedipal conflicts between sons and fathers. Further investigation revealed that in Trobriand society, the maternal uncle was in charge of discipline and training and received his nephews' resentment. Although Trobriand males did not seem to desire their mothers sexually, they did manifest a repressed lust for their forbidden sisters. Malinowski thus did not deny the Oedipal complex completely, but he did attempt to refute the alleged universality of the particular pattern Freud had identified. Freud had greatly overgeneralized from his clinical instances, and anthropology, if conducted scientifically, provided a corrective for such cultural blinders.[43]

Like Lynd, Lasswell saw the most important work in the social sciences as being done by individuals tracing the connections between culture and personality. As early as 1927 he had joined Lynd and other supporters in trying to get increased funding for such work from the ssrc. He was a close friend and great admirer of Edward Sapir, liberally quoted Boas, Benedict, and Paul Radin, and even called for extensive research in cross-cultural child development in the official Freudian journal *Imago*. Lasswell saw the field of personality and culture as essential to his purposive aims; only through its integrative function could social scientists achieve a coherent perspective on social behavior and possibly effect social change.[44]

Freud's belief in universal individual development took on particular significance for Lasswell as for many other Americans because it led directly to his cultural pessimism. Freud believed that the self-centered drives of the id derive from common experiences during infancy. One simply cannot ever fully tame one's aggressive instincts or sublimate them into socially responsible acts: "Every individual is virtually an enemy of civilization. . . . There are present in all men destructive, and therefore anti-social and anticultural trends. . . . Thus, civilization has to be defended against the individual." If one could not control individual human behavior, one surely could not mold an entire culture. Although Freud favored certain social reforms, he scorned mass efforts such as Russian communism, because they assumed that selfish social conduct resulted from cultural conditioning rather than biological nature. Freud tough-mindedly suggested that humankind might simply have to learn to live with its deficiencies.[45]

In *Psychopathology and Politics* Lasswell developed a "politics of prevention" which countered Freud's thinking on this very point and reflected the optimistic viewpoint of American psychiatry and its adaptation of Freud. Lasswell maintained that the proper goal of politicians and political experts should be the reduction of strain and maladjustment in society. Politicians should prevent problems rather than solve them. This view clearly assumed that cultural rather than biological factors caused individual anxieties and neuroses. Lasswell simply denied the Freudian belief in the dominance of assertive biological drives; tendencies toward compromise were simultaneously present and "easily organized." "Although the instinctive nature of man is in principle nonsocial and in important particulars anti-social, man is capable of socializing his destructive impulses to a very high degree." Since compromise was possible, and from Lasswell's perspective quite probable, humankind *could* achieve a harmonious utopia. Lasswell never—even during World War II and the Vietnam War—lost his faith that utopia would someday be achieved. His vision of the powers of social science and psychoanalysis to effect a mass cure represented one of the most optimistic uses of Freudian psychology ever developed.[46]

Lasswell's optimistic use of psychoanalysis conformed to its typical reception in the United States. Ever since Freud had stressed the optimistic and practical nature of psychoanalysis in his 1908 Clark University lectures, American psychiatrists and social thinkers had viewed it as a tool to be used for the betterment of society. Ironically, American eclectic psychiatrists such as White and Meyer and neurologists such as James Jackson Putnam welcomed psychoanalysis in their battle against a pessimistic psychiatry that viewed mental disorders as hereditary, physiological, and incurable. Psychoanalysis, with its faith in the individual's ability to discover the basis of his or her neuroses with the aid of an analyst and the power of catharsis, appeared to offer a way to combat and cure mental disease. Putnam, the Harvard Medical School professor whom Freud considered his most important American convert, accepted psychoanalysis because of its respect for the individual patient and the possibility of self-cure. Putnam prized psychoanalysis chiefly for its ethical implications; he had dedicated his life to curing the sick and seeking social justice, and he valued ideas and techniques that contributed to those goals.[47]

Lasswell shared Putnam's goals. He made clear that he saw psychoanalysis as a humanistic approach to individual psychology which offered individuals the opportunity to improve their personal and collective lives. Unlike behaviorism or Edward Titchener's "existential psychology," psychoanalysis looked at the situation from the individual's perspective. Moreover, it gave individuals the right and ability to choose their own goals through recognizing their personal situations. Psychoanalysis did not impose values; it gave patients the information necessary to choose their own. By liberating the individual from irrational behavior, psychoanalysis enabled people to act rationally. They could actually make decisions in their own best interests and construct a society that met their needs. Psychoanalysis thus provided the foundation for a purposive science of politics.[48]

American psychiatry shared Lasswell's goals in another way. Beginning roughly around 1908 with the establishment of the National Committee for Mental Hygiene under the direction of former mental patient Clifford Beers and with the support of Meyer, American psychiatry began to emphasize the prevention of mental illness. Since psychiatrists like Meyer and Boston Psychopathic Hospital's director E. E. Southard believed that much mental illness derived from environmental causes, they had begun to send out psychiatric social workers as early as 1905. Meyer proclaimed that "just as bacteriology studies the water supply and the air and food of communities, schools, and homes, so we psychopathologists have to study more effectively the atmosphere of the community and must devise safeguards in the localities from which the patients come, and to which they are to return." Meyer's close associate Stewart Paton could declare in 1924 that current crises required physicians and psychiatrists with their superior knowledge to take leadership roles in managing human affairs in order "to stabilize, perfect, and ensure the progress of civilization." By the year of *Psychopathology's* publication, White could call for a preventive psychiatry and declare that the immediate goals of the mental hygiene movement was the prevention of "all forms of social maladjustment and even of unhappiness."[49]

Given Lasswell's work with Mayo and his immersion into psychiatric literature, he could hardly have overlooked this familiar theme. The mental hygiene movement spread rapidly into industrial psychology in the 1920s, and Mayo noted his general conformance with its insights on several occasions. Moreover, Lasswell had worked with Hamilton, who was Meyer's student as well as the director of the Bureau of Social Hygiene's Division of Psychobiological Research. At Boston Psychopathic, Mayo and Lasswell's superior was McFie Campbell, another Meyer student and associate. The whole concept of preventive psychiatry conformed to Lasswell's vision of a harmonious society. Its one chief deficiency, as Lasswell patiently explained for the next decade, was psychiatry's relative ignorance of society and collective attitudes. One of his chief goals would become to convince psychiatrists and others that no true preventive psychiatry could exist without a politics of prevention.[50]

Lasswell's politics of prevention represents his first enumeration of the normative ideals toward which he insisted social scientists should strive. Before this he was quite vocal about the need for social researchers to work for ethical ends but, like many of the objectivists, painfully unclear about the exact nature of these goals. The politics of prevention, on the other hand, was a relatively clear normative statement, and social scientists' role in its achievement was likewise definite. But the nature of Lasswell's harmonious society had disturbing implications. He called for the alleviation of personal insecurities through "adjustment." But was harmonious society to be achieved by adjusting society to individual needs or by adjusting individuals to existing social institutions? Dewey, Lynd, and Beard advocated the former; Mayo and the American psychiatrists clearly accepted the latter. Lasswell, with his knowledge of how propaganda had successfully "adjusted" individuals to the demands of a militaristic state, opposed the latter interpretation. Nevertheless, the specific social institutions of Lasswell's harmonious society to which adjustment should take place remained undefined, as did the vexing problem of how social psychiatrists were to attain influential positions. The worldwide economic depression, the rise of totalitarianism, and the resultant increase of social tensions across the world pressured Lasswell to come up with answers to these questions.

Lasswell believed that the crises of the 1930s required a shift to what his friend and fellow advocate of political psychiatry Arnold Rogow later termed "applied psychoanalysis." With the exponential growth of social tensions during the 1930s, individual analysis seemed a luxury. Social forces were producing neurotics and psychotics faster than an army of psychiatrists could hope to cure them. Lasswell turned away from a study of the individual political participant to collective behavior. Although politics was a collection of individual behavior, one could and must approach it from a collective standpoint. "If we begin with a political pattern and view it against the private histories of actual people, we find the pattern takes on variable meanings from one group to another, but that broad groupings of associated meanings are possible of ascertainment." This shift conformed to Lasswell's insistence that his study of individual psychology derived from his wish to understand and eventually control the social process. A politics of prevention, unlike preventive psychiatry, dealt with groups, not individuals.[51]

In the early 1930s Lasswell wrote a series of articles in which he explained social institutions and behavior according to their roots in individual needs and desires. His most successful use of applied psychoanalysis was his early analysis of Hitler's psychological appeal to the German people. Lasswell knew Germany well; he had studied there in 1923 and 1928–29, undertook the preliminary outline of the German civic education study, and had noted the potential power and appeal of the Nazis as early as 1925. In "Psychology of Hitlerism" (1933) Lasswell attributed Hitler's success to his alleviation of the personal insecurity of many Germans. Suffering from their defeat in World War I and the economic deprivation of the 1920s, Germans longed to feel strong and powerful again. The Weimar Republic had failed to create symbols or policies that appealed to them, and Hitler successfully appropriated the authoritarian imperial symbols. They were particularly popular with the lower middle class, who felt threatened by both the proletariat and the upper bourgeoisie. Hitler used the Jews as a scapegoat to unite his followers through a common enemy. Germans could blame all national and personal problems on the Jews and eliminate their own problems and insecurities. Fascism used the libidinal energy thus released in political and paramilitary actions.[52]

The key work of applied psychoanalysis and Lasswell's most important seminal work was the 1934 *World Politics and Personal Insecurity*. Of all his works, it remains the most confusing—not merely because of its abstruse language but from the sheer number of hypotheses and suggestions it advances. Using a confusing and, I believe, eventually detrimental method he called "the configurative analysis," Lasswell examined the intricate subject of world politics from as many perspectives as possible. Most significantly, he added a Marxist perspective that emphasized change and the structure of power to his individualistic Freudian analysis. The result is a sometimes too accurate re-creation of the booming, buzzing confusion of reality. Yet, as Lasswell's original title, "The Future of War and Insecurity: A Contribution to Political Psychiatry," makes clear, the goal of the work was to predict and prevent the outbreak of war. In its clear depiction of a specific goal and a role for social scientists in the achievement of it, *World Politics* ranks as Lasswell's first truly purposive work.[53]

Lasswell adopted the configurative analysis for both scientific and purposive reasons. He argued that conventional disciplinary boundaries and their encouragement of one-dimensional cause-and-effect relationships did not adequately describe the social process. Reality was much more complicated than that. Just as he had earlier tried to add somatic and other considerations to the standard analytic interview, he now insisted on a truly holistic view of the social situation. The only way to make certain that one possessed sufficient information was to study the problem "from *every promising point of view.*" The more perspectives on a subject an analyst used, the better the chance of exposing new relationships. Since every social institution and event was unique, the most useful viewpoint depended on the particular situation. The expert could not know which was the most useful until he or she had studied them all.[54]

Despite Lasswell's obvious and consistent concern for a scientific methodology, he also developed the configurative analysis for purposive reasons. Although he talked about the equality of all factors, in *World Politics* he placed the major emphasis on the need to study events in a time frame, or "developmental analysis." This represented the primary attraction of Marxism for Lasswell. Conventional students of international relations had unanimously relied on an "equilibrium analysis," which viewed events within a fixed time frame and lacked any conception of ongoing development of social trends and possible futures. Marxist theory, on the other hand, provided a time-oriented analysis and predicted future trends. A preventive politics depended on some conception of the future so that positive developments could be encouraged and negative ones discouraged. "Trends have a way of changing direction; and often we can contribute to these changes by the skillful management of factors that condition them." To succeed, a politics of prevention must stop wars before they begin. The only way to do this, Lasswell thought, was to recognize the tendencies leading toward war and eliminate them at the root.[55]

In *World Politics* Lasswell developed for the first time the two complementary roles of the social scientist. First, social scientists needed to view social and political events from the "contemplative attitude" of describing and predicting the social process. This contemplative approach was not, however, sufficient in itself. Once the expert had predicted the trends, he or she should state his or her preferences and attempt to manipulate events to reach the desired social goals. Lasswell referred to this approach as the "manipulative attitude" to social science. The role of social experts, then, was to use their knowledge to aid in the achievement of a new and better society by encouraging alternatives to the institutions and behaviors that prevented individuals from reaching their true potential.[56]

World Politics and Personal Insecurity is a mixture of Marxist and

Freudian analysis as well as contemplative and manipulative attitudes. From Marx, Lasswell pointed out that conflict often arises out of competition for the goods and benefits of a society. Throughout the late 1920s and early 1930s, Lasswell had noted the omnipresence of Marxist insights and hypotheses among European social scientists and their total absence from the United States. In *World Politics* Lasswell berated American political scientists such as Merriam who permitted the United States's relative freedom from group conflict to blind them to the international and interclass struggle for power. Lasswell had earlier learned the conflict theory of Ludwig Gumplowicz and Gustav Ratzenhofer from Park and Albion Small. Yet Chicago conflict theory largely overlooked the significance of economic issues and did not see these conflicts in relation to the struggle for control of material and psychological resources. Lasswell saw Marxism as a far more sophisticated, scientific, and normative perspective.[57]

Despite the importance of a Marxist perspective for *World Politics*, the book's central hypotheses were Freudian. Again Lasswell returned to the theme of "Patriotism" and *Psychopathology and Politics*: individuals sublimated their personal insecurities in allegiance to political and social institutions. Individuals indulged their libidinal drives for power by their identification with symbols like nations or a particular social class. In an attempt to relieve their anxiety, individuals became the tools of dictators and happily rushed off to war. Lasswell laid the blame for international conflicts and their horrors squarely on the pervasive social anxiety of humankind.[58]

Although Lasswell had noted the significance of anxiety for mass political violence throughout his career and had been among the first social scientists to recognize and publicize the insights of Karen Horney and Harry Stack Sullivan on the "whip" of individual anxieties and fears, he accentuated this point during the 1930s. He saw the world tottering on the edge of an explosion. Outbreaks of mass violence were always possible, but the material want of the depression combined with decreased self-concept and feelings of dignity among millions of individuals presented ruthless demagogues with a perfect opportunity for exploitation. Now was the time for social scientists to assume the manipulative attitude. Lasswell pleaded with public officials to recognize the importance of individuals' feelings about themselves and attempt to provide work and welfare in a manner not damaging to the recipient's sense of self-worth. If society was to prevent war, so attractive for the alleviation of insecurities, especially in this time of increasing technological complexity and tightened economic circumstances, social experts must take an active role in eliminating the causes of anxiety and fear. Although achieving a preventive politics would surely be difficult, it was not impossible. "Wars, though likely, are not inevitable if we continually practice preventive politics."[59]

Lasswell placed his hopes for preventive politics on the ability and skills of trained social scientists. He emphasized, even more than in *Psychopathology*, that the future happiness of the world depended on a ruling elite "based on footnotes, questionnaires, and conditioned responses" rather than on violence. He continued his campaign to convince social experts that they should actively seek control of society. The knowledge they possessed necessarily gave them the power to do so. He warned, as Beard was doing at the same time, that if social scientists were not willing to use their knowledge to create a harmonious society, then competing elites would happily control society on behalf of their own interests and goals.[60]

To achieve their goal, the technocratic elite had to create ways of managing society as a whole. Although Lasswell believed in the merit of individual therapy, "in these trying times . . . the main application of the psychiatric method to politics is in devising expedients of mass management." Since humans were not rational, social scientists had to exercise control by manipulating emotions. They could best accomplish this by creating a myth based on symbols appealing to the populace. Since the problem was international tension, the most successful means of meeting insecurity was a world myth based on idealistic goals of justice and equality. Such a myth would serve as a rallying point for all nationalities and classes and would enable the accepted, benevolent elite to institute ways of reducing collective insecurities by abolishing their sources. Lasswell maintained that only by channeling man's irrationality could social scientists create the good society.[61]

Lasswell's turn to myth as a pragmatic tool was hardly unique in contemporary social thought. Marx's revolution of the proletariat was a conscious myth designed to provide the working class with a belief in their inevitable triumph. The French social critic Georges Sorel likewise devised the myth of a general strike to convince workers of their superior power. Sorel recognized that this myth was not a truthful description of reality, but if people acted as if it were, the myth would become fact. The Italian sociologist-economist Vilfredo Pareto similarly viewed all political ideologies and theories as wish fulfillment and set out to establish his own ideology. Even Karl Mannheim, who so brilliantly exposed the limits of objectivity in ideology, turned in his old age to the creation of a faith appropriate to modern needs. In the United States during the 1930s, thinkers as diverse as Reinhold Niebuhr, Max Eastman, and Thurman Arnold advocated the use of myths to aid their social organizations.

Lasswell never approached Arnold's celebratory attitude toward myth. His customary declarative tone quickly shifted to the conditional *may*, and he dealt with the concept thoroughly in only two places, a 1933 *International Journal of Ethics* article, "The Problem of World-Unity: In Quest of a World Myth," and the concluding chapter of *World Politics*, "In Quest of a Myth: The Problem of Unity." As their titles suggest, the two are nearly identical, with Lasswell rephrasing some of his abstruse language into more comprehensible prose for the journal. Lasswell clearly recognized that applied psychoanalysis had come to have applications far removed from the original analytic insights. He had consistently praised analysis for liberating the individual from the blinders of earlier experiences and allowing rational choice. In the hands of a psychiatric elite, however, myth was turned around to manipulate and blind individuals collectively. Lasswell did realize to a certain degree the moral dangers of such action. He specifically warned against political psychiatrists placing their skills in the hands of any organization. Moreover, he called for the use of myth for only one specific purpose: the prevention of war through the creation of a sense of world unity. Like Beard, Lasswell's horror of war was so great that he was willing to take drastic action to prevent it.[62]

Lasswell's optimistic view of the social scientists' easy control over myth was much too simple. If myths, like propaganda, were possible, the issue was not whether they would be used but rather who would use them. How could Lasswell, immersed in Marxist thought, believe that political psychiatrists would come to power through their own strength? Lasswell, like Arnold, tried to dodge this issue by calling for purposive social scientists to ally themselves with the class or group most concerned with the proper ethical goals of society and to use their skills in the battle for power. This would ensure both a concern for normative ends and a position within the controlling elite where they could use their techniques to bring about these ethical goals.

In his classification of his chapters in *World Politics and Personal Insecurity*, Lasswell placed "In Quest of a Myth" last and alone under the category of "Control." Here Lasswell was following, perhaps better than he knew, his original conception of a propaganda trilogy. *Propaganda Technique in World War I* and the related articles deal clearly with the "technique" of mass persuasion. *Psychopathology and Politics* and the other uses of psychology, psychiatry, and psychoanalysis are concerned with the "causes" or basis of the appeal of propaganda. Applied psychoanalytic works such as "The Psychology of Hitlerism" and World Politics and Personal Insecurity deal with the mass "consequences" of propaganda. Now, in his discussion of myth and the goals for propaganda, Lasswell turned to the final and most important issue of the "control" of propaganda: how propaganda was to be used, by whom, and for what purpose. In the final analysis, Lasswell's purposive social science would rise or fall on the treatment of this issue.[63]

Ironically, the key book for this phase of his career was the one generally considered his most amoral, Politics: Who Gets What, When, How. The first paragraph reflected Lasswell's behavioralism: "The study of politics is the study of influence and the influential. The science of politics states conditions; the philosophy of politics justifies preferences. This book, restricted to political analysis, declares no preferences. It states conditions." Lasswell had begun World Politics the year before by urging social analysts to study how the possessors of the desired values had changed over time in each society. Now he took this first paragraph and elaborated it into a behavioral study of the various techniques those elites used to obtain the majority of values in a society. Lasswell perceived power as the ability to make decisions allocating values to various groups and individuals in a society. Any institution or group that made such decisions came under the purview of political science. In a New England mill town, for example, one would study the factory superintendent who made the truly important decisions for the community.[64]

In many ways, Politics follows the behavioral approach of Lasswell's first article on Chicago ward politics. He continued to denounce vigorously institutional taxonomy and proclaimed the behavioral interpretation of politics as "the working attitude of working politicians." His goal was simply to describe the actual techniques used by politicians and other elites to seek and obtain power. Politics differs from conventional political science in its strict behavioralism, its interest in the issue of power, its recognition of the existence of powerful elites, and its latent psychoanalytic insights. It was a combination that confirmed Lasswell's reputation as the enfant terrible of political science.[65]

Lasswell made two important assumptions in Politics. First, politics deals with the struggle for power. Second, elites dominate society. Politics begins with a chapter on the elite, and Lasswell quietly repeated Bryce's dictum that "government was always government by the few, whether in the name of the one, the few, or the many." If political science was, as Lasswell maintained, the study of power, analysts must begin to recognize that a disproportionate few made the important decisions in every society. Whether one preferred this was an entirely different matter; the contemplative attitude of *Politics* demonstrated its validity, despite American political scientists' lack of attention to the subject.[66]

Yet, for all of its behavioralism and alleged lack of belief in democracy, *Politics: Who Gets What, When, How* is implicitly the most activist of all of Lasswell's works. It was also the first book Lasswell directed at a mass audience. He replaced the technical vocabulary of *World Politics* with more commonplace language and removed all the footnotes. Although he began by stating that the book declared conditions rather than preferences, he admitted in his preface that many "practical implications" followed from the analysis. As Lasswell pointed out later in the work, while political science is naturalistic and political philosophy normative, "in practice these distinctions are of relative emphasis rather than total exclusion." Knowledge can never be totally separated from its potential uses. Lasswell had not abandoned his manipulative approach to politics. Indeed, he specifically noted that his analysis in *Politics* sought to answer such questions as "How may elites be attacked or defended? How may specific objectives be reached by means of symbols, violence, goods, practices?" *Politics* is, in short, a primer designed to school individuals in the use of effective techniques for the acquisition and retention of power.[67]

In *Politics*, Lasswell quietly but clearly pointed out the applications of his and others' research, but he went further than that. In *Politics* and more clearly in several companion articles he actually selected the specific social class he wanted to use them. Although the complexity and size of modern society necessitated decision making by elites, certain elites had demonstrated more concern for the common good than others. The task of the purposive social scientist was thus to use the manipulative approach to aid those "better" elite groups in their struggle for power. The preferable elite was one that distributed values most equitably among all members of society. In contemporary Western civilization this was the "middle-income skill group."[68]

Lasswell's perception of this group as the rising social class of modern society buoyed his hopes for their accession to power. Relying on recent economic statistics, Lasswell demonstrated that contemporary technological society was depending more and more on skilled white-collar workers and less on the unskilled proletariat. He further argued that the element of skill and the shared experience of sacrifice to obtain that skill had replaced level of income as the key source of group identification. For instance, Lasswell maintained that a well-to-do physician shared more common goals and perspectives with a skilled middle-income bureaucrat than with a wealthy industrialist. He criticized modern political science for not recognizing the growth of the middle class at the expense of both the rich and the poor and its hold on the balance of power in contemporary society.[69]

Lasswell saw evidence for his hypothesis in the recent revolutions in Italy, Germany, and Russia. The bureaucrats—technicians and managers—were the one group that benefited at the expense of both the plutocracy and proletariat in the rise of these three dictatorships. Lasswell's representation of fascism as the violent reaction of the middle class to the threat of a proletarian revolution was a common thesis, but he also maintained that intellectuals, engineers, and technicians ran the alleged dictatorship of the proletariat in the Soviet Union. The Russian elite, like that of Germany and Italy, remained predominantly members of the middle-income skill group.[70]

Despite the harm that had resulted from the rise of the middle class to power in Germany and Russia, Lasswell actively welcomed its emerging predominance worldwide. He explained the reasons behind his preference in a 1935 *International Journal of Ethics* article, "The Moral Vocation of the Middle-Income Skill Group." This work, like many of his articles, describes Lasswell's personal preferences and makes explicit several of the implications found in his books. In it he maintained that the sole hope for a moral and efficient America was to replace a venal and parasitic plutocracy with a middle-class technical elite who would manage people rather than things. The middle class deserved extra values because they made personal sacrifices to acquire a socially useful skill. Also, they remained committed to the individualistic ethic of working and sacrificing to obtain rewards, while members of the plutocracy relied solely on their position within the system. As he summarized in "The Moral Vocation," "the political destiny of the middle-income skill group is revealed; it is nothing less than the re-moralization of society."[71]

Lasswell sought to aid this group in its struggle for power by suggesting means helpful to its goal. He regarded the most important of these as the liberation of the middle class from its allegiance to big business and the attainment of its own class consciousness. Until the middle class developed its own organizations and spokesmen, it would remain wedded to and would serve the interests of big business and not its own. For example, Lasswell recommended in both *World Politics* and *Politics* that the middle class demand the "ruthless" use of the income tax to eliminate great fortunes and force a more equal distribution of income. The social expert could serve the cause of the middle class in two ways. He could identify the group's best interests and the most effective means of obtaining them. Equally important in this situation, the expert could create symbols and a program designed to bring the middle class together into a cohesive force. In these roles, social scientists would become the directors of the new elite.[72]

Lasswell was not alone in recognizing and supporting the rise of the American middle class. On the right, American fascist Lawrence Dennis called on the middle class to seize power to achieve its ends. On the left, Alfred Bingham, editor of the independent radical journal *Common Sense*, argued in his 1935 *Insurgent America: The Revolt of the Middle Classes* that an alliance of workers and the technical and managerial middle class was America's only hope for meaningful social reform. That same year Marxist critic Lewis Corey likewise called for the economically oppressed middle class to revolt in his *Crisis of the Middle Class*. While the three differed violently on the proper goals to be sought, each agreed that the one major obstacle blocking the rise of the middle class to power was its lack of a shared ideology and class consciousness.[73]

The individual who most shared Lasswell's position on the practical and ethical role of the middle class in American politics was University of Chicago philosopher T. V. Smith, whose *Beyond Conscience* formed part of a trilogy with *World Politics* and Merriam's *Political Power*. In his preface to *Politics*, Lasswell noted the parallels between his conclusions and those of his "friend, colleague, and [United States] representative" Smith in his book *The Promise of American Politics*. In this work Smith cited Lasswell's *World Politics*, "Moral Vocation," the rough draft of *Politics*, and Lasswell's personal observations as the source for his arguments on the moral role of the middle class. Smith, like Lasswell, identified the middle class as the one group that could successfully remoralize society. Members of the middle class served society through their skills, and the possession of those skills provided them with self-respect and individual dignity. Smith hoped to build the good society around this skilled class and, like Lasswell before him, planned a campaign to strengthen its class consciousness. The most important element of Smith's plan was to defeat both the fascism of the plutocracy and the communism of the proletariat. He bluntly stated that the victory of either would defeat any hopes for a just America. Smith opposed the lower and unskilled classes because they lacked the moral quality that produced good men and condescendingly informed them that the victory of the middle class would give them the cherished opportunity to become skilled—and hence moral— themselves.[74]

Smith's identification of the dangers of fascism and communism reflected Lasswell's feelings. Indeed, Lasswell's support of the middle-income skill group tied in directly with his fears of an impending war for several reasons. First, the development of normative goals directed toward increasing individual potential would significantly decrease mass insecurities and the consequent threat of war. Second, the new goals would provide an alternate ideology and set of symbols to forestall the appeal of totalitarianism for the middle class. Third, possession of a useful skill gave the individual a sense of security which weakened the appeal of totalitarian ideologies. Lasswell was not blind to the potential for destructiveness, having been among the first to note the middle-class nature of communism abroad and of fascism in Europe and the United States. "If the United States escapes Fascism, in the sense of mass movements of violent protest, this will be a matter of able management." From Lasswell's perspective, this would have to be management by skilled individuals of the middle class for middle-class goals.[75]

By 1937 all the elements of Lasswell's purposive social science seemed to be in place. He had established a specific ethical goal based on a sophisticated understanding of human psychology and desires and had elaborated an activist role for social scientists in its attainment. Just as Lynd had turned to consumers and community organizations and Beard to educators as both audiences for their work and actors in the quest for a more just society, Lasswell selected the middle-income skill group. If his social psychiatrists in alliance with the moral middle class could manipulate the amoral pump handle of propaganda skillfully enough, the world might avoid the war Lasswell so dreaded and return to a concern for the truly important issues, social justice and human dignity. Within five years all those hopes would be totally destroyed. The outbreak of mass violence combined with drastic changes in Lasswell's academic life caused him to change his audience and immediate goals to the pattern established by the objectivists.

Beginning in 1937, Lasswell's career demonstrated that personal insecurity could affect the politics of social science as well as world politics. During that year Robert Hutchins, using the same type of brilliant insight that had led him to hound Mead and Gosnell out of the university, again refused to promote Lasswell to full professor because he was a "faddist" and a "monument" to one of Merriam's "passing whims." Insulted as much by Merriam's lack of protest as by Hutchins's decision, Lasswell left Chicago despite his positive feelings for the institution and the lack of a secure offer elsewhere. Protesting Chicago's "framework of a crystallized structure," Lasswell joined up with Edward Sapir and Harry Stack Sullivan at the Washington School of Psychiatry. Despite Lasswell's grandiose schemes to raise millions of dollars for the school from "rich pricks" through his personally selected public relations expert, few funds came in, and the bad feelings caused by what Sullivan referred to as Lasswell's "agile opportunism" led to a final split between Lasswell and Sullivan shortly after the death of their mutual friend Sapir. Although Lasswell held lectureships at the New School for Social Research and Yale Law School for the next seven years, these were primarily honorary positions involving a few lectures per semester and a postal address. Lasswell's financial support came from the General Education Board of the Rockefeller Foundation and his position as the director of research for the Rockefeller-funded Wartime Communications Research Project, headquartered first at the Library of Congress and later in the Office of War Information. The situation obviously required some mental adjustment for an individual who had long complained that foundations and governments molded the research they sponsored. Most important among these adjustments was Lasswell's decision to develop a career as a trainer of technical experts in the analysis and direction of propaganda.[76]

Lasswell's turn to technical analysis did not derive solely from his need for an academic position. He felt that the rush toward World War II and the proliferation of propaganda, especially the extremely able work of fascists and Communists, called for an immediate response in the creation of a proficient corps of propagandists to serve the democratic states. The goal of increasing equality in these democracies might have to wait. Adopting a contemplative attitude for the moment, Lasswell noted the exponential growth of press agents, public relations counsels, advertising men, and journalists and announced dramatically: "This is the Age of Propaganda." Since propaganda was pervasive and people behaved irrationally, especially when in groups, Lasswell developed a strategy of counterpropaganda. If totalitarian propaganda used emotional symbols and half-truths to reach the mass insecurities of the population, democratic propaganda would counter it with more effective techniques. Importantly, Lasswell's response did not bother to point out the inconsistencies and emotional manipulation of totalitarian propaganda. Such an appeal to rationality was doomed by definition. Rather, democratic propaganda would use more appealing and successful symbols to win loyalty.[77]

Although he projected a very optimistic view of the positive potential for propaganda, Lasswell was well aware of the negative effect of totalitarian propaganda in this time of mass insecurity. He made several trips to Germany and the Soviet Union during the 1930s, was in contact with exiled European psychoanalysts and social scientists at the New School for Social Research and elsewhere, studied the propaganda of American fascists and Huey Long and his allies, and during a lectureship in China had noted the impact of Japanese propaganda shortly before their successful invasion. Although propaganda could serve the beneficial purpose of acting as a catharsis when insecurity was low, during periods of intense mass frustration it increased insecurity and often led to violent outbreaks. The situation became a vicious cycle with increasing insecurity leading to more propaganda, which in turn produced more insecurity. In the United States other counterelites such as the fascists, whose concerns were inimical to Lasswell's normative ideals, were using propaganda to fuel their own drive to power.[78]

Lasswell argued that the side with the best propaganda would win the struggle for power and that any hope for the creation of a just and harmonious society lay in training the most skilled technicians. Lasswell set out to study propaganda scientifically, which for him meant the configurative analysis of as many different perspectives as possible. He abandoned the historical approach of *Propaganda Technique* and adopted an extremely complicated methodology. By the late 1930s Lasswell's perceived audience was other specialists in propaganda, and neither his language nor his approach made any concessions to the general public.

If one wished to study and explain propaganda, one should study the apex of the art. Although Lasswell conceded that fascist propaganda contained "brilliant examples" of the appeal to conscience, he retained his greatest admiration for Marxist propaganda. Marxism realized that a revolutionary propaganda needed to break the traditional bonds of the superego and replace them with an appeal to a higher conscience. Thus, it identified itself as the harbinger of true social justice by attacking the inhumanity of capitalism and the unfairness of lazy individuals living on the "surplus value" of the workers. Yet it couched these moralistic appeals in self-proclaimed scientific and objective language. Even the vagueness of the Marxist utopia helped its cause, as individuals were able to view their own ideals as the perfect society and avoid quarreling over details.[79]

Using this Freudian perspective, Lasswell and his associate, Dorothy Blumenstock, applied the configurative analysis to four years of communist propaganda in Chicago. They noted the various channels of propaganda transmittal, various techniques and the amount of each used, and finally, successes and failures. Lasswell and Blumenstock even attempted to quantify not only how many people received the propaganda but also how much time they spent studying or thinking about it. Lasswell hoped that such intensive studies of specific propaganda would eventually produce a comprehensive theory of the effect of propaganda on individuals and collectives.[80]

World Revolutionary Propaganda convinced the Rockefeller Foundation of the potential practicality of Lasswell's analysis of propaganda, and in 1939 the foundation gave him and his junior associates a large grant to study propaganda during wartime conditions. The immediate practicality of such a study for a powerful nation surrounded by war was obvious, and Lasswell assured his already convinced listeners that the quantification of communications ensured "scientific and policy gains." Lasswell's content analysis concentrated initially on measurement; some of the earlier work simply calculated the amount of space given to international news in the *New York Times*. By the war years, however, the group was doing sophisticated research comparing analyses of the same material by different techniques and developing rigidly defined categories. In addition to its methodological work the group utilized content analysis to study propaganda in various nations. It determined what information and opinions various nations were giving their civilians and classified them according to specific categories. This information, they hoped, would provide clues to the intentions and conditions of potential enemies and allies and aid military and civilian authorities in their policymaking. Lasswell and Sergius Yakobson's study of Soviet May Day slogans from 1918 to 1943, for example, noted a consistent trend away from internationalism and world revolutions and toward nationalism and domestic concerns.[81]

The government found such information useful and in 1941 transferred the Wartime Communications Research Project first to the Office of Facts and Figures and later to its successor, the Office of War Information (OWI). The group's most important work was to apply content analysis to American fascist propaganda, specifically William Dudley Pelley's periodical the *Gallilean*. Using a complex eight-part test, Lasswell conclusively demonstrated that the journal consistently followed the Nazi line, and in *United States* v. *William Dudley Pelley* an impressed district judge found the defendant guilty. The Justice Department found Lasswell's method useful in its prosecution of alleged subversive publications and called on him to testify in several other cases as well.[82]

Lasswell's activist hopes for the project, however, generally remained unfulfilled. Roosevelt personally chose the name of the Office of Facts and Figures (OFF) and emphasized to its director, Archibald MacLeish, his wish to limit the department to those two aspects. Roosevelt was reluctant to emphasize ideology for two reasons. As a former member of Wilson's wartime cabinet, he remembered well the hatred and postwar turmoil engendered by the Committee on Public Information and Wilsonian propaganda during World War I and wanted to avoid a similar situation. Also, he needed the support of Republicans and conservative southern Democrats for his military measures and correctly predicted their portrayal of all ethical discussions as New Deal indoctrination. When MacLeish later tried to encourage enthusiasm for democratic goals in his new position as assistant director for policy development of the OWI, Assistant Director Milton Eisenhower peremptorily blocked all his efforts and informed him that the OWI was an information, not a policymaking, agency.[83]

Roosevelt's failure to act and Eisenhower's obstruction directly precluded Lasswell's goal of positive movement toward a more just society and his perception of the social scientist's activist role in its achievement. With his dream of psychiatrist-kings apparently so close to fruition, Lasswell fought to convert his superiors to his perspective. Shortly after the government assumed control over the research project, Lasswell wrote a lengthy memorandum to Secretary of the Treasury Henry Morgenthau outlining the resources his group could offer the government. He argued that without a sophisticated and positive approach, the appeal of fascism internationally and even within the United States would seriously hamper the war effort. As he proclaimed publicly at the time, "If democracy is to endure, democracy must make propaganda in favor of itself and against propaganda hostile to itself." When he did not hear from Morgenthau, he descended on OFF director MacLeish and bombarded him with an array of technical material and verbiage. MacLeish, an internationally recognized poet and cultural critic, certainly realized and respected the power of words and ideas. But he recollected that this meeting left him unconvinced and ignorant of Lasswell's main points. The project remained purely a research project, and Lasswell had to seek other outlets for his activism.[84]

Lasswell's experiences with the Wartime Communications Project appear from this perspective ironic and somewhat sad. Only a few years earlier he had announced grandiloquently that the psychiatrist not only "*may* decide to become the advisor of the 'King'" but might in a case of continued ignorant action on the part of the rulers "unseat the King and actualize in the realm of fact the 'philosopher-king' of Plato's imagination." Although Lasswell found himself closer to the seat of power, no one would listen to his policy proposals and certainly no one was thinking of turning power over to him and his associates. He was purely a technician, providing techniques and data on demand that might help in the achievement of preconceived policies. As an astute student of power, Lasswell should have predicted such a response. He and his propagandists were not members of the ruling elite and had not aided in its rise to power. Nor did Morgenthau, Eisenhower, and his other superiors necessarily share his conception of the proper normative values. In his haste to gain access to the corridors of power and access to funding, Lasswell abandoned the middle-income skill group whose ethical values and desires coincided with his own belief in what was best for the nation. Although Lasswell specifically took Wesley Mitchell to task in 1942 for concentrating on empirical research to the exclusion of concern for the proper goals of a society, he was guilty of exactly the same actions and had far less influence.[85]

Lasswell's encounter with MacLeish was even more ironic and sad. MacLeish did share many of Lasswell's normative goals and in his later position at the OWI tried to develop programs to counter apathy and provide normative ideals for America's civilian population. Yet when the two met, MacLeish literally could not understand Lasswell. In part this may have been the result of MacLeish's negative connotations of propaganda. Mostly it derived from Lasswell's allegedly scientific technical vocabulary. Lasswell's concentration on training technical experts prevented him from communicating with anyone outside his specialized group. Lasswell, the student of communication, could not communicate with MacLeish, whose poetry and public statements showed him to be one of the ablest communicators of the age. Indeed, it is hard to think of anyone better than MacLeish—poet, outspoken liberal, public figure, and future librarian of Congress—to represent the morality of Lasswell's middle-income skill group. How Lasswell and his associates hoped they could help this group come into power when they could not explain either their procedures or purposes to them is difficult to comprehend.

Lasswell's work on propaganda had further disturbing implications for a purposive science of society, best seen in a 1938 pamphlet he wrote for Sullivan's journal, *Psychiatry*. One of the journal's regular features was to be a section edited by Lasswell called the Political Symbol Series. The section would present a propaganda pamphlet whose author then explained the techniques used in devising it. Lasswell began the series with a contribution entitled "Continental Security" in which he made a Beardian argument for a noninterventionist position in current world affairs, then proceeded to explain how he had based his argument on "well-rooted clichés" and "thin" rationalizations and the use of strong words like *independence* and *continent* to describe the United States. When he wished to oppose a certain position, he gave it a negative name like "monopolism" or "unfree." He also appealed to the reader's emotions by making such statements as "Our soldiers died by fraud" and by keeping all his statements short and terse. "Continental Security" was both an excellent piece of propaganda and an excellent explanation of its techniques.[86]

That, indeed, was exactly the point. Lasswell's propaganda skills were so effective that it was impossible to tell whether he believed in "Continental Security" or not. Only contradictory evidence exists. In his analysis he specifically warned readers not to equate the political position of the document with that of the author and noted that it involved "thin rationalizations of a doubtful case." In 1941 he attended a conference on North American relations with England in which he suggested methods for increasing Americans' support for the British cause. Yet Lasswell also showed definite signs of being an isolationist. Ever since *Propaganda Technique* he had noted his agreement with isolationist critics such as Harry Elmer Barnes, who argued that America's entrance into World War I was unnecessary and caused in part by Allied and American big business propaganda. The language of "Continental Security" mirrored that of Beard and Barnes. Most important, the right-wing isolationist publication *Scribner's Commentator,* whose editor had previously been a longtime publicity agent and public relations counsel for an agency of the Japanese government, reproduced excerpts of one of Lasswell's similar radio broadcasts. In it, Lasswell and coauthor Albert Williams retold the story of the American Revolution from the perspective of the colonists' desire for an independent United States free from international ties and quarrels. These "American voices" from the past now feared that their "precious heritage" was being "sacrificed for a foreign cause." This broadcast certainly shows isolationist sentiment.[87]

Did the broadcast reflect Lasswell's beliefs, or was it merely another exercise in creating effective propaganda? Lasswell might say that it really did not matter, but obviously it did. *Scribner's Commentator* used it and used it well to support its isolationist position. More to the point, in their position as government propagandists would Lasswell and his associates create propaganda for the government without regard to their own goals and beliefs? Surely Lasswell had proven that he could do so. What if Roosevelt asked him to become the new George Creel and create anti-German propaganda that would inspire the population at the cost of creating hatred for German Americans and immigrant groups in general? Lasswell might argue that scientific evidence had proven positive propaganda to be superior to negative, but this would not necessarily preclude the government's decision. How could Lasswell in his clearly powerless position ensure the direction of the propaganda he was ordered to create? The image that comes to mind is Randolph Bourne's depiction of John Dewey as the child on the back of the mad elephant of World War I, trying to direct it toward socially positive purposes.

Lasswell tried to overcome this apparent lack of control through an explicit ordering of his normative values. In what he called the "developing science of democracy," he tried to come up with a specific definition of democratic values. A majority of the population in Lasswell's truly democratic society would participate in central decisions and would share equally the values of safety, income, and deference. Extreme efforts would be made to decrease individual insecurity and, above everything else, increase the sense of human dignity. But questions remained. How does one increase an individual's dignity by manipulating emotions? How does one reconcile an all-knowing philosopher-king with equally shared decision making? How, indeed, does one square a belief in people's irrationality and consequent need for conscious manipulation with a commitment to democracy and its belief in individual rationality? Lasswell's promising original goal of combining the normative goals of the purposivists with the careful attention to detail of the objectivists resulted, sadly, in emphasizing the worst of both positions. His work on propaganda contained the antidemocratic strains of social scientists as rulers or at least as privileged decision makers while retaining an implicit policy of narrowly trained technicians routinely following the existing system. That is, elitism became totally separated from the original ethical rationale, leaving a social science more ethically bankrupt than anything Mitchell, Merriam, or even Arnold ever devised.[88]

Lynd and Beard were also working on the issue of propaganda at this time. In 1937 Clyde Miller of Columbia's Teachers College organized the Institute for Propaganda Analysis to conduct objective, nonpartisan studies of contemporary propaganda. The results were then published in monthly bulletins. Lynd and Beard became charter members of the advisory board and remained active on it until the organization disbanded on America's entrance into World War II. Miller and the institute agreed with Lasswell that propaganda involved simply an exchange of information designed to influence or persuade and by itself was neither good nor bad. Propaganda was vicious only when it was monopolized. Yet the institute's approach differed from Lasswell's in one important respect. In the preface to the first bulletin, Miller argued that one could deal with propaganda in only three ways: suppress it, attack it with counterpropaganda, or analyze it. Lasswell chose the second way; the institute selected the third. By "analysis," the institute members meant the explanation of the strategy of propaganda, which they described in simple, uncomplicated language complete with suggestions for discussion and further thought at the end of the article. "Most books on propaganda are for the benefit of the propagandist rather than the public. Others are in technical terms understood only by persons with the nomenclature of psychology or sociology." The institute's self-pronounced goal from the very beginning was to develop critical thinking by helping readers understand the function of propaganda, creating a situation in which, in the words of its last bulletin, "Each One [Is] His Own Analyst." Lasswell would have probably choked if he had read it.[89]

Although the institute declared its strict nonpartisanship, it certainly was not noncontroversial. The bulletins did study the propaganda of Nazi Germany and the Soviet Union, although they concentrated on American varieties. This included not merely the tiny lunatic fringe like Pelley but powerful groups and individuals such as Father Coughlin, the anti-Semite Henry Ford, and the House Un-American Activities Committee (HUAC). Several of the institute's positions reflected the specific concerns of Lynd and Beard. One bulletin featured a devastating critique of ex-Communist turned superpatriot J. B. Matthews's accusations against the consumer movement before the Dies Commission, and bulletins frequently pointed out Britain's attempts to "woo America" through such propaganda techniques as sending royalty over to visit. Indeed, the November 1939 bulletin, "Mr. Roosevelt's Foreign Policy," repeats Beard's critique almost word for word and studies Roosevelt's foreign policy speeches—especially the quarantine speech that Beard hated so much—according to the criteria of propaganda.[90]

Despite considerable public support and the publication of Alfred McClung Lee's classic study of Father Coughlin, *The Fine Art of Propaganda*, the institute became steadily weaker. The primary problem was financial. The old Progressive E. A. Filene had supported the institute generously until his death, but his family foundation withdrew its support after he died due to the institute's "controversiality." In 1939 the institute, like Lasswell, applied for funds from the Rockefeller Foundation. While Lasswell and his associates received a large amount for their "practical" research, the foundation dismissed the institute's work as not "unassailably scientific." By 1941, the HUAC was attacking the institute as subversive and making it difficult even to find a publisher for its bulletins. As former board members such as Hadley Cantril, Leonard Doob, and Ralph Casey resigned in order to work for the government, often with the Wartime Communications Project, the financial and institutional rewards of institutional social science were again made manifest. It was a lesson a financially insecure Lasswell had learned well. As the fury of World War II and an ensuing torrent of government and foundation support poured down on Lasswell and his fellow social scientists, a dominant paradigm emerged, at least temporarily. It was one that made all of them, even the objectivists, nervous.

CONCLUSION

As the 1930s ended, the purposive school seemed on the verge of replacing the objectivist approach as the dominant movement within American social science. The rise of totalitarian regimes and their effective use of social technicians compelled the service intellectuals to rethink many of their basic theories. For individuals such as Mitchell and Merriam, the basic goal behind empiricism had always been to strengthen democratic society. Many social scientists came to the conclusion that for now, at least, the most pressing need was not more facts and skilled technicians but the construction of a normative theory to guide both themselves and common citizens in their actions. As the journalist and social thinker Max Lerner declared in his 1939 *Ideas Are Weapons*, "We have come to see that . . . we have had to manufacture an ideology of whose existence we had hitherto been only dimly aware." Purposive thinkers were joined by previous champions of the social science of technique in a virtual outpouring of attempts to establish ethical goals for American society. As one of Lerner's reviewers wearily noted, "If talk and writing about democracy will save it [democracy], salvation is for sure."[1]

Nineteen thirty-nine was also the year Lynd's *Knowledge for What?* was published, and the public response to it demonstrated the growing appeal of the purposive critique of social science. Nonspecialists such as Lerner and Stuart Chase joined purposive thinkers such as Beard, Lasswell, and Harry Elmer Barnes in commending the book for its "unashamed instrumentalism" and commitment to an activist social science. Erich Fromm called it the most important work in recent social thought for its reassertion of the significance of the individual in the face of totalitarianism, and Howard Tolley of the Department of Agriculture's Bureau of Agricultural Economics made the book required reading for the division's social scientists and planners. More significant, objectivist social scientists joined in the chorus of praise. While a few such as the economist and social technician John Rogers Commons tried to transform *Knowledge for What?* into a call for "research that will aid the practical administrator of affairs," most, including Mitchell, accepted the general outline of Lynd's critique. The only strong criticism came from Lynd's Columbia colleague and opponent Robert MacIver and those like him who felt that Lynd did not separate himself sufficiently from the objectivist position.[2]

The challenge to mainstream social science took place even in its strongholds. On December 1 and 2, 1939, the leaders of objectivist social science and their foundation supporters met in Chicago to celebrate the tenth anniversary of the Social Science Research Building. Merriam in his opening address chortled, "We analyzed and synthesized; we integrated and disintegrated; we added, subtracted, multiplied; we coordinated, correlated and co-efficienated; the bewildered facts fled in defeat." Less rhapsodically but with equal enthusiasm, the chief dinner speaker, Henry Bruere, cofounder of the New York Bureau of Municipal Research and at that time director of the New York Life Insurance Company, noted the heightened esteem of social scientists among the public and their increased employment by governments and businesses. The 1930s had proven "to be the period of greatest employment for the social sciences that America had known."[3]

Not everyone at the meeting joined in the celebration. The toastmaster of the dinner, University of Chicago President Robert Hutchins, preceded Bruere's speech by sourly condemning the entire enterprise of social science as useless and even immoral. Hutchins had spent much of the ten years since his perfunctory address at Eleven Twenty-six's dedication calling and working for the replacement of men of facts with those concerned with the rational analysis of first principles. Now he scornfully repeated his claims that "more money, building, staff and equipment . . . doesn't amount to much if you don't know what you are going to do with them" and that a naturalistic science by definition could never provide such direction.[4]

Although the organizers expected and could easily discount Hutchins's tirade, they probably did not expect criticism erupting within the sessions. Yet that is exactly what happened. During the session on interrelationships between the social sciences, Social Science Research Council President Robert Crane, speaking from prepared notes, discounted the integration of the social sciences as unfeasible and even undesirable. Lynd, the next scheduled speaker, put aside his scheduled remarks to inquire if that was what Crane had really meant to say. Upon receiving a positive answer, Lynd launched an impromptu blistering attack on organized American social science and its "sahibs at the top" for neglecting purposively oriented integrated research. Many of the session's participants quickly supported Lynd, with even Beardsley Ruml expressing "profound doubt" as to the utility of existing disciplinary boundaries. The issue was, as Northwestern University political scientist A. R. Hatton remarked, one of social problems and the consequent determination of values.[5]

A similar situation arose in the session "Social Science and Social Action," significantly scheduled last on the program. When William Ogburn insisted that social scientists should be concerned solely with the accumulation of knowledge and should not act "until all the evidence is in," the panel exploded. Agricultural economist John Black emphatically replied that government social scientists already successfully combined science and action on a daily basis. Nor were he and several others willing to accept Merriam's distinction between technical personnel and decision makers. They argued that social researchers, often the most knowledgeable individuals in the process, must help choose proper goals for any program.[6]

Still, if the threat of World War II had provided ammunition for the purposivists' attack, the outbreak of the war definitely strengthened technical social science. As in World War I, once mobilization began, the federal government turned to technical experts to help run the war. The federal government had learned the value of social scientists during World War I and actively recruited them; the Civil Service Commission sent out individual letters and job listings on several occasions to every member of the American Economics Association. Social scientists were happy to join up, working in such areas as intelligence testing and job classification, price controls and rationing, fiscal and financial planning and operation, product and manpower mobilization, propaganda and cultural analysis, and military and civilian morale. A Civil Service Commission expert estimated that the number of social science positions within the federal government doubled to roughly sixteen thousand within the first six months of the war alone. One such social technician exulted, "World War II can . . . be said to have been a social scientist's war."[7]

Yet, as always with technical social science, definite limitations remained on the social scientists' roles. During World War II Roosevelt sought to gain business support and forestall the xenophobic outbreaks of World War I by consciously removing all ideological aspects from the war effort, and military personnel were unconcerned about the ethical dimensions and goals of the war. Every one of the official commentators on the role of social scientists within the government complained of political restrictions, manipulation of data, lack of adequate consultation, and absence of overall goals concerning the ends of their research.[8]

Despite such reservations, objectivist social science accepted the continuing and increased sponsorship of government and business after the war. The federal government officially recognized the utility of the social sciences with the 1946 establishment of the Council of Economic Advisors and its staffing with professional economists. Businesses and private foundations eagerly funded research institutions in such newly developed areas as social surveys, electoral behavior, and international relations. The Ford Foundation alone pumped twenty-three million dollars into the study of political behavior. Again, as in the 1920s, fledgling social scientists recognized the professional success of technical social scientists and patterned their own careers after them. Political scientist Bernard Berelson, himself such a model, maintained in a highly influential report on graduate education that it "should aim at training the skilled specialist—not the 'educated man,' 'cultivated man,' [or] 'wise man.' "[9]

Given such an emphasis on the empirical description of reality, postwar social science turned decidedly away from normative concerns. Ethical issues and goals were not the concern of the social scientist. Indeed, since normative theory was by definition not about facts, most postwar social scientists denied its very possibility. To them, theory was empirical and descriptive, not normative and prescriptive. Theory described and attempted to explain social reality as it existed. Talcott Parsons and David Easton explained the social and political sciences, respectively, using equilibrium models. When issues such as democracy arose, theorists such as Robert Dahl and Gabriel Almond described ongoing allegedly democratic systems such as the United States and posed them as ideal models against alternative systems. American social science had fulfilled Lynd's worst fears: it was consciously celebrating what *is* as what *ought* to be. As Lynd's Columbia colleague and former student Seymour Martin Lipset cheerfully concluded, "This change in Western political life reflects the fact that the fundamental problems of the industrial revolution have been solved."[10]

Objectivist social science and empirical theory were two important manifestations of the end-of-ideology movement of postwar American social thought. Indeed, sociologist Edward Shils first introduced the phrase and fellow sociologist Daniel Bell popularized it. The major tenets of the school were the lack of important issues of conflict, absence of ideology even in international politics, an absolute moral and cultural relativism, and, especially, a commitment to the existing American system as a positive good. Historians such as Daniel Boorstin and Arthur Schlesinger, Jr., described America's past as lacking significant conflict and praised American political thought lavishly for its practical empirical orientation. The goal was, as it had been for Arnold, a non-normative political and social system in which competing elites agreed on basic issues and turned to trained technicians to boost economic production, run the social system smoothly, and assist malcontents in their adjustment and acceptance of the system. Although the perspective drew much of its appeal from the terrors of fascism and Stalinism, one must also recognize that its acceptance of the status quo and the high status of social technicians met the needs of objectivist social science perfectly.[11]

In such an environment, the old debate of the 1920s and 1930s seemed empty. Significantly, Mitchell, Merriam, and Lasswell joined Lynd and Beard in their general distaste for contemporary social science. Cut off from their assumptions of the correlation between knowledge and social reform, the older objectivists watched the triumph of the Ogburns, Cranes, Lundbergs, and Lazarfelds with mixed emotions. Mitchell and Merriam had opposed Ogburn's attempts to separate knowledge and action during the Recent Social Trends survey; during World War II Ogburn and his allies used their appeal to government and business to gain the upper hand not only over the purposive school but over their objectivist predecessors as well.

Of the three, Mitchell accepted the new developments best. In 1939 Mitchell was president of the American Association for the Advancement of Science (AAAS) one of the few social scientists ever honored with that position. In his presidential address and a similar talk to the American Science Teachers Association, Mitchell demonstrated his continued commitment to technical social science. Science, he said, should not be prejudiced by either outside influences or the scientist's feelings. Science has advanced, and social science can advance only by its "single-minded, critical, austere spirit." The infusion of normative goals into scientific research defeats its purpose and blocks its true service to society.[12]

As he had been during World War I, Mitchell was a champion of social science service to the government during World War II. Five days after Pearl Harbor he urged the Columbia Economics Club in the first of several wartime talks to conduct factual research for the government so that it might perform most efficiently. His annual report as the director of research for the National Bureau of Economic Research was a summary of what the bureau was and could be doing for the war effort. The long-term goal for economists and other social scientists was to produce as much specific information as possible so they could prove their value to postwar governments and businesses and continue to increase their impact on society.[13]

Simultaneously, Mitchell expressed doubts as to the implications of empirical research. In his AAAS presidential address he insisted that while social scientists should keep their normative goals out of their research, they *must* take a public stand and become involved in social affairs. If they had special competence in an issue, "they should contribute what they knew, whether formally invited to do so or not." In two admittedly "personal confessions expressed in a layman's language," Mitchell explained the dilemma between "feeling and thinking" and "values and facts." A "cold head" was indispensable for research while a "warm heart" was not. Yet these emotional feelings cannot and should not be totally removed, because social scientists have "a moral duty toward society." Only through a clear conception of social ideals can social scientists ever hope to achieve their ultimate goals. In a formal discussion at the 1943 American Economics Association convention he emphatically declared, "I have always supposed that the importance of economics derives from the contribution it may make to welfare. . . . And does not contributing to welfare involve action?" Aghast, Joseph Dorfman, historian of American economic thought, biographer of Veblen, and a great admirer of Mitchell, protested this link between science and social reform. To Dorfman as to Ogburn, knowledge was its own goal. Mitchell firmly disagreed and reaffirmed his beliefs. Five years later he died, working and dreaming up to the very end of his business cycle research and its implications.[14]

Merriam's reaction to the triumph of objectivism was both simpler and more contradictory. Despite his vocal support for a purely technical, or, as he came to call it, an "administrative" social science, he relied on very clear normative values—values so deeply ingrained that he no longer even noticed their existence. As fascism with its appeal to violence threatened the domination of his beloved reason, Merriam for once seemed to try to articulate these values. In two 1939 works he posited the central values of all social life: the dignity of man, equal opportunity for individual and social progress, and popular decision making through rational discussion and choice. In an insight found nowhere else in his work, Merriam even noted that without commitment to such values his beloved administrators could actually serve evil. "The organization of violence is a technical question, to answer which, men of reason will be called. There is no reason why bandits and gangsters and gorillas should be given the secrets of the laboratory, of management, of psychology, of medicine for their bandit purposes alone." By the 1940s Merriam and the National Resources Board had attempted a concrete expression of America's basic philosophy, a "New Bill of Rights" to go along with the ethical ideals of Roosevelt's Four Freedoms.[15]

Merriam did not seem to realize the possible contradiction between this discovery of normative values and his earlier advocacy of technique. He simply could not conceive that anyone could not believe in such obvious truths. His longtime friend and colleague Leonard White noted that the core of Merriam and his thinking lay in his "confidence in the future and certainty of the values of democracy." Such progressive faith was unfashionable in the postwar years, and he no longer possessed the organizational backing he had had in the 1920s and 1930s. After Roosevelt's sacrifice of the National Resources Planning Board to conservative demands in 1943, Merriam's sole government service was an unhappy year on Harry Truman's Loyalty Review Board, which tacitly supported witch hunting. At the time of his death in 1953 in Washington, he had long ceased to be a major force in either social science or government.[16]

Lasswell demonstrated the most complicated and changeable reaction to the change in social science, characteristically reflecting his chameleonlike tendency to conform to his surroundings. At first his attainment of a permanent institutional home at Yale Law School through the intercession of Professor of International Law Myres McDougal caused him to return to his concern for normative goals for social science. Yet his inability to crystallize these goals—and, more important, the specific beneficiaries of them—combined with his increasing association with foundation-supported think tanks resulted in him again turning away from ends and concentrating on techniques.

McDougal had met Lasswell while he was teaching for a year at the University of Chicago and, despite considerable faculty and alumni opposition, had succeeded in bringing Lasswell to Yale to develop what he called "affirmative" jurisprudence. McDougal, like many legal thinkers of the day, opposed the rising power of natural law but concurred with its criticism of legal realism as "only a means to an end" lacking in the necessary ethical dimension of law. In 1943, McDougal and Lasswell produced a classic reformulation of the purposes and goals of legal education based on an integration of democratic values, law, and the social sciences. In what McDougal himself graciously acknowledged as "pre-eminently Lasswell's creation," they sought to replace the accepted narrow definition of law, the outmoded curriculum based on unthinking reliance on formalistic legal concepts and the case study approach, and especially the purely technical nature of education with law as policy-making. They hoped that the crisis of World War II would shock the profession into dealing with the central problem of legal education, the "belief that law is and can be nothing but a method." Such an attitude thwarted proper legal education because "law cannot, like golf or surgery, be taught only as technique; its ends are not so fixed or certain. What law 'is' and hence what should be taught as 'law' depends primarily, as we have seen, upon the ends preferred."[17]

Legal education would thus necessarily involve ethical choices. Lawyers must recognize the lack of objectivity in the law and consciously work toward policies in line with democratic goals. Indeed, a large part of Lasswell and McDougal's proposal simply listed normative goals very similar to those advanced by Merriam in his 1939 works and based, according to Lasswell, on enhancing human dignity. Although many practitioners roundly criticized McDougal at that year's Association of American Law Schools meeting for abandoning the Holmesian tradition of the lawyer as a neutral "craftsman," he insisted that the concern of law schools must extend beyond such technique to lawyers' personal choices and values. It was necessary to replace the purely "destructive" phase of legal scholarship with the positive activity of applying available knowledge to solving social problems. Neither McDougal, Lasswell, or their critics ever defined human dignity, its relationship to specific cultures or historical periods, or its relationship to the equally unclear list of values.[18]

In a letter to Merriam, Lasswell noted that his positive experience with legal education had encouraged him to search for a similar unifying approach to the social sciences. Reacting to Merriam's anger at the Social Science Research Council for ignoring his advice in its turn to a value-free objectivism, he suggested that they join together to form an opposing, activist organization based on the idea of the policy sciences. This new organization would pursue three major goals: provide the public with information clarifying long-term policy goals and alternatives, furnish data either supportive or critical of recent decisions, and supply unpaid consultants to decision makers. Its overall goal would be "to enhance the possibility that preferred future events will occur."[19]

Lasswell's plan reflects his consistent failure to face up to the possibility that decision makers might refuse to accept recommendations or might oppose an independent source suggesting alternative possibilities to an unruly public. It was one thing for an old Progressive like Merriam to ignore this. Lasswell, on the other hand, had written widely on the power of elites and was simultaneously noting how research organizations, reflecting their funding sources, encouraged "applied" work and ignored policy and social change issues.[20]

The fact is that Lasswell seemed constitutionally unable to accomplish such a task. His indirect reference to himself as "a horse for single harness, not cut out for tandem or team work . . . with a marked lack of desire for direct association with men and women," not to mention his incredibly dense terminology, prevented him from engaging in the sort of organizational and propaganda work that Lynd and Beard did. In a definitional article of the policy sciences written six years after his first note to Merriam, he identified their goals as developing a science of policy formation and execution and improving the information available to policymakers. In this shift derived from the article's publication in *The Policy Sciences* under the auspices of Stanford's Center for the Advanced Study of the Behavioral Sciences, exactly the type of status quo–oriented research institution Lasswell had previously criticized. This classic volume consists largely of articles by such objectivists as Lazarfeld and Rensis Likert that show policymakers how to use probability methods, sample interviews, typologies, and other techniques in their work.[21]

The history of the policy sciences, despite the efforts of such leaders as William Ascher, has consisted of a progressive abandonment of its normative roots for a concentration on empirical and administrative techniques. Lasswell and McDougal's normative approach to the law has likewise been relatively ignored, except in McDougal's own specialty of international law. Lasswell's intense desire for practical results and his dependence on such think tanks as the Center for the Advanced Study of the Behavioral Sciences and the RAND Corporation resulted in an inability to separate himself from the social science of technique despite his recognition of its limitations.[22]

If Merriam, Lasswell, and even Mitchell viewed the future with trepidation, Beard and Lynd reacted with anger, desperation, and even bitterness. They had warned their fellow social scientists to repent before it was too late. Now their worst fears had come true, and they perceived themselves more and more as lonely voices crying in the wilderness.

As usual, Beard served as a lightning rod for opponents of the purposive position. Although he drew back from isolationism before America

262 / Social Science in the Crucible

entered the war and even publicly bought war bonds, his refusal to re-think his overall position on the proper goals for foreign policy pro-vided an opening for his previously dormant enemies. Beard was publicly jeered at the annual AHA and APSA conventions, and even his old friend and neighbor Lewis Mumford attacked him as an "active abettor of tyr-anny, sadism, and human defilement."[23]

Although such attacks coupled with his declining health and hearing obviously hurt Beard, he continued to research New Deal foreign policy. At the end of the war he published *American Foreign Policy in the Mak-ing 1932–1940*, which argues that Roosevelt designed his allegedly isola-tionist policies of those years to disguise his true interventionist feelings. In 1947 Beard followed with "the toughest job I ever tackled," *President Roosevelt and the Coming of the War 1941*, which accuses FDR of acting in an increasingly duplicitous, dictatorial, and unethical manner and directly challenging the Japanese government. More important, Roose-velt failed to live up to his responsibility to the American people. Even if he had been correct about the need for intervention, he had a moral duty as president of a democracy to educate the public and help them choose the true national interest without manipulating them. In good pragmatic fashion, Beard entitled his epilogue to *President Roosevelt* "Interpreta-tions Tested by Consequences." According to Beard, those consequences were the triumph of Stalin in Russia and Eastern Europe, and on the home front "a kind of an armed camp for defense," a huge national debt, a large increase in taxes, the suppression of civil liberties, and general disintegration of American values.[24]

Beard's difficulties in researching *American Foreign Policy* and *Presi-dent Roosevelt* further bore out his critique of the social science of tech-nique. After the end of World War II, many governmental figures, most notably Secretary of War Robert Patterson, began to fear the emergence of a postwar historical revisionism similar to that which had appeared after World War I. They consequently shipped most of the relevant gov-ernment documents to the privately operated Franklin Roosevelt Hyde Park Library, which denied Beard permission even to examine the tran-scripts of press conferences. The library did provide such access to two "objective" scholars funded by the Rockefeller Foundation and spon-sored by the Council on Foreign Relations. These two, CIA Director of Research William Langer and National Security Council executive S. Everett Gleason, proved their objectivity by allowing the State Depart-ment and former secretary of state Cordell Hull to "correct" any "inac-curacies" in their finished work. Beard publicly raged against "subsidized history of this kind, prepared to serve a purpose fixed in advance," especially since its factual basis could not be tested by other scholars. "It is a primary axiom of despotism that archives shall be kept shut and that freedom of historical research shall be suppressed." Even after Beard was able to gain access to some of the documents through his connections with his former researcher George H. E. Smith, who had become the director of the Senate Republican Policy Committee, he still refused to be officially associated with it or any other governmental institution. "I want no *official* business whatever, no money, no thanks, nothing." Beard was suspicious about preparing a report for individuals whose positions required them to be partisan and who would use his work for their own purposes. This was the subservience of the service intellectual, and even his hatred of his archenemy Roosevelt could not tempt him to go that far.[25]

With the completion of *President Roosevelt* in 1947, Beard seemed to step back from the frenetic pace of the previous several years. Now that he had given the public his view of foreign policy, he began to contemplate once again the nature of the social sciences and their unfulfilled potential. In a note to his old friend Stuart Chase, Beard stated that he was unimpressed with the actual accomplishments of the physical sciences. Given the complexities of social relations, the social sciences required more ability and had achieved equal advances. But as long as the empirical, objectivist model was dominant, he feared that social science would consist of mere description. Later that same year, his former student, successor at Columbia, and longtime friend Arthur Macmahon asked him to give a special address to the APSA convention. Beard tried to beg off by noting his past "public offenses" but was soon persuaded, much to the delight of Mary, who thanked Mcmahon for giving her husband the chance to "speak his mind again." As usual, Beard did exactly that. Just as he had done twenty-one years ago, he began by noting the progress in political research and then concentrated on its deficiencies. He criticized political science for ignoring interdisciplinary topics, historical perspectives, and crucial topics such as war in favor of "almost frantic specialization." Such errors stemmed from the chimera of exact knowledge and the "arrogance" of the objectivist model. One had to recognize the personal and ethical dimensions of social reality or risk "trivializ[ing] the mentality of the teaching profession."[26]

Although Beard's words were characteristically bold, his tone was tired and sour. When he had spoken before his social science colleagues in the past, he had been certain of the victory of his ethical vision. The ability of social scientists to educate and arouse an intelligent citizenry was one of the keys to his belief, summed up in the closing words of *Rise of American Civilization*, that "this was the dawn, not the dusk of the gods." By 1948 he was far from certain about the future of social science and of the world itself. He would write to Counts that "day and night I tremble for the future of my country and mankind." Less than a year after his APSA speech, he was dead.[27]

While Beard had gone his solitary and defiant way, Robert Lynd characteristically tried to oppose the impending changes in American society and social science from a consensual direction. In 1940 he had attempted to form a government-sponsored institute that would serve as a check on the natural abuses of democratic rights during wartime. Although this institute, not surprisingly, never received government support, Lynd as an individual attacked the conduct of the war for strengthening business's control and blocking the influence of unions and planning groups. As early as 1940, in his plans for the wartime institute, he publicly criticized social science for its acceptance of the status quo and its consequent abdication of responsibility: "Our concern with polling surface attitudes and opinions regarding a miscellany of public issues is yielding areas of superficial data, but very little on the deep motivational why's of people, and our how's for achieving social motivations from these studies go little beyond hints of propaganda technique." When the greatest achievement of this wartime sponsorship of social research, *The American Soldier*, by Samuel Stouffer and his associates, appeared in 1949, Lynd condemned it with uncharacteristic viciousness. Although he admired the technical virtuosity of the study, he could not overlook the fact that social science was being used "to sort out and control men for purposes not of their own willing." The book symbolized the descent of social science from an institution trying to solve problems of democracy to an instrument of mass control in the hands of private and undemocratic institutions and consequently an enormous threat to true democracy.[28]

Lynd attributed the increasing subservience of social scientists to the growing power of business interests during the 1930s and the war: "We academic folk are middle-class people and therefore vulnerable when power applies pressure to us and our work." Social technology was not neutral, and "political tides" were turning it toward increasingly political uses. In the United States, these tides were the power of big corporations, which threatened to control all of American society and create a fascistic state. The only possible choices for social scientists in such a situation were working for a big-business state heading toward fascism or striving for the greater extension of democracy. The proper choice was obvious to Lynd. Institutional alterations alone were insufficient; it was necessary to work for a permanent change in the structure of power by transforming the social structure of the country through the formation of a militant working-class Labor party. Lynd encouraged the growth of labor and community groups and warned them about the "propaganda" of consensual social science. He thought that class barriers were actually increasing, and he pleaded with union leaders not to ignore the important issues in their search for improved economic benefits and supposed inclusion among the power elite.[29]

The price for his social activism was high. Many of his practically oriented students transferred to work with Lazarsfeld, and the more theoretically inclined went with Merton. As early as 1942 Lynd found himself labeled a Communist. Helen Lynd was called before the Jenner Hearings as an alleged party member, and in the 1950s *Middletown* and their other books were removed from United States Information Agency libraries throughout the world. Moreover, he became increasingly depressed about the state of American society. He recognized that American society lacked truly competitive institutions such as the British Labor party, and that their future development was unlikely. Yet, even if "the single decent man was never so impotent as today . . . because organization is power and in the saddle," the intellectual's "subversive" approach was never more important for understanding and articulating the inadequacies of the time. Shortly after writing these remarks in 1954, Lynd, tormented by a not completely unfounded paranoia, descended into a long period of mental and physical illness leading to his death.[30]

While Beard and Lynd continued to rain body blows on the apparently defenseless science of technique, neither they nor any of their purposive colleagues ever delivered a knockout punch. Some of the reasons for their failure are manifest in Sidney Blumenthal's analysis of the New Right in recent American politics. In a new introduction written to accompany the 1988 reissue of his 1986 *Rise of the Counter-Establishment*, Blumenthal argued that the New Right had spent so much time in opposition sharpening their weapons against the hated liberalism that they had never fully developed a positive program of their own. The bureaucratic state was such an easy target that they almost seemed to welcome Ronald Reagan's defeat so that they could again go on the attack. Actual governing had been far more difficult and less rewarding. Somewhat similarly, purposivists like Lasswell, Beard, Lynd, and, in the 1950s, C. Wright Mills demonstrated the glaring weaknesses of objectivist social science from both practical and theoretical standpoints. They could even identify exactly how to solve its deficiencies; unfortunately, they could never solve their own.[31]

Surely part of the purposive thinkers' difficulties derived from their continued attachment to the basic philosophy of social science. They too shared the traditional desire for the certainty of the scientific method combined with the ideal of social betterment. Unlike the neo-Thomists or true historical relativists like Carl Becker, they were unwilling to base their goals on philosophy or personal subjectivism alone. Their object, unlike Becker's, included public education—convincing the masses of the moral and empirical correctness of their objectives. The American public, especially in the high opinions of Lynd and Beard, generally made good decisions and demanded facts on which to make them. Moreover, if social scientists qua intellectuals qua public intellectuals were to serve their audience well, their judgments had to be based on facts. Although Beard called for a leap of faith, it was always an informed leap based on empirical data. Purposive thinkers both welcomed and feared the impossibility of objectivity. Beard noted in an interview late in his life, "I don't say that you ought to write history on the basis of your assumptions—but I say you do." The best social scientists of the interwar period grappled, as had Mitchell in the last years of his life, with the necessity of combining the apparently irreconcilable: "feeling and thinking" and "facts and values." While the purposive thinkers insisted on the feeling and values side, they did not deny the importance of facts.[32]

Although practitioners of neither school were able to completely integrate the two, their efforts seem valiant in comparison with the present morass of contemporary social science. As numerous critics within the various disciplines have noted, the drive toward "hyperspecialization" has created a situation in which social scientists often seem to care little about either facts or values. Certainly the tendency toward service intellectuals has accelerated. Daniel Bell even asserted that intellectuals in postindustrial society must serve some institution and suggested the five possible alternatives of university, military, medicine, government, and business. The new masters of technique lack Merriam's unsophisticated but touching faith in the possibilities of objectivity and data collection. Although they fully recognize the limitations of their approach, they simply do not care. It works well for their clients' goals of marketing products and politicians and predicting short-term tendencies. Its lack of utility for long-term social reconstruction is irrelevant from their perspective.[33]

Even more disturbing is the path followed by those attempting to discover a normative theory on which to base their science of society. The flood of European refugee scholars during the war led to a "deprovincialization of the American mind," especially in the social sciences. Most relevant to the problem of the facts and values dichotomy was a Marxist-Freudian synthesis known as critical theory developed by a group of German émigrés associated with the Institute for Social Research on the Columbia campus. The critical theorists sought to create a combination of theory and practice, referred to by the Marxist term *praxis*, which would transcend the limitations of the status quo and in effect transform it. Like the purposive thinkers, they focused on that extremely difficult, sometimes seemingly impossible, step between what already exists and what ought to be. Their search was for what their undisputed leader, Max Horkheimer, called *"ein ganz Anderes"* (an entirely other) outside empirical reality. Horkheimer and his associates strongly rejected "positivism" for its fatal separation of objectivity and values and insisted on the historical and social roots of all knowledge.[34]

Critical theory attracted many purposive thinkers, and some of the institute's closest contacts with American social science were with Lynd, Beard, and Lasswell. Lynd and Beard were two of the original proponents of the institute's affiliation with Columbia; Beard and Lasswell were the first of the few Americans or noninstitute members ever to contribute to the official journal, *Zeitschrift für Sozialforschung*; and Lasswell is the only one ever to contribute more than one article. The closest connection was with Lynd. The institute's official connection at Columbia was with the sociology department, and Lynd alone among department members fought to obtain at least one official professorship for it. Lynd had a deep, almost reverential, respect for institute political scientist Franz Neumann, and his historian son, Staughton, did his first serious historical research with Neumann.[35]

Despite the institute's goal of combining theory and empiricism, even such widely acclaimed works as Theodor Adorno's *The Authoritarian Personality* failed to provide a sufficient empirical basis for its theory. The situation worsened as many postwar Americans continued to search for answers from European thinkers and were necessarily influenced by their bitter disillusionment with Marxist categories. Following Roland Barthes and his study of semiotics, literary and social thinkers, especially those most critical of modern society, have emphasized the subjective nature of language, and thus reality. Unlike Dewey and Beard, who somewhat similarly noted the social and individual construction of reality, poststructural theorists deny the validity of any knowledge and have consequently paid scant attention to empiricism or their own value as intellectuals. The potential liberation of Michel Foucault's smashing of the conventional categories of social deviance is obstructed by his insistence on the relativistic position of his and all knowledge. He is simply one unique "text" studying other "texts," and nothing exists outside of such texts. Jean Baudrillard goes even further. In studying consumption under capitalism, Baudrillard argues that commodities become separated from human moral relations and even from individual needs. He further asserts that in present society only artificial needs exist. A search like Lynd's or Lasswell's for what people really want and need is hopeless and even ludicrous. But if no real human needs exist, on what foundation does one build a humane society to replace the present inhuman one?[36]

For all their criticism of the contemporary world, poststructural thinkers, or "linguistic leftists" as one of their critics caustically referred to them, have little to offer to its reconstruction. One prominent literary critic angrily denied that the role of the intellectual should include "a service function." Certainly their abstruse language, which makes Lasswell seem like Hemingway in comparison, precludes any public role. Their language limits their audience to other specialists like themselves trained in their own increasingly narrow areas. Although one can attribute much of this style to a healthy concern for shared discourse and meaning, one must also note the protective coloration it provides. As Russell Jacoby pointed out in *The Last Intellectuals*, contemporary academics seem to possess absolute academic freedom as long as they do not become involved in the public arena. One can be as radical as one wants as long as one is writing to and for other academics and the general public cannot understand one. Indeed, one of the few points that Jacoby missed in his condemnation of contemporary intellectuals' abandonment of their public role is the lack of recognition of the role that academic intellectuals like Lynd, Ruth Benedict, Margaret Mead, and even Mitchell, Merriam, and Arnold played during the 1920s and 1930s. The differences lie not so much, as Jacoby asserted, between freelance and academic intellectuals as between types of academic intellectuals. Yet hyperspecialization has its roots in the objectivists' reliance on foundation funds and desire for practicality, while Jacoby's so-called fetishism of theory can trace its beginnings back to the purposivists' denial of complete rationality and objectivity.[37]

Nevertheless, many American social scientists continue to maintain the disciplines' traditional emphasis on facts *and* values. All the disciplines have strong advocacy movements that call for direct involvement of social scientists and their scholarship in social reform. Even the somewhat waspish Jacoby grudgingly sees some hope among historians. Most important, a number of philosophers, including Richard Bernstein, Hilary Putnam, William Sullivan, and especially Richard Rorty, are attacking the dominant analytical philosophy and attempting to reconstruct a public role for philosophy and central roles for scholarship, and especially for human action. Significantly, each has independently turned to John Dewey's work as a key source for their different viewpoints. Like the purposive thinkers before them, they find Dewey's respect for the scientific method when directed by a normative vision a way out of the false choice between a mindless empiricism and an uncontrolled subjectivism.[38]

Max Weber perhaps most eloquently expressed the need for such vision tempered by facts and for informed individuals willing to make such judgments: "No one knows who will live in this cage in the future, or whether at the end of this tremendous development entirely new prophets will arise, or there will be a great rebirth of old ideas and ideals, or, if neither, mechanized petrification, embellished with a sort of compulsive self-importance. For of the last stage of this cultural development, it might be truly said: 'Specialists without spirit, sensualists without heart; this nullity imagines that it has attained a level of civilization never before achieved.' But this brings us to the world of judgments, of value, and of faith."[39]

NOTES

ABBREVIATIONS USED IN THE NOTES

Journals

AAAPSS *Annals of the American Academy of Political and Social Science*
AER   *American Economic Review*
AHR   *American Historical Review*
AJS   *American Journal of Sociology*
APSR   *American Political Science Review*
NR   *New Republic*

Manuscript Collections

AEA   American Economics Association Records, Joseph Regenstein Library, University of Chicago.

TWA   Thurman W. Arnold Collection, American Heritage Center, University of Wyoming Library, Laramie.

CMB   Charles A. and Mary Ritter Beard Collection, The Archives of DePauw University and Indiana United Methodism, DePauw University Library, Greencastle, Indiana.

ENB   Emily Newell Blair Papers, National Recovery Administration Papers, National Archives, Washington, D.C.

HEB   Harry Elmer Barnes Papers, American Heritage Center, University of Wyoming Library, Laramie.

GSC   George S. Counts Collection, Special Collections, Morris Library, University of Southern Illinois, Carbondale.

REF   Ralph E. Flanders Collection, George Arents Research Library, Syracuse University, New York.

ACK   Augustus C. Krey Collection, University of Minnesota Archives, Minneapolis.

RHL   Robert S. and Helen Merrell Lynd Collection, Manuscript Division, Library of Congress, Washington, D.C.

AWM   Arthur W. Macmahon Collection, Butler Library, Columbia University, New York.

CEM   Charles E. Merriam Collection, Joseph Regenstein Library, University of Chicago.

WCM   Wesley C. Mitchell Collection, Butler Library, Columbia University, New York.

WFO   William Fielding Ogburn Collection, Joseph Regenstein Library, University of Chicago.

GHS   George H. E. Smith Collection, Yale University Library, New Haven, Connecticut.

SC   Stuart Chase Collection, Manuscript Division, Library of Congress, Washington, D.C.

INTRODUCTION

1. Bert F. Hoselitz, "Economics," in *A Reader's Guide to the Social Sciences*, ed. Bert F. Hoselitz (New York: Free Press, 1970), 240–45, 265; Ira W. Howerth, "Present Conditions of Sociology in the United States," *AAAPSS* 5 (September 1894): 260–69, cited in Dorothy Ross, *The Origins of American Social Science* (Cambridge: Cambridge University Press, 1991), 131; L. L. Bernard, "The Objective View in Sociology," *AJS* 25 (November 1919): 305; Richard J. Bernstein, *The Restructuring of Social and Political Theory* (New York: Harcourt Brace Jovanovich, 1976), 52.

2. L. L. Bernard and Jessie Bernard, *Origins of American Sociology: The Social Science Movement in the United States* (New York: Thomas Y. Crowell, 1943); Bernard and Bernard, "A Century of Progress in the Social Sciences," *Social Forces* 11 (May 1933): 488–505; Floyd Nelson House, *The Development of Sociology* (New York: McGraw-Hill, 1936); George W. Stocking, Jr., "On the Limits of 'Presentism' and 'Historicism' in the Historiography of the Behavioral Sciences" (1965), in *Race, Culture, and Evolution: Essays in the History of Anthropology* (New York: Free Press, 1968), 1–12; Stocking, Introduction to *Functionalism Historicized: Essays in British Social Anthropology*, ed. Stocking, vol. 2 of *History of Anthropology* (Madison: University of Wisconsin Press, 1984); Stocking, "Radcliffe-Brown and British Social Anthropology," in *Functionalism Historicized*, esp. 136–37, n. 2; Paul Lazersfeld, Foreword to *The Establishment of Empirical Sociology:*

Studies in Continuity, Discontinuity, and Evolution, ed. Anthony Ober-
schall (New York: Harper and Row, 1972), xii–xiii; Edward T. Silva and
Shelia A. Slaughter, *Serving Power: The Making of the Academic Social
Science Expert* (Westport, Conn.: Greenwood Press, 1984). More recently,
several historians of the social sciences have specifically criticized this
Whiggish interpretation. Most important are two works in the Cambridge
University Press Ideas in Context series: Dorothy Ross, *Origins of American
Social Science,* and Peter Novick, *That Noble Dream: The "Objectivity
Question" and the American Historical Profession* (Cambridge: Cambridge
University Press, 1988). Two pioneers in this externalist criticism are Doro-
thy Ross and Henrika Kuklick. Particularly insightful for this perspective
are Ross, "Professionalization and the Transformation of American Social
Thought," *Journal of Economic History* 38 (June 1978): 494–99; Ross, "The
Development of the Social Sciences," in *The Organization of Knowledge in
Modern America, 1860–1920,* ed. Alexandra Oleson and John Voss (Bal-
timore: Johns Hopkins University Press, 1979), 107–38; Kuklick, "Boundary
Maintenance in American Sociology," *Journal of the History of the Be-
havioral Sciences* 16 (July 1980): 201–19; Kuklick, "The Organization of
Social Science in the United States: A Review Essay," *American Quarterly*
28 (Spring 1976): 124–41; and especially, Kuklick, "Restructuring the Past:
Toward an Appreciation of the Social Context of Social Science," *Sociological Quarterly* 21 (Winter 1980): 5–21.

3. For a study of the debate between believers in the scientific method and
those in a natural law, see Edward A. Purcell, Jr., *The Crisis of Democratic
Theory: Scientific Naturalism and the Problem of Value* (Lexington: University of Kentucky Press, 1973).

4. David A. Hollinger, "Historians and the Discourse of Intellectuals," in
New Directions in American Intellectual History, ed. John Higham and Paul
Conkin (Baltimore: Johns Hopkins University Press, 1979), 42–63.

5. Robert C. Bannister, *Sociology and Scientism: The American Quest for
Objectivity 1880–1940* (Chapel Hill: University of North Carolina Press,
1987), 5.

6. Lewis A. Coser, *Men of Ideas: A Sociologist's View* (New York: Free
Press, 1965), 136–43; Edward Shils, "The Intellectuals and the Powers: Some
Perspectives for Comparative Analysis," in *On Intellectuals: Theoretical
Studies/Case Studies,* ed. Phillip Rieff (Garden City, N.Y.: Anchor Books,
1970), 43–44.

7. Coser, *Men of Ideas,* viii; Shils, "The Intellectuals," 34–35.

8. Charles A. Beard, with George H. E. Smith, *The Open Door at Home: A
Trial Philosophy of National Interest* (New York: Macmillan, 1934), 4.

9. Among innumerable other choices for representative service intellec-

tuals, one might include the legal thinker and New Deal administrator Thurman Arnold, sociologist William Ogburn, and the other "scientistic" thinkers examined in Robert Bannister's *Sociology and Scientism*; or Harold Moulton and his fellow Brookings Institution scholars. See Donald T. Critchlow, *The Brookings Institution, 1916–1952: Expertise and the Public Interest in a Democratic Society* (DeKalb: Northern Illinois University Press, 1985), for the latter. Because of the Whiggish nature of the history of social science, comparable works on the purposivists do not exist. Other purposive thinkers who might have been included are anthropologists Ruth Benedict, Edward Sapir, Melville Herskovits, and Margaret Mead; sociologist Louis Wirth; legal realist Jerome Frank; economists Walton Hamilton and Clarence Ayres; and historian James Harvey Robinson.

10. Robert S. Lynd, *Knowledge for What? The Place of Social Science in American Culture* (Princeton: Princeton University Press, 1939), ix.

11. Purcell, *Crisis*; Barry D. Karl, *Charles E. Merriam and the Study of Politics* (Chicago: University of Chicago Press, 1974); Guy Alchon, *The Invisible Hand of Planning: Capitalism, Social Science and the State in the 1920s* (Princeton: Princeton University Press, 1985); Critchlow, *Brookings Institution.*

1 AMERICAN SOCIAL SCIENCE: MORALISM AND THE SCIENTIFIC METHOD

1. Daniel J. Boorstin, *The Americans: The Colonial Experience* (New York: Vintage Books, 1958); *The Americans: The Democratic Experience* (New York: Vintage Books, 1973); and *The Genius of American Politics* (Chicago: University of Chicago Press, 1953).

2. John Winthrop, "A Modell of Christian Charitie" (1630), in *The Puritans: A Sourcebook of Their Writings*, ed. Perry Miller and Thomas Johnson (New York: Harper and Row, 1938), 197–98. The best overview of the moral aspects of American social thought is Wilson Carey McWilliams, *The Idea of Fraternity in America* (Berkeley: University of California Press, 1973).

3. Robert Owen, "A New View of Society or Essays on the Principle of the Formation of the Human Character" (1813), in *A New View of Society and Other Writings*, ed. G. D. H. Cole (New York: E. P. Dutton, 1927), 16.

4. Daniel J. Wilson, *Science, Community, and the Transformation of American Philosophy 1860–1930* (Chicago: University of Chicago Press, 1990), 2, 56; Francis Wayland, *Elements of Political Economy* (Boston: Gould, Kendall, and Lincoln, 1837), iv.

5. Arthur T. Vidich and Stanford M. Lyman, *American Sociology: Worldly Rejections of Religion and Their Direction* (New Haven: Yale University Press, 1985), 9–19; L. L. Bernard and Jessie Bernard, *Origins of American Sociology: The Social Science Movement in the United States* (New York: Thomas Y. Crowell, 1943), 223–36.

6. Robert C. Davis, "Social Research in America Before the Civil War," *Journal of the History of the Behavioral Sciences* 8 (January 1972): 69–85; John Koren, "The American Statistical Association 1839–1914," in *The History of Statistics: Their Development and Progress in Many Countries*, ed. Koren (New York: Macmillan, 1918), 5–8.

7. Michael Gordon, "The Social Survey Movement and Sociology in the United States," *Social Problems* 21 (Fall 1973): 284–93; Carl C. Taylor, *The Social Survey, Its History and Methods*, University of Missouri Bulletin 20, no. 28 (1930): 11, 23.

8. George M. Fredrickson, *The Inner Civil War: Northern Intellectuals and the Crisis of Union* (New York: Harper and Row, 1965), esp. 98–112; Franklin Sanborn, quoted in Thomas L. Haskell, *The Emergence of Professional Social Science: The American Social Science Association and the Nineteenth Century Crisis of Authority* (Urbana: University of Illinois Press, 1977), vi.

Some of the associations that began in the ASSA are the National Institute of Arts and Letters, the American Historical Association, the American Economic Association, the National Conference on Charities and Corrections (later the National Conference on Social Work), the American Anthropological Association, the American Political Science Association, and the American Sociological Society.

9. Edward T. Silva and Shelia A. Slaughter, *Serving Power: The Making of the Academic Social Science Expert* (Westport, Conn.: Greenwood Press, 1984), 42–45; Haskell, *Emergence*, 63–74, 87–90, 100–104; Albion W. Small, "Fifty Years of Sociology in the United States," *AJS* 21 (May 1916): 729; Eaton, quoted in Bernard and Bernard, *Origins*, 599.

10. Franklin B. Sanborn, "The Social Sciences: Their Growth and Future," *Journal of Social Science* 21 (September 1886): 6; Sanborn, "The Threefold Task of Social Science," *Journal of Social Science* 14 (November 1881): 31.

11. Haskell, *Emergence*, 146–67; Dorothy Ross, "Socialism and Academic Liberalism: Academic Social Thought in the 1880s," *Perspectives in American History* 11 (1977–78): 5–10, 30–35.

12. Thomas Bender, "The Culture of Intellectual Life: The City and the Professions," in *New Directions in American Intellectual History*, ed. John Higham and Paul Conkin (Baltimore: Johns Hopkins University Press, 1979), 181–85. Ernest Greenwood, "Attributes of a Profession," *Social Work* 2 (July

1955): 45–55; William J. Goode, "Community Within a Community: The Professions," *American Sociological Review* 22 (April 1957): 194–200; Goode, "Encroachment, Charlatanism, and the Emerging Professions," *American Sociological Review* 25 (December 1960): 902–14.

13. Small, "Fifty Years," 726; Dorothy Ross, "The Development of the Social Sciences," in *The Organization of Knowledge in Modern America,* ed. Alexandra Oleson and John Voss (Baltimore: Johns Hopkins University Press, 1979), 118–21.

14. Ira Remsen, "Scientific Investigation and Progress," quoted in Wilson, *Science, Community,* 23; Norval D. Glenn and David Werner, "Some Trends in the Social Origins of American Sociologists," *American Sociologist* 4 (November 1969): 291–96; Frank W. Blackman and John L. Gillin, *Outlines of Sociology* (New York: Macmillan, 1915), 36.

15. Richard T. Ely, "The American Economic Association, 1885–1909," *American Economic Association Quarterly* 11 (January 1910): 46; Joseph Dorfman, *Thorstein Veblen and His America* (New York: Viking Press, 1934), 207–8.

16. Ross, "Socialism," 36–47; Dorothy Ross, *The Origins of American Social Science* (Cambridge: Cambridge University Press, 1991), 172–86.

17. Albion W. Small, "The Significance of Sociology for Ethics," *Decennial Publications of the University of Chicago* 4 (1903): 119; Small, "The Social Value of the Academic Career," *University of Chicago Record* 2 (1906): 21–31; Small, "Fifty Years"; Vernon K. Dibble, *The Legacy of Albion Small* (Chicago: University of Chicago Press, 1975).

18. Richard Hofstadter and Walter P. Metzger, *The Development of Academic Freedom in the United States* (New York: Columbia University Press, 1955), 335–38, 400–401, 412; Mary O. Furner, *Advocacy and Objectivity: A Crisis in the Professionalization of American Social Science 1865–1905* (Lexington: University of Kentucky Press, 1975), passim; Joseph Dorfman, *The Economic Mind in American Civilization.* Vol. 3: *1865–1918* (New York: Viking Press, 1949), 61–65, 257–58; Benjamin G. Rader, *The Academic Mind and Reform: The Influence of Richard T. Ely in American Life* (Lexington: University of Kentucky Press, 1966), 130–222; Silva and Slaughter, *Serving Power,* 88–89. Even German universities, supposedly the epitome of academic freedom, had social scientists dismissed from the faculty during this time for their controversial political and social views. See Hofstadter and Metzger, *Development,* 389–90.

19. Dorfman, *Economic Mind,* 477; Carol Gruber, *From Mars to Minerva: World War I and the Uses of Higher Learning in America* (Baton Rouge: Louisiana State University Press, 1975), 95–102, 109–10, 117; George T. Blakely,

Historians on the Homefront: American Propagandists for the Great War (Lexington: University of Kentucky Press, 1970); William E. Leuchtenberg, "The New Deal and the Analogue of War," in *Change and Continuity in Twentieth-Century America*, ed. John Braeman, Robert H. Bremner, and Everett Walters (Columbus: Ohio State University Press, 1964), 81–143.

20. Loren Baritz, *The Servants of Power* (New York: John Wiley and Sons, 1960), 48–49, passim; Otis L. Graham, Jr., *Toward a Planned Society: From Roosevelt to Nixon* (New York: Oxford University Press, 1976), 12; Wesley C. Mitchell, "The National Bureau's Social Function," in *Twelfth Annual Report of the Director of Research* (New York: National Bureau of Economic Research, 1940), 20.

21. Raymond B. Fosdick, *The Story of the Rockefeller Foundation* (New York: Harper, 1952), 193, 213; Donald Fisher, "Philanthropic Foundations and the Social Sciences: A Reply to Martin Bulmer," *Sociology* 18 (November 1984): 580–89; Elihu Root, "The Need for Organizations in Social Research," *Bulletin of the National Research Council* 1 (October 1919): 8–10; David M. Grossman, "American Foundations and the Support of Empirical Research, 1913–29," *Minerva* 20 (Spring–Summer 1982): 64–66, 78–79.

22. Silva and Slaughter, *Serving Power*, 259–63; Barbara Howe, "The Emergence of Scientific Philanthropy, 1900–1920: Origins, Issues, and Outcomes," in *Philanthropy and Cultural Imperialism: Foundations at Home and Abroad*, ed. Robert F. Arnove (Bloomington: Indiana University Press, 1982), 33–48. John, Jr., and the Rockefeller advisers learned well from the King episode about how to handle the social sciences. When John, Sr., once mumbled about withholding salaries from allegedly socialist instructors at the University of Chicago, his personal attorney quickly pointed out the public relations danger of such an action and blocked it. Charles E. Harvey, "John D. Rockefeller and the Social Sciences: An Introduction," *Journal of the History of Sociology* 4 (Fall 1982): 8–9.

23. Fosdick, *The Story*, 198–201; *Laura Spelman Rockefeller Memorial Final Report* (New York: privately printed, 1933), 10–11.

24. Barry D. Karl, "Presidential Planning and Social Science Research: Mr. Hoover's Experts," in *Perspectives in American History* 3, ed. Donald Fleming and Bernard Bailyn (1969): 373; L. L. Bernard, "Sociological Research and the Exceptional Man," *Publications of the American Sociological Society* 27 (1933): 3–4; Harold Laski, "Foundations, Universities, and Research," in his *The Dangers of Obedience and Other Essays* (New York: Harper, 1930), 174–75. Laski was particularly cutting, constantly referring to the "big man . . . the very big man" who could control social research. Ruml was very obese. Ibid., 169–70.

25. Thurman W. Arnold, *The Folklore of Capitalism* (New Haven: Yale University Press, 1937), 120; National Planning Board, *Final Report* (Washington, D.C.: U.S. Government Printing Office, 1934), 55.

26. Joseph Dorfman, *The Economic Mind in American Civilization*. Vols. 4 and 5: *1918–1933* (New York: Viking Press, 1959), 674; letter from Frederick E. Deibler to S. M. Foster, July 8, 1930, AEA, Box 23, Folder 5; Morris R. Cohen (chairman), "Generalization in the Social Sciences: A Round-Table Discussion," in *Eleven Twenty-six: A Decade of Social Science Research*, ed. Louis Wirth (Chicago: University of Chicago Press, 1940), 247; George Lundberg, *Can Science Save Us?* (New York: Longmans, Green, 1947), 47–48.

27. Leonard D. White, "The Local Community Research Committee and the Social Science Research Building," in *Chicago: An Experiment in Social Science Research*, ed. White (Chicago: University of Chicago Press, 1929), 26–27; Fred H. Matthews, *Quest for an American Sociology: Robert E. Park and the Chicago School* (Montreal: McGill–Queen's University Press, 1977), 109.

28. Wesley C. Mitchell, "Research in the Social Sciences," in *The New Social Science*, ed. Leonard D. White (Chicago: University of Chicago Press, 1930), 4–15.

29. John C. Merriam, "The Significance of the Border Areas Between Natural and Social Sciences," in White, ed., *The New Social Science*, 31–32; Beardsley Ruml, "Recent Trends in Social Science," in ibid., 99.

30. Barry Karl, *Charles E. Merriam and the Study of Politics* (Chicago: University of Chicago Press, 1974), 155; Charles E. Merriam, "Dedication of the Social Science Building at the University of Chicago," unpublished address, December 17, 1929, CEM; Frederick C. Mills (chairman), "Quantification: The Quest for Precision—A Round-Table Discussion," in Wirth, ed., *Eleven Twenty-six*, 169, 177.

31. C. Judson Herrick, "The Scientific Study of Man and the Humanities," in White, ed., *The New Social Science*, 112–22.

32. Fred Rodell, "Fun into Fundamentals: Review of *The Folklore of Capitalism*, by Thurman Arnold," *NR* 92 (December 15, 1937): 175; Harold J. Laski, "Review of *The Folklore of Capitalism*, by Thurman Arnold," *Brooklyn Law Review* 7 (May 1938): 535–37; Stuart Chase, "Review of *Symbols of Government*, by Thurman Arnold," *Common Sense* 5 (April 1936): 24–25; Henry Hazlitt, "This 'Folklore' of Capitalism: Review of *The Folklore of Capitalism*, by Thurman Arnold," *New York Times Book Review*, February 13, 1938, 2; Richard Hofstadter, *The Age of Reform: From Bryan to F.D.R.* (New York: Alfred A. Knopf, 1955), 320; Howard Zinn, ed., *New Deal Thought* (Indianapolis: Bobbs-Merrill, 1966), xviii–xxi.

33. Karl N. Llewellyn, *The Common Law Tradition* (Boston: Little, Brown, 1960), 508–10; Llewellyn, "Some Realism about Realism—Responding to Dean Pound," *Harvard Law Review* 44 (June 1931): 1236; Edward A. Purcell, Jr., *The Crisis of Democratic Theory: Scientific Naturalism and the Problem of Value* (Lexington: University of Kentucky Press, 1973), 91. The best works on legal realism are Laura Kalman, *Legal Realism at Yale 1927–1960* (Chapel Hill: University of North Carolina Press, 1986); and Wilfred E. Rumble, Jr., *American Legal Realism: Skepticism, Reform and the Judicial Process* (Ithaca: Cornell University Press, 1968).

34. John W. Johnson, "Adaptive Jurisprudence: Some Dimensions of Early Twentieth Century Legal Culture," *Historian* 40 (November 1977): 27–29; Arnold to Frank Hogan, March 19, 1934; Arnold to J. E. Kerrigan, February 9, 1933; Arnold to James F. Aishie, Jr., March 23, 1933, last three in TWA; Llewellyn, quoted in Kalman, *Legal Realism*, 6–7; William O. Douglas, Introduction to *Selections from the Letters and Legal Papers of Thurman Arnold*, ed. Victor H. Kramer (Washington: Merkle Press, 1961), viii.

35. Thurman W. Arnold, "Government," unpublished address delivered at the third session of the *New York Herald Tribune* Forum, Waldorf-Astoria Hotel, New York, October 26, 1938, 3, 6, TWA; Arnold, "Oral History of Thurman Arnold," conducted by Paul Greenberg, June 1962, Washington, D.C., 13; Arnold to Royal Hunt Balcom, May 26, 1934, TWA; Arnold, *The Symbols of Government* (New Haven: Yale University Press, 1935), 73; Arnold, *The Folklore of Capitalism* (New Haven: Yale University Press, 1937), 10, 39, 62, 116–17, 138; Arnold, "Theories about Economic Theory," *AAAPSS* 172 (March 1934): 27.

36. Thurman W. Arnold, "Apologia for Jurisprudence," *Yale Law Journal* 44 (March 1935): 739; Arnold, *Symbols*, 215; Arnold, "Theories about," 26; Arnold, "The Folklore of Mr. Hook—A Reply," in *Reason, Social Myths, and Democracy*, by Sidney Hook (New York: Humanities Press, 1940), 55–56; Arnold, *Folklore*, 207–29; Arnold, "The Antitrust Laws: Their Past and Future," Radio address over station wjsv, Washington, D.C., August 19, 1939, 2, TWA.

37. George Dykhuizen, *The Life and Mind of John Dewey* (Carbondale: Southern Illinois University Press, 1973), 297; Sidney Hook, *Reason, Social Myths, and Democracy* (New York: Humanities Press, 1940), 28–29, 41–61.

38. For surveys of the search for values, see Robert S. McElvaine, *The Great Depression* (New York: Times Books, 1984), 196–223; and Richard Pells, *Radical Visions and American Dreams* (New York: Harper and Row, 1973), passim.

39. Edward B. Tylor, *Primitive Culture* (Boston: Estes and Lauriat, 1874) 2:453.

40. Ruth Benedict, *Patterns of Culture* (Boston: Houghton Mifflin, c. 1934; reprint, 1959), 96; Paul Valery, quoted in Herbert Marcuse, *One-Dimensional Man: Studies in the Ideology of Advanced Industrial Society* (Boston: Beacon Press, 1964), 68.

41. Robert S. Lynd, *Knowledge for What? The Place of Social Science in American Culture* (Princeton: Princeton University Press, 1939), 16.

42. Edwin Nourse, "The Development of Council Policy: Report of the Problems and Policy Committee of the Social Science Research Council," Minutes of the meeting of the Board of Directors of the Social Science Research Council, Buck Hill Falls, Pa., September 13–15, 1938, 1–2, CEM; Wesley C. Mitchell (chairman), "The Social Sciences, One or Many: A Round Table Discussion," in Wirth, ed., *Eleven Twenty-six*, 122–23; James Harvey Robinson, "The Newer Ways of Historians," *AHR* 35 (January 1930): 245–47.

43. Edward Sapir, "Cultural Anthropology and Psychiatry" (1934), reprinted in *Culture, Language, and Personality: Selected Essays*, ed. David G. Mandelbaum (Berkeley: University of California Press, 1956), 146, 156–57; Lynd, *Knowledge for What?*, 53, 189–97, 250.

44. John E. Smith, *Themes in American Philosophy* (New York: Harper, 1970), 8. Two of the best histories of pragmatism emphasize this central theme of knowledge and action in their very titles: H. S. Thayer, *Meaning and Action: A Study of American Pragmatism* (Indianapolis: Bobbs-Merrill, 1973), and John E. Smith, *Purpose and Thought: The Meaning of Pragmatism* (New Haven: Yale University Press, 1978).

45. John Dewey, *Psychology* (New York: Harper and Brothers, 1887), 10.

46. John Dewey to T. V. Smith, quoted in a letter from Smith to Wesley Mitchell, December 18, 1929, WCM; Dewey, "The Influence of Darwinism on Philosophy" (1909), in *The Influence of Darwinism on Philosophy* (New York: Henry Holt, 1910), 1–19; Dewey, "Intelligence and Morals" (1908), in ibid., 46–76; Dewey, "Interpretation of the Savage Mind," *Psychological Review* 9 (May 1902): 219.

47. Smith, *Purpose and Thought*, 96–98; Dewey, "The Influence," 17; Robert B. Westbrook, *John Dewey and American Democracy* (Ithaca: Cornell University Press, 1991), 140.

48. Lewis Feuer, "America's Medicine Man: Review of *Young John Dewey: An Essay in American Intellectual History*, by Neil Couglan," *Times Literary Supplement*, December 3, 1976, 1507; Arthur M. Schlesinger, Jr., *The Politics of Upheaval* (Boston: Houghton Mifflin, 1960), 151; Eric F. Goldman, *Rendezvous with Destiny* (New York: Alfred A. Knopf, 1952), 122–23; Darnell Rucker, *The Chicago Pragmatists* (Minneapolis: University of Minnesota Press, 1969), 132, 141.

49. John Dewey, *Reconstruction in Philosophy* (Boston: Beacon Press, c. 1920; reprint, 1948), 26–27 and passim; Lawrence A. Cremin, *The Transformation of the School: Progressivism in American Education 1876–1957* (New York: Vintage Books, 1961), 235–36; Dykhuizen, *Life and Mind of Dewey*, 235–36.

50. John Dewey, "Philosophy," in *Research in the Social Sciences: Its Fundamental Methods and Objectives,* ed. Wilson Gee (New York: Macmillan, 1929), 241–65.

51. Mark DeWolf Howe, *Holmes-Pollock Letters: The Correspondence of Mr. Justice Holmes and Sir Frederick Pollack, 1874–1932* (Cambridge: Harvard University Press, 1941), 2:287.

52. For an excellent examination of the centrality of the scientific perspective for developments in philosophy and psychology in the late nineteenth and early twentieth centuries, see Daniel J. Wilson, *Science, Community, and the Transformation of American Philosophy, 1860–1930* (Chicago: University of Chicago Press, 1990).

53. Morton White, *Science and Sentiment in America: Philosophical Thought from Jonathan Edwards to John Dewey* (New York: Oxford University Press, 1972), 3, 218, passim; William Milligan Sloane, ed., *The Life of James McCosh: A Record Chiefly Autobiographical* (New York: C. Scribner's Sons, 1896), 234–35; David A. Hollinger, "Inquiry and Uplift: Late Nineteenth Century Academics and the Moral Efficacy of Scientific Practice," in *The Authority of Experts: Studies in History and Theory,* ed. Thomas L. Haskell (Bloomington: Indiana University Press, 1984), 142–56.

54. Dykhuizen, *Life and Mind of Dewey,* 17–18; Neil Coughlan, *Young John Dewey: An Essay in American Intellectual History* (Chicago: University of Chicago Press, 1973), 25–29, 80–82; John Dewey, "The New Psychology" (1884), in *The Early Works of John Dewey, 1882–1898,* ed. JoAnn Boydston (Carbondale: Southern Illinois University Press, 1969), 1:48–60; Dewey, "Renan's Loss of Faith in Science" (1893), in ibid., 4:17–18.

55. Dewey, "Logical Conditions," 229–32; Dewey, "Theory of Valuation," in *International Encyclopedia of the Unified Sciences* 2 (Chicago: University of Chicago Press, 1939).

56. Lewis Mumford, *The Golden Day: A Study in American Literature and Culture* (Boston: Beacon Press, c. 1926; reprint, 1957), 136.

57. White, *Science and Sentiment.*

58. Louis Hartz, *The Liberal Tradition in America: An Interpretation of American Political Thought since the Revolution* (New York: Harcourt, Brace, and World, 1955), 59; Charles Sanders Peirce, "Evolutionary Love," in *Chance, Love, and Logic: Philosophical Essays by the Late Charles S. Peirce,*

ed. Morris R. Cohen (New York: Harcourt, Brace, 1923), 272–75; William James, "The Will to Believe," in his *The Will to Believe and Other Essays in Popular Philosophy* (New York: Longmans, Green, 1897), 22.

59. Coughlan, *Young John Dewey*, 67–68; John Dewey, "From Absolutism to Experimentalism" (1930), in *John Dewey on Experience, Nature and Freedom*, ed. Richard J. Bernstein (New York: Liberal Arts Press, 1960), 10–11; Dewey, *Liberalism and Social Action* (New York: Capricorn Books, c. 1935; reprint, 1963), 23–25; Dewey, "The Ethics of Democracy" (1888), in Boydston, ed., *Early Works of John Dewey*, 1:233; Dewey, "Ethics and Physical Science" (1887), in ibid., 1:217–18.

60. John Dewey, *The Quest for Certainty: A Study of the Relation of Knowledge and Action* (New York: G. P. Putnam's Sons, c. 1929; reprint, 1960), 255.

61. Ibid., 262, 312; John Dewey, *The Public and Its Problems* (New York: Swallow Press, c. 1927; reprint, 1954), 141, 174–76, 199; Dewey, "Human Nature," in *Encyclopedia of the Social Sciences* 8 (New York: Macmillan, 1932), 531–36; Dewey, "Science and Society," in *Philosophy and Civilization* (New York: G. P. Putnam's Sons, 1931), 320; Dewey, "Philosophy and Democracy" (1918), in *Characters and Events: Popular Essays in Social and Political Philosophy*, ed. Joseph Ratner (New York: Henry Holt, 1929), 2:844–45.

62. John Dewey, "Social Science and Social Control," *NR* 76 (July 29, 1931): 276–77; Dewey, *Liberalism*, 47–48; Dewey, "Liberating the Social Scientist," *Commentary* 4 (October 1947): 379, 385.

63. Dewey, *Liberalism*, 38–41, 55; Dewey, *Individualism Old and New* (New York: Capricorn Books, c. 1929; reprint, 1962), 33–34, 101–45.

64. James Harvey Robinson and Charles A. Beard, *The Development of Modern Europe* (New York: Ginn, 1907), 1:iii; Charles M. Andrews, "These Forty Years," *AHR* 30 (January 1925): 225–44.

65. James Harvey Robinson, "Newer Ways," 247–55; Carl Becker, "Everyman His Own Historian," *AHR* 37 (January 1932): 229–33; Charles A. Beard, "Written History as an Act of Faith," *AHR* 39 (January 1934): 220–23, 227–29.

66. Charles H. McIlwain, "Bias in Historical Writing," *History* 11 (October 1926): 197; McIlwain, "The Historian's Role in a Changing World," *AHR* 42 (January 1937): 207–24. The best debate is Theodore Clarke Smith, "The Writing of American History in America from 1884 to 1934," *AHR* 40 (April 1935): 439–49; and Charles A. Beard, "That Noble Dream," *AHR* 41 (January 1936): 74–87.

67. Charles E. Merriam, "Progress in Political Research," *APSR* 20 (February 1926): 1–13.

68. Charles Merriam to Charles Beard, November 3, 1925, CEM; Charles A. Beard, "Review of *American Political Ideas, 1865–1917*, by Charles E. Merriam," *NR* 25 (January 19, 1921): 235–36; Charles A. Beard, "Review of *The New Democracy and the New Despotism*," *APSR* 33 (October 1939): 884–86; Karl, *Charles E. Merriam*, 184–85.

69. Charles A. Beard, "Time, Technology, and the Creative Spirit in Political Science," *APSR* 21 (February 1927): 1–11.

70. Jacob Hollander, "The Economist's Spiral," *AER* 12 (March 1922): 8–16; Wesley C. Mitchell, "Quantitative Analysis and Economic Theory," *AER* 15 (March 1925): 1–12; Edwin F. Gay, "Historical Records," *AER* 20 (March 1930): 1–8; E. L. Bogart, "Pushing back the Frontiers," *AER* 22 (March 1932): 4–9; Alvin Johnson, "The Economist in a World of Transition," *AER* 27 (March 1937): 1–3.

71. James Q. Dealey, "Eudemics, The Science of National or General Welfare," *Publications of the American Sociological Society* 15 (1920): 1–7; Bernard, "Sociological Research," 3–12; John Lewis Gillin, "The Development of Sociology in the United States," *Publications of the American Sociological Society* 21 (1926): 17–25; William F. Ogburn, "The Folkways of a Scientific Sociology," *Publications of the American Sociological Society* 24 (1929): 1–11.

72. Robert C. Bannister, *Sociology and Scientism: The American Quest for Objectivity* (Chapel Hill: University of North Carolina Press, 1987), 188–214; Patricia Lengermann, "The Founding of the American Sociological Review," *American Sociological Review* 44 (April 1979): 185–99; Norbert Wiley, "The Rise and Fall of Dominating Theories in American Sociology," in *Contemporary Issues on Theory and Research: A Metasociological Perspective*, ed. William E. Snizek, Ellsworth R. Fuhrman, and Michael K. Miller (Westport, Conn.: Greenwood Press, 1979), 47–71.

2 WESLEY MITCHELL AND THE QUANTITATIVE APPROACH

1. Arthur F. Burns, "Introductory Sketch," in *Wesley Clair Mitchell: The Economic Scientist*, ed. Arthur F. Burns (New York: National Bureau of Economic Research, 1953), 23, 51; Rexford G. Tugwell, "Wesley Mitchell: An Evaluation," *NR* 92 (October 6, 1937): 240; Adolf A. Berle, "Wesley Clair Mitchell: The Economic Scientist," *Journal of the American Statistical Association* 48 (June 1953): 169; Joseph Dorfman, "A Professional Sketch," in Burns, ed., *Wesley Clair Mitchell*, 125–38; John Maurice Clark, "Memorial Address," in ibid., 139.

2. Joyce Antler, *Lucy Sprague Mitchell: The Making of a Modern Woman* (New Haven: Yale University Press, 1987), 330; Lucy Sprague Mitchell, *Two Lives: The Story of Wesley Clair Mitchell and Myself* (New York: Simon and Schuster, 1953), 387.

3. Lucy Mitchell, *Two Lives*, 21, 80; David Seckler, *Thorstein Veblen and the Institutionalists: A Study in the Social Philosophy of Economics* (Boulder: Colorado Associated University Press, 1975), 100; Antler, *Lucy Sprague Mitchell*, 337; Lynd to Mitchell, April 22 and May 30, 1939; Mitchell to Lynd, April 24, 1939, all in WCM.

4. Lucy Mitchell, *Two Lives*, 8–9; Antler, *Lucy Sprague Mitchell*, 164, 227–28, 314.

5. Robert L. Heilbroner, *The Worldly Philosophers: The Lives, Times, and Ideas of the Great Economic Thinkers* (New York: Simon and Schuster, 1967), 308; Wesley C. Mitchell, "Lectures on Current Types of Economic Theory," Lecture notes of 1934–35, transcribed by Augustus M. Kelley (New York: Augustus M. Kelley, 1937), 509, 646; Joseph Dorfman, "The Department of Economics," in *A History of the Faculty of Political Science, Columbia University*, by R. Gordon Hoxie, Sally Falk Moore, et al. (New York: Columbia University Press, 1955), 191–93; Mitchell to Davis Dewey, July 31, 1914, AEA, Box 65, Folder 31.

6. Wesley C. Mitchell, "Fifty Years as an Economist," Talk to the Economics Club, Columbia University, New York, May 11, 1945, WCM.

7. Wesley C. Mitchell, ed., *What Veblen Taught: Selected Writings of Thorstein Veblen* (New York: Viking Press, 1936), xxxvi–xlvii; Mitchell, "Quantitative Analysis in Economic Theory" (1925), in his *The Backward Art of Spending Money and Other Essays* (New York: McGraw-Hill, 1937), 29; Mitchell, "The Rationality of Economic Activity," *Journal of Political Economy* 13 (February 1910): 205–12; Philip A. Klein, "The Neglected Institutionalism of Wesley Mitchell's Theoretical Basis," *Journal of Economic Issues* 17 (December 1983): 867–99; Joseph Dorfman, *Thorstein Veblen and His America* (New York: Viking Press, 1934), 394; Mitchell, "Thorstein Veblen, 1857–1929," *NR* 60 (September 4, 1929): 66–68.

8. Wesley C. Mitchell, Notes for "Fifty Years as an Economist," May 11, 1945; Mitchell to Lucy Sprague, October 18, 1911, both in WCM.

9. Wesley C. Mitchell, "Appendix: The Author's Own Account of His Methodological Interests," in *Methods in Social Science: A Case Book*, ed. Stuart A. Rice (Chicago: University of Chicago Press, 1929), 676–77; Mitchell, "The Public Relations of Science," *Science* 90 (December 29, 1939): 606; Mitchell to Dewey, December 7, 1934, WCM.

10. Wesley C. Mitchell, "J. Lawrence Laughlin," *Journal of Political Econ-*

omy 49 (December 1941): 879–80; Robert L. Church, "Economists as Experts: The Rise of an Academic Profession in the United States 1870–1920," in *The University in Society,* ed. Lawrence Stone (Princeton: Princeton University Press, 1974), 581–83.

11. Wesley C. Mitchell, "The Role of Money in Economic Theory" (1916), in *The Backward Art,* 158, 160, 165–77; Alfred Marshall, *Principles of Economics* (New York: Macmillan, c. 1890; reprint, 1940), 1:22.

12. Lucy Mitchell, *Two Lives,* 294; Mitchell, "Lectures," 13–16, 41, 61, 93–94; Mitchell, "Review of *Risk, Uncertainty, and Profit,* by Frank Knight," *AER* 12 (June 1922): 275.

13. Mitchell, "Appendix," 673–80; Mitchell, "Institutes for Research in the Social Sciences" (1930), in *The Backward Art,* 59.

14. Wesley C. Mitchell, "The Real Issues in the Quantity-Theory Controversy," *Journal of Political Economy* 12 (June 1904): 403–8; Mitchell, "Fifty Years."

15. Mitchell, "Lectures," 9–13; Mitchell to Sprague, October 18, 1911, WCM.

16. Tugwell, "Wesley Mitchell," 238–39.

17. Mitchell to Sprague, October 18, 1911, WCM.

18. Wesley C. Mitchell, *A History of Greenbacks with Special Reference to the Economic Consequences of Their Issue 1862–65* (Chicago: University of Chicago Press, 1903), 136–37, 198–99, 238–56, 279, 339–47.

19. F. R. Clow, "Review of *The History of Greenbacks,* by Wesley Clair Mitchell," *Journal of Political Economy* 12 (June 1904): 424; Mitchell to Sprague, June 8, 1909, quoted in Lucy Mitchell, *Two Lives,* 176.

20. Lucy Mitchell, *Two Lives,* 176.

21. Wesley C. Mitchell, *Business Cycles,* Memoirs of the University of California 3 (Sacramento: University of California Press, 1913), 20, 191–93; Mitchell, "Quantitative Analysis," 26–27; Mitchell, "Economics 1904–1929," (1931) in *The Backward Art,* 400–401; Joseph Dorfman, *The Economic Mind in American Civilization.* Vol. 2: *1606–1865* (New York: Viking Press, 1949), 842.

22. John Maurice Clark, "Wesley C. Mitchell's Contribution to the Theory of Business Cycles," in Rice, ed., *Methods,* 662; Mitchell, *Business Cycles,* vii.

23. Mitchell, "Lectures," 591; Lucy Mitchell, *Two Lives,* 92; Mitchell, "Research in the Social Sciences," in *The New Social Science,* ed. Leonard D. White (Chicago: University of Chicago Press, 1930), 7; Gerald N. Grob, *Edward Jarvis and the Medical World of Nineteenth Century America* (Knoxville: University of Tennessee Press, 1978); Donald A. MacKenzie, *Statistics*

in Britain 1865–1930: The Social Construction of Scientific Knowledge (Edinburgh: Edinburgh University Press, 1981).

24. Wesley C. Mitchell, *Business Cycles: The Problem and Its Setting* (New York: National Bureau of Economic Research, 1927), 201–5, 357–60; Mitchell, "The Making and Using of Index Numbers," Bulletin 656 (Washington: U.S. Government Printing Office, 1938).

25. James Bryce, *The American Commonwealth* (New York: Macmillan, c. 1888; reprint, 1924), 1:12; Geoffery H. Moore, "Wesley Mitchell in Retrospect," *Journal of Economic Issues* 12 (June 1978): 281; Mitchell, *Business Cycles*, 204–5; Mitchell and Arthur F. Burns, *Measuring Business Cycles*, Studies in Business Cycles 2 (New York: National Bureau of Economic Research, 1946), 12; Mitchell, "How the National Bureau's Program Is Made," unpublished address, no date, (c. 1939), WCM.

26. Allyn Abbott Young, "Economics," in *Research in the Social Sciences: Its Fundamental Methods and Objectives*, ed. Wilson Gee (New York: Macmillan, 1929), 72–77; Wesley C. Mitchell, "The Prospects of Economics," in *The Trend of Economics*, ed. Rexford Guy Tugwell (New York: F. S. Crofts, 1924), 21–24; Frederick C. Mills, "On Measurement in Economics," in Tugwell, ed., *The Trend*, 37.

27. Mitchell, "The Prospects"; Joseph Dorfman, *The Economic Mind in American Civilization*. Vol. 4: *1918–1933* (New York: Viking Press, 1959), 202; Dorfman, *The Economic Mind in American Civilization*. Vol. 3: *1865–1918* (New York: Viking Press, 1949), 477.

28. Guy Alchon, *The Invisible Hand of Planning: Capitalism, Social Science, and the State in the 1920s* (Princeton: Princeton University Press, 1985), 27–30.

29. Lucy Mitchell, *Two Lives*, 96–97; Mitchell to Sprague, October 18, 1911; Mitchell to Joseph Willits, December 29, 1941, both letters in WCM; Mitchell, "The Prospects," 27–28; Mitchell, "Empirical Research and the Development of Economic Science," in *Economic Research and the Development of Economic Science and Public Policy* (New York: National Bureau of Economic Research, 1946), 8.

30. Wesley C. Mitchell, Stenographic notes taken from his May 1, 1918, lecture in the course "Current Types of Economic Theory," quoted in Dorfman, *Economic Mind*, 4:111, 490; Mitchell, "The Prospects," 21; William E. Leuchtenberg, "The New Deal and the Analogue of War," in *Change and Continuity in Twentieth-Century America*, ed. John Braeman, Robert H. Bremner, and Everett Walters (Columbus: Ohio State University Press, 1964), 81–143.

31. Wesley C. Mitchell, "Statistics and Government" (1918), in *The Backward Art*, 49–50; Mitchell to Willits, December 29, 1941, WCM.

32. Herbert Heaton, *A Scholar in Action: Edwin F. Gay* (Cambridge: Harvard University Press, 1952), 91–93; David M. Grossman, "American Foundations and the Support of Economic Research, 1913–29," *Minerva* 20 (Spring–Summer 1982): 64–66.

33. Heaton, *A Scholar*, 93–95.

34. Charles Merriam, "Impressions of Hanover," Unpublished notes, September 1927, CEM; Mitchell, *History*, dedication page.

35. Heaton, *A Scholar*, 197.

36. Dorfman, *Economic Mind*, 4:365; Wesley C. Mitchell, "The National Bureau Enters Its Twentieth Year," in *Report of the Director of Research of the National Bureau of Economic Research* (New York: A. Colish, 1939), 9–11; Mitchell, "How the National Bureau's"; Mitchell, "The National Bureau's Social Function," in *Twentieth Annual Report of the Director of Research of the National Bureau of Economic Research* (New York: National Bureau of Economic Research, 1940), 9.

37. Grossman, "American Foundations," 70–73; Alchon, *Invisible Hand*, 54–55; Mitchell, "National Bureau Enters," 9; Mitchell, "What the National Bureau Is and Does," Talk at a dinner meeting of the Advisory Council on Fiscal Research of the National Bureau of Economic Research, October 19, 1939, WCM.

38. Wesley C. Mitchell, Introduction to *Income in the United States: Its Amount and Distribution 1909–1919* (New York: National Bureau of Economic Research, 1922), v, ix; Mitchell to Willits, November 21, 1941, WCM; Mitchell, "National Bureau's Social," 15.

39. Wesley C. Mitchell, "The Problem of Business Instability," *Proceedings of the Academy of Political Science* 12 (July 1927): 650; President's Conference on Unemployment, *Business Cycles and Unemployment* (New York: McGraw-Hill, 1923), 32; Gay to Mitchell, September 16, 1921 WCM; Joseph Dorfman, *The Economic Mind in American Civilization*. Vol. 5: *1918–1933* (New York: Viking Press, 1959), 551–52.

40. Mitchell, "Statistics and Government," 52–53; Mitchell, "Economics and Social Engineering," in *Science and Social Change*, ed. Jesse E. Thornton (Washington: Brookings Institute, 1939), 312; Mitchell, "Empirical Research," 4–6; Mitchell, "Economics 1904–1929," 401; Maurice G. Kendall, "Measurement in the Study of Society," in *Man and the Social Sciences*, ed. W. A. Robson (London: Allen and Unwin, 1972); Dorfman, *Economic Mind*, 3:70–73; Mitchell, "Fifty Years"; Mitchell to Sprague, October 18, 1911, WCM.

41. Hoover to Mitchell, July 29, 1921; Mitchell to Hoover, August 3, 1921, both in WCM; Antler, *Lucy Sprague*, 234–35.

42. Wesley C. Mitchell, Letter to the editor, *New York Evening Post*,

March 21, 1920, quoted in Lucy Mitchell, *Two Lives,* 337–38; Mitchell to William Ogburn, January 21, 1932, WFO; R. F. Harrod, "Wesley Mitchell in Oxford," *Economic Journal* 59 (September 1949): 460.

43. Mitchell, "Appendix," 678; Mitchell, "Lectures," 11–12, 23–24; Mitchell to Gay, November 18, 1924; Mitchell, "Problems of Methods in Economics," Talk to the Economics Club, Columbia University, January 12, 1944, last two in WCM.

44. Raymond T. Bye, *An Appraisal of Frederick C. Mills' "The Behavior of Prices"* (New York: Social Science Research Council, 1940), 202.

45. Wesley C. Mitchell, "Intelligence and the Guidance of Economic Evolution" (1936), in his *The Backward Art,* 127; Mitchell, "Lectures," 19, 135, 266–67; Mitchell, "Review of *An Introduction to Tooke and Newmarch's A History of Prices of the State of the Circulation from 1792 to 1956,* by T. E. Gregory," *Economica* 26 (June 1929): 215.

46. Barry D. Karl, "Presidential Planning and Social Science Research: Mr. Hoover's Experts," in *Perspectives in American History* 3, ed. Donald Fleming and Bernard Bailyn (1969): 364–65, 374; Craig Lloyd, *Aggressive Introvert: A Study of Herbert Hoover and Public Relations Management 1912–1932* (Columbus: Ohio State University Press, 1972), 22–25, 97–102, passim.

47. Alchon, *Invisible Hand,* 81–87, 109–10; Ellis W. Hawley, "Economic Inquiry and the State in New Era America: Antistatist Corporatism and Positive Statism in Uneasy Coexistence," in *The State and Economic Knowledge,* ed. Mary O. Furner and Barry Supple (Cambridge: Cambridge University Press, 1990), 287–324.

48. Ogburn to Mitchell, September 6, 1929, WFO.

49. Minutes of the meeting of the President's Research Committee on Social Trends, offices of the Social Science Research Council, New York, February 8, 1930, WFO.

50. Barry D. Karl, *Charles E. Merriam and the Study of Politics* (Chicago: University of Chicago Press, 1974), 211; Karl, "Presidential Planning," 369; Minutes of the second meeting of the President's Committee on Social Trends, Chicago, Illinois, December 19, 1929, WFO.

51. Robert E. L. Faris, *Chicago Sociology 1920–1932* (Chicago: University of Chicago Press, 1967), 113–19; Robert Bannister, *Sociology and Scientism: The American Quest for Objectivity 1880–1940* (Chapel Hill: University of North Carolina Press, 1987).

52. William F. Ogburn, "Memorandum to the Investigators for the President's Research Committee on Social Trends: Note on Method," unpublished memorandum, February 15, 1932, 1–2, 4–6, 13–14, CEM and WFO; Ogburn to Mitchell, January 10, 1932, WCM.

53. Minutes of the meeting of the President's Research Committee on Social Trends, 230 Park Avenue, New York, June 20 and 30, 1932, WFO.

54. Ogburn to Merriam, May 11, 1932; Hunt to Merriam, May 4, 1932; Gosnell to Ogburn, May 13, 1932, all in CEM.

55. Ogburn to Mitchell, February 10, 1932; Minutes of the meeting of the President's Research Committee on Social Trends, 230 Park Avenue, New York, June 20, 1932, both in WFO.

56. Wesley C. Mitchell, "A Review of Findings by the President's Research Committee on Social Trends," in *Recent Social Trends in the United States: Report of the Committee on Social Trends* (New York: McGraw-Hill, 1933), xi–xx, lx–lxxv.

57. Editorial, "What Is Happening in America: Review of *Recent Social Trends in the United States*, by the President's Research Committee on Social Trends," *Spectator* 151 (July 21, 1933): 88; Adolf A. Berle, "The Trend of the Turn: Review of *Recent Social Trends*," *Saturday Review of Literature* 9 (April 15, 1933): 533–35; Charles A. Beard, "Facts, Opinions, and Social Values," *Yale Review* 22 (March 1933): 595–97; Beard, "Limitations to the Application of Social Science Implied in *Recent Social Trends*," *Social Forces* 11 (May 1933): 505–10.

58. Alchon, *Invisible Hand*, 156.

59. Mitchell, "Economics and Social," 312; Mitchell, Address at the Tenth Anniversary Dinner of the Social Science Research Council, September 14, 1933, WCM.

60. Dorfman, *Economic Mind*, 4:196–200; Soule to Mitchell, February 10, 1937; Mitchell to Soule, February 12, 1937, both in WCM.

61. Wesley C. Mitchell and Arthur F. Burns, *Statistical Indicators of Cyclical Revivals*, National Bureau of Economic Research Bulletin 69 (New York: National Bureau of Economic Research, 1938), 1–2, 12; Mitchell, "A Review," in *Recent Economic Changes in the United States: Report of the Committee on Recent Economic Changes* (New York: McGraw-Hill, 1929), 2:861–62; Mitchell and Arthur F. Burns, *Production During the American Business Cycle of 1927–1933*, National Bureau of Economic Research Bulletin 61 (New York: National Bureau of Economic Research, 1936), 1.

62. Robert H. MacIver, James W. Angell, et al., *Economic Reconstruction: Report of the Columbia University Commission* (New York: Columbia University Press, 1934), 82.

63. Ibid., 82, 87–104.

64. Lucy Mitchell, *Two Lives*, 254; Mitchell, "Economic and Social," 302–4, 315–16.

65. Edward A. Purcell, Jr., *The Crisis of Democratic Theory: Scientific*

Naturalism and the Problem of Value (Lexington: University of Kentucky Press, 1973), 179–96.

66. Mitchell, "The National Bureau's Social," 8–15.

67. Bye, *An Appraisal*, 232–36, 299–300; Wesley C. Mitchell, "Discussion of 'Political Science, Political Economy, and Values,' " *AER* 34, suppl. (March 1944): 49–50; Mitchell, "Problems of Methods in Economics," Talk to the Economics Club, Columbia University, January 12, 1944, WCM.

68. Mitchell, "Feeling," 229–32; Mitchell, "Facts and Values in Economics," *Journal of Philosophy* 41 (April 1944): 219; Mitchell, "Science and the State of Mind," *Science* 79 (January 6, 1939): 2–3.

69. Wesley C. Mitchell, "Public Relations," 605–7; Mitchell, "Intelligence," 127; Mitchell, "Science," 3; Mitchell to Willits, November 21, 1941, and May 22, 1942; Mitchell, "Economics and the Formation of Public Policies," Talk to the Economics Club, Columbia University, December 12, 1941, last three in WCM.

70. Mitchell, "Economic Research"; Mitchell, "Testimony on Science Legislation," Hearings Before the Subcommittee on War Mobilization, Committee on Military Affairs, U.S. Senate, 79th Congr., 1st sess., 1945, 781.

71. Mitchell, "Problems of Methods"; Mitchell, "Fifty Years"; Mitchell, "Economics in a Unified World," *Social Research* 11 (February 1944): 7.

3   CHARLES MERRIAM AND TECHNICAL EXPERTISE

1. Charles Merriam, "Impressions of Hanover," Unpublished notes, CEM. For a concise and eloquent statement of Merriam's importance for social science, see Harold Orlans, "The Advocacy of Social Science in Europe and America," *Minerva* 14 (Spring 1976): 6–32.

2. Robert M. Crunden, *Ministers of Reform: The Progressives' Achievement in American Civilization* (New York: Basic Books, 1982); Barry D. Karl, *Charles E. Merriam and the Study of Politics* (Chicago: University of Chicago Press, 1974), 2–13; Merriam to Herbert Croly, October 19, 1921, CEM; Harold L. Ickes, *The Secret Diary of Harold L. Ickes: The First Thousand Days 1933–36* (New York: Simon and Schuster, 1954), 281.

3. Steven J. Diner, *A City and Its Universities: Public Policy in Chicago 1892–1919* (Chapel Hill: University of North Carolina Press, 1980); Charles E. Merriam, "The Education of Charles E. Merriam," in *The Future of Government in the United States*, ed. Leonard D. White (Chicago: University of Chicago Press, 1942), 5; Lincoln Steffens, *The Autobiography of Lincoln Steffens* (New York: Harcourt, Brace, and World, 1931), 2:428.

4. Maureen A. Flanagan, "Charter Reform in Chicago: Political Culture and Urban Progressive Reform," *Journal of Urban History* 12 (February 1987): 109–30. Merriam's personal attitude toward immigrants and their role within American politics and life is unclear. In direct contrast with Robert Park and the Chicago school of sociology, Merriam rarely mentioned immigrants, even in his work on city politics. However, his brother John, the president of the National Research Council, was a disciple of the racist geologist Joseph LeConte, spoke disparagingly of immigrants in general, and was a close friend of Madison Grant, a vehement anti-Semite and author of *Passing of the Great Race*. Ellen Condeliffe Lagemann, *The Politics of Knowledge: The Carnegie Corporation, Philanthropy and Public Policy* (Middletown, Conn.: Wesleyan University Press, 1989), 81.

5. Charles Merriam, "The Task of Politics," Unpublished memorandum, no date, CEM; Merriam, *New Aspects of Politics* (Chicago: University of Chicago Press, c. 1925; reprint, 1970), 51, 53; Robert H. Wiebe, *The Search for Order 1877–1920* (New York: Hill and Wang, 1967); John C. Burnham, "Progressivism: An Essay," in *Progressivism*, by John D. Buenker, John C. Burnham, and Robert M. Crunden (Cambridge: Schenckman, 1977), 3–30; Samuel P. Hays, *Conservation and the Gospel of Efficiency: The Progressive Conservation Movement 1890–1920* (Cambridge: Harvard University Press, 1959); Samuel Haber, *Efficiency and Uplift: Scientific Management in the Progressive Era* (Chicago: University of Chicago Press, 1964); Merriam, *Civic Education in the United States* (New York: Charles Scribner's Sons, 1934), xvii, 28.

6. Charles E. Merriam, "Progress in Political Research," *APSR* 20 (February 1926): 14; Merriam, *Political Power: Its Composition and Incidence* (New York: McGraw-Hill, 1935), 202–3; Merriam, *The Role of Politics in Social Change* (New York: New York University Press, 1936), 61–66; Merriam, "The National Resources Planning Board: A Chapter in American Planning Experience," *APSR* 29 (December 1944): 1086; Merriam, Foreword to *Our Cities: Their Role in the National Economy. Report of the Urbanism Committee of the National Resources Committee* (Washington, D.C.: U.S. Government Printing Office, 1937), v; Merriam, "The Possibilities of Planning," *AJS* 49 (March 1944): 407.

7. Charles E. Merriam, *What Is Democracy?* (Chicago: University of Chicago Press, 1941), 41–43; Merriam, *New Aspects*, 326–27; Merriam, "Education," 2.

8. Merriam to John Merriam, October 15, 1928, CEM; Merriam, *New Aspects*, 249, 252; Merriam, *Civic Education*, 26; Frederic C. Howe, *The Confessions of a Reformer* (Chicago: Quadrangle Books, c. 1925; reprint, 1961), 322.

9. Charles E. Merriam, *The New Democracy and the New Despotism* (New York: McGraw-Hill, 1939), 262; Merriam, *New Aspects*, 190; Merriam, *Political Power*, 221; Merriam, *The Role of Politics*, 14, 17–24; Merriam, "Modern Socialism," Unpublished essay, Columbia University, 1897, 12–13, 18–19, CEM.

10. Merriam, *New Aspects*, 35, 47–48.

11. Merriam, "Progress in Political Research," 4; Merriam, *Chicago: A More Intimate View of Politics* (New York: Macmillan, 1929).

12. Official Minutes of the Conference of Psychologists called by the Laura Spelman Rockefeller Foundation, Hanover, N.H., August 26–September 3, 1925, 319, CEM.

13. Merriam, *New Aspects*, 37–38, 57.

14. Ibid., 57; Dorothy Ross, *The Origins of American Social Science* (Cambridge: Cambridge University Press, 1991), 450; Charles E. Merriam, "American Publicity in Italy," *APSR* 13 (November 1919): 546–47, 553–54; Merriam, *New Aspects*, 95, 137, 290–91; Merriam, *Civic Education*, 126–27.

15. Merriam, *New Aspects*, 95, 166; Merriam and Harold Foote Gosnell, *Non-Voting: Causes and Methods of Control* (Chicago: University of Chicago Press, 1924), 17–18; Merriam, *Chicago*, 178; Carroll Woody to Merriam, November 15, 1926; Wallas to Merriam, November 20, 1926, both in CEM; Harold F. Gosnell, "Some Practical Applications of Psychology in Government," *AJS* 28 (May 1923): 735–48; Merriam, *Civic Education*, xxii.

16. Tang Tsou, "Fact and Value in Charles E. Merriam," *Southwestern Social Science Quarterly* 36 (June 1955): 10–11; Merriam and Gosnell, *Non-Voting*, 1–24; Martin Bulmer, *The Chicago School of Sociology: Institutionalization, Diversity, and the Role of Social Research* (Chicago: University of Chicago Press, 1984), 164.

17. Merriam, *New Aspects*, 74, 189, 195–96, 202–4, 208; Merriam, "Public Administration and Political Theory," *Journal of Social Philosophy* 5 (July 1940): 300.

18. Merriam, *New Aspects*, 74, 213; Karl, *Charles Merriam*, 155; Merriam, "Dedication of the Social Science Building at the University of Chicago," Unpublished address, December 17, 1929, CEM; Proceedings of the President's Research Committee for Social Trends, June 3–4, 1932, meeting at 320 Park Avenue, New York, 231, WFO; Merriam to Lynd, January 12, 1929, RHL; Merriam to Lawrence Frank, February 10, 1926, CEM.

19. Charles Merriam, Notebook for "History of Political Economy," Professor E. R. A. Seligman, Columbia University, Fall 1897, inside cover, CEM; Merriam, "Progress in Political Research," 7; Merriam, "Physics and Politics," *APSR* 40 (June 1946): 445–47.

20. Charles E. Merriam, *Systematic Politics* (Chicago: University of Chi-

cago Press, 1945), 328; John C. Merriam, "Science and Belief," in *A Century of Social Thought: A Series of Lectures Delivered at Duke University During the Academic Year 1938–39* (Durham: Duke University Press, 1939), 95–96; John C. Merriam, *Ultimate Values of Science* (Washington, D.C.: Carnegie Institution of Washington Division of Publications, 1935), 4–5.

21. Merriam, *New Aspects*, 97, 102–3, 205, 219.

22. Charles E. Merriam, "William Archibald Dunning," *APSR* 16 (November 1922): 693–94; Merriam, "William Archibald Dunning," in *American Masters of Social Science*, ed. Howard Odum (New York: Henry Holt, 1927), 138, 140.

23. Charles E. Merriam, *History of the Theory of Sovereignty since Rousseau* (New York: Columbia University Press, 1900), 227; Merriam, *New Aspects*, 58–59, 65, 136–37; Merriam to Harold Lasswell, April 26, 1944, CEM.

24. Merriam, *New Aspects*, 83.

25. Leonard D. White, "Co-operation with Local and Civic Agencies," in *Chicago: An Experiment in Social Science Research*, ed. T. V. Smith and Leonard D. White (Chicago: University of Chicago Press, 1929), 35–39; Sophonisba Breckenridge and Leonard D. White, "Urban Growth and Problems of Social Control," in Smith and White, eds., *Chicago*, 194; Bulmer, *The Chicago School*, 129–50; Merriam, *New Aspects*, 68.

26. Merriam to Ruml, November 11, 1925; Merriam to Raymond Fosdick, October 8, 1923, and April 20, 1926, all in CEM; Raymond B. Fosdick, *The Story of the Rockefeller Foundation* (New York: Harper, 1952), 215.

27. Louis Wirth, "Report on the History, Activities, and Policies of the Social Science Research Council," Unpublished document prepared for the Committee on Review of Council Policy, August, 1937, 6, 11; Merriam to Lynd, December 5, 1927; Merriam, "History and Purposes of the Social Science Research Council," Unpublished memorandum, no date; John Fairlie to Merriam, February 5, 1929, all in CEM; and Karl, *Charles Merriam*, 116.

28. Merriam to Lynd, December 5, 1927; John Merriam to Merriam, December 11, 1923; Merriam to John Merriam, December 19, 1923; Ogburn to Merriam, April 30, 1924; Mitchell to Merriam, January 9, 1924; Wirth, "Report," all in CEM; Joseph Dorfman, *The Economic Mind in American Civilization.* Vol. 3: *1865–1918* (New York: Viking Press, 1949), 325.

29. Merriam to John Merriam, October 15, 1928; Merriam to Mitchell, July 17, 1926, both in CEM.

30. Donald Fisher, "Philanthropic Foundations and the Social Sciences: A Response to Martin Bulmer," *Sociology* 18 (November 1984): 584–85; Wirth, "Report," 18.

31. Merriam, *New Aspects*, 81, 325; Merriam, *Civic Education*, 40; italics are Merriam's.

32. Merriam, "Education"; Orlans, "Advocacy," 21.

33. Merriam, "Education," 15.

34. Merriam, "Public Administration," 305.

35. Merriam, Foreword to *Our Cities*, vii, xiii; Merriam, *Chicago*, introduction, 176–77.

36. Charles E. Merriam, "Democracy and Management," *Public Management* 27 (January 1945): 3; Merriam, "Mayors and Managers," Lecture 5 of the Walgreen Lectures delivered at the University of Chicago, spring 1948; Merriam, "Memorandum on Proposed Public Administration Service," Unpublished memorandum, no date; Merriam to Ruml, November 19, 1925; Merriam to Clarence Ridley, October 6, 1933, last four in CEM.

37. Lynd to Merriam, October 25, 1928, CEM; Merriam, "Political Science in the United States," *Contemporary Political Science: A Survey of Methods, Research and Teaching* (Paris: UNESCO, 1950), 243; Fosdick, *Story*, 140–41, 205–8; Barry D. Karl, "Presidential Planning and Social Science Research: Mr. Hoover's Experts," in *Perspectives in American History* 3, ed. Donald Fleming and Bernard Bailyn (1969): 376.

38. Minutes of a meeting of the Commission on Public Service Personnel, July 13, 1934; Minutes of the Board of Directors of the Social Science Research Council, April 8, 1933, both in CEM.

39. Merriam to Crane, August 21, 1933; Memorandum to members of the Committee on Commissions of Inquiry, from Robert Crane, unpublished memorandum, September 29, 1933; Crane to Merriam, September 23, 1933, all in CEM.

40. Commission of Inquiry on Public Service Personnel, *Better Government Personnel: Report of the Commission of Inquiry on Public Service Personnel* (New York: McGraw-Hill, 1935), 2.

41. Charles E. Merriam, "Danger Zones Between Politics and Administration," *Public Management* 28 (October 1946): 290–91; Merriam, *New Democracy*, 129.

42. Eugenie Ladner Birch, "Advancing the Art and Science of Planning: Planners and Their Organizations," *Journal of the American Planning Association* 46 (January 1980): 28–30.

43. Merriam, "Danger Zones," 290–91; Merriam, "Discussion," Summarized Report of the Public Administration Clearing House Conference at Chateau d'Ardenne, September 1937, 7, CEM; Merriam, "Review of *The Road to Serfdom*, by Frederick A. Hayek," *AJS* 50 (November 1944): 233–34; Merriam, *What Is Democracy?*, 25.

44. Crane to Merriam, September 23, 1932; Gulick to Merriam, March 20 and 23, 1934, all in CEM.

45. Commission of Inquiry, *Better Government Personnel*, 3, 5–6, 29–30, 35.

46. Gulick to L. D. Coffman, December 15, 1934, CEM.

47. *Annual Report of the Social Science Research Council, 1934–35* (New York: Social Science Research Council, 1935), 3; *Annual Report of the Social Science Research Council, 1936–37* (New York: Social Science Research Council, 1937), 2; Minutes of the annual meeting of the Board of Directors of the Social Science Research Council, New York, April 15–16, 1939, CEM.

48. Minutes of the annual meeting of the Board of Directors of the Social Science Research Council, New York, September 4–6, 1936, 6–7; Merriam to George Soule, January 27, 1933, and August 26, 1935, all in CEM.

49. Frank A. Warren III, *Liberals and Communism: The "Red Decade" Revisited* (Bloomington: Indiana University Press, 1966); John A. Vieg, "Developments in Governmental Planning," in White, ed., *The Future*, 64.

50. Phillip W. Warken, "A History of the National Resources Planning Board, 1933–1943" (Ph.D. diss., Ohio State University, 1969), 15; Franklin D. Roosevelt, "Actualities of Agricultural Planning" (1931), in *America Faces the Future*, ed. Charles A. Beard (Boston: Houghton Mifflin, 1932), 333; Roosevelt, "Growing up by Plan," *Survey Graphic* 21 (February 1, 1932): 483–85, 506.

51. Karl, *Charles Merriam*, 55; Roosevelt to Governor Frank Lowden, November 20, 1929, CEM; Ickes, *Secret Diary*, May 25, 1936, 610.

52. John D. Millet, *The Process and Organization of Governmental Planning* (New York: Columbia University Press, 1947), 144; Albert Lepawsky, "The Planning Apparatus: A Vignette of the New Deal," *Journal of the American Institute of Planners* 42 (January 1976): 22–23.

53. Merriam, *New Democracy*, 179; Merriam, "Possibilities of Planning," 398.

54. Merriam, *Prologue to Politics*, 96; Memorandum, Merriam to Morris Cooke, first draft, no date (c. 1935–36), CEM; Merriam, *Role of Politics*, 127, 131–40; Merriam, "Possibilities of Planning," 401–3.

55. Warken, "History," 49; Memorandum from National Planning Board to city, county, regional, and state planning organizations, unpublished, November 16, 1933, CEM; Charles E. Merriam, Preface to *State Conservation of Resources*, by Clifford J. Hynning (Washington, D.C.: U.S. Government Printing Office, 1939), iii–iv; Merriam, "The National Resources Planning Board: Symposium on the Executive Office," *Public Administration Review* 1 (August 1940): 120; Merriam, "Observations on Centralization and Decentralization," *State Government* 16 (January 1943): 2–4, 18.

56. Merriam, "National Resources Planning Board: Symposium," 116; Na-

tional Resources Board, *A Report on National Planning and Public Works in Relation to Natural Resources and Including Land Use and Water Resources with Findings and Recommendations, December 1, 1934* (Washington, D.C.: U.S. Government Printing Office, 1934), 76.

57. Merriam, "National Resources Planning Board: Symposium," 116; President's Committee on Administrative Management, *Administrative Management in the Government of the United States* (Washington, D.C.: U.S. Government Printing Office, 1937), 26; Report of the National Resources Committee to the President, November 12, 1935; Committee of the Social Science Research Council, "The Aid Which the Social Sciences Have Rendered and Can Render to National Planning," unpublished memorandum prepared for the National Planning Board, 1934, 1–4, 8–9, 19–20, last two in CEM.

58. Ibid., 4–6; Charles Merriam, "Post-War Changes in the Structure and Functioning of Government," Address before a joint meeting of the American Political Science Association, American Economic Association, American Statistical Association, and American Sociological Association, December 26, 1934, 13; Conference of the National Resources Committee with the President at the White House, February 11, 1936, CEM; Merriam, "Governmental Planning," 505.

59. First Report of the National Planning Board, Federal Agency of Emergency Public Works, September 16, 1933, CEM; National Resources Board, "A Report," 85.

60. Karl, *Charles Merriam*, 245–46; Merriam, "Governmental Planning," 502; Official Minutes of the National Resources Board, July 2, 1934; Executive Action by Franklin D. Roosevelt, June 7, 1934, last two in CEM. The official name of the NPB's successor was the National Resources Board, which was soon transformed into the National Resources Committee. These two agencies were different in name only, and I refer to the two of them collectively as the National Resources Committee.

61. Frederic Delano, Memorandum concerning Revision of Drainage Basin Report, in connection with letter from Mr. McNinch dated January 11, 1938, January 17, 1938; Merriam to Delano, January 11, 1938; Official Minutes of the National Resources Board meeting, November 20, 1934; Official Minutes of the National Planning Board meeting, Newburg, N.Y., June 16, 1934, all in CEM. Lewis L. Lorwin, *Time for Planning: A Social-Economic Theory and Program for the Twentieth Century* (New York: Harper and Brothers, 1945), contains portions of this critique.

62. Dern to Delano, September 28, 1934, CEM; Warken, "History," 98–100.

63. Charles E. Merriam, *Four American Party Leaders* (New York: Macmillan, 1926), vii, xi–xii; Merriam, *Political Power*, 33–35 and passim.

64. Notes on the National Resources Planning Board conference with the President at the White House, September 6, 1939, noon, CEM.

65. Notes on a conference of the President's Committee on Administrative Management with the President at the White House, February 11, 1936; Charles Merriam, Notes concerning conference with the President, February 20, 1936; Merriam to Brownlow, February 20, 1936, all in CEM.

66. Barry Dean Karl, *Executive Reorganization and Reform in the New Deal: The Genesis of Administrative Management, 1900–1939* (Cambridge: Harvard University Press, 1963), 213, 222; Richard Polenberg, *Reorganizing Roosevelt's Government: The Controversy over Executive Reorganization 1936–1939* (Cambridge: Harvard University Press, 1966), 17.

67. Merriam, *New Democracy*, 125, 256; President's Committee, *Administrative Management*, v.

68. Donald Critchlow, *The Brookings Institute 1916–1952: Expertise and the Public Interest in a Democratic Society* (DeKalb: Northern Illinois University Press, 1985), 105–34; Dwight Waldo, *The Administrative State: A Study of the Theory of American Public Administration* (New York: Ronald Press, 1948), 118–20.

69. Polenberg, *Reorganizing Roosevelt's Government*, 35–36, 41, passim; James T. Patterson, *Congressional Conservatism and the New Deal: The Growth of the Conservative Coalition in Congress, 1933–1939* (Lexington: University of Kentucky Press, 1967), 214–29.

4   ROBERT LYND AND KNOWLEDGE FOR WHAT?

1. Robert S. Lynd, "Problem of Being Objective in Studying Our Own Culture," Lecture delivered at Princeton University, December 9, 1938, 3, RHL; Lynd, *Knowledge for What? The Place of Social Science in American Culture* (Princeton: Princeton University Press, 1939), 32–37, 153, n. 33; Lynd, "Family Members as Consumers," *AAAPSS* 160 (March 1932): 91; Lynd to Mitchell, February 6, 1937, April 22 and May 30, 1939, WCM; Lynd, "A Review of *Harold Laski: A Biographical Memoir*, by Kingsley Martin," *Nation* 176 (May 16, 1953): 418; Lynd to Lucy Sprague Mitchell, December 25, 1954, RHL.

2. Lynd, *Knowledge for What?* 119–20, 144.

3. Ibid., 120–22, 142–47, 221–22.

4. Ibid., 3, 146–49, 185–86.

5. Ibid., 26; Lynd to Mitchell, April 22 and May 8, 1939, December 22, 1941, and May 30, 1944, WCM.

6. S. M. Miller, "The Struggle for Relevance: The Lynd Legacy," *Journal of the History of Sociology* 2 (Fall–Winter 1979–80): 64, n. 3; Wesley C. Mitchell, "Book Review of *Knowledge for What? The Place of Social Science in American Culture*, by Robert Lynd," Unpublished review delivered before the Columbia Economics Club, May 2, 1939, WCM; also Lucy Sprague Mitchell, *Two Lives: The Story of Wesley Clair Mitchell and Myself* (New York: Simon and Schuster, 1953), 553–68.

7. Mitchell to Lynd, April 24 and May 9, 1939, and May 31, 1944, WCM.

8. Helen Merrell Lynd, *Possibilities* (Youngstown, Ohio: Ink Well Press, 1983), 30–32; Helen Lynd, "Oral History," interview by Mrs. Walter Gellhorn, Columbia Oral History Project, March 27–May 7, 1973, 34, 39–40; Robert S. Lynd, "Miscellaneous Items about Robert S. Lynd, 3/9/54," Unpublished memorandum, March 9, 1954, RHL.

9. Helen Lynd, "Oral History," 39–40; Staughton Lynd, "Robert S. Lynd: The Elk Basin Experience," *Journal of the History of Sociology* 2 (Fall–Winter 1979–80): 14; "Interview with Robert Lynd," *Daily Princetonian*, March 25, 1938; [Robert S. Lynd], ". . . But Why Preach?" *Harper's* 142 (June 1921): 81–82.

10. [Lynd], ". . . But Why Preach?"; Robert S. Lynd, "Crude Oil Religion," *Harper's* 144 (September 1922): 425; Staughton Lynd, "Robert S. Lynd," 14; Lynd to Lewis Corey, November 24, 1950, RHL; John A. Hobson, *Work and Wealth: A Human Valuation* (New York: Macmillan, 1914), v–ix and passim.

11. Susan J. Turner, *A History of The Freeman: Literary Landmark of the Early Twenties* (New York: Columbia University Press, 1963); Van Wyck Brooks, *Days of the Phoenix: The Nineteen-Twenties I Remember* (New York: E. P. Dutton, 1957), 52–75; Robert S. Lynd, "The Book Industry," *Saturday Review of Literature* 8 (January 16, 1932): 459.

12. Lynd, "Crude Oil Religion," 425, 429, 433–34; Richard Wightman Fox, "Epitaph for Middletown: Robert S. Lynd and the Analysis of Consumer Culture," in *The Culture of Consumption: Critical Essays in American History 1880–1980*, ed. Fox and T. Jackson Lears (New York: Pantheon Books, 1983), 107–8; Helen Merrell Lynd to author, December 12, 1978; [Lynd], ". . . But Why Preach," 85.

13. [Lynd], ". . . But Why Preach?" 83–84; Lynd, *Knowledge for What?*, 238–39; Lynd, "Creed—R.S.L.," 1922, RHL.

14. [Lynd], ". . . But Why Preach?" 84–85.

15. Henry Sloane Coffin, *A Half-Century of Union Theological Seminary*,

1876–1945 (New York: Charles Scribner's Sons, 1954), 32–34 and passim; Robert S. Lynd, "Addenda to Lynd's copy of John D. Rockefeller's article 'A Promise of Better Days,' " March 1963, RHL.

16. Robert S. Lynd, "Has Preaching a Function in Adult Reeducation?" Unpublished seminar paper for homiletics course, Union Theological Seminary, Fall 1922, RHL.

17. Lynd, "Addenda to Lynd's copy"; Lynd, "Crude Oil Religion," 425–34; Helen Lynd, "Oral History," 26; Lynd, "A Critique of Preaching from the Standpoint of Modern Educational Method," Unpublished Union Seminary paper, Spring 1923, 1–2, RHL.

18. Robert S. Lynd, "Addendum to Robert Lynd's copy of 'Crude Oil Religion,' " no date, RHL; Lynd, "Done in Oil," *Survey* 49 (November 1, 1922): 147–48.

19. Lynd, "Addendum to 'Crude Oil' "; John D. Rockefeller, Jr., "A Promise of Better Days," *Survey* 49 (November 1, 1922): 147–48.

20. Robert S. Lynd, "The Implications of Economic Planning for Sociology," *American Sociological Review* 9 (February 1944): 14; Daniel Bell, "Review of *Knowledge for What?*, by Robert S. Lynd," *Modern Quarterly* 11 (Fall 1939); Helen Lynd, "Oral History," 252, 261.

21. Lynd to Mitchell, April 22, 1939; Lynd to Fosdick, June 16, 1926, both in RHL; Helen Lynd, "Oral History," 18, 50, 62.

22. Lynd, "Addenda to 'A Promise' "; Lynd, "Sixteen Million Voices," *Survey* 49 (December 1, 1922): 341.

23. Donald Meyer, *The Protestant Search for Political Realism, 1919–1941* (Berkeley: University of California Press, 1960), 113–14; Charles E. Harvey, "Religion and Industrial Relations: John D. Rockefeller, and the Interchurch World Movement of 1919–20," *Research in Political Economy* 4 (1981): 200; Charles E. Harvey, "John D. Rockefeller and the Social Sciences: An Introduction," *Journal of the History of Sociology* 4 (Fall 1982): 8–11; Galen Merriam Fisher, *The Institute of Social and Religious Research 1921–1934: A Sketch of Its Development and Work* (New York: Institute of Social and Religious Research, 1934), 5–8, 10–35; Lynd, "Problem of Being Objective," 2–3.

24. Fox, "Epitaph for Middletown," 116–18.

25. Lynd, "A Critique of Preaching," 10–11; Fisher, *The Institute*, 12; Robert S. Lynd and Helen Merrell Lynd, *Middletown in Transition: A Study in Cultural Conflicts* (New York: Harcourt, Brace, and World, 1937), ix–xi; Lynd, "Sociology as Social Research," Unpublished outline submitted as a basis for discussion at a meeting of the seminar Sociology 320, May 15, 1932, 5, RHL; Lynd, "Problem of Being Objective," 216.

26. Shelby M. Harrison, "Development and Spread of Social Surveys," in *A Bibliography of Social Surveys*, ed. Allen Eaton and Shelby Harrison (New York: Russell Sage Foundation, 1930), xi–xlviii; Carl C. Taylor, *The Social Survey, Its History and Methods*, University of Missouri Bulletin 20, no. 28 (1923); Michael Gordon, "The Social Survey Movement and Sociology in the United States," *Social Problems* 21 (Fall 1973): 284–98; Fox, "Epitaph for Middletown," 117–18; Fisher, *The Institute*, 15–21; Lynd to Fisher, April 7, 1924, RHL; Lynd and Helen Merrell Lynd, *Middletown: A Study in Modern American Culture* (New York: Harcourt, Brace, and World, 1929), 3, 6.

27. John Madge, *Origins of Scientific Sociology* (Glencoe, Ill.: Free Press, 1962), 125–61; Maurice R. Stein, *The Eclipse of Community: An Interpretation of American Studies* (Princeton: Princeton University Press, 1960), 55–56; Lynd and Lynd, *Middletown*, 505–10.

28. Lynd to Mitchell, May 30, 1944, WCM; Malcolm Cowley, Foreword to *Books That Changed Our Mind*, ed. Cowley and Bernard Smith (New York: Doubleday, Doran, 1939), 18; Lynd and Lynd, *Middletown*, 42, 57, 80–88, 225, 443; Lynd and Lynd, *Middletown in Transition*, 62, 246, 268, 280, 421–22; Lynd, *Knowledge for What?*, 5, 34, 58, 73, 76, 171; Lynd, "Miscellaneous items"; Helen Lynd, "Oral History," 32–33; Charles H. Page, *Fifty Years in the Sociological Enterprise* (Amherst: University of Massachusetts Press, 1982), 42–46.

29. Clark Wissler, Foreword to Lynd and Lynd, *Middletown*, v–vii; Wissler to Lynd, June 7, 1926; Sapir to Lynd, March 1, 1929; Herskovitz to Harcourt, Brace, and World, no date, last three in RHL; Lynd and Lynd, *Middletown*, 3–4.

30. Lynd and Lynd, *Middletown*, 4–5, 21, n. 1, 249, n. 39, 439, n. 4; A. R. Radcliffe-Brown, *The Andaman Islanders* (Cambridge: Cambridge University Press, 1922), 229–45, 324–25; Cowley, Foreword, 18; Anne Marie de Waal Malefijt, *Images of Man: A History of Anthropological Thought* (New York: Alfred A. Knopf, 1974), 192–94; George W. Stocking, Jr., "Radcliffe-Brown and British Social Anthropology," in *Functionalism Historicized: Essays on British Social Anthropology*, vol. 2 of *History of Anthropology*, ed. Stocking (Madison: University of Wisconsin Press, 1984), 153.

31. Lynd and Lynd, *Middletown*, 21, 84, 186, 296, 311, 402–3; Edward Shils, "The Calling of Sociology," in his *The Calling of Sociology and Other Essays in the Pursuit of Learning* (Chicago: University of Chicago Press, 1980), 5–6.

32. Lynd and Lynd, *Middletown*, 5–6, 81–82, 498.

33. H. L. Mencken, "A City in Moronia: Review of *Middletown: A Study in Modern American Culture*, by Robert and Helen Lynd," *American Mer-*

cury 16 (March 1929): 379–81; Mencken, "A Treatise on the Americans: Review of *Middletown: A Study in Modern American Culture,* by Robert and Helen Lynd," *Baltimore Evening Sun,* January 14, 1929; Helen Lynd, *Possibilities,* 34–37; Helen Lynd, "Oral History," 56–57; Lynd and Lynd, *Middletown in Transition,* xviii, 144–45.

34. F. Jack Hurley, *Portrait of a Decade: Roy Stryker and the Development of Documentary Photography in the Thirties* (Baton Rouge: Louisiana State University Press, 1972), 96–98; Roy Emerson Stryker and Nancy Wood, *In This Proud Land: America 1935–1943 as Seen in the FSA Photographs* (Boston: New York Graphic Society, 1973), 8, 187; Robert S. Lynd, "Manhattan Boom-Town," *Survey* 68 (October 1, 1932): 465.

35. Thorstein Veblen, *Absentee Ownership and Business Enterprise in Recent Times* (New York: B. W. Huebsch, 1923), 142–52; Richard Lingeman, *Small Town America: A Narrative History 1620 to the Present* (Boston: Houghton Mifflin, 1980), 274–391; Stuart M. Blumin, *The Urban Threshold: Growth and Change in a Nineteenth-Century American Community* (Chicago: University of Chicago Press, 1976).

36. Lingeman, *Small Town America,* 260–61, 392–94.

37. Lynd, "Problem of Being Objective," 9–13.

38. Lynd and Lynd, *Middletown,* 214–15, 222.

39. Ibid., 59, 469.

40. Ibid., 431, 483.

41. Helen Lynd, "Oral History," 93; Fosdick to Fisher, November 20, 1925, quoted in Harvey, "John D. Rockefeller," 15; Minutes of a staff conference of the Institute of Social and Religious Research concerning the Small City Study, January 11, 1926; Conference on Lynd's manuscript on the study of a small industrial city, Institute of Social and Religious Research meeting at Town Hall Club, November 16, 1926; Went to Lynd, May 26, 1927; Notes on the Lynd manuscript by C. Luther Fry, May 6, 1927; General comments by Went on Section I of the Small City Study, May 5, 1927, last five in RHL.

42. Lynd to Fosdick, June 16, 1926, RHL; Lynd, "Problem of Being Objective," 4; Helen Lynd, "Oral History," 99–102; Lynd to William Ogburn, "Saturday evening" (c. January 1930); Harrison to Ogburn, January 14, 1930, last two in WFO.

43. Robert S. Lynd, "The Future of Our Educational Research," Unpublished memorandum to Max Farand, July 26, 1926; Lynd, Unpublished memorandum on social studies, May 6, 1926; Lynd, "A Suggested Program for Educational Research," Unpublished memorandum to Barry C. Smith, May 1927, all in RHL.

44. Frank to Merriam, no date, CEM; Mitchell to Lynd, January 2 and

September 2, 1929, RHL; Helen Lynd, "Oral History," 67; E. B. Wilson to Merriam, October 30, 1930; Merriam to Woodworth, May 12, 1931, last two in CEM.

45. Lynd to Mitchell, January 9 and 12, 1929; Lynd, Unpublished memorandum to J. Steele Gow, executive director of the Maurice and Laura Falk Foundation, December 4, 1930, both in RHL; *Fourth Annual Report of the Social Science Research Council, 1927–28* (New York: Social Science Research Council, 1928), 13; Mortimer J. Adler, *Philosopher at Large: An Intellectual Autobiography* (New York: Macmillan, 1977), 133–34; Adler, "The Social Scientist's Misconception of Science," Unpublished lecture delivered before the Social Science Research Council Summer Conference at Hanover, N.H., August 1930, copy in author's possession; Lynd to Merriam, October 25, 1928, and April 16, 1929, CEM; Frederick Deibler to M. B. Hammond, October 14, 1930; Deibler to Mitchell, December 19, 1930, both in AEA.

46. Robert Lynd, "Confidential Notes for the Committee on Problems and Policy of the Social Science Research Council," Unpublished memorandum, July 15, 1929, RHL.

47. Lynd and Lynd, *Middletown*, 158; Lynd, Confidential memorandum for the Committee on Problems and Policy of the SSRC on the work of the committee and its advisory committees, August 15, 1928; Lynd, Unpublished memo to Gow, December 4, 1930, last two in RHL; Proceedings of the President's Research Committee on Recent Social Trends, Social Science Building, University of Chicago, May 15–16, 1932, 151–52, CEM.

48. Ogburn, quoted in Lynd, "Problem of Being Objective," 16; Confidential copy of notes made at a discussion of future policy of the Social Science Research Council, Hanover, N.H., August 1929, 50–52, CEM; William F. Ogburn, "The Folkways of Scientific Sociology," *American Sociological Society Publications* 24 (1930): 1–11; Lynd, "Sociology as Practical Science," Unpublished talk before Professor Robert MacIver's Sociology 320 seminar, May 15, 1938, 7–8; Merriam to Lynd, January 12, 1929, last two in RHL.

49. Robert C. Bannister, *Sociology and Scientism: The American Quest for Objectivity 1880–1940* (Chapel Hill: University of North Carolina Press, 1987), 162–68; Dorothy Ross, "American Social Science and the Idea of Progress," in *The Authority of Experts: Studies in History and Theory,* ed. Thomas L. Haskell (Bloomington: Indiana University Press, 1984), 169; Ogburn, "Folkways," 8–9; Lynd to Ogburn, July 11, 1930; Ogburn to Lynd, July 15, 1930, last two in WFO.

50. Ogburn to Lynd, July 15, 1930; Lynd to Ogburn, July 11 and August 16, 1930, all in WFO; Lynd, with Alice C. Hanson, "The People as Consumers," in *Recent Social Trends in the United States: Report of the President's Re-*

search Committee on Recent Social Trends (New York: McGraw-Hill, 1933), 857, 866–68, 885, 911.

51. Ogburn to Lynd, January 15, 1932, WFO; Proceedings of the Board of Directors of the President's Research Committee on Social Trends, February 13, 1932, CEM; Craig Lloyd, *Aggressive Introvert: A Study of Herbert Hoover and Public Relations Management 1912–1932* (Columbus: Ohio State University Press, 1972), passim; E. E. Hunt to Ogburn, April 22, 1932; Ogburn to Lynd, May 24, 1932, last two in WFO.

52. Wilma Ruth Slaight, "Alice Hamilton: First Lady of Industrial Medicine" (Ph.D. diss., Case Western Reserve University, 1974), 158–61; Proceedings of the meeting of the President's Research Committee on Social Trends, Social Science Building, University of Chicago, May 15–16, 1932, 141–57, CEM; Adolf A. Berle, "The Trend of the Turn: Review of *Recent Social Trends*," *Saturday Review of Literature* 9 (April 15, 1933): 535.

53. Robert S. Lynd, "Democracy's Third Estate: The Consumer," *Political Science Quarterly* 51 (December 1936): 486, 514; Lynd and Lynd, *Middletown in Transition*, 46–47, 247, n. 6; Lynd, "Power in American Society as Resource and Problem," in *Problems of Power in American Democracy*, ed. Arthur Kornhauser (Detroit: Wayne State University Press, 1957), 31–32.

54. Lynd, "Democracy's Third Estate," 481–95; Lynd, "Family Members," 88, 91–92; Lynd, Introduction to *The Consumer*, ed. J. C. Brainerd, *AAAPSS* 173 (1934): xi–xii.

55. Helen Sorenson, *The Consumer Movement and What It Means* (New York: Harper and Brothers, 1941), 9–10; Stuart Chase and F. J. Schlink, *Your Money's Worth: A Study in the Waste of the Consumer's Dollar* (New York: Macmillan, c. 1927; reprint, 1934); Arthur Kallet and F. J. Schlink, *100,000,000 Guinea Pigs: Dangers in Everyday Food, Drugs, and Cosmetics* (New York: Grosset and Dunlap, 1933), 195–250; J. B. Matthews, *Guinea Pigs No More* (New York: Covici Freide, 1936).

56. Gardiner C. Means, "The Consumer and the New Deal," *AAAPSS* 173 (1934): 7–13; P. G. Agnew, "The Movement for Standards for Consumer Goods," *AAAPSS* 173 (1934): 64; Herbert Tily, "Codes and Consumers," *AAAPSS* 173 (1934): 112; Sorenson, *Consumer Movement*, 154–59, 165; Robert S. Lynd, "The Consumer Becomes a Problem," *AAAPSS* 173 (1934): 3; Lynd, Foreword to *Consumer Representation in the New Deal*, by Persia Campbell (New York: Columbia University Press, 1940), 9.

57. Sorenson, *The Consumer Movement*, 46–50; Norman Isaac Silber, *Test and Protest: The Influence of Consumers Union* (New York: Holmes and Meier, 1983), 18–27, 139, n. 12.

58. Lynd, "Democracy's Third Estate," 498; Ellis W. Hawley, *The New*

Deal and the Problem of Monopoly: A Study in Economic Ambivalence (Princeton: Princeton University Press, 1966), 72–79, 102–3, 133–34, passim; Bernard Bellush, *The Failure of the NRA* (New York: W. W. Norton, 1975); Arthur M. Schlesinger, Jr., *The Coming of the New Deal* (Boston: Houghton Mifflin, 1958), 86–176; Persia Campbell, *Consumer Representation*, 31.

59. Frederick J. Schlink, "Safeguarding the Consumer's Interest—An Essential Element in National Recovery," *AAAPSS* 173 (1934): 112–16; Schlink, "What Government Does and Might Do for the Consumer," *AAAPSS* 173 (1934): 140–42; Matthews, *Guinea Pigs*, 248–58; Robert S. Lynd, "A New Deal for the Consumer," *NR* 77 (January 3, 1934): 220–22.

60. Chase and Schlink, *Your Money's Worth*, 4–5, 183–217; Agnew, "Movement," 62–63; D. W. McConnell, "The Bureau of Standards and the Ultimate Consumer," *AAAPSS* 173 (1934): 148–50; Consumer Advisory Board Committee on Consumer Standards, "A Proposal to Develop Standards for Consumer Goods by Establishing a Consumer Standards Board and Funds for Basic Testing," RHL; Lynd, "Democracy's Third Estate," 491, 503, 506; Lynd, "New Deal," 220–21.

61. Emily Newell Blair, "The Valedictory of the Advisory Board," *Consumer* 1 (October 15, 1935): 11–14; Lynd, Unpublished memo to Gow; Lynd, "Consumer Gains under the New Deal," Unpublished memorandum to the Executive Committee of the National Recovery Administration, June 3, 1935, ENB; Sorenson, *The Consumer Movement*, 11–15.

62. Bannister, *Sociology and Scientism*, 71, passim; Seymour Martin Lipset, "The Department of Sociology," in *A History of the Faculty of Political Science, Columbia University*, by Gordon Hoxie, Sally Falk Moore, et al. (New York: Columbia University Press, 1955), 292–97, 302; Helen Lynd, "Oral History," 106; Robert S. Lynd, "Intelligence Must Fight," *Survey Graphic* 28 (August 1939): 498; Lynd, "Sociology as Social Research"; Lynd, "Sociology as Practical Science"; Robert M. MacIver, "Enduring Systems of Thought: A Review of *Knowledge for What?* by Robert Lynd," *Survey Graphic* 28 (August 1939): 496–97; Robert M. MacIver, *As a Tale That Is Told: The Autobiography of Robert M. MacIver* (Chicago: University of Chicago Press, 1968), 137–38.

63. Helen Lynd, "Oral History," 107–8; Nico Stehr, "A Conversation with Paul Lazersfeld," *American Sociologist* 17 (August 1982): 151–52; Miller, "The Struggle," 60–63; Page, *Fifty Years*, 39.

64. Helen Lynd, "Oral History," 114; Lynd and Lynd, *Middletown in Transition*, 4.

65. Dorothy Ross, *The Origins of American Social Science* (Cambridge: Cambridge University Press, 1991), 359.

66. Lynd and Lynd, *Middletown in Transition*, 5–7, 67–68, 408, 427–28, 489–90.

67. Ibid., xiv, 427–28, 442–43, 465, 481–84, 509–10.

68. Ibid., 124–25, 136, 399, n. 28, 509–10.

69. Lynd, *Knowledge for What?* ix, 9, 115–16, 177, 181, 207, 250; italics are Lynd's.

70. Ibid., 163–64, 178; Lynd, "Miscellaneous Items."

71. Lynd, *Knowledge for What?* 17–19, 35–37, 123, 128; italics are Lynd's.

72. Ibid., 35, 121, n. 7, 123, 171–74, 183; Lynd, "Sociology as Practical Science."

73. Lynd, *Knowledge for What?* 71, 122, n. 7; Edward A. Purcell, Jr., *The Crisis of Democratic Theory: Scientific Naturalism and the Problem of Value* (Lexington: University of Kentucky Press, 1973).

74. Lynd, *Knowledge for What?* 65–74, 81–87, 97–103, 109–13, 196, 220, 232.

75. Ibid., 24–25, 160; Lynd, "Confidential Notes," 20–21.

76. Lynd, "Intelligence Must Fight," 499; Lynd, *Knowledge for What?* 21–23, 32, 37–41; Helen Lynd, "Oral History," 26–27; Robert S. Lynd, "What Are Social Studies?" *School and Society* 25 (February 19, 1927): 218; Lynd, Unpublished outline for a study of the impact of the depression on family organization and function, presented before the Columbia Council on Research Projects, May 1, 1933, RHL; Lynd, *Knowledge for What?* 51–52.

77. Franz Boas, "History and Science in Anthropology: A Reply" (1936), in *Race, Language and Culture* (New York: Free Press, 1940), 305–11; John J. Honigmann, *The Development of Anthropological Ideas* (Homewood, Ill.: Dorsey Press, 1976), 208–9; Lynd, Unpublished outline; Louis Wirth, "Report on the History, Activities, and Policies of the Social Science Research Council," prepared for the Committee on Review of Council Policy, August 1937, CEM; Lynd, *Knowledge for What?* 52; italics are Lynd's.

78. Lynd, *Knowledge for What?* 56, 158; Lynd, "Sociology as Social Research"; Lynd and Lynd, *Middletown in Transition*, 402–3, 469, n. 59; Alfred L. Kroeber, ed., *Ruth Fulton Benedict: A Memorial* (New York: Viking Fund, 1949), 22–24, 31–33; Margaret M. Caffrey, *Ruth Benedict: Stranger in This Land* (Austin: University of Texas Press, 1989), 275–76; Lyman Bryson, Introduction to *Society as the Patient: Essays in Culture and Personality*, by Lawrence K. Frank (New Brunswick, N.J.: Rutgers University Press, 1948), v–vi; Lawrence K. Frank, "Society as the Patient," in Frank, ibid., 8–9; Lawrence K. Frank, "The Fundamental Needs of the Child," *Mental Hygiene* 22 (July 1938): 353–79; Regina Darnell, "Personality and Culture: The Fate of the Sapirian Alternative," in *Malinowski, Rivers, Benedict and Others: Essays in Culture and Personality*, vol. 4 of *History of Anthropology*, ed.

George W. Stocking, Jr. (Madison: University of Wisconsin Press, 1986), 166; Edward Sapir, "The Emergence of the Concept of Personality in a Study of Cultures" (1934), in *Culture, Language, and Personality: Selected Essays,* ed. David G. Mandelbaum (Berkeley: University of California Press, 1956), 200–201; Richard Handler, "Vigorous Male and Aspiring Female: Poet, Personality and Culture in Edward Sapir and Ruth Benedict," in *Malinowski, Rivers,* 147; Benedict to Mead, November 30, 1932 in Margaret Mead, *An Anthropologist at Work: The Writings of Ruth Benedict* (New York: Atherton Press, 1966), 201.

79. Lynd, *Knowledge for What?* 42–44, 112, 192–97, 200–201, 234–35. See Franz Neumann, "Review of *Knowledge for What? The Place of Social Science in American Culture,* by Robert Lynd," *Studies in Philosophy and Social Science* 8 (November 3, 1939): 469–74; and Oskar Morgenstern, "Review of *Knowledge for What?* by Robert Lynd," *Princeton Alumni Weekly* 29 (May 5, 1939): 647–48, for insightful critiques by two German émigrés on the biases and dangers of Lynd's values.

80. Lynd, *Knowledge for What?* 13–21, 50, 166–70.

81. Ibid., 51, 70, 139–41, 209–19.

82. Bingham to Merriam, June 22 and October 9, 1939; Frank to Merriam, September 27, 1940, all in CEM; Robert S. Lynd, "Proposed Study of Potentialities of Democratic Processes in a Period of Mobilization" (Princeton: American Committee for International Studies, 1940); Staughton Lynd, "Robert S. Lynd," 19; Robert S. Lynd, "The Place of the University in 1940," *Columbia University Quarterly* 31 (December 1939): 241–51.

83. Frank to Merriam, September 27, 1940; Merriam to Frank, October 2, 1940; Bingham to Merriam, October 9, 1939, all in CEM.

5   CHARLES BEARD AND ACTIVIST SOCIAL SCIENCE

1. John Higham, *Writing American History: Essays on Modern Scholarship* (Bloomington: Indiana University Press, 1970), 131.

2. Malcolm Cowley, Foreword to *Books That Changed Our Mind,* ed. Malcolm Cowley and Bernard Smith (New York: Doubleday, Doran, 1939), 7–9, 19–20; Charles A. Beard, "The Role of Administration in Government," in *The Work Unit in Federal Administration: Papers Read at a Meeting of the Washington Chapter of the Society for the Advancement of Management* (Chicago: Public Administration Service, 1937), 1; George H. E. Smith to Beard, February 6, 1935, GHS; Mary Beard to Rosika Schwimmer, July 25, 1936, quoted in John Braeman, "Charles A. Beard: The Formative Years in

Indiana," *Indiana Magazine of History* 78 (July 1982): 127; Charles A. Beard, *The Nature of the Social Sciences in Relation to Objectives of Instruction* (New York: Charles Scribner's Sons, 1934), 61.

3. Charles A. Beard, "That Promise of American Life," *NR* 81 (February 6, 1935): 352.

4. Alvin Johnson, *Pioneer's Progress* (Lincoln: University of Nebraska Press, 1952), 279; Miriam Beard Vagts, in *Mary Ritter Beard: A Sourcebook,* ed. Ann J. Lane (New York: Schocken Books, 1977), 4–5; Charles A. Beard, "A Memorandum from an Old Worker in the Vineyard," *Social Education* 2 (September 1938): 384–85; Max Lerner, *Ideas Are Weapons: The History and Use of Ideas* (New York: Viking Press, 1939), 152; Matthew Josephson, *Infidel in the Temple* (New York: Alfred A. Knopf, 1967), 38.

5. Arthur W. Macmahon, "Charles Beard: The Teacher," in *Charles A. Beard: An Appraisal,* ed. Howard K. Beale (Lexington: University of Kentucky Press, 1954), 224; Beard to Moley, August 29, 1916, quoted in Ellen Nore, *Charles A. Beard: An Intellectual Biography* (Carbondale: Southern Illinois University Press, 1983), 56.

6. Erik Goldman, *Rendezvous with Destiny* (New York: Alfred A. Knopf, 1952), 149; George S. Counts, "Charles Beard, the Public Man," in Beale, ed., *Charles A. Beard,* 233; Miriam Beard Vagts, quoted in Peter A. Soderbergh, "Charles A. Beard, the Quaker Spirit, and North Carolina," *North Carolina Historical Review* 46 (January 1969): 24–25.

7. Eric F. Goldman, "Charles A. Beard, an Impression," in Beale, ed., *Charles A. Beard,* 2.

8. Hubert Herring, "Charles A. Beard, Freelance among the Historians," *Harper's* 178 (May 1939): 641.

9. Charles A. Beard, *The Open Door at Home: A Trial Philosophy of National Interest* (New York: Macmillan, 1934), 69; Beard, "The Frontier in American History," *NR* 97 (February 1, 1939): 361; Beard, "Turner's 'The Frontier in American History,'" in Cowley and Smith, eds., *Books That Changed Our Mind,* 69–70; Detleu Vagts, "A Grandson Remembers His Grandfather," in *Charles A. Beard: An Observance of the Centennial of His Birth,* ed. Marvin G. Swanson (Greencastle, Ind.: DePauw University, 1976), 20; Charles A. Beard, Letter to the editor, *Knightstown Banner,* July 23, 1948, CMB; Mary Beard to Arthur Macmahon, November 17, 1948, AWM.

10. Clifton J. Phillips, "The Indiana Education of Charles A. Beard," *Indiana Magazine of History* 55 (March 1959): 5, 11.

11. Alfred Vagts, Personal note, no date, CMB.

12. Ross E. Paulson, *Radicalism and Reform: The Vrooman Family and American Social Thought 1837–1937* (Lexington: University of Kentucky

Press, 1968), 149–50, 154–55; John Ruskin, *Unto This Last*, ed. John L. Bradley (New York: Appleton-Century-Crofts, c. 1862; reprint, 1967), 87–88; John Braeman, "Charles A. Beard: The English Experience," *Journal of American Studies* 15 (1981): 177. Beard took credit in a 1940 letter to the principal of Ruskin Hall for suggesting and even insisting on the name Ruskin College. Beard to A. Barrett Brown, July 7, 1940, quoted in Burleigh T. Wilkins, "Charles A. Beard on the Founding of Ruskin Hall," *Indiana Magazine of History* 52 (September 1956): 280. Among Beard's later citations of Ruskin and his importance are Beard, "Political Science," in *Research in the Social Sciences: Its Fundamental Methods and Objectives*, ed. Wilson Gee (New York: Macmillan, 1929), 288; Beard, "Ruskin and the Babble of Tongues," *NR* 87 (August 5, 1936): 370–72.

13. Wilkins, "Charles Beard," 283; Harlan B. Phillips, "Charles Beard: The English Lectures, 1899–1901," *Journal of the History of Ideas* 14 (June 1953): 451, 453; Charles A. Beard, *The Industrial Revolution* (London: S. Sommenschein, 1901), 90.

14. Herring, "Charles Beard," 643; Lane, *Mary Ritter Beard*, 18–24; Braeman, "English Experience," 187–88.

15. Burleigh Taylor Wilkins, "Frederick York Powell and Charles A. Beard: A Study in Anglo-American Historiography and Social Thought," *American Quarterly* 11 (Spring 1959): 36.

16. Nore, *Charles Beard*, 19; Wilkins, "Frederick York Powell," 26–27.

17. Charles A. Beard, "Politics," in *Columbia University Lectures on Science, Philosophy, and Art 1907–08* (New York: Columbia University Press, 1908), 8, 18; Beard, *American Government and Politics* (New York: Macmillan, 1910), 1, 280–88; Beard, "A Socialist History of France," *Political Science Quarterly* 21 (March 1906): 112.

18. Quoted in Bert James Lowenberg, *American History in American Thought: From Christopher Columbus to Henry Adams* (New York: Simon and Schuster, 1972), 382–83.

19. John Higham, with Leonard Krieger and Felix Gilbert, *History* (Englewood Cliffs, N.J.: Prentice-Hall, 1965), 13, 45–46; W. Stull Holt, "The Idea of Scientific History in America," in *Historical Scholarship in America and Other Essays* (Seattle: University of Washington Press, 1967), 17; J. Franklin Jameson, *The History of Historical Writing in America* (Boston: Houghton Mifflin, 1891), 132–33.

20. Beard, "Politics," 10; Beard, "The Study and Teaching of Politics," *Columbia University Quarterly* 12 (June 1910): 269; Beard, "Recent Activities of City Clubs," *National Municipal Review* 1 (August 1912): 435.

21. Peter Novick, *That Noble Dream: The "Objectivity Question" and*

the American Historical Profession (New York: Cambridge University Press, 1988), 68–70; Richard Hofstadter, *The Progressive Historians* (New York: Alfred A. Knopf, 1968), 28–30; Charles A. Beard, "James Ford Rhodes: Review of *History of the United States, 1877–1896,* by James Ford Rhodes," *NR* 21 (December 17, 1919): 82–83; Beard, "Frontier," 350.

22. James Harvey Robinson and Charles A. Beard, *The Development of Modern Europe,* vol. 1 (New York: Ginn, 1907), iii; Charles A. Beard, "A Plea for Greater Stress upon the Modern Period," *Minutes of the Sixth Annual Convention,* Middle States Council for the Social Studies (1908), 12.

23. Nore, *Charles Beard,* 36; Burleigh Taylor Wilkins, *Carl Becker: The Development of an American Historian* (Cambridge: MIT Press, 1961), 56; James Harvey Robinson, "History," in *Columbia University Lectures on Science, Philosophy, and Art, 1907–08* (New York: Columbia University Press, 1908), 26; James Harvey Robinson, *The New History: Essays Illustrating the Modern Historic Outlook* (New York: Macmillan, 1912), 24, 61, 252.

24. Charles A. Beard and Mary R. Beard, *The Rise of American Civilization: The Industrial Era* (New York: Macmillan, 1927), 789; Beard, *Open Door,* 30–33, 144–46; Beard, Letter to the editor: "Beard on Liberalism," *NR* 81 (January 30, 1935): 334; Beard, "Neglected Aspects of Political Science," *APSR* 42 (April 1948): 213; Charles A. Beard and Mary R. Beard, *The American Spirit: A Study of the Idea of Civilization in the United States* (New York: Macmillan, 1942), 665–70.

25. Charles A. Beard, *Contemporary American History, 1877–1913* (New York: Macmillan, 1914), v–vi; Beard to Mayers, January 21, 1913, CMB.

26. Charles A. Beard, *The Supreme Court and the Constitution* (New York: Macmillan, 1912), 1, 13–14, 126.

27. Ibid., 76–77; Charles A. Beard, *An Economic Interpretation of the Constitution of the United States* (New York: Free Press, c. 1913; reprint, 1935), 14, 19–51, 63, 73, 290.

28. Beard, *Economic Interpretation,* vi, 5–6, 15; Charles A. Beard, *The Economic Basis of Politics* (New York: Alfred A. Knopf, 1922).

29. Beard, *Economic Interpretation,* 10–12; Lerner, *Ideas Are Weapons,* 35.

30. Goldman, *Rendezvous with Destiny,* 153–54; Herring, "Charles Beard," 644.

31. Beard to Mayers, July 1 and August 22, 1913, CMB; Beard to Max Farrand, May 5, 1913, quoted in Novick, *That Noble Dream,* 97.

32. Charles A. Beard, "The University and Democracy," *Dial* 64 (April 11, 1918): 335.

33. Carol S. Gruber, *From Mars to Minerva: World War I and the Uses of*

Higher Learning in America (Baton Rouge: Louisiana State University Press, 1975), 73–74; Thomas C. Kennedy, *Charles A. Beard and American Foreign Policy* (Gainesville: University of Florida Press, 1975), 18–19, 29; [Charles A. Beard], "Atrocities," in *War Cyclopedia: A Handbook for Ready Reference to the Great War*, ed. Frederick L. Paxson et al. (Washington, D.C.: Committee on Public Information, 1918), 22; *New York Times*, January 26, 1919, 8; "Professor Beard Resigns," *New York American*, October 9, 1917, 1.

34. Charles A. Beard, "A Statement of Facts in the Matter of the Committee of Education of the Board of Trustees of Columbia University and Professor Charles A. Beard," Undated memorandum, CMB.

35. Charles A. Beard, "A Statement by Charles A. Beard," *NR* 13 (December 29, 1917): 249–51; Herring, "Charles Beard," 644; Mary Beard to Macmahon, September 21, 1947, AWM.

36. Herring, "Charles Beard," 644; Wilkins, *Carl Becker*, 75; Charles A. Beard, "The Quest for Academic Power," *Journal of Higher Education* 3 (December 1932): 466–67; Beard, "Charles A. Beard's Letter of Resignation from Columbia University (October 8, 1917)," *School and Society* 6 (October 13, 1917): 466–67; Nicholas Murray Butler, *Scholarship and Service* (New York: Columbia University Press, 1921), 21; Carol Signer Gruber, "Academic Freedom at Columbia University, 1917–1918: The Case of James McKeen Cattell," *American Association of University Professors Bulletin* 58 (March 1972): 300–301; Mary Ritter Beard, *The Making of Charles A. Beard* (New York: Exposition, 1955), 22; Beard to Mussey, no date, quoted in Nore, *Charles Beard*, 83.

37. Beard, "Political Science," 288–90; Beard, Letter to the editor, *Freeman* 3 (July 20, 1921): 450–51.

38. Nore, *Charles Beard*, 83, 249, n. 38.

39. Charles A. Beard, "Municipal Research Abroad and at Home," *Journal of Social Forces* 3 (March 1925): 497; Beard, *American Government and Politics*, 4th ed., rev. (New York: Macmillan, 1924), 38–41; Beard, "Role," 3.

40. Charles A. Beard, "It Is Not True," in *In Review* (Washington, D.C.: Governmental Research Association, 1948), 2; Beard, "Methods of Training for Public Service," *School and Society* 2 (December 25, 1915): 910–11; Beard, "Rebuilding in Japan," *Review of Reviews* 68 (October 1923): 382; Beard, "Municipal Research," 495.

41. Martin J. Schiesel, *The Politics of Efficiency: Municipal Administration and Reform in America, 1880–1920* (Berkeley: University of California Press, 1977), 99–101, 111–15, 118, 121, 126; Jane S. Dahlberg, *The New York Bureau of Municipal Research: Pioneer in Government Administration* (New York: New York University Press, 1966), 60–61; William Allen, "Efficiency in City Government," *City Club Bulletin* 2 (April 22, 1908): 127.

42. Dahlberg, *New York*, 6; Luther Gulick, "Beard and Municipal Reform," in Beale, ed., *Charles A. Beard*, 50.

43. Gulick, "Beard," 51–53.

44. Dahlberg, *New York*, 133, 241. Interestingly, Cleveland had left the bureau for the University of Pennsylvania shortly before, when the Rockefeller Foundation refused to fund his proposal for a fiscal study of the executive branch and instead turned it over to Merriam's future enemy, the safer and more malleable W. F. Willoughby. Donald T. Critchlow, *The Brookings Institution, 1916–1952: Expertise and the Public Interest in a Democratic Society* (DeKalb: Northern Illinois University Press, 1985), 29–34.

45. Charles A. Beard, *The Administration and Politics of Tokyo*, (New York: Macmillan, 1923), 9, 26–36, 112, 174, passim.

46. Ibid., 1, 11, 43–60.

47. Ibid., v–vii.

48. Charles A. Beard, "Goto and the Rebuilding of Japan," *Our World* 5 (April 1924): 11, 14, 18; Nore, *Charles Beard*, 108.

49. Marshall E. Dimock, "The Criteria and Objectives of Public Administration," in *Frontiers of Public Administration*, ed. John Gaus, Leonard White, and Dimock (Chicago: University of Chicago Press, 1936), 116–33; Dimock, "The Meaning and Scope of Public Administration," in ibid., 1–12; E. Pendleton Herring, *Public Administration and the Public Interest* (New York: McGraw-Hill, 1936); Dwight Waldo, *The Administrative State: A State of the Political Theory of American Public Administration* (New York: Ronald Press, 1948); Charles A. Beard, "Some Aspects of Regional Planning," *APSR* 20 (May 1926): 281–83; Beard, "Conflicts in City Planning," *Yale Review* 17 (October 1927): 66.

50. Beard, *Administration of Tokyo*, 163; Beard, "Government Research: Past, Present, and Future," Address to annual meeting of the Governmental Research Conference, Rochester, N.Y., November 23, 1926, 8; Beard, "Life Is Not a Table of Logarithms," *Public Management* 11 (July 1929): 511; Beard, "The Place of Administration in Government," *Plan Age* 2 (December 1936): 6–10.

51. Nore, *Charles Beard*, 128–29.

52. Charles A. Beard, "Review of *Primary Elections*, by Charles E. Merriam," *Political Science Quarterly* 24 (June 1909): 317; Beard, "Review of *American Political Ideas*, by Charles E. Merriam," *NR* 25 (January 19, 1921): 235; Barry D. Karl, *Charles E. Merriam and the Study of Politics* (Chicago: University of Chicago Press, 1974), 182–83; Beard to Merriam, November 3 and 15, 1924, CEM.

53. Charles A. Beard, "Time, Technology, and the Creative Spirit in Political Science," *APSR* 21 (February 1927): 5–9.

54. Beard, "Political Science," 269–91.

55. Charles A. Beard, "Method in the Study of Political Science as an Aspect of Social Science," *Essays on Research in the Social Sciences* (Washington, D.C.: Brookings Institute, 1931), 51, 54–63.

56. Thomas H. Reed (chairman), "Report of the American Political Science Association Committee on Policy," *APSR* 24, suppl. (1930): 1; Charles A. Beard, "Conditions Favorable to Creative Work in Political Science," *APSR* 24, suppl. (1930): 25–29.

57. Howard Odum to William Ogburn, February 21, 1933, WFO; Charles A. Beard, "Facts, Opinion, and Social Values: Review of *Recent Social Trends*," *Yale Review* 22 (March 1933): 595–97; Beard, "Limitations to the Application of Social Science Implied in *Recent Social Trends*," *Social Forces* 11 (May 1933): 505–10.

58. Beard, *Open Door*, 28–30; Beard, "The Historian and Society," *Canadian Historical Review* 14 (March 1933): 2–3.

59. Beard, *Nature of the Social Sciences*, 71; Beard, *Open Door*, 16–17, 32, 138, 216.

60. Beard, *Open Door*, 31; Charles A. Beard, "A Search for the Centre: A Challenge to the Competent Mind," *Scribner's* 91 (January 1932): 2; Beard, "Freedom in Political Thought," in *Freedom: Its Meaning*, ed. Ruth Nanda Anshen (New York: Harcourt, Brace, 1940), 301.

61. Charles A. Beard, "The Historical Approach to the New Deal," *APSR* 28 (February 1934): 12; Beard and Alfred Vagts, "Currents of Thought in Historiography," *AHR* 42 (April 1937): 460, 483; Beard, *The Discussion of Human Affairs* (New York: Macmillan, 1936), prefatory note, 82–83.

62. Beard and Vagts, "Currents," 462–65; Emerton and Beard to Dodd, July 30, 1927, quoted in Novick, *That Noble Dream*, 90, 158; Higham, *History*, 98; Vagts to Cushing Strout, October 31, 1958, CMB.

63. Charles A. Beard, "Review of *The Problem of Historical Knowledge: An Answer to Relativism*, by Maurice Mandelbaum," *AHR* 44 (April 1939): 572; Beard and Vagts, "Currents," 478–79; Beard, *Discussion*, 85–87.

64. Beard to Mr. Lowell, March 29, 1944, CMB; Becker to Beard, September, 1938, in *What Is the Good of History? Selected Letters of Carl Becker, 1900–1945*, ed. Michael Kammen (Ithaca: Cornell University Press, 1973), 261; Novick, *That Noble Dream*, 270.

65. Charles A. Beard, "Written History as an Act of Faith," *AHR* 39 (January 1934): 220–21, 225–27.

66. Beard and Vagts, "Currents," 480–81; Beard, "Written History," 225–26, 228.

67. Beard, "James Ford Rhodes," 83; Beard, "Review of *Political Thought*

in England from Locke to Bentham, by H. J. Laski," *NR* 24 (November 17, 1920): 303; Cowley, Foreword, 19; Beard, "Historians at Work: Brooks and Henry Adams," *Atlantic Monthly* 171 (April 1943): 88, 92.

68. Beard to Lowell, March 29, 1944, CMB; Beard, Introduction to *The Idea of Progress: An Inquiry into Its Origin and Growth,* by J. B. Bury (New York: Macmillan, 1932), ix.

69. Beard to Ralph E. Flanders, February 9, 1930, REF; Beard, Introduction, ix, xl; J. B. Bury, *The Idea of Progress: An Inquiry into Its Origin and Growth* (New York: Macmillan, c. 1920; reprint, 1932), 1–4, 7, passim. Beard used Bury's quote to open his introduction to the American edition.

70. Charles A. Beard, "That Promise of American Life," *NR* 81 (February 6, 1935): 351; Herring, "Charles Beard," 652.

71. Beard and Beard, *Rise of American Civilization,* 544; Beard, Introduction, xxvii.

72. Beard, *Open Door,* 152; Beard, "Idea of Let Us Alone," *Virginia Quarterly Review* 15 (October 1939): 505.

73. Beard and Beard, *American Spirit,* v, 3, 9, 544, 581, 672–74.

74. Higham, *History,* 78–81; Theodore Clarke Smith, "The Writing of American History in America, from 1884 to 1934," *AHR* 40 (April 1935): 445–49; Roy F. Nichols, *A Historian's Progress* (New York: Alfred A. Knopf, 1968); John Herman Randall, Jr., and George Haines IV, "Controlling Assumptions in the Practice of American Historians," in *Theory and Practice in Historical Study: A Report of the Committee on Historiography* (New York: Social Science Research Council, 1946), 51.

75. Beard, "Methods of Training," 909; Diane Ravitch, *The Troubled Crusade: American Education 1945–1980* (New York: Basic Books, 1983), 59–60; Beard, *The Unique Function of Education in American Democracy* (Washington, D.C.: National Education Association of the United States, 1937).

76. Charles A. Beard, *A Charter for the Social Sciences in the Schools* (New York: Charles Scribner's Sons, 1932), vii; A. C. Krey, "History and Other Social Sciences in the Schools," *Annual Report of the American Historical Association for the Year 1926* (Washington, D.C.: U.S. Government Printing Office, 1930), 114.

77. Krey, "History," 110–16, 119–20; A. C. Krey, "Purpose of the Commission on the Social Studies in the Schools," *School and Society* 40 (November 17, 1934): 663–64.

78. Krey, "History," 114–15; Novick, *That Noble Dream,* 70–72, 191, 199–200.

79. Krey, "History," 120; Beard to Krey, July 5, 1933, ACK; Peter A. Soder-

bergh, "Charles A. Beard and the Commission on the Social Studies 1929–1933: A Reappraisal," *Social Education* 31 (October 1967): 466.

80. Charles A. Beard, "Objectives," Unpublished memorandum to the Committee on Objectives of the Commission on the Social Studies of the American Historical Association, no date, 10, 13–22, 36–46, 49–51, CEM.

81. Interview with George Counts, no date, part 1:12, 17–18, 22, GSC; Lawrence J. Dennis, *George S. Counts and Charles A. Beard: Collaborators for Change* (Albany: State University of New York Press, 1989), 11.

82. Interview with Counts, part 3: 9; George S. Counts, *Dare the School Build a New Social Order?* (New York: John Day, 1932), 5–6, 11–14, 33; Counts, Personal diary, unpublished, 26–27, GSC; Counts, *The Social Foundations of Education* (New York: Charles Scribner's Sons, 1934), 277–79, 533–36; Counts, *The American Road to Culture: A Social Interpretation of Education in the United States* (New York: John Day, 1930), 93–94, 180–82.

83. George S. Counts, *A Call to the Teachers of America* (New York: John Day, 1933), 18–23, 25–26; Counts, *Dare the School,* 9–10, 25–26, 44–46, 54; Counts, *American Road,* 189; Counts, "The Opportunity of the Social Studies Teacher," *Proceedings of the Middle States Association of Middle School Teachers* 33 (1935): 31, 34–35; Counts, "Secondary Education and the Social Problem," *School Executives Magazine* 51 (August 1932): 520.

84. Beard to Counts, December 25, 1933; Interview with Counts, part 1: 24–25, both in GSC; Dennis, *George Counts,* 8; Gerald L. Gutek, *George S. Counts and American Civilization* (Atlanta: Mercer University Press, 1984), 72; Beard to Counts, April 23, 1930, and August 5, 1934; Counts to Beard, April 19 and May 16, 1930, and August 3 and 9, 1933, all in GSC.

85. Beard to Counts, February 7 and 11, 1933, GSC; Krey to Counts, October 3, 1933, ACK.

86. American Historical Commission on the Social Studies, *Conclusions and Recommendations of the Commission* (New York: Charles Scribner's Sons, 1934), ix–x, 67–73, 91–94, 98–101, 104, 110, 145; Beard to Krey, December 9, 1932, ACK; Beard to Counts, November 23, 1933, GSC; Dennis, *George Counts,* 90.

87. American Historical Association, *Conclusions and Recommendations,* 3–4, 7–19, 33–43, 49, 122–34.

88. W. H. Harper, *Social Beliefs and Attitudes of American Educators,* Teachers College, Columbia Contributions to Education, no. 294 (New York: Columbia University Press, 1927).

89. Beard to Counts, December 22, 1933, GSC.

90. Krey to Counts, August 1933, GSC; Krey to Counts, January 14, 1934, ACK; Soderbergh, "Charles Beard and Commission," 467; Krey to Frederick

Keppel, quoted in Dennis, *George Counts*, 95; Counts to Merriam, September 19, 1933, CEM.

91. Merriam to Counts, April 20, 1934; Merriam to Edmund Day, April 7, 1934; Merriam to J. J. Pugh, June 20, 1934, all in CEM; Merriam, *Civic Education in the United States* (New York: Charles Scribner's Sons, 1934), xi, xvi, xxi; Merriam, *Chicago: A More Intimate View of Politics* (New York: Macmillan, 1929), 85.

92. Merriam, *Civic Education*, xvii, 33–34, 39–42, 177–80; Merriam to John Merriam, July 10, 1925, CEM.

93. Transcript of the AHA commission meeting, October 12, 1933, quoted in Dennis, *Charles Beard*; Soderbergh, "Charles Beard and Commission," 467; Counts, "Charles Beard," 219; Krey to Day, February 12, 1934; Krey to Merriam, January 13 and March 6, 1934; Krey to Counts, March 7, 1934; Merriam to Krey, March 9, 1934, all in ACK; Counts to Merriam, April 3, 1934, CEM.

94. Counts to Beard, January 9, 1934, GSC; Counts to Krey, February 7(?) and March 12, 1934; Krey to Counts, January 24, 1934, all in ACK.

95. Krey to Day, April 19, 1934, ACK; Dennis, *George Counts*, 66, 72, 97–100; Frank Ballou, "Statement Concerning the Report of the Commission on the Investigation of History and the Other Social Studies of the American Historical Association," *School and Society* 39 (June 2, 1934): 702; Newlon to Krey, February 3, 1933; Krey to Counts, January 24, 1934; Day to Conyers Read, April 20, 1934 (copy), last three in ACK.

96. John S. Brubaker, "Book Review of *Conclusions and Recommendations* of the Commission," *AHR* 40 (January 1935): 301–5; American Historical Association, *Conclusions and Recommendations*, 146–47; C. A. Bowers, *Progressive Educator and the Depression: The Radical Years* (New York: Random House, 1969), 34.

97. Some of the best examples of positive reviews are "On with This Revolution," [editorial], *Christian Century* 51 (May 23, 1934): 686–87; Ernest E. Bayles, "More Comment on Bobbitt's Criticism," *School and Society* 40 (November 24, 1934): 690–91; and Edgar B. Wesley, "Book Review of *Conclusions and Recommendations of the American Historical Association*," *Journal for Educational Research* 28 (January 1935): 367–69. The best critique from a radical perspective is Julian Aronson, "The Pedagogues Sound the Tocsin," *School and Society* 41 (January 19, 1935): 95–97. Among the numerous attacks by the technocratic essentialists are Franklin Bobbitt, "Questionable Recommendations of the Commission on the Social Studies," *School and Society* 40 (August 18, 1934): 201–8; Bobbitt, "Preparing Citizens for Difficult Years Ahead: Review of *Conclusions and Recommendations of the*

Commission," *School Review* 42 (September 1934): 547–50; A. S. Barr, "Book Review of *Conclusions and Recommendations*," *Journal of Educational Research* 28 (January 1935): 365–67; and Percival W. Hutson, "Opinions on Instruction in the Social Studies: Conclusions and Recommendations of the Commission," *Elementary School Journal* 35 (March 1935): 549–51.

98. Charles A. Beard, "A Five Year Plan for America," *Forum* 86 (July 1931): 8; Beard, *Open Door*, 308–9; Nore, *Charles Beard*, 144–47; Smith to Beard, January 4, 1933; Beard to Smith, October 28, 1933, both in GHS.

99. Beard, "Five Year Plan"; Beard, "The Myth of Rugged Individualism," *Harper's* 164 (December 1931): 13–22; Beard to Ralph Flanders, July 4, 1931, REF; Beard, "The Rationality of Planned Economy," in *America Faces the Future*, ed. Beard (Boston: Houghton Mifflin, 1932), 403.

100. Charles A. Beard, with George H. E. Smith, *The Idea of National Interest: An Analytical Study in American Foreign Policy* (New York: Macmillan, 1934), 525–35, 541–45; Beard, *Giddy Minds and Foreign Quarrels* (New York: Macmillan, 1939), 43–44; Beard to Smith, January 8, 1935, GHS.

101. Beard to Smith, August 4, 1933, GHS.

102. Beard to Smith, January 6, 1933, GHS; Beard, *The Devil Theory of War: An Inquiry into the Nature of History and the Possibility of Keeping out of War* (New York: Vanguard, 1936), 109; Beard, *A Foreign Policy for America* (New York: Alfred A. Knopf, 1940), 6.

103. Beard and Smith, *Idea*, 1–29, 311–406; Beard, "Review of *Washington and the Riddle of Peace*, by H. G. Wells," *Nation* 114 (March 8, 1922): 289–90; Beard and George H. E. Smith, *The Future Comes: A Study of the New Deal* (New York: Macmillan, 1933), v; Beard, "Five Year Plan," 9.

104. Beard to Smith, January 14 and August 29, 1933, GHS; Beard, *Open Door*, v–viii, 34, 210, 228–32, 261–62, 273–74.

105. Beard, *Open Door*, 66–69, 134, 210–15, 221.

106. Charles A. Beard and Mary R. Beard, *America in Midpassage*, vol. 3 of their *The Rise of American Civilization* (New York: Macmillan, 1939), 451–52.

107. Beard, "Five Year Plan," 8–9; Beard, *Open Door*, 269.

108. Charles A. Beard, "Review of *Freedom of Speech*, by Zachariah Chafee, and *Collected Legal Papers*, by Oliver Wendell Holmes," *National Municipal Review* 10 (April 1921): 247–48; Beard, "War with Japan: What Shall We Get out of It?" *Nation* 120 (March 25, 1925): 312; Beard, "The Future of Democracy in the United States," *Political Quarterly* 8 (October 1937): 505.

109. Beard to Arthur Macmahon, July 16, 1917, AWM; Novick, *That Noble Dream*, 131; Beard to Curti, April 15, 1945, and January 29, 1947, quoted in Nore, *Charles Beard*, 111; Kennedy, *Charles Beard*, 50; Mary Beard, *The Making*, 26–27.

110. Charles A. Beard and George Radin, *The Balkan Pivot: Yugoslavia—A Study in Government and Administration* (New York: Macmillan, 1929), 75, 87, 162; Goldman, *Rendezvous with Destiny*, 283.

111. Herring, "Charles Beard," 646; Charles A. Beard, Testimony before the House Foreign Affairs Committee, in *New York Times*, February 11, 1938, quoted in Warren I. Cohen, *The American Revisionists* (Chicago: University of Chicago Press, 1967), 193; Beard and Radin, *Balkan Pivot*, 46.

112. Beard, *American Government*, 355; Beard, *Devil Theory*, 22; Beard, *Rise*, 2:631–32, 643; Beard, "Historical Approach," 13–14.

113. Beard, *Giddy Minds*, preface; Beard, *Devil Theory*, 22; Kennedy, *Charles Beard*, 38–39.

114. Charles A. Beard, "Big Navy Boys: Part I," *NR* 39 (January 20, 1932): 258–62; Beard, "Big Navy Boys: Part II," *NR* 39 (January 27, 1932): 287; Beard, "Big Navy Boys: Part III," *NR* 39 (February 3, 1932): 318; Beard, "Making a Bigger and Better Navy," *NR* 68 (October 14, 1931): 223–26; Beard, *Open Door*, 101–2, 263–64; Beard, Testimony before the House Committee on Naval Affairs, February 9, 1938, quoted in Kennedy, *Charles Beard*, 88–89.

115. Charles A. Beard, "Peace for America: Solving Domestic Crises by War," *NR* 86 (March 11, 1936): 127–29; Beard, "Peace for America: In Time of Peace Prepare for Peace," *NR* 86 (March 18, 1936): 156–59; Manfred Jonas, *Isolationism in America 1935–1941* (Ithaca: Cornell University Press, 1966), 1; Harry W. Baehr, "A Cycle of Revisionism Between the Two Wars," in *Essays in American Historiography: Papers Presented in Honor of Allen Nevins*, ed. Donald Sheehan and Harold C. Synett (New York: Columbia University Press, 1960), 279.

116. Charles A. Beard, "National Politics and War," *Scribner's* 97 (February 1935): 70.

117. Ibid., 157–58; Charles A. Beard, "We're Blundering into War," *American Mercury* 46 (April 1939): 399; Beard, *Devil Theory*, 118; Beard, "Future," 506; Chase, quoted in Jonas, *Isolationism*, 128; Beard, "Democracy and Education in the United States," *Social Research* 4 (September 1937): 393; Beard, "Peace for America: In Time," 158–59.

118. Beard to Barnes, May 1940, HEB.

6 HAROLD D. LASSWELL AND THE LOST OPPORTUNITY OF THE PURPOSIVE SCHOOL

1. Duane Marvick, "Introduction: Context, Problems, and Methods," in *Harold D. Lasswell on Political Sociology*, ed. Duane Marvick (Chicago: University of Chicago Press, 1977), 17–18, 21–22; Harold D. Lasswell to

author, March 26, 1974; Lasswell, "Review of *Sovereignty*, by Paul W. Ward," *AJS* 34 (November 1928): 559; Lasswell, *A Pre-View of Policy Sciences* (New York: American Elsevier, 1971), xiv; Lasswell, *Psychopathology and Politics* (Chicago: University of Chicago Press, 1930), 196; Daniel Lerner, "Managing Communication for Modernization: A Developmental Construct," in *Politics, Personality, and Social Science in the Twentieth Century: Essays in Honor of Harold D. Lasswell*, ed. Arnold Rogow (Chicago: University of Chicago Press, 1969), 172; Lasswell, "Review of *Knowledge for What? The Place of Social Science in American Culture*, by Robert S. Lynd," *Public Opinion Quarterly* 2 (December 1939): 725–26; Lasswell, "The Policy Orientation," in *The Policy Sciences: Recent Developments in Scope and Method*, ed. Daniel Lerner and Lasswell (Stanford: Stanford University Press, 1951), 7–8.

2. Lasswell, "Policy Orientation," 11; Lasswell, "The Developing Science of Democracy," in *The Future of Government in the United States: Essays in Honor of Charles E. Merriam*, ed. Leonard D. White (Chicago: University of Chicago Press, 1942), 25, 34, 48; Lasswell, "The Future of the Social Sciences as Policy Sciences," Unpublished memorandum, no date (c. 1947), 1, 4–6, CEM; Harold D. Lasswell, "What Psychiatrists and Political Scientists Can Learn from One Another," *Psychiatry* 1 (February 1938): 33–39.

3. Oscar Jaszi, "Review of *Beyond Conscience*, by T. V. Smith, *Political Power*, by Charles Edward Merriam, and *World Politics and Personal Insecurity*, by Harold D. Lasswell," *International Journal of Ethics* 45 (July 1935): 448; Floyd W. Matson, *The Broken Image: Man, Science, and Society* (New York: George Braziller, 1964), 14, 100–115; David Easton, "Harold Lasswell: Policy Scientist for a Democratic Society," *Journal of Politics* 12 (September 1950): 455, 469–71; Paul Mandelstam, "The Freudian Impact upon Contemporary Political Thought: An Analysis of the Political Ideas of Sigmund Freud, Arthur Koestler, Erich Fromm, Harold D. Lasswell, and Abram Kardiner" (Ph.D. diss., Harvard University, 1952), 201, n. 3.

4. John Dollard, quoted in Saul Padover, "Lasswell's Impact on the Study of Power in a Democracy," *Social Research* 29 (Winter 1962): 491; Edward Shils, "Some Academics, Mainly at Chicago," *American Scholar* 50 (Spring 1981): 192–96; Leo Rosten, "A Memoir," in Rogow, ed., *Politics, Personality*, 11; Harold D. Lasswell, "Radio as an Instrument of Reducing Political Insecurity," *Studies in Philosophy and Social Science* 9 (1941): 59; Lasswell, "Why Be Quantitative?" in *Language of Politics: Studies in Quantitative Semantics*, by Lasswell, Nathan Leites, and Associates (Cambridge: MIT Press, c. 1949; reprint, 1965), 43–50; Lasswell, "The Problem of Adequate Personality Records: A Proposal," *American Journal of Psychiatry* 8 (May

1929): 1057–66; Lasswell, "The Scientific Study of Human Biography," *Scientific Monthly* 30 (January 1930): 79–80; Lasswell, *World Politics and Personal Insecurity* (New York: McGraw-Hill, 1935), 5–6; Lasswell, "Intensive and Extensive Methods of Observing the Personality-Culture Manifold," *Yenching Journal of Social Studies* 1 (June 1938): 74–88.

5. Marvick, "Introduction," 15–17; Morris Janowitz, "Content Analysis and the Symbolic Environment," in Rogow, ed., *Politics, Personality,* 157.

6. Mary Harrington Hall, "A Conversation with Harold Lasswell," *Psychology Today* 1 (October 1968): 63.

7. Harold D. Lasswell, "Chicago's Old First Ward: A Case Study," *National Municipal Review* 12 (March 1923): 127–31.

8. Harold D. Lasswell, "Political Policies and the International Investment Market," *Journal of Political Economy* 31 (June 1923): 380–92, 397–400.

9. Harold D. Lasswell, "Review of *The Chicago Primary of 1926,* by Carroll Hill Woody," *AJS* 32 (March 1927): 84–49; Lasswell, "The Comparative Method of James Bryce," in *Methods in Social Science: A Case Book,* ed. Stuart Rice (Chicago: University of Chicago Press, 1931), 479; Lasswell, "Review of *Farmers and Workers in American Politics,* by Stuart Rice," *AJS* 21 (July 1925): 108. Revealingly, Rice, whom Lasswell praised at this time for his scientific technique, would be the specific object of his barb about "counting some" twenty years later.

10. Harold D. Lasswell and Willard E. Atkins, *Labor Attitudes and Problems* (New York: Prentice-Hall, 1924), iii–vi, xiii, 212–14, 348–50, 416.

11. Charles E. Merriam, "Recent Advances in Political Methods," *APSR* 18 (May 1923): 275–95; Merriam, *New Aspects of Politics* (Chicago: University of Chicago Press, 1925), 149–83; Lasswell to Merriam, August 4, September 7, and November 5, 1923, CEM; Merriam and Lasswell, "Current Public Opinion and the Public Service Commissions," in *Public Utility Regulation,* ed. Morris L. Cooke (New York: Ronald Press, 1924), 276–95; Lasswell, Introduction to his *Propaganda Technique in World War I* (Cambridge: MIT Press, 1970), ix–x.

12. Merriam to Kosok, December 11, 1925; Lasswell to Merriam, October 8, 1923, August 2, 1925, January 13 and November 1, 1926; Merriam to John Gaus, March 10, 1926; Lasswell, "German Civic Psychology: Preliminary Notes," Unpublished Manuscript, October 1, 1925, passim; Merriam, "Memorandum on Comparative Civic Training," Unpublished memorandum from Merriam to Beardsley Ruml, no date, all in CEM; Harold D. Lasswell, "A Crypto-Heretic on Nationalism," *NR* 49 (December 8, 1926): 94; Lasswell, "Two Forgotten Studies in Political Psychology," *APSR* 19 (November 1925): 712.

13. Charles Beard and Mary Beard, *The Rise of American Civilization* (New York: Macmillan, 1927), 640; Harold D. Lasswell, "The Status of Research on International Propaganda and Opinion," *Publications of the American Sociological Society* 20 (July 1926): 198–200.

14. Marvick, "Introduction," 18–19; Charles E. Merriam, "American Publicity in Italy," *APSR* 13 (November 1919): 541–55; Harold D. Lasswell, *Propaganda Technique in the World War* (New York: Alfred A. Knopf, 1927), 114–15; Merriam, *New Aspects*, 304; Lasswell to Merriam, January 23, 1926, CEM.

15. Lasswell, *Propaganda Technique*, 5, 9, 12–14; Lasswell, "The Function of the Propagandist," *International Journal of Ethics* 38 (April 1928): 264; Lasswell, "Propaganda," in *Encyclopedia of the Social Sciences*, ed. Edwin Seligman and Alvin Johnson (New York: Macmillan, 1933), 11:524–25; Lasswell, "Why Be Quantitative?" 42; Lasswell, *Politics: Who Gets What, When, How* (New York: McGraw-Hill, 1936), 13.

16. Lasswell, "Why Be Quantitative?" 40–42; Lasswell, *Propaganda Technique*, 94–96, 133, 209–12.

17. Lasswell, *Propaganda Technique*, 82, 157–60.

18. Lasswell, "Propaganda," 523–26; Lasswell, "The Theory of Political Propaganda," *APSR* 21 (August 1927): 631; Lasswell, "Review of *Influencing Human Behavior*, by H. A. Overstreet," *AJS* 32 (July 1926): 141–42; Lasswell, "Review of *The Phantom Public*, by Walter Lippmann," *AJS* 31 (January 1926): 534–35.

19. Harold D. Lasswell, "Proposed Institute of Political Research," Undated memorandum to Charles Merriam, c. 1948, CEM; Lasswell, "Theory of Propaganda," 627–28; Lasswell, *Psychopathology and Politics* (New York: Viking Press, c. 1930; reprint, 1960), v, 1; Lasswell and Abraham Kaplan, *Power and Society* (New Haven: Yale University Press, 1950), 14, n. 17.

20. Lasswell to Merriam, "Monday" (1923), October 8, and November 5, 1923, CEM; Dwight Waldo, "Graham Wallas: Reason and Emotion in Social Change," *Journal of Social Philosophy and Jurisprudence* 7 (January 1942): 142–60.

21. Harold D. Lasswell, "Psychology and Political Science in the U.S.A.," in *Contemporary Political Science: A Survey of Methods, Research and Teaching* (Paris: UNESCO, 1950), 536; Floyd H. Allport, "Political Science and Psychology," in *The Social Sciences and Their Interrelationships*, ed. William F. Ogburn and Alexander Goldenweiser (Boston: Houghton Mifflin, 1927), 260–62.

22. Barry D. Karl to author, March 11, 1974; interview with Karl, University of Chicago, January 19, 1979; Harold D. Lasswell, "The Cross-

Disciplinary Manifold: The Chicago Prototype," in *The Search for World Order: Studies by Students and Colleagues of Quincy Wright*, ed. Albert Lepawsky, Edward H. Boehrig, and Lasswell (New York: Appleton-Century-Crofts, 1971), 419, 422–24; Lasswell to Merriam, no date (1934), CEM.

23. George Herbert Mead, *Mind, Self, and Society* (Chicago: University of Chicago Press, 1934), 7–8, 134, passim; Marvick, "Introduction," 21–22; James T. Carey, *Chicago and Public Affairs: The Chicago School* (Beverly Hills: Sage, 1975), 187–88; Lasswell to author, March 26, 1974; Lasswell, "Personality Studies," in *Chicago: An Experiment in Social Science Research*, ed. T. V. Smith and Leonard D. White (Chicago: University of Chicago Press, 1929), 177–83; Lasswell, "The Cross-Disciplinary Manifold," 418; Robert Park, "The City as a Social Laboratory," in Smith and White, eds., *Chicago*, 12; Lasswell to Fred H. Matthews, in *Quest for an American Sociology: Robert E. Park and the Chicago School*, by Matthews (Montreal: McGill–Queen's University Press, 1977), 119, 145–48; Park to Merriam, May 6, 1926, CEM; Shils, "Some Academics," 194.

24. Ernest W. Burgess, ed., *Personality and the Social Group* (Chicago: University of Chicago Press, 1929), vii; W. I. Thomas, "The Behavior Pattern of the Situation," in ibid., 1.

25. Harold D. Lasswell, "Types of Political Personalities," in Burgess, ed., *Personality*, 151–61; Mead, *Mind, Self, and Society*, 1–2; Charles W. Morris, Introduction to ibid., xv, xxv–xxvi.

26. Charles E. Merriam, "The Education of Charles E. Merriam," in *The Future of Government in the United States: Essays in Honor of Charles E. Merriam*, ed. Leonard D. White (Chicago: University of Chicago Press, 1942), 17; Richard C. S. Trahair, *The Humanist Temper: The Life and Work of Elton Mayo* (New Brunswick, N.J.: Transaction Books, 1984), 96–98, 120–21, 143–66.

27. Elton Mayo, *The Human Problems of an Industrial Civilization* (New York: Macmillan, 1933), 55–121, 131–33; Mayo, "The Maladjustment of the Individual Worker" (1928), in *Wertheim Lectures on Industrial Relations* (Cambridge: Harvard University Press, 1929), 172; F. J. Roethlisberger and William J. Dickson, *Management and the Worker* (Cambridge: Harvard University Press, 1933).

28. Trahair, *Humanist Temper*, 38–41, 103, 181–85, 200–202; Minutes of the conference of psychologists called by the Laura Spelman Rockefeller Memorial, Hanover, N.H., August 26–September 3, 1925, 195, CEM; Richard C. S. Trahair, "Elton Mayo and the Early Political Psychology of Harold D. Lasswell," *Political Psychology* 3 (August 1982): 179–80; Padover, "Impact," 490; Marvick, "Introduction," 27; Hall, "Conversation," 63.

29. Mayo, *Human Problems*, 176–77.

30. Mayo to Merriam, February 9 and October 15, 1927; Merriam to Mayo November 3 and 20, 1925; Lasswell to Merriam, October 11 and December 3, 1926, all in CEM; Trahair, "Elton Mayo," 179.

31. Mayo, *Human Problems*, 131–33; Mayo, "Sin with a Capital 'S,'" *Harper's* 154 (April 1927): 537–44.

32. Harold D. Lasswell, "Impact of Psychoanalytic Thinking on the Social Sciences," in *Psychoanalysis and Social Science*, ed. Hendrik M. Ruitenbeck (New York: E. P. Dutton, c. 1956; reprint, 1962), 8; Trahair, *Humanist Temper*, 93–99, 200–201; Abraham Zalesnik, "Foreword: The Promise of Elton Mayo," in ibid., 7–9; Charles E. Harvey, "John D. Rockefeller and the Social Sciences," *Journal of the History of Sociology* 4 (Fall 1982): 20–21.

33. Mayo to Ruml, January 10, 1923, quoted in Trahair, *Humanist Temper*, 164; Minutes of the conference of psychologists, 190–91, CEM; Harold D. Lasswell and Robert Rubenstein, *The Sharing of Power in a Psychiatric Hospital* (New Haven: Yale University Press, 1966).

34. Mayo to Merriam, March 6, 1925, and March 10, 1926; Lasswell to Merriam, January 23, 1926, CEM.

35. G. V. Hamilton, *A Research in Marriage* (New York: Albert and Charles Boni, 1929), xii–xiii, passim; Lasswell to Merriam, January 29, 1927; "This Week Wednesday" (January 1927); Mayo to Merriam, February 9, 1927, last three in CEM.

36. Harold D. Lasswell, "Patriotism," Unpublished manuscript, no date (c. 1927), chap. 1, 1–2, 8, 15–16; chap. 2, 12–16; chap. 3, 77–79; chap. 4, 7, 16, CEM; Mayo, "Sin"; Trahair, *Humanist Temper*, 135–36.

37. Martin Bulmer, Interview with Gosnell, March 23, 1982, quoted in Bulmer, *The Chicago School of Sociology: Institutionalization, Diversity and the Rise of Sociological Research* (Chicago: University of Chicago Press, 1984), 194; Trahair, Interview with Lasswell, May 6, 1975, in Trahair, "Elton Mayo," 180.

38. Trahair, "Elton Mayo," 180; Rosten, "Harold Lasswell," 6; Hall, "Conversation," 63; Lasswell and Atkins, *Labor Attitudes*, 114.

39. Paul Roazen, *Freud and His Followers* (New York: Alfred A. Knopf, 1971), 326–27; Lasswell to author, March 26, 1974; Lasswell, "Afterthoughts: Thirty Years Later," in his *Psychopathology and Politics* (New York: Viking Press, 1960), 275; Fred L. Greenstein, Introduction to *Psychopathology and Politics*, by Lasswell (Chicago: University of Chicago Press, 1977), ix.

40. Lasswell, *Psychopathology and Politics*, 75–76, 184–85; Lasswell, "Chauvinism," in *Encyclopedia of the Social Sciences*, ed. Edwin Seligman and Alvin Johnson (New York: Macmillan, 1930), 3:361; Lasswell, *Power and Personality* (New York: W. W. Norton, 1948), 38.

41. Sigmund Freud, "Character and Anal Eroticism" (1908), in *The Standard Edition of the Complete Psychological Works of Sigmund Freud*, ed. James Strachey (London: Hogarth Press, 1959), 9:167–75; Lasswell, *Psychopathology and Politics*, 8–9, 14–16, 78–79, 103–4.

42. Martin Birnbach, *Neo-Freudian Social Philosophy* (Stanford: Stanford University Press, 1961), 157; Harold D. Lasswell, "Review of *The Structure and Meaning of Psychoanalysis as Related to Personality and Behavior*, by William Healy, Augusta F. Browner, and Anna Mae Bowers," *AJS* 36 (January 1931): 653; Lasswell, "Review of *Civilization and Its Discontents*, by Sigmund Freud," *AJS* 37 (September 1931): 330.

43. Trahair, *Humanist Temper*, 83–85; Harold D. Lasswell, "Tentative Analysis for Case Book," Unpublished memorandum, no date (c. 1928), CEM; Lasswell, "A Hypothesis Rooted in the Preconceptions of a Single Civilization Tested by Bronislaw Malinowski," in Rice, ed., *Methods in Social Science*, 481–85.

44. Lasswell, "Future of Social Sciences," 1–2; Lasswell to Robert Lowie, August 31, 1927; Charles Merriam, "Impressions of Hanover," Unpublished notes, September 1929, last two in CEM; Lasswell, "The *Encyclopedia of the Social Sciences* in Review," *International Journal of Ethics* 46 (April 1936): 392; Lasswell, *Psychopathology and Politics*, 13; Lasswell, "Collective Autism as a Consequence of Cultural Contact: Notes on Religious Training and the Peyote Cult at Taos," *Zeitschrift für Sozialforschung* 4 (1935): 237; Lasswell, "Psychoanalyze and Sozioanalyze," *Imago* 19 (1933): 377–83.

45. Sigmund Freud, *The Future of an Illusion*, trans. W. D. Robson-Scott, ed. and rev. James Strachey (Garden City, N.Y.: Doubleday, c. 1927; reprint, 1957), 3, 5; Philip Rieff, *The Triumph of the Therapeutic: Uses of Faith After Freud* (New York: Harper and Row, 1966), 29–107; Philip Rieff, *Freud: The Mind of the Moralist* (New York: Viking Press, 1959); Freud, *Civilization and Its Discontents*, trans. James Strachey (London: Hogarth Press, c. 1930; reprint, 1949), 142–44.

46. Lasswell, *Psychopathology and Politics*, 196–98; Lasswell, "Compromise," in *Encyclopedia of the Social Sciences*, ed. Edwin Seligman and Alvin Johnson (New York: Macmillan, 1931), 4:147–49; Lasswell, "Conflict, Social," in ibid., 4:495; Bruce Lannes Smith, "The Mystifying Intellectual History of Harold D. Lasswell," in Rogow, ed., *Politics, Personality*, 73.

47. Nathan G. Hale, Jr., *Freud and the Americans: The Beginning of Psychoanalysis in the United States 1865–1917* (New York: Oxford University Press, 1971), 5–6, 115, 332–33, 370–76.

48. Lasswell, *Psychopathology and Politics*, 218, 250–51; Lasswell, "The Contribution of Freud's Insight to the Social Sciences," *AJS* 45 (April 1939): 387–90; Lasswell, *Public Opinion in Peace and War: How Americans Make*

up Their Minds (Washington, D.C.: National Education Association, 1943), 45; Lasswell, "Intensive," 77; Lasswell, "Impact," 44–45.

49. Barbara Sicherman, "The Quest for Mental Health in America, 1880–1917" (Ph.D. diss., Columbia University, 1967), 286–89, 311–12, 325, 332–33; George K. Pratt, "Twenty Years of the National Committee for Mental Hygiene," *Mental Hygiene* 14 (April 1930): 399–428; Adolf Meyer, "The Purpose of the Psychiatric Clinic," in *Collected Papers of Adolf Meyer: Psychiatry*, ed. Eunice E. Winters (Baltimore: Johns Hopkins University Press, c. 1913; 1951), 2:178; Stewart Paton, "Protecting Civilization: The Physician's Duty in the Reorganization of Society," *Harper's* 148 (January 1924): 165–66, 170; William Alanson White, "The Origin, Growth and Significance of the Mental Hygiene Movement," *Science* 72 (July 25, 1930): 2.

50. Sicherman, "Quest," 422–23; Mayo, "Sin," 544; Elton Mayo, "Orientation and Attitude: Mental Hygiene in Industry," in *The Psychological Foundations of Management*, ed. H. C. Metcalfe (New York: Shaw, 1927), 261–90; Lasswell, "What Psychiatrists," 33–39; Lasswell, "Political Psychiatry: The Study and Practice of Integrative Politics," in *Mental Health*, ed. Forest Ray Moulton, Publication of the American Association for the Advancement of Science, no. 9 (Lancaster, Pa.: Science Press, 1939), 269–75.

51. Arnold Rogow, "Toward a Psychiatry of Politics," in Rogow, ed., *Politics, Personality*, 127–28; Lasswell, *Psychopathology and Politics*, 240–46, 258.

52. Lasswell, "German Civic Psychology," 21; Lasswell, "The Psychology of Hitlerism," *Political Quarterly* 4 (July–September 1933): 373–84.

53. Harold D. Lasswell, "The Problem of World Unity: In Quest of a Myth," *International Journal of Ethics* 44 (November 1933): 68, n. 1.

54. Lasswell, "The *Encyclopedia*," 395–96; Lasswell, "Power, Personality, Group, Culture," *Psychiatry* 2 (November 1939): 542; Charles E. Merriam and members of the Department of Political Science of the University of Chicago, Unpublished memorandum, no date (c. 1931), 25, CEM; Lasswell, *World Politics*, 5–6; Lasswell, "Developing Science," 39; italics are Lasswell's.

55. Lasswell, *World Politics*, 4–6, 22–24, 201–3; Lasswell and Myres S. McDougal, "Legal Education and Public Policy: Professional Training in the Public Interest," *Yale Law Journal* 52 (March 1943): 214; Lasswell and Dorothy Blumenstock, *World Revolutionary Propaganda: A Chicago Study* (New York: Alfred A. Knopf, 1939), vi; Lasswell, "The *Encyclopedia*," 393–94; Lasswell, "Strategy of Revolutionary and War Propaganda," in *Public Opinion and War Politics*, ed. Quincy Wright (Chicago: University of Chicago Press, 1933), 196–97.

56. Lasswell, *World Politics*, 5–6; Lasswell, *Politics*, 24; Lasswell, *Power and Personality*, 9; Lasswell, "The Relation of Skill Politics to Class Politics and National Politics," *Chinese Social and Political Science Review* 21 (May 1937): 299.

57. Marvick, "Introduction," 17, 28; Lasswell to Merriam, "Monday" (1923), CEM; Smith, "Mystifying," 64–66; Lasswell, *World Politics*, 214–17; Lasswell to author, March 26, 1974; Jurgen Herbst, *The German Historical School in American Scholarship: A Study in the Transfer of Culture* (Ithaca: Cornell University Press, 1969), 154–59; Albion W. Small, "Fifty Years of Sociology in the United States," *AJS* 21 (May 1916): 818–19; Lasswell, "German Civic Psychology," 7.

58. Lasswell, *World Politics*, 39, 73–79.

59. Lasswell and Atkins, *Labor Attitudes*, 309–11; Lasswell, *Propaganda Technique*, 57, 190; Lasswell, "Review of *The Structure*," 653; Harry Stack Sullivan, *The Interpersonal Theory of Psychiatry* (New York: W. W. Norton, 1953), 102; Lasswell, "Impact," 7–8; Lasswell, *World Politics*, 75, 214, 231, 273, 285; Lasswell, *Politics*, 147; Lasswell, *Democracy Through Public Opinion* (Menasha, Wisc.: George Banta, 1941), 49, 65–66; Lasswell, *World Politics Faces Economics* (New York: McGraw-Hill, 1945), 8.

60. Lasswell, *World Politics*, 19–21.

61. Ibid., 233, 237–54; Lasswell, "Problem of World-Unity."

62. Lasswell, *World Politics*, 283–85; Lasswell, "Problem of World-Unity."

63. Lasswell, "Proposed Institute of Political Research."

64. Lasswell, *Politics*, 13; Lasswell, *World Politics*, 3; Lasswell, Postscript to *Politics: Who Gets What, When, How* (New York: World, 1958), 195–96; Lasswell and Associates, "The Politically Significant Content of the Press: Coding Procedures," *Journalism Quarterly* 19 (March 1942): 12–13.

65. Lasswell, *Politics*, 7–8; Heinz Eulau, "The Maddening Methods of Harold D. Lasswell: Some Philosophical Underpinnings," in Rogow, ed., *Politics, Personality*, 15–16; Eulau, "Elite Analysis and Democratic Theory: The Contribution of Harold D. Lasswell," in *Elite Recruitment in Democratic Politics: Comparative Studies Across Nations*, ed. Eulau and Moshe M. Czudnowski (New York: John Wiley and Sons, 1976), 8.

66. Lasswell, *Politics*, 13–27, 168; T. B. Bottomore, *Elites and Society* (London: C. A. Watts, 1964), 7. According to Heinz Eulau, one of the leaders in the field of elite analysis during the 1950s and 1960s, Lasswell and Walter Lippmann were the only 1930s thinkers who seriously studied the subject. Eulau, "Elite Analysis," 8.

67. Lasswell, *Politics*, 8–9, 13, 24, 107.

68. Ibid., 32–33.

69. Ibid., 20; Harold D. Lasswell, "The Garrison State," *AJS* 46 (January 1941): 460; Lasswell, "The Relation of Ideological Intelligence to Public Policy," *Ethics* 53 (October 1942): 34.

70. Lasswell, *World Politics*, 266, 279–80; Lasswell, "The Moral Vocation of the Middle-Income Skill Group," *International Journal of Ethics* 45 (January 1935): 127, 131; Lasswell, "Strategy," 213–14; Lasswell, "Review of *Rebels and Renegades*, by Max Nomad," *AJS* 38 (September 1932): 466.

71. Lasswell, "The Moral Vocation," 130–31; Lasswell, *Politics*, 100.

72. Lasswell, "The Moral Vocation"; Lasswell, *World Politics*, 177, 232; Lasswell, *Politics*, 127, 172, 175; Lasswell, "Relation of Skill," 306–7, 310–13.

73. Matthew Josephson, *Infidel in the Temple* (New York: Alfred A. Knopf, 1967), 321; Alfred Bingham, *Insurgent America: Revolt of the Middle Classes* (New York: W. W. Norton, 1935); Lewis Corey, *The Crisis of the Middle Class* (New York: Covici Friede, 1935), 20–25, 32–35, passim.

74. Lasswell, *Politics*, 9; T. V. Smith, *The Promise of American Politics* (Chicago: University of Chicago Press, 1936), ix–x, 223–30, 239–44, 272–74, 279; Smith, *Beyond Conscience* (New York: McGraw-Hill, 1934), xiii.

75. Lasswell, "Moral Vocation," 136–37; Lasswell, "Relation of Skill"; Lasswell, *Politics*, 222; Lasswell and Blumenstock, *World Revolutionary Propaganda*, 356.

76. Hutchins to Karl, November 13, 1970, quoted in Karl, *Charles Merriam*, 286; author's interview with Karl, January 19, 1979; Marvick, "Introduction," 32; Shils, "Some Academics," 195–96; Helen Swick Perry, *Psychiatrist of America: The Life of Harry Stack Sullivan* (Cambridge: Harvard University Press, 1982), 366–73; Lasswell to Merriam, October 13, 1939, CEM; J. Michael Sproule, "Propaganda Studies in American Social Science: The Rise and Fall of the Critical Paradigm," *Quarterly Journal of Speech* 73 (February 1987): 69, 77, n. 30.

77. Harold D. Lasswell, "Propagandist Bids for Power," *American Scholar* 8 (Summer 1939): 354–57; Lasswell, "Person: Subject and Object of Propaganda," *AAAPSS* 179 (1935): 190–93; Lasswell, "Research on the Distribution of Symbol Specialists," *Journalism Quarterly* 12 (June 1935): 146–56; Lasswell and Blumenstock, *World Revolutionary Propaganda*, 3–4.

78. Lasswell to Merriam, undated (1937), CEM; Lasswell, *World Politics*, 114; Lasswell, "Person, Subject," 188; Lasswell, "The Study and Practice of Propaganda," in *Propaganda and Promotional Activities: An Annotated Bibliography*, ed. Lasswell, Ralph D. Casey, and Bruce Lannes Smith (Minneapolis: University of Minnesota Press, 1935), 26; Lasswell, "The Propagandist," 357.

79. Harold D. Lasswell, "Propaganda in a Planned Society," in *Planned Society Yesterday, Today, Tomorrow*, ed. Findlay MacKenzie (New York: Prentice-Hall, 1937), 637; Lasswell, "Psychology of Hitlerism," 375; Lasswell, "The Scope of Research on Propaganda and Dictatorship," in *Propaganda and Dictatorship: A Collection of Papers*, ed. Harwood Lawrence Childs (Princeton: Princeton University Press, 1936), 111; Lasswell, "Strategy," 202–9; Lasswell, *World Politics*, 128–33; Lasswell, "Study and Practice," 13; Lasswell and Dorothy Blumenstock, "Techniques of Slogans in Communist Propaganda," *Psychiatry* 1 (November 1938): 507, 514.

80. Lasswell and Blumenstock, *World Revolutionary Propaganda*, 102–3, 121, 218, 277–300, 350–58.

81. Lasswell, "Why Be Quantitative?" 46, 51–52; Abraham Kaplan and Joseph M. Goldsen, "The Reliability of Content Analysis Categories," in Lasswell, Leites, et al., eds., *Language of Politics*, 83–112; Irving L. Janis, "The Problem of Validating Content Analysis," in ibid., 55–82; Sergius Yakobson and Lasswell, "Trend: May Day Slogans in Soviet Russia," in ibid., 233–97.

82. Harold D. Lasswell, "Detection: Propaganda Detection and the Courts," in Lasswell, Leites, et al., eds., *Language of Politics*, 177–78; Lasswell, "Why Be Quantitative?" 387, n. 14, 392, n. 9; "Mosquito," *Time Magazine* 39 (June 1, 1942): 52–54.

83. Allan M. Winkler, *The Politics of Propaganda: The Office of War Information, 1942–1945* (New Haven: Yale University Press, 1978), 1–7, 23, 40–42, 54, 64–72, 112–29; John Morton Blum, *V Was for Victory: Politics and American Culture During World War II* (New York: Harcourt Brace Jovanovich, 1976), 5, 13–16.

84. Harold D. Lasswell, "Morale Symbols," Unpublished memorandum from Lasswell to Morgenthau, February 17, 1941, CEM; Lasswell, *Democracy Through Public Opinion*, 98; Blum, *V Was for Victory*, 27–29.

85. Lasswell, "What Psychiatrists," 39; Lasswell, "Developing Science," 27; italics are mine. Lasswell's occasional slips into grand conceit seem to coincide with periods of great personal anxiety. He wrote this article immediately after his unwilling departure from Chicago. Like his associate at the time, Harry Stack Sullivan, Lasswell appeared driven by the "whip" of anxiety and in times of great personal stress overcompensated through claims of grandiosity. For Sullivan, see Perry, *Psychiatrist of America*.

86. Harold D. Lasswell, "Materials for the Study of Propaganda: Number One," *Psychiatry* 1 (August 1938): 421–47.

87. Ibid., 440, 444; Harold D. Lasswell, *Public Opinion and British-American Unity*, Document no. 4, Conference on North American Rela-

tions, Prout's Neck, Maine, September 4–9, 1941 (Princeton: American Committee for International Studies, 1941), 1–9; Lasswell, "Review of *The Merchants of Death*, by H. C. Engelbrecht and F. C. Hanighen," *APSR* 28 (November 1934): 1135; Lasswell and Albert N. Williams, "American Voices," *Scribner's Commentator* 9 (November 1940): 109–11.

88. Lasswell, "Developing Science," 26–27, 32–33, 46–47; Lasswell, "Psychology Looks," 334–35; Lasswell, *Democracy Through Public Opinion*, 133–34.

89. The Institute of Propaganda Analysis, *The Fine Art of Propaganda: A Study of Father Coughlin's Speeches*, ed. Arthur McClung Lee and Elizabeth Briant Lee (New York: Harcourt, Brace, 1939), title page; Clyde Miller, *What Everybody Should Know about Propaganda: How and Why It Works* (New York: Commission for Propaganda Analysis—Methodist Federation for Social Action, 1948), 3; "Propaganda Techniques of German Fascism," in *Propaganda Analysis: A Bulletin to Help Intelligent Citizens Detect and Analyze Propaganda* 1, no. 8 (May 1938): 37; Clyde Miller, Preface to *Propaganda Analysis* 1, no. 1 (September 1937): iii–v; "Announcement: *Propaganda Analysis*; a Bulletin to Help the Intelligent Citizens Detect and Analyze Propaganda," *Propaganda Analysis* 1, no. 2 (October 1937): 2–3; "Some ABC's of Propaganda Analysis," *Propaganda Analysis* 1, no. 3 (December 1937): 11; "We Say Au Revoir," *Propaganda Analysis* 4, no. 13 (January 9, 1942): 6.

90. "Announcement," 4; Institute, *Fine Art*; "The Ford Sunday Evening Hour," *Propaganda Analysis* 1, no. 10 (July 1938): 57–60; "Propaganda: Some Illustrations," *Propaganda Analysis* 1, no. 12 (September 1938): 68; "Mr. Dies Goes to Town," *Propaganda Analysis* 3, no. 4 (January 15, 1940); "The A and P Campaign," *Propaganda Analysis* 2, no. 3 (December 1, 1938): 6; "Britain Woos America," *Propaganda Analysis* 2, no. 10 (June 10, 1939); "Mr. Roosevelt's Foreign Policy," *Propaganda Analysis* 3, no. 2 (November 15, 1939).

CONCLUSION

1. Edward A. Purcell, Jr., *The Crisis of Democratic Theory: Scientific Naturalism and the Problem of Value* (Lexington: University of Kentucky Press, 1973), 115–232; Max Lerner, *Ideas Are Weapons: The History and Use of Ideas* (New York: Viking Press, 1939), 8–9; N. Clarence Nixon, "Review of *It Is Later Than You Think: The Need for a Militant Democracy*, by Max Lerner," *Journal of Politics* 1 (August 1939): 317.

2. Max Lerner, "The Revolt Against Quietism: Review of *Knowledge for What? The Place of Social Science in American Culture*, by Robert Lynd," *NR* 99 (July 5, 1939): 257–58; Stuart Chase, "Review of *Knowledge for What? The Place of Social Science in American Culture*, by Robert Lynd," *Books: New York Herald Tribune Book Review* 15 (July 2, 1939): 7; Charles A. Beard, "Review of *Knowledge for What?* by Robert Lynd," *APSR* 33 (August 1939): 711–12; Harold D. Lasswell, "Review of *Knowledge for What? The Place of Social Science in American Culture*, by Robert Lynd," *Public Opinion Quarterly* 4 (December 1939): 725–26; Harry Elmer Barnes, "Review of *Knowledge for What? The Place of Social Science in American Culture*, by Robert Lynd," *AHR* 45 (October 1939): 185; Erich Fromm, *Escape from Freedom* (New York: Holt, Rinehart and Winston, 1941), 274–75; Richard S. Kirkendall, *Social Scientists and Farm Policies in the Age of Roosevelt* (Columbia: University of Missouri Press, 1966), 184–85; John R. Commons, "Review of *Knowledge for What? The Place of Social Science in American Culture*, by Robert Lynd," *AER* 22 (September 1939): 635; Wesley C. Mitchell, "Book Review of *Knowledge for What? The Place of Social Science in American Culture*, by Robert Lynd," Unpublished review delivered to the Columbia Economics Club, Columbia University, May 2, 1939, WCM; Robert Mac-Iver, "Enduring Systems of Thought: A Review of *Knowledge for What?* by Robert Lynd," *Survey Graphic* 28 (August 1939): 496–98; Franz Neumann, "Review of *Knowledge for What? The Place of Social Science in American Culture*, by Robert Lynd," *Studies in Philosophy and Social Science* 8 (November 3, 1939): 469–74; Oskar Morgenstern, "Review of *Knowledge for What?* by Robert Lynd," *Princeton Alumni Weekly* 29 (May 5, 1939): 647–48.

3. Charles E. Merriam, "Urbanism," in *Eleven Twenty-six: A Decade of Social Science Research*, ed. Louis Wirth (Chicago: University of Chicago Press, 1940), 30; Henry Bruere, "The Social Sciences in the Service of Society," in ibid., 5–22.

4. Purcell, *The Crisis*, 139–52; Robert Maynard Hutchins, "Address at the Dinner Celebrating the Tenth Anniversary of the Dedication of the Social Science Research Building," in Wirth, ed., *Eleven Twenty-six*, 2–4.

5. Wesley C. Mitchell (chairman), "The Social Sciences, One or Many," in Wirth, ed., *Eleven Twenty-six*, 122–51.

6. John H. Williams (chairman), "Social Science and Social Action," in ibid., 274–95.

7. John McDiarmid, "The Mobilization of Social Scientists," in *Civil Service in Wartime*, ed. Leonard White (Chicago: University of Chicago Press, 1945), 74–76, 79–80, 85; Gene M. Lyons, *The Uneasy Partnership: Social*

Science and the Federal Government in the Twentieth Century (New York: Russell Sage Foundation, 1969), 87–101; Paul T. Homan, "Economics in the War Period," *AER* 37 (December 1946): 865–71; Harold F. Gosnell and Moyca C. David, "Public Opinion Research in Government," *APSR* 43 (June 1949): 564–72; Darwin Cartwright, "Social Psychology in the United States During the Second World War," *Human Relations* 1 (November 1947): 334–39; Walter Dill Scott et al., *Personnel Management* (New York: McGraw-Hill, 1954), 251.

8. David Brody, "The New Deal and World War II," in *The New Deal: The National Level*, ed. John Braeman, Robert H. Bremner, and Brody (Columbus: Ohio State University Press, 1975), 1:267–309; John Morton Blum, *V Was for Victory: Politics and American Culture During World War II* (New York: Harcourt Brace Jovanovich, 1976), 21–48; Allan M. Winkler, *The Politics of Propaganda: The Office of War Information 1942–1945* (New Haven: Yale University Press, 1978); Homan, "Economics," 870; Gosnell and David, "Public Opinion," 569–70; Cartwright, "Social Psychology," 330.

9. Peter J. Seybold, "The Ford Foundation and the Triumph of Behavioralism in American Political Science," in *Philanthropy and Cultural Imperialism: The Foundations at Home and Abroad*, ed. Robert F. Arnove (Bloomington: Indiana University Press, 1980), 272; Bernard Berelson, *Graduate Education in the United States* (New York: McGraw-Hill, 1960), 235.

10. Seymour Martin Lipset, *Political Man: The Social Bases of Politics* (Garden City, N.Y.: Doubleday, 1959), 442.

11. Robert Booth Fowler, *Believing Skeptics: American Political Intellectuals, 1945–1964* (Westport, Conn.: Greenwood Press, 1978); Chaim I. Waxman, ed., *End of Ideology Debate* (New York: Simon and Schuster, 1968); Daniel Bell, *The End of Ideology: On the Exhaustion of Political Ideas in the Fifties* (New York: Free Press, 1960), 110–221.

12. Wesley C. Mitchell, "The Public Relations of Science," *Science* 90 (December 29, 1939): 604–8; Mitchell, "Science and the State of Mind," *Science* 89 (January 6, 1939): 1–4.

13. Lucy Sprague Mitchell, *Two Lives: The Story of Wesley Clair Mitchell and Myself* (New York: Simon and Schuster, 1953), 373–82; Wesley C. Mitchell, "Problems of Methods in Economics," Unpublished talk given to Columbia Economics Club, January 12, 1944; Mitchell, "Fifty Years as an Economist," Unpublished talk given to Columbia Economics Club, May 11, 1945, last two in WCM; Mitchell, "Economic Research in War and Reconstruction," in *Twenty-second Annual Report of the Director of Research of the National Bureau of Economic Research* (New York: National Bureau of Economic Research, 1942), 9–43; Mitchell, "Empirical Research and the De-

velopment of Economic Science," *Economic Research and the Development of Economic Science and Public Policy* (New York: National Bureau of Economic Research, 1946), 19.

14. Mitchell, "Public Relations," 605–7; Mitchell, "Feeling and Thinking in Scientific Work," *Social Science* 15 (July 1940): 229–32; Mitchell, "Facts and Values in Economics," *Journal of Philosophy* 41 (April 13, 1944): 213–19; Mitchell, "Discussion of 'Political Science, Political Economy, and Values,'" *AER* 34, suppl. (1944): 50; Dorfman to Mitchell, undated (c. 1944), WCM; Joyce Antler, *Lucy Sprague Mitchell: The Making of a Modern Woman* (New Haven: Yale University Press, 1987), 338–39.

15. Charles E. Merriam, *The New Democracy and the New Despotism* (New York: McGraw-Hill, 1939), 6–8, 11–12, 237; Merriam, *Prologue to Politics* (Chicago: University of Chicago Press, 1939), 3, 17, 45, 51–52, 99–100; Merriam, "Make No Small Plans," *National Municipal Review* 32 (January 1943): 65; Merriam, "The National Resources Planning Board: A Chapter in American Planning Experience," *APSR* 38 (December 1944): 1079–80; John D. Millet, *The Process and Organization of Government Planning* (New York: Columbia University Press, 1947), 118–21.

16. Leonard D. White, Preface to *The Future of Government in the United States: Essays in Honor of Charles E. Merriam*, ed. White (Chicago: University of Chicago Press, 1942), v.

17. Laura Kalman, *Legal Realism at Yale 1927–1960* (Chapel Hill: University of North Carolina Press, 1986), 148–49, 176–84; Myres S. McDougal, "Fuller vs. the American Legal Realists: An Interpretation," *Yale Law Journal* 50 (May 1941): 832–37; Myres S. McDougal, "Legal Education for a Free Society: Our Collective Responsibility," in *Politics, Personality, and Social Science in the Twentieth Century: Essays in Honor of Harold D. Lasswell*, ed. Arnold A. Rogow (Chicago: University of Chicago Press, 1969), 383; Harold D. Lasswell and Myres S. McDougal, "Legal Education and Public Policy: Professional Training in the Public Interest," *Yale Law Journal* 52 (March 1943): 203–12, 244–45.

18. Lasswell and McDougal, "Legal Education," 212, 217–32; McDougal, "Legal Education," 396; McDougal, "Policy-making as the Center of Emphasis," *Association of American Law School Proceedings* 43 (1943): 52; "General Discussion of Dr. McDougal's Speech," *Association of American Law School Proceedings* 43 (1943): 55–67; McDougal, "The Law School of the Future: From Legal Realism to Policy Science in the World Community," *Yale Law Journal* 56 (September 1947): 1346–49.

19. Lasswell to Merriam, March 6, 1951, and April 10, 1945; Lasswell, "The Future of the Social Sciences as Policy Sciences," Unpublished memo-

randum, undated (c. 1945), 7, all in CEM; Lasswell, *Power and Personality* (New York: W. W. Norton, 1948), 126.

20. Harold D. Lasswell, "The Policy Orientation," in *The Policy Sciences: Recent Developments in Scope and Method*, ed. Daniel Lerner and Lasswell (Stanford: Stanford University Press, 1951), 7–11, 15.

21. Harold D. Lasswell, *World Politics and Personal Insecurity* (New York: McGraw-Hill, 1935), 216; Lasswell, "Policy Orientation," 2–3; Lerner and Lasswell, *The Policy Sciences*, 22; William Ascher, "The Evolution of the Policy Sciences: Understanding the Rise and Avoiding the Fall," *Journal of Policy Analysis and Management* 5 (Winter 1986): 365–73; Bruce A. Ackerman, "*Law and the Modern Mind*, by Jerome Frank," Twentieth Century Classics Revisited, *Daedalus* 103 (Winter 1974): 129, n. 28; Edward Shils, "Some Academics, Mainly at Chicago," *American Scholar* 50 (Spring 1981): 195.

23. Matthew Josephson, *Infidel in the Temple* (New York: Alfred A. Knopf, 1967), 413–14; Lewis Mumford, Letter to the editor, *Saturday Review of Literature* 27 (December 2, 1944): 27; Peter Novick, *That Noble Dream: The "Objectivity Question" and the American Historical Profession* (New York: Cambridge University Press, 1988), 292.

24. Beard to George H. E. Smith, November 11, 1947, GHS; Beard to Oswald Villard, April 13, 1948, quoted in Ronald Radosh, *Prophets on the Right: Profiles of Conservative Critics of American Globalism* (New York: Simon and Schuster, 1975), 60; Beard, *President Roosevelt and the Coming of the War 1941: A Study in Appearance and Realities* (New Haven: Yale University Press, 1948), 575–82; Beard and Mary R. Beard, *A Basic History of the United States* (Philadelphia: Blakiston, 1944), 472–79.

25. Ellen Nore, *Charles A. Beard: An Intellectual Portrait* (Carbondale: Southern Illinois Press, 1983), 204–8; Charles A. Beard, "Who's to Write the History of the War," *Saturday Evening Post* 220 (October 4, 1947): 172; Beard, Letter to the editor, *Washington Post*, November 9, 1947; Beard "Review of *The Idea of History*, by Robin Colingwood," *AHR* 52 (July 1947): 708; Smith to Beard, July 7 and December 2, 1945, and January 27 and April 10, 1946; Beard to Smith, January 29 and March 2, 5, and 12, 1946, all in GHS.

26. Charles A. Beard, "Some Reflections on the Social Sciences after Fifty-odd Years of Studying the Same," personal note to Stuart Chase, January 7, 1947, SC; Beard to Macmahon, September 18, 1947; Mary Beard to Macmahon, September 21, 1947, AWM; Beard, "Neglected Aspects of Political Science," *APSR* 42 (April 1948): 213–22.

27. Charles A. Beard and Mary R. Beard, *The Rise of American Civilization*. Vol. 2: *The Industrial Era* (New York: Macmillan, 1927), 800; George S.

Counts, "Charles Beard, The Public Man," in *Charles A. Beard: An Appraisal,* ed. Howard K. Beale (Lexington: University of Kentucky Press, 1954), 235.

28. Robert S. Lynd, "Proposed Study of Potentialities of Democratic Processes in a Period of Mobilization" (Princeton: American Committee for International Studies, 1940), 1–4, 20–22, RHL; Lynd, "Not That Way, Mr. Nelson," *Nation* 154 (April 4, 1942): 393–95; Lynd, "The Structure of Power," *Nation* 157 (November 9, 1942): 597, 600; Lynd, "Our Racket Society," *Nation* 173 (August 25, 1951): 152; Lynd, "The Implications of Economic Planning for Sociology," *American Sociological Review* 9 (February 1944): 18; Lynd, "The Science of Inhuman Relations," *NR* 121 (August 29, 1949): 22–24.

29. Lynd, "Implications," 17; Lynd, "Is Technology Politically Neutral?" in *The Engineer in the Post-war World: Speeches and Addresses Delivered at the Public Conference Held in New York City on March 4, 1944* (New York: Research Bureau for Post-war Economics, 1944), 37–38, 42–43; Lynd, "The Structure," 597–99; Lynd, Foreword to *Business as a System of Power,* by Robert A. Brady (New York: Columbia University Press, 1943), vii–xviii; Lynd, "Power in American Society as Resource and Problem," in *Problems of Power in American Democracy,* ed. Arthur Kornhauser (Detroit: Wayne State University Press, 1957), 20–31; Lynd, "Capitalism's Happy New Year," *Nation* 163 (December 28, 1946): 749; Lynd, "Role of the Middle Class in Contemporary Social Change," Unpublished lecture delivered to Harvard John Reed Society, November 3, 1947, 14–14b; Lynd, "Integrating the Union More Effectively into the Life of the Community in Which It Functions," Unpublished lecture to a Quaker group near Swarthmore, no date, 4, last two in RHL; Lynd, *You Can Do It Better Democratically,* UAW-CIO Education Department, no. 192 (Detroit: UAW-CIO Education Department, 1949).

30. Lynd to R. Keith Kane, Office of Facts and Figures, March 4, 1942, RHL; Helen Lynd, "Oral History," Columbia Oral History Project, interviewed by Mrs. Walter Gellhorn, March 27–May 7, 1973, 181–84, 189–90; Robert S. Lynd, Foreword to *Agrarian Socialism: The Cooperative Commonwealth Federation in Saskatchewan,* by Seymour Martin Lipset (Berkeley: University of California Press, 1950), viii; Lynd, "Open Statement," Talk presented at meeting of Columbia University Chapter of American Association of University Professors, April 14, 1953; Lynd, "Miscellaneous Items about Robert S. Lynd, 3/9/54," Unpublished memo, March 9, 1954, last two in RHL; Helen Lynd to author, December 12, 1978.

31. Sidney Blumenthal, Preface to the Perennial Library Edition of *The Rise of the Counter-Establishment: From Conservative Ideology to Politi-*

cal Power (New York: Harper and Row, 1988), x–xiv. For Mills, see esp. C. Wright Mills, "The Professional Ideology of Social Pathologists" (1943), in *Power, Politics and People: The Collected Essays of C. Wright Mills,* ed. Irving Louis Horowitz (New York: Oxford University Press, 1963), 525–52; Mills, *White Collar* (New York: Oxford University Press, 1951); Mills, *The Sociological Imagination* (New York: Oxford University Press, 1959); Mills, "Letter to the New Left" (1960), in Horowitz, ed., *Power, Politics, and People,* 247–59.

32. Hubert Herring, "Charles A. Beard: Freelance among the Historians," *Harper's* 178 (May 1939): 651.

33. Raymond Seidelman, *Disenchanted Realists: Political Science and the American Crisis* (Albany: State University of New York Press, 1985), 190, passim; Howard S. Becker, "Whose Side Are We On?" *Social Problems* 14 (Winter 1967): 239–47; Wilbert E. Moore, "The Utility of Utopias," *American Sociological Review* 31 (December 1966): 765–72; A. W. Coats, "The Current 'Crisis' in Economics in Historical Perspective," *Nebraska Journal of Economics and Business* 16 (Summer 1977): 3–16; David M. Ricci, *The Tragedy of Political Science: Politics, Scholarship, and Democracy* (New Haven: Yale University Press, 1984); Paul A. Attewell, *Radical Political Economy since the Sixties* (New Brunswick, N.J.: Rutgers University Press, 1984); Daniel Bell, "The New Class: A Muddled Concept," in *The Winding Passage* (1980), 158–59, cited in Russell Jacoby, *The Last Intellectuals: American Culture in the Age of Academe* (New York: Basic Books, 1987), 108.

34. H. Stuart Hughes, "Social Theory in a New Context," Unpublished lecture delivered at the Smithsonian Institution, 1980, quoted in Lewis A. Coser, *Refugee Scholars in America: Their Impact and Their Experiences* (New Haven: Yale University Press, 1984), 10; Martin Jay, *The Dialectical Imagination: A History of the Frankfurt School and the Institute of Social Research 1923–1950* (Boston: Little, Brown, 1973), 3–4, 42, 46–48, 55–56, 67, 81–82; Max Horkheimer, Foreword to *Dialectical Imagination,* xii.

35. Jay, *Dialectical Imagination,* 169, 289, 353; Charles H. Page, *Fifty Years in the Sociological Enterprise* (Amherst: University of Massachusetts Press, 1982), 31; Coser, *Refugee Scholars,* 198; Helen Lynd, "Oral History," 219–20.

36. Michel Foucault, *Archaeology of Knowledge,* trans. A. M. Sheridan-Smith (New York: Pantheon Books, 1972); Jean Baudrillard, *For a Critique of the Political Economy of the Sign* (St. Louis: Telos Press, 1981).

37. Steven Watts, "Point of View: Academe's Leftists Are Something of a Fraud," *Chronicle of Higher Education,* April 29, 1992, A40; Jacoby, *Last Intellectuals,* 130–90, 198.

38. William H. Simon, "The Ideology of Advocacy: Procedural Justice and Professional Ethics," *University of Wisconsin Law Review* (January 1978): 30–144; George H. Weber and George J. McCall, eds., *Social Scientists as Advocates: Views from the Applied Disciplines* (Beverly Hills: Sage, 1978); Richard J. Bernstein, *Praxis and Action* (Philadelphia: University of Pennsylvania Press, 1971); Richard J. Bernstein, *John Dewey* (New York: Washington Square Press, 1966); Hilary Putnam, *Realism with a Human Face* (Cambridge: Harvard University Press, 1990), esp. chap. 11, "Objectivity and the Science/Ethics Distinction," 163–78; William M. Sullivan, *Reconstructing Public Philosophy* (Berkeley: University of California Press, 1982); Richard Rorty, *Consequences of Pragmatism* (Minneapolis: University of Minnesota Press, 1982).

39. Max Weber, *The Protestant Ethic and the Spirit of Capitalism*, trans. Talcott Parsons (New York: Charles Scribner's Sons, 1958), 182. 1958), 182.

Index

MARK C. SMITH is Assistant Professor of American Studies and
History at the University of Texas at Austin.

Library of Congress Cataloging-in-Publication Data

Smith, Mark C.
Social science in the crucible: the American debate over
objectivity and purpose, 1918–1941 / Mark C. Smith.
p. cm.
Includes bibliographical references and index.
ISBN 0-8223-1484-3 (cloth). — ISBN 0-8223-1497-5 (pbk.)
1. Social sciences—United States—History—20th century.
2. Social sciences—United States—Philosophy. I. Title.
H53.U5S57 1994
300'.973'09049—dc20 94-7823 CIP